AMERICA'S
Bread Book

By the same author:

Mary's Bread Basket and Soup Kettle

AMERICA'S
Bread Book

≡≡≡≡≡

*300 authentic recipes for
America's favorite homemade breads,
collected on a 65,000-mile journey
through the fifty United States*

BY MARY GUBSER

Illustrated by Pat Biggs

WILLIAM MORROW AND COMPANY, INC · NEW YORK

Library of Congress Cataloging in Publication Data

Gubser, Mary.
America's bread book.

Includes index.
1. Bread.   2. Cookery—United States.   I. Title.
TX769.G77   1985   641.8'15   84-27283
ISBN 0-688-04176-0

Printed in the United States of América

First Edition

1 2 3 4 5 6 7 8 9 10

BOOK DESIGN BY LINEY LI

For My Grandchildren

CHARLES

STEVEN

SASHA

CHRISTI

HEATHER

JOHN

Preface

Early in the winter of 1946, the bakers in the city of Tulsa went on strike. World War II was definitely over. I opened one of my three cookbooks to the bread section and baked my first bread. Never shall I forget the thrill of pulling those golden loaves from the oven. The aroma permeated our home and my three young sons and their father were elated with my success. So the die was cast.

Through the ensuing years, I collected recipes from friends, the food pages of newspapers wherever we were, and magazines. I tried different flours, working out my own problems, for there were no bread books for guidance. In 1969 my husband built me a kitchen I had designed, with a house around it. Within a very short time, I realized I had unintentionally created a perfect teaching area, for my kitchen is open to the family room, with a long counter between them. With a close friend, I plunged into teaching. Classes mushroomed, for a revival of the art of breadmaking was sweeping across the United States. My students taught me what they needed and wanted to learn. I wrote *Mary's Bread Basket and Soup Kettle,* which to my delight was accepted by the Book-of-the-Month Club. My kitchen had changed my life—many doors were now opened and I began teaching and appearing on television in other cities. I had a new life-style and career, as well as becoming a grandmother.

Throughout our many years of marriage, my husband and I have traveled extensively in the United States for both pleasure and business. Although I've had many journeys abroad, there is still no greater pleasure to me than packing my car and driving anywhere in my country. So, in 1974, I was dismayed, along with the rest of my fellow citizens, by the prospect of a serious gasoline crisis. But I had faced difficulties before and found they could often be turned into opportunity. My mind began to whirl with ideas. Then an acquaintance said to me, "Mary, why don't you write a cookbook and include some of your travels and put your own personality into it?" With only nebulous thoughts in my head,

I suggested to my husband that we travel the United States during the next few years, for it just might be our last chance. I proposed to go to each of the fifty states to find breads. Travel becomes even more pleasurable when it has an interesting purpose. The organization of such an adventure had not clearly manifested itself—just the urgency and motivation had been created. We started with a journey into Texas that proved most successful. I was encouraged and felt that my idea was possible. Even my editor approved.

I learned quickly how to find people in the bread world, but the frosting on the bread was the people I met accidentally, as you will read. I enjoyed visiting bakeries, often purchasing bread and re-creating the recipe, or designing my own to fit a particular area. Ethnic traditions of all kinds abound in our nation, but this book was never intended to be an ethnic or a regional cookbook. *America's Bread Book* reflects the diversity to be found everywhere in the country, and each journey uncovered recipes of wide variety and different origins.

When I finished my journeys, I settled down at home to test, taste, research, and write. At this point, I was most fortunate, because three wonderful women volunteered their time and abilities. For over a year, each Wednesday they arrived early, apron in hand, to spend the day baking an assortment of breads and coffeecakes, and then took more recipes home to test. A wonderful camaraderie developed, which has continued even though the book is finished. They are ready to assist with classes or any special cooking that needs to be done. These great friends lead the list in the Acknowledgments that I owe to so many.

All these events occurred during a five-year period, as *America's Bread Book* gradually developed in my mind, my journals took shape, and a manuscript was written that finally became a book. I was motivated through it all by love for my country and a great desire to see every possible corner of it. The creation of homemade bread everywhere in our fifty states is exciting and proves to me that the American pioneer spirit is fully alive, from the vast open West to the densely populated East.

Acknowledgments

From sea to shining sea I have met millers, bakers, farmers, housewives, professors, librarians, business executives, innkeepers, fine chefs, writers, curators of museums, and reporters, who generously shared their time, knowledge, and research into the world of grains, flours, and breads. Those who gave me specific recipes are credited where their recipes appear in the book. But without the assistance of very special friends, *America's Bread Book* could never have achieved the depth and wide variety I wanted to share with you.

Three friends, Dora Malone, Kathy Major, and Jo Spencer, stepped into my life and my kitchen and volunteered for over a year to test, taste, and wash all those bowls and pans. To these three women, I shall forever be grateful.

My gratitude extends across our nation, and I made contact with both old and new friends. I would like to thank these special "connections":

Judy Bell of Portland, Oregon
Linda Davis of Kansas City
Evolyn Melville of Fairbanks, Alaska
Annie Wappler and Clyde Hester of San Antonio
Ethel Kulhanek of Lawton, Oklahoma
Gladys Girard of Honolulu and San Diego
Helen Tessler of Bristol, Rhode Island
Ruth Rasmussen of St. Louis
Howard Weber of New Glarus, Wisconsin
Shirley and Earl Stewart of Albuquerque
Lois Powell of Atlanta
Shushan Teager of Boston
Margaret Gubser of Aspen, Colorado

Nelle G. Meints of Hinsdale, Illinois
Rosalie Talbott of Taos, New Mexico
Margaret and Pete Boysen of Bemidjii, Minnesota

Throughout my travels and in my own city, further contacts gave me constructive advice and brought me in touch with excellent cooks. I am most appreciative of the help given by all the following:

JoEdith Watt, Millie Ladner, Suzanne Holloway, Gig and Jack Harlow, Mary Harris, Irene Holland, Mary Louise and Howard Cowan, Dolores Pfaff, Colonel Francis Wilson, Dr. Leon Horowitz, Carl Wolfe, Kathleen Kelly, Marilyn Joyo, Joe Lundberg, Urbane Peachy, Jerry Engram, Faye Wick, Donald L. Haight, Marguerite Stetson, Jag Mehta, Janet Saghaletian, Dr. Robert C. Wakefield, Robert Pedersen, Chip Seigal, Mary Cooke, Jack Ferrell, Rose Deets, Richard and Marian Hail, Janet Loring, Carolyn Crawley, the Minnesota State Fair Board, The Shaker Inn at Pleasant Hill in Kentucky, Oklahoma Northeastern State University, Universal Foods, and the National Park Service.

My family has given me the needed encouragement and practical help and assisted in research during the five years of traveling and writing. I love them all for their optimistic outlook.

My husband, Gene, has driven, sailed, flown, walked, and waited patiently. I thank each of my remarkable daughters-in-law, Margaret, Annie, and Laura, and their husbands, my sons, Nick, Peter, and Mike. My special thanks to Eulala James for her exceptional assistance through ten years of classes and to Edna James, my housekeeper, for her steadfast devotion.

It is my privilege to thank my editor, Narcisse Chamberlain, who with great diligence and professional expertise has pulled together a massive manuscript to make a handsome book.

Contents

AMERICA'S
Bread Book

Introduction

"Turn right at the bomb, ma'am. You cain't miss it."

Taken aback by this startling but explicit direction, I looked at the service-station woman for assurance. "Right at the bomb?" I repeated.

"Five miles north of town, turn right at the bomb and drive ten more miles across the valley. You'll see a bunch of buildings and, oh, yes, lots of geese. The Hutterites are real friendly folks."

Slightly dazed, I settled back in the car and we drove north out of Cascade, Montana (two service stations, one bar, one café), on a well-graded gravel road. My husband noted the mileage on the odometer, for we certainly did not want to miss the "bomb."

Sure enough, there was a fork in the road and to our left, the "bomb." Surrounded by a high strong fence was a military installation where presumably there resided a buried missile. What's the difference—bomb, missile—they all do the same thing. The big Montana sky stretched over the clearest of air, and we relished the view of this magnificent valley of rolling, golden wheat fields. Not only could I easily see the group of buildings ten miles away, but also across the fifty miles of valley surrounded by low mountains. A summer storm streaked over a tiny area at the top of one mountain, sending out vivid flashes of lightning. The state of Montana has a solid, rustic beauty that gives one a marvelous feeling of expansiveness and a great desire to breathe deeply.

As we came closer to the colony, my husband grinned at me with a question, "Exactly what are you going to say when we do arrive?" Now, being a P.K. (preacher's kid), I figured something would pop out.

The Hutterites were part of a sect that separated from the Roman Catholic Church five hundred years ago. They are Germanic in origin and related to the Mennonites and Amish. This particular religious group was named after John Hutter, who was burned at the stake.

15

Many of the Mennonites, Amish, and Hutterites went into the Ukraine to avoid religious persecution and had to move on again under the tsar one hundred years later. Immigration began to the United States and Canada. The Hutterites settled in the Dakotas, but left during World War I to avoid the U.S. draft. Later, groups returned and settled again in the Dakotas, Idaho, Montana, and the state of Washington—all wheat-growing states. The Hutterites live quite a different life from that of their sister religions. Each group is a self-contained colony and all work is shared, but unlike the Amish, they believe in buying and using the finest of modern, mechanized equipment on their farms and in their communal kitchens.

Our car skittered to a stop on the gravel in the center of the colony. Handsome barns and low buildings, small, freshly painted white houses trimmed in green, an enormous pen holding magnificent geese, and a lush, grassy area for a children's playground completed this compact, neatly arranged settlement.

A dozen men were working on huge farm machinery. Two small boys and a teenager wore hard black caps and black pants held up by suspenders over brightly printed shirts. I was greeted by a smiling young man of about twenty-five, probably the public relation expert of the colony. Quickly I explained my interest in making breads, he nodded understandingly, and turned to enter one of the small houses. He came back with a middle-aged woman wearing a gaily flowered cotton dress that reached to her ankles and black hose and shoes. An apron of a different print protected the dress and her dainty white blouse, buttoned high up the neck, was trimmed with lace and pearl buttons. Her cap matched the printed dress and was pinned tightly across the back of her hair, which was pulled primly into a bun at the nape of her neck. Three small girls playing on the grass were dressed exactly like our hostess.

Graciously she invited us into the building that housed the communal kitchen and dining room. On the stove in the center of the kitchen was an enormous restaurant soup kettle bubbling with mutton stew sufficient to feed one hundred eighteen people for that evening's supper. She lifted the lid, I took a delicious sniff, and followed her into the bakery. Close to a work table was a Hobart mixer capable of mixing fifty pounds of flour. A huge trough was available to receive the dough for proofing. She told me that thirty-eight gigantic loaves plus six smaller ones are baked each week. Two women share the cooking chores for one week and then are replaced by another two.

The oven, large enough to hold all forty-four loaves, was a masterpiece, built by the men of the colony. How I envied such a handsome oven lined with bricks. Proudly our hostess displayed the extra-large bread pans made by a Hutterite blacksmith more than sixty years ago. A huge walk-in refrigerator plus a closet to hold the many sacks of flour completed the bakery.

We returned through the kitchen into the communal dining room. Four teenage girls, each dressed in replicas of our hostess's costume (they surely must have purchased bolts and bolts of that flowered print), were preparing fine German noodles with a restaurant-size pasta machine. Noodles were spread over the twenty tables to dry. The room was completely simple, with no decorations on walls or floors. A small pulpit stood in one corner of the dining room. This area seemed to be the church, the dining room, and I am certain the place where important decisions are made by the men. Obviously Hutterites spend money carefully, only on practical needs—and bolts of material.

At this colony the Hutterites prepare only one kind of bread. Their sweets are cookies, pies, and cakes. Our hostess laughed and said I would probably not use a recipe for a hundred pounds of flour and three cups of sugar, plus water, yeast, and lard. It is simple, wholesome bread, with an excellent crust created by that magnificent oven. An adaptation of the Hutterite bread will be found on page 146.

As we walked outside, I asked where the children attended school. A teacher is brought in from the outside world, so the Hutterites are at peace with the Montana school system. There are no TVs, no radios, and no telephone was visible. There is more to their communal way of production than wheat and breadmaking, for they brew their own beer, make a little wine, and I had been shown a tub full of homemade bottled root beer for the children. One thousand geese chattered in that huge pen. The women make all their own down pillows and comforters and sell the geese to local ranchers. When a colony becomes too large, a group breaks away, new land is purchased, and another community begins. The Hutterites are devoted to their families, religion, and wheat farming. They are superb farmers, contribute much to our nation, and are grateful to live as they wish.

The visit with the Hutterites was only one of the most charming recorded in the journal I kept during our travels. In time, people from Maine to Hawaii shared recipes with me. I experienced the warm, open friendliness and delightful sense of humor of Americans in all fifty states and admired their resilience and versatility.

With the exception of two short journeys, my husband joined me in traveling thousands of miles by automobile, plane, bus, and boat, visiting regions we knew well and discovering splendid new areas in my search for good breads to share with you. There were a few disappointing moments, and I will share those, too. Each state is unique and has a personality and beauty of its own. I loved traveling on the superhighways, turning off onto state and county roads, and sometimes winding up on a cow path.

Sit back, relax, and come on the journey with me, for this is a cookbook to read, with stories to amuse you, and much to learn about one of our most important and interesting foods— the great variety of breads made in these United States.

GUIDE TO
THE BASICS
OF
BREADMAKING

You will be plunging into a special art form in the world of cooking that will bring the greatest personal satisfaction and pleasure to your family and friends. Take the time to read this basic information on the methods of breadmaking to understand how to construct a loaf of bread. The shaping of breads, equipment, ingredients, a bit of history, and problems—all these are described in these first pages. Use this section as a reference if a question arises, for the answer will be here.

TERMS TO UNDERSTAND

Following are explanations of a few terms as they will be used throughout the book.

• **Proofing:** Both proofing and rising mean the inflation of dough after kneading. They also mean the combining of yeast with a liquid. The two words can be used interchangeably.

• **Butter:** To eliminate having to state "brush a bowl or pan with butter, margarine, or shortening," I have chosen to use the word "butter." Recipes say "brush a bowl with melted butter" or "a buttered bowl," but melted margarine or vegetable shortening may be substituted. Do not use oil unless specified. Oil soaks into a dough, whereas the other ingredients coat it and prevent a dry crust from forming. A hundred years ago, lard was the main cooking fat. Lard does make an unusually crusty bread, but it has become difficult to find and is overloaded with cholesterol.

• **Flour:** The term "all-purpose flour" has been shortened to "flour." The word "flour" in all recipes means a commercially milled all-purpose flour or an unbleached white flour. When other flours are to be used, they are specifically designated.

• **Active Dry Yeast:** In all my testing of recipes, active dry (instant) yeast has been used. I can find no difference in the action of compressed and dry yeasts. Because it is readily available, and I know the majority of cooks use dry yeast, that has been my choice. All recipes specify active dry yeast, but compressed yeast may be substituted.

INGREDIENTS

This section describes the many ingredients that can go into making a loaf of bread. We are fortunate to have a wealth of flours available to prepare any kind of bread, from high protein wheat to nongluten rice flour. The following entries tell exactly what the flours are and what they accomplish in breadmaking.

• **Stone-Ground Flour:** Originally, all flour was stone ground. In this process, a grist mill uses two large, heavy, carved round stones; one is stationary, the other moves slowly as the grain flows down between the two stones. The process is slow and cool, preserving the bran and germ, keeping intact all the vitamins and nutrition of each kernel. Stone-ground flours are excellent flours, which I love to feel, smell, and work with. Any of the stone-ground flours may be substituted throughout my book where whole grain flour such as whole wheat, rye, corn, or triticale is called for. Often I prefer a beginning sponge made with such flours, for they are slower to absorb the liquid. Because the stone-ground flours are coarse, add them slowly during the kneading process. Enjoy stone-ground flours not only for the nutritive value, but also for the superb flavor.

As our country developed, thousands of community grist mills were built where water power was available. In 1878 the first fast, all-roller mill was installed in Minneapolis. With this newly acquired speed, quantities of bread could be made and shipped, creating a need for additives and preservatives. The picturesque grist mill was outmoded and bread was changed. Recently, however, there has been a resurgence of interest in stone-ground flours, and at this writing there are 429 working grist mills in the United States.

• **Wheat Flour:** Ancient man chewed a primitive wheat called emmer and einkorn that still grows wild in remote areas of Iran. As early as 6700 B.C., man ground grains with rocks. Four thousand years ago Egyptians accidentally discovered that the addition of yeast puffed up bread dough, making it more palatable and handsome. No attempt was made to discover how this amazing leavening worked, but bread became a vital part of the economy in Egyptian life, for workers were paid in bread and beer. With more expertise in milling, the beauty of white bread became synonymous with the aristocracy, and for centuries we have been burdened with a powdery light flour, while the vitamin-filled

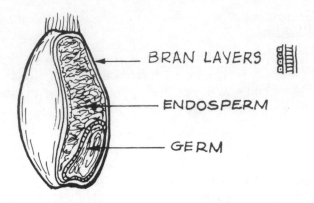

germ and hearty bran has been thrown to the peasants and livestock. The upper classes of each succeeding dominant country—Egypt, Greece, Rome, France, and England—demanded elegant white bread. The love for white bread sailed right over the ocean with the immigrants to the New World.

Why are wheat flours so important to breadmaking? All wheat has a percentage of protein. The hard spring and winter wheat has a higher proportion than soft wheat. Within wheat protein is gluten, which has the exciting ability to stretch when combined with yeast and warm liquid (remember the sticky flour paste you made as a child?). The yeast huffs and puffs, blowing all kinds of bubbles which expand the gluten strands into a lovely bread dough. Carbon dioxide has been created by the yeast's feeding on sugar and starches. The dough depends on the elasticity of the gluten to hold the gas. High-protein flour containing more and stronger gluten will make a better bread. Therefore wheat is so important because, while other grains have a minimal amount of gluten, nothing compares with wheat.

Much is happening in that bowl of dough you have created, and to me it is always a marvel to walk into my kitchen and see the bread bowl filled with a smooth inflated dough.

• **All-Purpose Flour:** A combination of soft and hard wheat composed primarily of the endosperm (the starchy portion of wheat grains), with chemical additives to supplement the wheat germ and bran that have been removed. Much of my testing for white breads has been done with commercial all-purpose flour simply because it is available in all fifty states. That does not mean I prefer using it personally. But it contains sufficient protein to make an agreeable bread. For those interested in adding more nutrition to all-purpose flour, read directions under Wheat Germ and Bran.

• **Unbleached White Flour:** High in protein count, with no chemical additives, this product is the finest white flour for breadmaking, particularly when purchased from one of the splendid mills listed under Sources of Supply, page 483. The wheat germ and bran have been removed, but may be added back by you if desired. It is an easy and delightful flour to handle, although more expensive than the regular all-purpose flour.

• **Bread Flour:** A white flour with a higher protein count than the all-purpose. But, because the flour contains additives, the dough rises too fast, becomes far too inflated when baked, and the bread ends up with little flavor. I have found it best to mix commercial bread flour with some other flour. Certain recipes in my book have been designed using a combination of bread flour with other flours that do not have the necessary gluten to make it alone. The New Hope Grist Mill located in the state of New York prepares an excellent bread flour.

• **Whole Wheat Flour:** Today, through popular demand, more whole wheat flour is being milled. Research has shown that the outer coating of bran may help decrease the chance of colon cancer. Whole wheat flour contains the complete wheat berry or kernel—the outer coating of bran, the endosperm, and the oil-rich germ. Commercially milled whole wheat flours are zipped through a fast process with chemical additives and make a heavier, darker loaf than all white flour—but it makes a most agreeable, flavorful bread. Whole wheat flour absorbs liquid quickly. When a recipe calls for adding more whole wheat flour, add it in small amounts. Otherwise the dough might become too stiff.

• **Graham Flour:** A misunderstood term for whole wheat flour, named for Dr. Sylvester Graham, a colorful devotee of health food in the nineteenth century. "Graham" became synonymous with whole wheat. It is not a specially milled flour, but only the special blend a company chooses to make; the content is printed on the sack. Usually, Graham flour is excellent to use, though perhaps more expensive than other whole wheat flours.

• **Gluten Flour:** Wheat flour from which most of the starch has been eliminated. To make a bread using only gluten flour is rather like bouncing a rubber ball—as you knead, the dough comes right back up into your hands. The practical use is the addition of one or two cups of gluten flour to a heavy, dense dough or to any recipe that needs lightening.

• **Cake Flour:** Composed of soft wheat, this fine white flour is designed for use in cakes and quick breads. Small amounts are occasionally added to yeast breads for a special texture.

• **Whole Wheat Pastry Flour:** Available in health food stores and health food departments of supermarkets. A finely ground, lovely whole wheat flour for pastries and cakes. Added to a yeast bread in small quantities, it produces a fine-textured bread.

• **Self-Rising Flour:** Similar to all-purpose flour, but with the addition of baking powder and sometimes salt. This flour is not interchangeable with all-purpose flour for bread recipes. When used in this book, it is specified.

• **Durum Wheat:** A hard, golden wheat grown especially to be milled into the coarse product, semolina, for the macaroni market.

• **Rye Flour:** Because of its sturdiness and resistance in the face of many difficult growing conditions, rye became the main grain grown in central Europe and Russia. The percentage of gluten in rye flour is low, making an all-rye bread dense but flavorful. Usually rye flour is combined with white or whole wheat or is used in a combination of flours as for making pumpernickel. Any dough that contains rye flour has a tendency to be sticky. Dust bits of flour on the kneading board and on your hands to make a smooth dough.

• **The Ancient Flours:** Millet, rye, oats, and barley as well as wheat were eaten by primitive man in the Old World from Europe to China. Corn was the grain of the New World. None of these except wheat and rye have the gluten content to create a leavened bread with yeast. Millet, oats, and barley are added in small amounts to wheat bread for flavor and nutritive value. With some exceptions, cornmeal is used primarily in quick breads.

• **Soy Flour:** Soy beans are ground into a dense, high-protein flour, which contains no gluten. For breadmaking, use soy flour in small quantities—½ to 1 cup may be added to recipes for its nutritive value.

• **Triticale:** The first man-made grain, produced from a cross between wheat *(Triticum)* and rye *(Secale)*. The name triticale (rhymes with daily) is derived from these two Latin terms. Although research has continued since the nineteenth century, it has only been within the last twenty years that efforts of Canadian and Mexican scientists have produced a positive grain and seed that grows and reproduces successfully. Since triticale combines the high protein of wheat and the sturdiness of rye, there is hope that ultimately it will be grown in those parts of the world in which only a hardy grain will survive. The gluten content is more fragile than in wheat. Triticale dough requires gentler kneading and only one bowl rising.

• **Wheat Germ and Bran:** One tablespoon of wheat germ per cup of flour will give the nutrition needed. The resulting bread will be speckled and have an earthy flavor. Bran flakes (miller's bran) meld easily with other ingredients. Wheat germ and bran are available in health departments of supermarkets and in health food stores as well as specialty shops. If you live in a remote area, both may be ordered through Sources of Supply, page 483. Some recipes call for bran cereal, which is available under a multitude of brand names in all supermarkets.

• **Cracked Wheat, Steel-Cut Oatmeal:** The grains of each have been cut in pieces. Nothing has been left out. Both are used in similar fashion. They are soaked in boiling water before being introduced into a bread dough.

• **Rolled Wheat, Oats, Oatmeal, Oat Flour:** Rolled wheat and oats are similar in that they have been "ironed" with rollers to make flat grains. Although oats in any form have no gluten, this grain gives bread an excellent texture and flavor.

• **Bulgur:** A form of wheat used extensively in the Middle East. The whole grains of wheat have been cooked and dried and then can be reconstituted to produce a healthful and lightly textured bread.

• **Buhr:** The artists who made grist mill stones preferred the French

Buhr stone for its hardness and ability to maintain the groove through countless millings. When a sack of flour is imprinted with the word "Buhr," the flour should have been ground on some of these old stones. But the word has become fashionable and is often used indiscriminately.

• **Bolted Flour:** Another confusing term you may encounter. Within the mechanism of a grist mill, there is a round drum which many years ago was tightly covered with a very fine silk. To obtain white flour, the bran and wheat germ were sifted out of the flour through this silk. My 95-year-old mother-in-law relates that her mother would be given this silk when it became filled with debris. She washed and ironed it and made elaborate embroideries on the material. Mr. Weed at the New Hope Mill gave us bolting material which is now made of nylon but is very similar to the silk formerly used.

• **Rice:** Cooked rice, particularly the brown whole grain, added to a recipe makes a different and interestingly textured bread. Rice flour is not often used, but it is certainly an excellent variation for a nongluten bread.

• **Potatoes:** Yeast is partial to warm potato water. Potatoes give sturdiness to bread and a tender, excellent texture that toasts well. I prefer using the baking Russet potato, but if you are short of time, use instant potato flakes. When preparing the fresh potato, put the cooked potato through a ricer to avoid lumps. When using instant potatoes, be sparing with water when mixing or the dough will be too moist. One tablespoon of instant potato flakes mixed with ½ cup of warm water is excellent for dissolving yeast.

• **Yeast:** It is an amazing fact that for centuries no one understood what yeast was or how it grew. Yeasts are a minuscule form of plant life that can multiply unbelievably under proper conditions. They are so tiny that it takes twenty billion to weigh ⅟₂₈ of an ounce as compressed yeast. As yeast grows, carbon dioxide gas is created and becomes trapped in the elastic strands of gluten found in flour. Yeast is the catalyst for that thrilling part of breadmaking—the rising of the dough.

There are two kinds of yeast available—active dry yeast and compressed fresh yeast. Active dry yeast is available in small packets, jars, large packages, and cans, all marked with an expiration date. But covered properly and refrigerated, dry yeast will keep for years. Compressed yeast also has a date of expiration and is far more fragile. The two yeasts may be used interchangeably. Active dry yeast is overwhelmingly the most popular, because of its availability and endurance.

To test either yeast, mix with ½ cup warm water (100°—110°F for dry, 90°F for compressed), 1 teaspoon sugar, and ¼ teaspoon ginger. Beat the mixture with a fork and set aside. Within 5 minutes, bubbles should appear, and in 10 minutes froth and bubbles. If nothing happens within 15 minutes, throw out the mixture and purchase new yeast.

One package of active dry yeast equals 1 scant tablespoon. Remember, yeast is a living plant. Liquid too hot will kill yeast, liquid too cold makes yeast sluggish. Follow these directions to avoid problems: Run water over your hand or wrist until there is a warm feeling with no bite, about 100°F. The limit is 110°F. Above that temperature, yeast will be destroyed. Test with a thermometer a few times, and soon you will have the "feel" of the correct temperature.

• **Baking Soda and Powder:** When mixed with an acid liquid such as buttermilk, baking soda produces carbon dioxide and an action similar to that of yeast. Soda functions quickly and often will be added at the end of a recipe, as in sourdough breads. To make soda more stable, baking powder is occasionally included. Baking powder is a combination of soda and flour or starch. When activated by liquid and heat, baking soda creates tiny bubbles causing the cake, quick breads, and pancakes to become light and filled with air. Baking soda and powder are sometimes used in yeast breads to obtain a desired texture and lightness.

• **Liquids:** Liquid is necessary to bind yeast and flour together. Water produces a crisp crust and excellent toasting bread. Yeast is eminently happy feeding on potato water, which is used extensively in breadmaking. Milk produces a velvet quality. Warm any milk to take off the chill—to about 110°F. Yeast dissolves more slowly in milk; let it sit for a minute or two and then stir. Raw milk should be scalded and cooled, but this is not necessary with pasteurized milk. Buttermilk is a great favorite of many cooks, for it seems to give an old-fashioned flavor to homemade bread. Do not worry if buttermilk curdles while heating. Instant dry skim milk is inexpensive, cuts down on calories, and is easy to use. All other milk products such as yogurt, evaporated milk, and cream should be heated just to a warm temperature. Fruit and vegetable juices create exciting flavors and should be at room temperature. The reason for warming liquids, as you have read, is that yeast loves a cozy, warm environment.

• **Fats:** Unsalted butter has been used exclusively in all my testing. Other kinds of butter certainly may be used, but the unsalted has a fresher flavor which blends best into the bread. Margarine and vegetable shortening are acceptable substitutes except in certain recipes. The light oils, safflower, sunflower, and corn oil are all excellent, particularly in health breads. If cholesterol is a problem for you, these oils can be substituted for butter. All fat products tenderize breads, increasing the volume by lubricating the gluten framework. Melted butter or margarine are the best to brush a proofing bowl and baking pans; do not use oil for this purpose unless specified as it soaks into a dough. Olive oil is explicitly called for in some recipes. Lard is limited primarily to old recipes; vegetable shortening may be substituted.

• **Sweeteners:** White, brown, and natural sugar, honey, and syrups add distinctive flavors and assist in browning breads. Basic breads with minimal amounts of sugar can be baked at a higher temperature than the very sweet breads and coffeecakes, for sugar burns easily. Honey and molasses are favorites of health food devotees and naturalists. Honey may be substituted for any of the sugars. Powdered or confectioner's sugar is used primarily for frosting cakes and buns.

Sugar substitutes may be used in a basic bread without harming the texture. Read directions on a package of sugar substitute and be careful of the amount you use, as it can be cloyingly sweet.

• **Salt:** An item that can be eliminated for a no-salt diet, or amounts can be cut in half. The bread will not be harmed, just not quite so tasty. Vary the salt content in recipes to suit your own taste or diet. Salt substitutes are unsatisfactory.

• **Eggs:** Color, flavor, and texture are enhanced by the addition of eggs. Beaten eggs in a dough help in the leavening process by tenderizing the gluten strands and relaxing the dough.

• **Cheese, Spices, Herbs, Fruits, and Nuts:** These ingredients have been used in breads since the flamboyant days of the Pharaohs. Such ingredients make bread intriguing and delightful for holidays and for gifts.

BASIC BREADMAKING METHODS

• **Conventional Method:** All ingredients are combined, mixed, kneaded, allowed to rise, formed into loaves to rise again, and baked.

• **Sponge Method:** The liquids, yeast, and a portion of the flour are combined, beaten until smooth, covered, and allowed to proof until light and bubbly—usually 30 minutes to 1 hour.

• **Overnight Sponge:** This may be accomplished in two different ways. A light sponge similar to the Sponge Method is combined, covered, and allowed to sit overnight. This is a method frequently used for sour-doughs. The second method is to combine all ingredients, knead, place in a warm bowl, cover, and allow to proof overnight. Many old recipes were prepared in this manner because homemade yeast was not as active as the yeast available today. The overnight sponge is particularly successful when a dough is rich with eggs, butter, and sugar; the result is a beautiful texture.

• **Batter Breads:** The liquids, yeast, butter, and eggs are combined with just enough flour to make a mixture similar to a heavy pancake batter. The mixture is beaten hard either by machine, rubber spatula, or by slapping the dough (see page 32) with one hand. Since this technique is the only kneading for a batter bread, the texture will be coarser than that of conventional dough.

• **Rapidmix:** A popular method evolved to combine all dry ingredients including the active dry yeast in a mixing bowl. The liquid is heated with butter and sugar to a specified temperature, usually 115°F, and is poured into the dry ingredients. The mixture is beaten thoroughly with a dough hook on a heavy-duty machine or by hand and finished in the conventional manner.

MAKING HOMEMADE BREAD

• **The Conventional Method:** Here is a step-by-step description of how to make a loaf of bread, with special advice for beginners, to give you a clear understanding of the complete process.
1. Select and read recipe; gather all ingredients in one area.

2. Sprinkle yeast over warm water (100°–110°F) and stir with a fork, the best instrument for breaking up yeast granules.

3. Combine sugar, butter, salt, and a warm liquid; add the yeast mixture.

4. Beat in 2–3 cups of flour until a smooth batter is formed.

5. Gradually add sufficient flour to form a soft, workable dough. The addition of flour is one of the exciting challenges of breadmaking, for each day it can be a little different. Do not worry if the same recipe requires more or less flour than on a previous day. Humidity makes a difference, sacks of flour can vary even though milled by the same company. Any well-written bread recipe will make allowance for differing amounts of flour by stating—"8 cups flour, approximately," or "7–8 cups flour."

Do not pack flour into a cup. When you buy a bag of flour, empty the contents into a container and loosen with a wooden spoon or scoop. In other words "stir" the flour. This avoids a packed cup of flour when measuring. To measure flour, scoop it up with measuring cup and scrape the excess flour from the top of the cup with a knife. Flour for breads need not be sifted unless specified in a recipe.

6. When enough flour has been added, the dough will pull away from the sides of the bowl. At this point, you are ready to knead. To knead by hand, turn the dough out onto a floured board, marble, or pastry cloth. With a dough scraper, lift up one edge of the dough and fold it toward the center, pressing down with the heel of your other hand. Give the

dough a quarter turn and lift and press one edge into the center again. You may have to use the scraper for the first few turns. As soon as the dough holds together, use both hands to knead. Pull a portion of the dough to the center and push firmly down with heels of both hands. (A baker usually kneads with one hand, but I use both!) Give another quarter turn and repeat. Keep turning and pressing down firmly, but avoid breaking the dough. Kneading activates the gluten to stretch and

hold the gas created by the action of the yeast. Breaking the dough will tear the dough structure.

You cannot knead too much. If you tire, throw a towel over the dough and rest—the dough will be happy to rest with you. *Knead, knead, knead,* for this is the heart and soul of making a beautifully textured bread. Rub flour on your hands, pick up the dough and dust the kneading surface, but, again, be careful about the amount of flour you add. My beginning students love to smother dough with flour but I make them brush it off. Knead until the dough becomes smooth, elastic, slightly damp to the touch of your hand, and bounces back when a finger is pressed into it.

To knead with a dough hook: Mix liquid ingredients plus yeast mixture in bowl of electric mixer. Beat in 2 to 3 cups of flour by hand until fairly smooth. Set the bowl on the machine and, at a medium-low speed, slowly add sufficient flour to make a soft, workable dough that pulls away from sides of the bowl. Knead 5 minutes by machine. Turn dough out on a lightly floured board and knead 1 minute by hand.

7. Rinse a bowl with warm water, dry thoroughly. Brush with melted butter and drop the dough into the bowl, turning it to coat the top with the butter. Cover loosely with plastic wrap (which helps prevent a dry crust from forming) and a towel. Place the bowl in a cozy corner of your kitchen. If you live in a very cold area or keep your house at 65°F, place the bowl in an unheated, draft-free oven with the pilot light on or with a bowl of hot water on the shelf below. A utility room, warm bathroom, or

even the top of a hot water tank are all possibilities. Yeast spores live in my kitchen by the billions, for there is no spot where the dough will not rise. Set a timer for proofing. After the dough has doubled, press a finger into the dough. If the indentation remains, the dough is ready for shaping.

8. Punch down the dough, turn out on a lightly floured board, and divide into equal portions. Knead each portion briefly, cover, and let rest 10–15 minutes, during which time the dough will relax and become easier to manipulate. Shape into regular loaves, following the instructions beginning on page 33.

9. Place the loaves in prepared loaf pans (a pan should be about half filled with dough, no more than two thirds), allow to rise to top of pan, and bake in a preheated oven for the specified time. If the loaves are golden brown all over, slide easily out of the pan, and sound hollow when thumped on the bottom, they are done. Let cool on wire racks.

• **Kneading a Batter Bread:** Without a heavy-duty mixer, stirring a batter or casserole bread with a rubber spatula or wooden spoon becomes a hard, dreary task. Throw both instruments aside, roll up the sleeve of your beating arm, place the bowl on a slightly wet tea cloth and begin, literally, to slap the dough with one hand. The batter feels silky, and the up-and-down motion is far easier on your arm than stirring 'round and 'round. When the batter becomes smooth and peels off your hand, it is ready for the next step.

• **High Altitude Baking:** The higher the altitude, the faster dough rises. Preparing bread in the mountains is discussed in detail in the chapter on a western journey through Colorado (page 247).

Special tips: Warm flour in the oven to remove any chill. Have all ingredients at room temperature. Find that cozy spot someplace in the kitchen or house for proofing. Flour dries out easily at high altitudes;

keep flour in airtight containers. Sometimes less yeast is needed. I have baked bread at eight thousand feet, at sea level, and in between with no difficulty.

• **Beginning Bakers:** Breadmaking can be delightfully relaxing and easy, for there are many variables and all of them work. When you muddle through your first batch of bread, the immediate thrill will be working with yeast, bringing it alive, catching a whiff of that wonderfully earthy aroma, and watching the yeast mixture bubble and froth. Learn to test the water for dissolving yeast by testing first with a thermometer and then checking by hand. Again, 100°F is excellent for dry yeast.

Be careful in the addition of flour; never dump the given amount in all at one time. The next real excitement is kneading, the splendid therapy of making bread by hand. Knead, knead, knead. Throw the dough around, slam it on the table. No damage can be inflicted once the ingredients are stuck together. Frustrations will fly out the window and soon kneading will become a rhythmic pleasure. When you give away your first loaf of bread and see the smile of the recipient, all that work was worth every floury minute.

Remember to read a recipe through, reread, and then plunge ahead. Select easy basic recipes in the beginning, then as you gain confidence, try a coffeecake. Remember, the dough is your friend. Give the loaves a love pat as you tuck them into pans.

Shaping Breads

When a dough is ready for shaping, punch it down and turn out on a lightly floured surface. Divide into the desired portions, knead each, and cover with a towel. *Let the dough rest 10–15 minutes.* If the dough pulls back during shaping, allow another 10 minutes rest.

• **Regular Loaf:** Roll one portion of dough into a rectangle, about as wide as the length of the baking pan and 12 inches long. Press along the edges if there are bubbles. Fold one third of the dough to the center. Fold the other portion on top (envelope style). Pinch the edge to seal and turn the loaf over so the seal is on the bottom. Tuck the ends under, pat and shape, and place in the pan (which you have brushed with melted butter, margarine or vegetable shortening). Tuck in the dough all around for a smooth loaf.

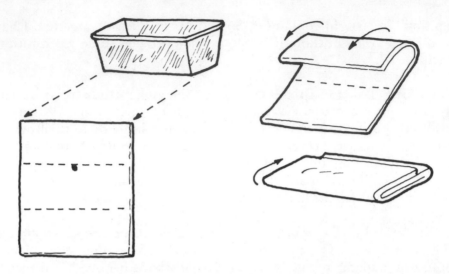

If the dough is quite soft, a loaf can simply be patted into shape. A third method is to roll out the dough into a rectangle as described and roll it up from the short side, jelly-role style. Pinch the seam and ends to seal. Turn the seam to the bottom when placing dough in the pan.

• **Round Loaf:** Knead a portion of dough into a round ball. Begin drawing one hand across the top, tightly, and to the bottom turning the loaf with your other hand. Repeat this tight smoothing across the top and under several times, turning constantly, and soon there will be a

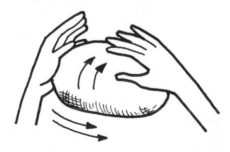

lovely round loaf. A round loaf can be baked in a casserole or cake tin, or on a baking sheet or a baking stone.

• **Snail:** Roll a portion of dough into a 30-inch rope. Do not attempt to make it perfectly smooth, for the pan proofing will eliminate lumps and bumps. Roll the rope in snail, or coil, fashion and place in a buttered cake tin or, if shaping a sturdy whole-grain dough as a free-form loaf,

on a buttered baking sheet. A snail loaf is particularly attractive if, before baking, it is brushed with an egg glaze (page 45) and sprinkled with poppy or sesame seeds.

• **Twist:** Divide a portion of dough in half. Roll each portion into a rope, overlap two ends and twist the two ropes. Seal both ends by pinching and tucking dough under. Place on a baking sheet and plump the loaf. Do not stretch the dough.

• **Cottage Loaf:** A charming loaf to make. Brush a 1-quart casserole or soufflé dish with melted butter. Cut off one quarter of the dough. Shape the larger portion into a round loaf, as described above, and place in the prepared casserole. Make an indentation in the center of the dough. Cup your hand over the smaller piece of dough and rotate quickly on a flat surface to make a perfectly round ball. Use no extra flour when making the small ball of dough. Place it in the indentation in

the larger portion. Stick your forefinger into some flour and then down into the center of the small ball, through the large round, to the bottom of the casserole. This glues the two pieces of dough together. Cover and let rise. Just before baking, stick your finger into the hole again.

For an even more attractive bread, sprinkle untoasted sesame seeds heavily over the buttered soufflé dish. When the loaf has risen, brush top with whole-egg glaze (page 45) and sprinkle with sesame seeds.

• **3-Strand Braid:** There are two methods for shaping a simple 3-strand braid.

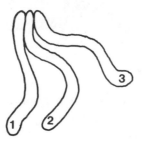 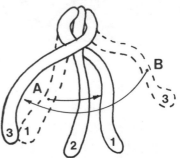

1. Divide the suggested amount of dough into 3 equal portions. Roll each portion into a smooth rope and place the 3 ends close together. Braid loosely from that end, then seal and tuck under both ends. Plump the braids.

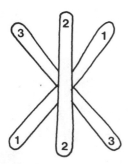 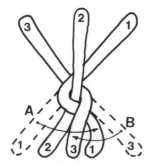 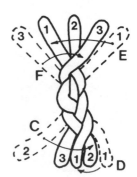

2. Roll 3 ropes of dough as directed above. Cross the 3 strands in the center and braid out toward each end. As you are forming the braid, do not be afraid to pick it up and move it around for your convenience in molding.

• **4- and 6-Strand Braided Loaves:** There are several recipes suggesting that the dough be shaped into multi-braided loaves. These are best described by my artist. My suggestion for a first experience is to tape a number at the end of each rope and then follow the diagrams. Both will result in beautiful braiding for very special breads.

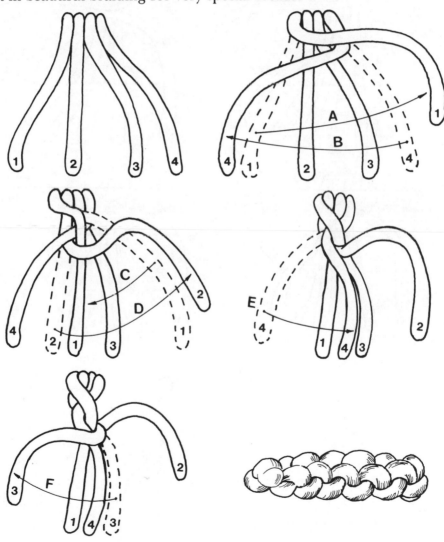

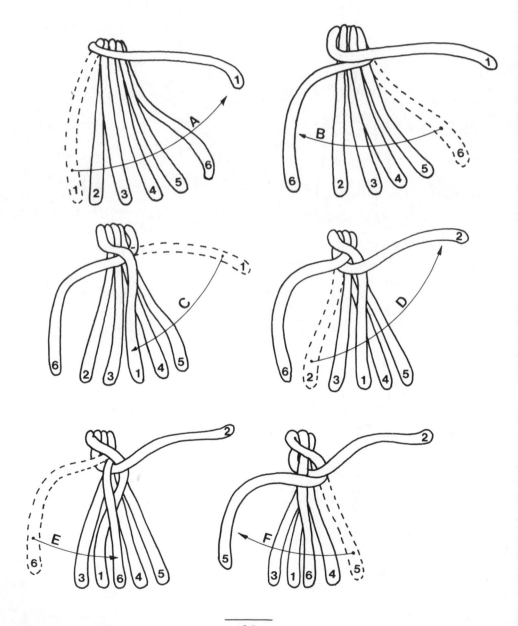

Shaping French Breads

From one recipe of French dough (page 32) five breads can be shaped. Each bread is given its French name with a phonetic spelling and explanation of the term. Most French loaves are slashed in some fashion. The best instrument is a razor, which makes a clean, sharp cut. Hint: My beautician gave me a folding razor and keeps me supplied with blades. Some slashing is also done with kitchen scissors.

Begin by dividing the French dough into 5 equal portions. The baguette, *tourte de seigle,* and *épi* each use one portion; the *couronne rosace* uses one and a half portions; and the *ficelle* is made from half a portion. Cover the unshaped dough while you mold each bread.

• **Baguette**—Ba-get'—long and slender: A crusty loaf and the most popular shape for French bread, both in France and the United States. Knead one portion of dough lightly, cover, and let rest 10 minutes. Roll into a rectangle 19–20 inches long, or the length of your baking sheet. Roll tightly from the long side, sealing the side and ends by pinching. (If the sealing pulls apart, there is too much flour in the dough.) Roll into a smooth loaf and place on a baking sheet, tapering or blunting the ends. Cover and let rise about 45–60 minutes. With a razor or knife make a series of short slashes or three long slashes in the top just before baking.

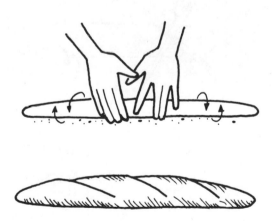

• **Tourte de Seigle**—Toort de seygl(uh)—round: Knead one fifth of the dough into a round. Place on a baking sheet and flatten slightly. Cover

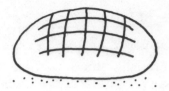

and let rise 45 minutes. Sprinkle flour on top, brushing off any excess. Slash in a crisscross fashion just before baking. *Seigle* means rye; this is an excellent way to slash a round loaf of rye or French country bread.

• **Épi**—Ay pee'—the head of a stalk of wheat: This is one of the most picturesque French loaves. Roll one fifth of the dough into a rectangle 20 inches long. Roll tightly from the long side, sealing the side and ends. Place on a baking sheet, cover with a light towel, and let rise 45–60 minutes. With kitchen shears, starting at one end, clip a deep slash into the top of the dough and pull that portion to one side. Clip further down and pull that portion to the opposite side. Continue down the loaf alternating the direction in which the slashed portions are pulled. (Each slashed portion represents one grain of the head of wheat.) The loaf is now ready to bake.

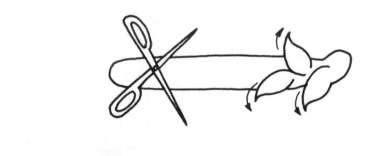

• **Couronne Rosace**—Koor-uhn' rohz-ahss'—crown: A lovely loaf to make. Cut one portion (one fifth) of the dough into 4 equal pieces. Divide another portion of dough in half, cover one half, and set aside

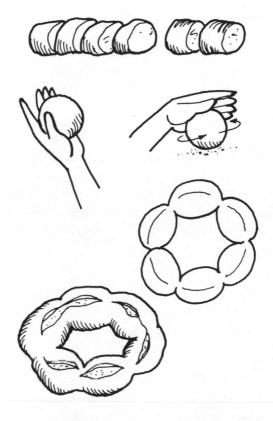

for a *ficelle*. Divide the remaining half into 2 pieces. Altogether you now have 6 equal portions. Cup your hand over one portion and rotate quickly to form a smooth ball. Continue rolling gently until the ball is slightly elongated. Repeat with remaining 5 portions of dough. On a baking sheet place the balls in a circle so that they just touch. Cover and let rise about 30 minutes, or until light. Slash down the center of each ball of dough just before baking.

• **Ficelle**—Fee-cell'—string: Roll the small portion of dough left from the *couronne rosace* into a rectangle about 12 inches long. Roll tightly from the long side and seal the side and ends. Plump the loaf gently and place on a baking sheet. Cover and let rise 30–45 minutes. Slash three times before baking.

Note: The best baking sheets for French breads are the heavy, black ones. Once they are seasoned, the baking sheets need not be brushed with any kind of fat. If using a nonseasoned baking sheet, brush lightly with vegetable shortening or use a canned spray.

SHAPING DINNER ROLLS

• **Parker House Rolls:** Divide the dough in half or into thirds for easier handling. Roll one portion in a rough circle about ¼–½ inch thick. Cut into rounds with a 2½-inch biscuit cutter. With the dull edge of a knife gently mark the tops of the rounds slightly off center. Brush with melted butter and fold the short sides of the rounds over so that the

edges barely meet. Seal and place on buttered baking sheet about 1 inch apart. Cover and let rise until double in bulk.

• **Cloverleaf Rolls:** Pinch or cut off small pieces of dough and form small balls. Whatever size you make, the dough will double in size. Have at hand a small bowl of melted butter, dip in each ball, then place in muffin tins, 3 balls to a cup. Cover and let rise until double in bulk.

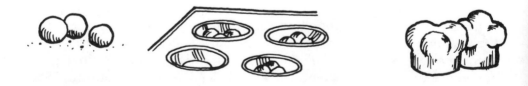

• **Fantans:** Roll a portion of dough into a rectangle about ¼ inch thick. Brush with melted butter. Cut the dough with a sharp knife or dough scraper into strips about 1 inch wide. Stack 6 strips on top of each other,

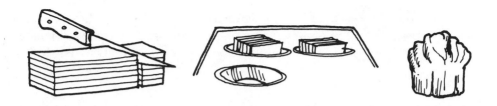

cut into pieces 1½ inches long, and place on end in buttered muffin tins. Cover and let rise until double in bulk.

• **Crescents:** Roll a portion of dough into a circle ¼ inch thick and 9 inches in diameter for an easily handled roll. Brush lightly with melted butter. Cut into 8 or 10 pie-shaped wedges. Beginning at the wide end, roll a wedge toward the narrow point and curve into a crescent. Place 1 inch apart on a buttered baking sheet. Cover and let rise until double in bulk.

• **Pan Rolls:** An easy roll to prepare. Shape one portion of dough into a long roll and divide evenly into pieces. Cup one piece in your hand and quickly rotate on a flat unfloured surface until a smooth ball is formed. (If there is too much flour, the dough will be so dry it cannot be rotated.) Place on buttered baking sheet ½ inch apart. If desired, the roll may be slightly elongated. Cover and let rise until double in bulk.

• **Bowknots:** These are fun, and children love to make and eat them. Roll a portion of dough ¼ inch thick. Cut in pieces about 7 inches long. Tie in a knot, place on a buttered baking sheet, and brush with melted butter. Cover and let rise until double in bulk.

FREEZING BAKED AND UNBAKED BREAD AND ROLLS

• **Freezing Baked Bread:** Let loaves cool completely, preferable overnight, in plastic bags. Wrap in aluminum foil, label, slip into a plastic bag, tie, and the bread will keep very well for a year in the freezer.

• **Freezing Dough:** Basic dough may be frozen for a short time. Let the dough rise, mold into loaves, wrap securely in plastic wrap or aluminum foil, label, and freeze for no longer than 4 weeks. Remove a loaf 6 hours before serving to allow time for defrosting and second proofing.

• **Freezing Rolls:** Basic dinner rolls may be shaped, placed on a buttered baking sheet, brushed with melted butter, and covered with a double thickness of plastic wrap or aluminum foil for freezing. When ready to use, remove from the freezer 3 hours before serving to allow time for thawing and rising. Brush again with melted butter and bake as directed. An excellent solution for a busy holiday dinner is to freeze the unbaked rolls several days ahead. If the rolls are to be kept longer, they may be removed from the baking sheet after they are frozen, placed in plastic bags, and kept 4–5 weeks. If a roll dough does not freeze well, I say so in the recipe.

GLAZES, TOPPINGS AND FROSTING

Glazes and toppings are the finishing touch for many breads. Most are interchangeable among breads—whether a soft buttery crust is desired; a hard, shiny, crisp finish; or a "glue" to hold seeds and nuts. For many basic breads, I prefer no finish, just the natural crust. Here are a number of toppings and glazes and an explanation of the effects they produce.

• **Egg Glaze:** Beat 1 whole egg or 1 egg yolk together with 1 tablespoon of either water or milk and brush on the loaves after they have risen, but before baking. A soft glaze for rich, sweet breads and for white breads to enhance the golden color. Also a good glue for sliced almonds or seeds.

• **Egg-White Glaze:** Beat 1 egg white together with 1 tablespoon of water until frothy. Before baking, brush the glaze on such loaves as French, rye, or pumpernickel for a shiny crust. This glaze is also used to hold nuts or seeds on the crust.

• **Rice Flour Topping:** An entrancing and different topping to enhance any plain basic bread. Combine 4 packages of active dry yeast with ⅔ cup warm water. Stir in 1 tablespoon of sugar, ¾ cup rice flour, and 2 teaspoons safflower oil. Set aside to rise until light and bubbly, about 30 minutes. The mixture will be a thick paste. Shape the basic loaves. Spread the rice topping over tops of loaves and cover with a light cloth. Let rise and bake as recipe directs. The result is a handsome cracked top.

• **Postum or Instant Coffee:** Mix a heaping tablespoon of either Postum or instant coffee into 2 tablespoons of water, stirring until dissolved. Brush on whole grain breads to give a dark, satiny finish; may be brushed on before baking or 5 minutes before bread is done.

• **Cornstarch:** For a soft, shiny finish, particularly for dark breads, combine 1 teaspoon of cornstarch with ½ cup of water in a saucepan. Bring to a boil and cook, stirring constantly, 3 minutes. Brush the glaze over the bread 5 minutes before it is done. Return to oven and finish baking.

• **Melted Butter:** Immediately after loaves are removed from the oven, brush the tops with melted butter for a soft crust. Or, brush loaves 5 minutes before removing from the oven.

• **Confectioner's Frosting or Icing:** Combine 1 cup of confectioner's sugar with 2 teaspoons of lemon juice and enough water to make a creamy frosting. Beat thoroughly with a whisk or fork until frosting is smooth and has reached the consistency desired. For most breads, the frosting should pour easily enough so that it drips down the sides of the bread.

Variations are limitless. Substitute for the lemon juice any of the following: lime or orange juice; liqueurs such as Curaçao, Grand Marnier, Amaretto, light or dark rum; vanilla; and even just milk or water.

Do not frost a bread that you are going to freeze. Use the icing only after the bread has defrosted.

• **Raisins:** Currants and raisins are often used in breads and rolls. Empty a box of raisins into a sieve and pour boiling or very hot water over them. Shake to eliminate some of the water and pour raisins out onto a double thickness of paper towels. Let dry and place in a container with a tightly fitting lid.

• **Cinnamon Sugar:** Combine 1 cup of granulated sugar with 2 tablespoons of cinnamon. Make up a quantity and keep in a labeled jar. If you prefer less cinnamon flavor, use only 1 tablespoon. For an even better flavor, measure the sugar into a glass jar. Add a piece of vanilla bean, cover, and leave it 2 weeks. Remove vanilla bean and add the cinnamon.

• **Nutmeg Sugar:** Prepare a jar of sugar with nutmeg—1 teaspoon of ground nutmeg for 1 cup of sugar. Nutmeg is strong in flavor and overuse results in a bitter taste.

Special glazes and frostings are given in recipes for many breads and rolls. When Cinnamon Sugar is used, directions will refer to page 46.

MAJOR EQUIPMENT

The twentieth-century kitchen is routinely equipped with many utensils needed for breadmaking, such as measuring cups and spoons, rubber spatulas, wooden spoons, sifter, rolling pins, kitchen shears, and many other small items. Not only from American industry, but also from other countries major utensils and machines are available, offering a variety of choices to aid the serious breakmaker. I list what has been of practical benefit to me through my years of teaching and making bread for my family.

• **Dough Scraper:** An inexpensive and invaluable utensil that does just what the name says—scrapes up the dough. When dough is first turned out of the mixing bowl onto a floured board, this marvelous but simply made utensil helps gather the dough into kneading order. It can scoop up the dough, pick up rolls, clean a countertop, even scrape a mess off the floor. Absolutely marvelous to pick up a broken egg! Available in all kitchenware stores.

• **Kneading Board:** Let's explore several. One of the best is a slab of marble. If you are building or redoing a kitchen, have a piece inserted into a kitchen counter top in the mixing area. Or purchase an unfinished slab of marble at your local tile store. Wood kneading boards are probably the most popular. I have had chopping board slabs built in as my kitchen cabinet tops, plus a marble slab. When I first began making bread forty years ago, I kneaded on a pastry cloth that worked well except that it would slip. Now one has been invented that has suction cups attached. See Sources of Supply, page 483. If you have none of these, kneading is quite successful on a Formica counter top.

• **Heavy-Duty Mixer:** Purchase the best and largest you can afford. For twelve years, my mixer has made countless batches of dough, saving my

energy for teaching and writing. For me it has been an invaluable appliance. KitchenAid, Braun, and Bosch are popular brands. Most electric mixers are equipped with a dough hook, so the breadmaker has a wide choice of machines.

• **Food Processor:** Excellent for whipping up a single loaf of bread. Dough recipes can easily be divided, whirled separately, and then combined for a final kneading before proofing, to make 2 or 3 loaves. Food processors are and will be made larger to handle more flour. Besides preparing bread dough, the processor speedily handles other needs in breadmaking—grating cheese; chopping nuts, candied fruits, and herbs; and puréeing fillings. It is ideal to have both a mixer and a processor; they will handle all the processes of breadmaking superbly.

For one loaf, it is best to add the dry ingredients with the butter to the processor bowl. Whirl to blend and slowly add the liquids, including the dissolved yeast. When the dough forms into a ball around the spindle, let it whirl or knead 1 minute. Remove and knead by hand 1–2 minutes. From that point, follow the recipe directions.

• **Proofing Bowls:** Invest in several heavy crockery bowls of various sizes. They may be found in kitchen shops, import stores, catalogs, and old fashioned hardware stores in small towns. When ready to proof the dough, warm the bowl with hot water, dry thoroughly, brush with melted butter, drop the dough in, swish it around, and turn over so the buttered side is up. Cover loosely with plastic wrap and a kitchen towel (preferably terry cloth). The dough will snuggle in such luxurious warmth and react lovingly by doubling in size. Plastic, metal, and glass bowls certainly may be used. Prepare them in the same manner.

• **Baking Stone:** This is not essential equipment, but it is marvelous for baking free-form loaves made of whole grains and great for pizzas. Baking stones are now available at most kitchenware stores and through catalogs.

• **Baking Pans:** Loaf pans made of a dark material will produce a lovelier golden color than bright, shiny pans. When using the latter, turn one loaf out in your towel-covered hand to check the color. If it is not to your satisfaction, pop the loaves back into the oven for another 5–10 minutes. I prefer to design a recipe using the 8½ × 4½ × 2½-inch loaf pans; the loaf cuts into slices of a good size to fit into a toaster and for sandwiches. A 9×5×3-inch pan is the next most popular. There are several smaller sizes available, including miniature loaf pans, which are excellent for making little loaves to serve individually or to slice for making melba toast to go with soups or to use as bases for appetizers.

• **Flour Mills:** It's a grand luxury to own a mill to grind grains into fresh, warm flour. The flavor of a bread made from grains freshly milled is incredibly delicious, with an earthy aroma and taste. There are a number of mills on the market, with the most popular at present the Magic Mill because of its neat and compact size. Others are listed in Sources of Supply.

• **A Necessary Assortment:** Sturdy baking sheets are a must for free-form loaves and coffeecakes. Look around your kitchen for other items on this list—most you will already have, and none are expensive: custard cups for large popovers and miniature plucket (or bubble) loaves. All sizes of muffin tins, including the tiny ones perfect for individual sweet rolls. A pancake griddle, waffle iron, deep-fat fryer, pastry wheel, wire racks for cooling, tube pans, brioche, Bundt, and Kuglehopf tins. By all means a timer to carry around in an apron pocket or on a cord around your neck to remind you the dough is proofing. As you delve deeper into the art of breadmaking, add to your collection. Forty years ago I began making bread with one cookbook, a pastry cloth, a rolling pin, an odd collection of bowls (mostly from my mother-in-law), a few loaf pans, no knowledge, but a strong arm.

PROBLEMS!

"My bread collapsed in the oven!"
    "What made that big crack on the side?"
    "There are such big holes all through my loaves!"
    "Do you think I killed the yeast?"
    "I can stick my finger between the bread and the top crust!"
    Problems do occur. I have found that many cooks, beginners and experienced, have a fear of handling yeast and bread dough. The fact is that the difficulties can be solved, clearing the way for making the kind of bread you want.

• **Bread collapses in oven:** Overrising in the bread pan. The dough has one final burst of rising during the first 15 minutes in the oven. When the dough has puffed too high during the second rising, the gluten strands, already overstretched, will break, the gas escapes, and the bread falls. When the dough has been formed into loaves, let it rise just to edges of the pan or slightly curved over the edges.

• **Bread has overrisen in the bowl:** A dough overrisen in the bowl will collapse and become heavy. Check the dough at the suggested time by punching one finger into it. If an indentation remains, the dough is ready for the next step. If the dough has collapsed, turn it out on a surface and knead 2–3 minutes. Cover, let rest 15 minutes, and form into loaves.

• **Pale bread:** If using shiny pans that reflect heat, extend baking time 5 minutes. Turn a loaf out into your hand (protected by towel) and, if not browned to your satisfaction, either place the loaf directly on the oven rack 5 minutes or return to the baking pan and oven 5 to 10 minutes longer. Glass pans absorb heat; reduce oven temperature by 25°F.

• **Crack on side of bread:** Several reasons—uneven heat, too much flour in the dough, or too much dough in the pan. Fill a bread pan no more than half to two thirds full. If there is a small crack, don't worry about it, for even bakers have a little trouble with bulging and breaking. And certainly, you do not want your loaves to be factory perfect—they would not look homemade!

• **Holes in bread:** Poor bread texture results from insufficient kneading and possibly from overproofing. You cannot overknead; the dough will love it as long as you can hold out. When ready to form loaves, divide dough as directed and knead each portion thoroughly to help take out those "holes."

• **Killing yeast:** Liquid over 110°F will kill either dry or compressed yeast. For active dry yeast, the liquid temperature should be 100° to 110°F—warm but not really hot. I have never had an old packet of yeast, but if you are concerned proof it in warm water 15 minutes. If the mixture is not bubbling by then, throw it out and purchase fresh yeast. For compressed yeast, the water should be cooler, about 90°F. Compressed yeast is fragile; check the date on the package. A fresh cube will have no aroma and will break cleanly. Cool water makes either type of yeast sluggish.

• **Omitting yeast:** This can happen. I prepared a basic dough on a television show, tucked it in the bowl, turned back to the camera, and to my horror, there sat my bubbling bowl of yeast and warm water which I had so carefully demonstrated. I grabbed the bowl of dough, frantically stirred my burbling bowl of yeast, and explained happily (?) what was going on as I poured the yeast on the dough. I threw flour on top, rekneaded in the bowl, and it all came out beautifully. Breadmaking has its pitfalls, but it is a most flexible art.

When a dough is sluggish, does not rise properly, and you feel the yeast has been killed or was old, proof fresh yeast and add to the bedraggled dough. Add a bit more flour and knead well. Let the dough rise, mold into loaves, and bake as directed. Then make bread crumbs and croutons. There is no need to waste a whole batch of dough.

• **Heavy streak at bottom:** Too much flour, not enough rising time, and possibly temperature too high on the bottom of the pan during proofing. Avoid placing dough in an oven with a pilot light or on a gas burner. Use an oven only when the kitchen is cold and drafty at high altitudes and cold temperatures. When baking, arrange pans in the oven with space between to let hot air flow freely.

• **Dry, crumbly bread:** Proofing period too long, too much flour added while kneading, oven temperature possibly too low. Follow directions given in recipe on timing. Add flour in small amounts—never all at once. Have your oven checked for correct temperature. The proofing bowl must be covered carefully or the dough will form a dry, crusty skin.

• **Emergencies:** A teacher calls, Johnny has been bitten by a dog, and your dough has just risen to perfection. Punch it down—the dough, not the dog—re-cover, and refrigerate. The dough can stay there overnight and be ready for you the next morning. By then you will need the therapy of reworking the dough. If the emergency is short (a skinned knee), just punch down the dough, re-cover, and let it rise again. A dough can rise several times and not be harmed. However, the rising period is shorter each time.

The dough has been molded and placed in the pans, has risen correctly, and is ready to pop in the oven. Emergency! Quickly brush the tops with melted butter and place the pans in the refrigerator. Cover with a towel. The dough will continue to rise slowly. When you return, it may be necessary to empty the pans, knead the dough thoroughly, and reshape the loaves.

And now, on to the recipes, which come from every state in this great nation. Plunge in, be fearless, and have a wonderful time!

A PORTION OF TEXAS

MILEAGE—1,559 MILES

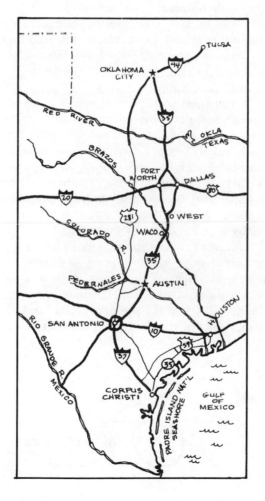

Blue Bonnet
TEXAS STATE FLOWER

arie Jerrabec opened the door and I stepped into my first experience looking for bread recipes in the United States. A blue norther
had zipped through Tulsa during the Christmas holidays. Any small show of
snow sends my husband scurrying south, so a quick decision put us onto Interstate 35E through Oklahoma City and into Texas, speeding madly at fifty-five
miles per hour. South of Fort Worth, a sign flashed by—Czechoslovakian Bakery. At my small scream, brakes were applied, and we skidded into West, a
village of three thousand where half the population is descended directly from
Bohemian immigrants. There proved to be three bakeries full of *kolaches*,
swirled breads, and all sorts of enticing Christmas cookies. Bakery clerks insisted I should meet Marie Jerrabec. I found her at home, introduced myself,
and she bid me enter with a warm Texas accent.

Marie was eighty, pretty, and strongly independent. Her grandfather had
left Bohemia because of religious persecution, found himself working in a
Pennsylvania mine, which was too confining for a farmer, and boarded a boat
to Galveston. Gradually he worked his way into the beautiful farming country
between Fort Worth and San Antonio.

A month later, I returned to West and spent a day with Marie making
kolaches. When I arrived she quickly stirred up the dough, plopped it in a bowl,
topped the bowl with a towel, and said, "Now let's meet my brothers." Our
whirlwind tour of this small Texas village took me into the back of a busy
butcher shop to rooms filled with kielbasa sausage in preparation, tongues mar-
inating in huge vats, carcasses of lamb and beef suspended on steel hooks, into
a curing room for hams and bacon, and to meet the three tall, handsome
brothers anxious to show off their domain. We made a quick stop at the local
newspaper operated by a young man of Portuguese ancestry, who published
both English and Czechoslovakian editions. Finally we stopped at one of the
bakeries to observe commercial *kolaches* being prepared. Marie assured me
their dough had to be much heavier than hers to go through the cutting machines. By this time I wondered what was happening to our own dough. We
found it light and high, quivering like the proverbial bowl of Jell-O. Following
is the recipe Marie shared with me, including a variety of fillings.

Bohemian Kolaches

Makes 50 kolaches

2 packages active dry
  yeast
¼ cup warm water
¾ cup plus 1 teaspoon
  sugar
⅜ pound (1½ sticks)
  butter, at room
  temperature
6 cups flour
2 egg yolks

2 cups warm milk, or one
  15-ounce can
  evaporated milk plus
  hot water to equal 2
  cups
2 teaspoons salt
melted butter
Kolache Fillings and
  Posipka, following
  recipes

Combine the yeast and water in a bowl, add 1 teaspoon of sugar, and stir until dissolved. Set aside. In a large mixing bowl cream the butter and the remaining sugar until light and fluffy. Add the yeast mixture and ½ cup of the flour. Blend in the egg yolks, milk, and salt. Gradually add the remaining flour by hand or machine, but do not use more than 6 cups. This is a very soft dough and is not kneaded. Beat the dough until glossy with a rubber spatula or with the flat beater of a heavy-duty mixer. Leave the dough in the mixing bowl and cover loosely with plastic wrap and a towel. Let rise until doubled, about 1 hour.

Butter 2 or 3 baking sheets.

The dough will be light, soft, and sticky. Cut or pull off small portions about the size of a medium egg, or smaller if you prefer a one-bite size. Marie used a tablespoon to shape the balls of dough, but I roll mine gently in the floured palms of my hands. Keep brushing your hands with flour as you handle the dough, but as a soft, sticky dough is the secret to tender, luscious *kolaches,* don't use too much flour or they will become dry. The rolls do not have to be perfect (you are not a cutting machine!). The next rising will eliminate lumps, bumps, and points. Place the balls of dough on the baking sheets about 1 inch apart. Brush with melted butter. Cover with a light cloth and let rise until light and puffy, about 45–60 minutes.

Preheat the oven to 400°F.

Unless you are using Cottage Cheese Filling (see the instructions on page 58), the risen *kolaches* are filled as follows: Make an indentation in each ball of dough with your thumb or two fingers. Place 1 tablespoon of filling in the center of each *kolache* and sprinkle with the *posipka* (topping). Bake about 15 minutes. Watch carefully, as the *kolaches* can burn easily because of their high sugar content. The rolls should be a light golden color when done. Remove from the oven and brush with melted butter. Remove the *kolaches* from the baking sheet and place on wire racks to cool. The rolls freeze very well.

Kolache Fillings and Topping

No one ever makes just a single kolache *filling. Instead, several are prepared and used to fill as many rolls as desired. The leftover fillings will keep for a week, well covered, in the refrigerator, or they can be frozen. Use the fillings in the recipe for Bohemian Coffeecake (page 59). Select the desired fillings and prepare them a day ahead. Then an assembly line of fillings and topping can be arranged while you wait for the rolls to rise in the bowl. Melt plenty of butter to brush on the* kolaches!

PRUNE FILLING

12 ounces pitted prunes
1 thick slice lemon, peeled
½ cup sugar
½ teaspoon vanilla

¼ teaspoon cloves
 (optional)
½ teaspoon cinnamon
 (optional)

Combine prunes, lemon, and sugar in water to cover in a saucepan. Bring to a boil, reduce heat, and simmer gently, uncovered, until soft and tender. Add the vanilla with cloves and cinnamon if you like a spicy touch. Let cool before using.

APPLE FILLING

3 cups peeled, cored, and
   coarsely chopped
   cooking apples
¼ cup water

3 tablespoons butter
¼ cup sugar
Grated rind of 1 lemon
1 teaspoon cinnamon

Combine all ingredients in a saucepan. Bring to a boil, reduce heat, and cook until thickened, stirring occasionally to avoid burning. Taste for seasoning. Let cool before using.

APRICOT FILLING

¾ pound dried apricots
¾ cup sugar

2–3 tablespoons Grand
   Marnier or Curaçao
   (optional)

Combine the apricots and water to cover in a saucepan. Simmer until water has evaporated, stirring occasionally to avoid burning. Remove from burner as soon as the water has evaporated (overcooking turns dried fruit dark), add the sugar and liqueur, if desired, and blend quickly in a food processor or with a wire whisk. Let cool before using.

POPPY SEED FILLING— THE CLASSIC CZECHOSLOVAKIAN FILLING

A delicious mixture for the kolaches; the poppy seeds must be ground, either with a poppy seed grinder or in a blender. If using a blender, whirl ⅓ cup at a time.

1 cup ground poppy seeds
4 tablespoons butter
¼ cup milk

2 teaspoons lemon juice
½ teaspoon vanilla
½ cup sugar

Blend all ingredients in a saucepan. Bring to a boil, reduce heat, and allow to simmer 5 minutes, or until thickened. Let cool before using.

COTTAGE CHEESE FILLING

1 pint dry cottage cheese
(See **Note**)
8-ounce package cream
cheese
1 egg yolk
½ cup sugar

Grated rind of 1 lemon
1 teaspoon lemon juice
10–12 soda crackers,
finely rolled (optional)
⅛ teaspoon salt

Note: If you cannot obtain dry cottage cheese, drain a pint of regular cottage cheese in a sieve placed over a bowl in the refrigerator overnight.

Combine all ingredients except the soda crackers and salt in a mixing bowl and stir until well blended, or place in a food processor and whirl two or three times. The mixture does not have to be smooth. If the cheese mixture seems too moist, add the soda crackers to absorb the liquid. Add the salt if you have not used soda crackers.

To fill the *kolaches*, after the first rising press a piece of the dough the size of a small egg into a circle and place 1 tablespoon of the filling in the center. Pull the edges over the filling and pinch together firmly. Place seam side down on a buttered baking sheet and brush top with melted butter. Let rise until light, about 30 minutes. Sprinkle with *posipka* and bake as directed on page 55.

POSIPKA OR CRUMB TOPPING (STREUSEL)
Makes enough topping for about 50 kolaches

1 cup sugar
¼ cup flour

1 teaspoon cinnamon
2 tablespoons melted
butter

Blend all ingredients in a small mixing bowl until the mixture resembles coarse cornmeal. Use a pastry blender or your hands—I like the latter. The *posipka*, which is a form of streusel or crumb topping, can be prepared and refrigerated several days in advance.

Bohemian Coffeecakes

Makes 3 coffeecakes

In the preparation of kolaches there will often be filling left over. The kolache dough adapts so well for both coffeecakes and rolls, I decided to make another batch and test several ideas to use those odds and ends.

1 recipe Bohemian *Kolache* dough, page 55	Cottage Cheese Filling, page 58
1 cup flour, approximately	Prune Filling, page 56
Apricot Filling, page 57	Melted butter
	Confectioner's Icing, page 45

Prepare the *kolache* dough as described and knead in enough additional flour to make a smooth dough that is not sticky. After the bowl rising punch down the dough and divide into 3 equal portions. Knead each piece, cover, and let rest 10–15 minutes.

Butter a baking sheet. Remove one portion of dough and roll into an 18 × 10-inch rectangle. With a rubber spatula spread one-third of the Apricot Filling (or whatever filling you have left) over the dough to within ½ inch of edges. Roll up the long side, jelly-roll style, and seal the seam. This is a lovely soft dough and will seal easily. If the dough tends to pull apart, there is too much flour—next time add less flour! Repeat directions with remaining portions of dough and fillings.

Place the rolls seam side down on the baking sheet, form into U shapes, and seal the ends. With kitchen scissors clip the tops with small slashes 1 inch apart. Cover and let rise until doubled, about 1 hour.

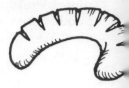

Preheat the oven to 350°F. Brush the rolls with melted butter and bake 35 minutes. Place on a wire rack to cool or frost with Confectioner's Icing and serve warm. The cakes freeze well, but eliminate any frosting.

Note: Sometimes, to make loaves of raisin bread, Marie would add 2 cups raisins, scalded and drained, 2 teaspoons cinnamon, and ½ cup chopped pecans to the above recipe. Let rise and shape into 3 loaves. Bake in preheated 375° oven 35 minutes.

San Antonio

Continuing south on Interstate 35W, the highway edges past Waco and Austin, the handsome capital city of Texas and home of the state's mammoth university. The Perdenales River winds through magnificent ranch country made famous by President Lyndon Johnson. Salado, a unique village of one street, is just off the highway and has one large hotel, an outstanding restaurant, bubbling springs that were an important stopping point on the Chisholm Cattle Trail, and a posh couturier shop, conveniently located for fly-in ranch women to purchase the latest designer clothes. Ninety miles south is San Antonio, one of our country's most charming cities.

There are three cities in the United States that have extravagant charm—San Antonio, New Orleans, and San Francisco. Each city has different ethnic groups, distinctive architecture, a rich history, and exceptionally fine cuisine. We walked beside the narrow, twisting, elegant river coursing through the center of San Antonio, were awed by the Alamo and its bloody history, fascinated with strutting peacocks on the grounds of Fort Sam Houston, and learned at the Institute of Texan Cultures that twenty-seven ethnic groups created the state of Texas. The large Mexican population bestows color and gaiety with its festivals, splendid dancing groups, and markets filled with brilliant handiwork.

Our special guide, Annie Wappler, a transplanted Tulsan, walked us past windows of Mexican bakeries displaying piles of tortillas and glass cases filled with pink-frosted rolls. To my surprise and delight Annie took us to a tiny street with a Russian bakery tucked in one corner. The bakery was owned by a young couple who had recently immigrated from Moscow. The wife (and baker) spoke no English, the husband just barely. There was no possibility of communication, but I poked around among the breads, coffee cakes, and rolls, purchased a variety, and decided I could adapt a Russian *krendel*.

Russian Krendel

Makes 2 coffeecakes

Krendel is a pretzel-shaped coffeecake, excellent for morning coffee or brunch. The cakes may be finished by two different methods, which are described at the end of the recipe. This is a far, far better bread than I had in Russia!

Dough:

2 packages active dry
    yeast
¼ cup warm water
3 tablespoons sugar
Grated rind of 1 lemon

1 cup warm milk
1 teaspoon salt
4 eggs, lightly beaten
½ cup melted butter
5 cups flour,
    approximately

Filling:

1 cup chopped dried
    prunes
1 cup chopped dried
    apples
1 cup chopped dried
    apricots

⅔ cup sugar
1 teaspoon cinnamon
¼ teaspoon nutmeg
Melted butter

Combine the yeast and water in a small mixing bowl, stirring until dissolved. In a large mixing bowl combine the sugar, grated rind, milk, salt, eggs, and butter. Blend well and add the yeast mixture. Beat in 2 cups of flour until mixture is smooth. Gradually add sufficient flour to make a soft dough that pulls away from the sides of the bowl. Turn out on a lightly floured surface and knead until smooth and satiny. Round into a ball and place in a warm buttered bowl, turning to coat the top. Cover loosely with plastic wrap and towel. Let rise until doubled, about 1½ hours.

To make the filling, combine the dried fruits in a bowl. In a separate bowl blend the sugar, cinnamon, and nutmeg. Punch down the dough, turn out on a lightly floured surface, knead lightly, cover, and let rest 10 minutes. Divide dough in half. Cover the portion not being worked on. Roll one piece of dough into a 28 × 9-inch rectangle. Brush with melted butter to within ¼ inch of the edges. Arrange half the fruit mixture over the dough. Sprinkle half the sugar mixture over the fruit. Roll up from a long side, jelly-roll style. When shaping such a long narrow roll, use a dough scraper to help control any stickiness. Seal the seam and ends. Twist the roll into a pretzel shape or a figure 8. Place on

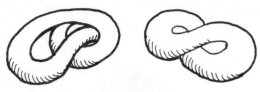

a buttered baking sheet and cover. Repeat directions with remaining portion of dough. Let rise until doubled, about 1 hour.

Preheat the oven to 350°F. Bake the *krendels* 35–40 minutes. Remove and let cool on wire racks.

Finishing the *krendel*: Prepare Confectioner's Icing (page 45) with your choice of flavoring and frost the cakes while warm. **A second method:** Beat 1 egg with 1 tablespoon of water. Brush cakes thoroughly just before baking. Sprinkle with sliced or slivered almonds.

T he vivid imagination of Mexican artisans turns breads into works of art. The simple tortilla is the main bread of Mexico, but bakers in both the United States and Mexico love working with yeast breads. Following are two fascinating Mexican braids. The *bolillo* is similar to French bread, but in Mexican hands the loaves are molded into fanciful forms. The second is a bread for All Saints' Day (our Halloween).

Bolillos

Makes 16 rolls or 12 combs or crescents

1 package active dry yeast
¼ cup warm water
2 cups hot water
¼ cup light oil or lard

2 tablespoons sugar
1½ teaspoons salt
6–7 cups flour

Combine the yeast and warm water in a small mixing bowl, stirring until dissolved, and set aside. In a large mixing bowl combine the hot water, oil, sugar, and salt. Stir until ingredients are dissolved and blended. Let cool to lukewarm. Stir in the yeast mixture and beat in 3 cups of flour until the mixture is smooth. Gradually add sufficient flour to make a soft, workable dough. Turn out on a floured surface and knead 10 minutes, or until smooth and silky. Round dough into a ball and place in a warm buttered bowl, turning to coat the top. Cover loosely with plastic wrap and a towel. Let rise until doubled, about 1 hour.

Rolls: Punch down the dough, knead 1 or 2 minutes, cover, and let rest 10 minutes. Butter a baking sheet. Divide the dough into 16 portions and cover dough not being worked on. Form each portion into a 4-inch roll. Place rolls on the sheet 2 inches apart. Cover and let rise until light and puffy, about 30–40 minutes. Before baking, slash down the center of each roll with a razor.

Combs: Butter a baking sheet. Divide dough into 12 pieces and cover dough not being worked on. Roll one portion into a 7-inch circle. Using the illustration as a guide, fold the circle so that the top edge does not quite meet the bottom edge. Around the curved edge of the half circle, cut ten 1-inch slashes through the dough with kitchen scissors or a sharp knife. Place on the sheet. Curve the two ends upward so the "comb" is spread out. Repeat with remaining portions of dough.

63

Crescents: Butter a baking sheet. Here are two ways for shaping rolls from a triangular piece of dough: Divide dough into 12 portions and cover dough not being worked on. Roll 1 piece into an elongated triangle, about 8 inches at the base. Roll up from the base, stretching the dough carefully as you roll. Place on the sheet and curve into a deep, long croissant shape. For a different formation, roll 1 piece of dough as directed, place on the baking sheet and form into an S shape.

Preheat the oven to 375°F. Any of the rolls may be brushed with an egg-white glaze (page 45) or with cold water. All rolls, of whatever shape, should be baked 25–30 minutes, or until golden brown. Serve immediately or let cool on wire racks. The rolls freeze well.

Pan de Muerto (BREAD OF THE DEAD)

Makes 2 breads

The name of this bread may sound depressing and macabre to you, but not to Mexicans or Filipinos. Picnics, games, and fun on November 1 and 2 are all in honor of loved ones that are gone, so celebrations frequently take place in cemeteries as well as parks. The Mexicans with their humorous imagination have created a delicious sweet bread in the shape of a spooky skull and crossbones.

1 package active dry yeast
¼ cup warm water
¾ cup warm milk
1 teaspoon salt

½ cup sugar
5 cups flour,
   approximately
3 eggs, lightly beaten

½ cup melted butter
1 teaspoon anise seeds,
   crushed
Grated rind of 1 lemon
1 egg white beaten with 1
   tablespoon water for
   glaze

4 agate marbles, if you
   can find them, or 8–12
   raisins
Slivered almonds

Combine the yeast and water in a small mixing bowl, stirring until dissolved, and set aside. In a large mixing bowl combine the milk, salt, and sugar. Add the yeast mixture and 1½ cups flour and beat thoroughly. Cover and let proof 1 hour.

Stir down the sponge, add the eggs, butter, anise (easily done with mortar and pestle), and grated rind. Gradually add sufficient flour to make a soft, workable dough that pulls away from sides of the bowl. Turn dough out on a lightly floured surface and knead until smooth and silky, about 8 minutes. Add as little flour as possible while kneading. Round dough into a ball and place in a warm buttered bowl, turning to coat the top. Cover loosely with plastic wrap and a towel. Let rise until doubled, about 1½ hours.

Turn the dough out and divide in half. Knead each piece about 1 minute, cover, and let rest 15 minutes. Keep 1 piece of dough covered while you shape the first half.

Preheat the oven to 350°F. Butter a large baking sheet.

Cut off one third of 1 of the pieces of dough. Round the larger portion into a smooth ball and flatten with your hands or a rolling pin into an oval about 8 inches long and 6 inches wide. Place on the sheet.

Cut off one third of the smaller piece of dough and set aside. Roll the larger portion into a circle 3–4 inches in diameter. Pull one edge of the circle, stretching and elongating it to give it the appearance of a skull. Brush the large oval on the sheet with the glaze. Place the elongated circle on the oval and press to be sure it adheres.

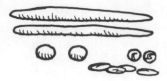

Divide the remaining small piece of dough in half. Snip off a tiny piece from each half to use for tears. With your hands form the larger pieces into 2 rolls long enough to fit across the top of the oval above the skull. Flatten the ends to simulate bones and press the rolls into the oval. Press the marble or raisins into the skull to make eyes, using 2 or 3 raisins for each eye. Shape the last 2 tiny pieces of dough into tears and place beneath the eyes. Insert slivered almonds for teeth. Brush the entire surface with glaze. Repeat with the other piece of dough.

Do not let the skulls rise; otherwise the bones will lose their shape and the skull will rise straight up! If you have only one oven, bake the first skull while you prepare the second one. Bake the breads about 30 minutes. Let cool on the baking sheet placed over a wire rack.

Note: Shaped into two 8½-inch loaves or plaited into two braids, this makes a wonderful sweet bread. After the breads are molded, cover and let rise until light, about 45 minutes. Bake in a preheated 350°F. oven 35–40 minutes. Let cool on wire racks.

Padre Island and Houston

C hecking a map, I found four interstate highways angling in different directions from San Antonio. Highway 37 continued south to Corpus Christi and Padre Island, which sounded lovely and warm. Padre Island, a National Seashore, is a long, slender key off the southern coast of Texas. The idea that it would be warm was ridiculous. The air was foggy, windy, no animals to be seen running through the long grasses, and not a bird in sight. The two of us seemed to be the only living things there and we were starving. We backtracked five miles from the entrance of the park and found The Catfish Inn.

Fresh, hot hush puppies were served immediately as we examined the paper place mats decorated with heads of magnificent animals from Africa. Then I realized the same handsome heads, beautifully mounted, graced the walls of this plain small restaurant. We asked for more hush puppies with our catfish and for the manager. I had to find out about those hush puppies.

A tall Texan with accent to match ambled slowly over to our table. I polished my Oklahoma accent and complimented him on those luscious hush puppies—and the amazing animal heads. My accent became stronger as I asked if it would be possible to obtain that recipe. He hitched his pants (all male Texans do that) and replied, "Wall now, ma'am, those things are our gimmick. You see, the snow birds flock down here in the summer and they just love those little puppies. Besides, ma'am, we took the cook out down the road one night, got him good and drunk and pried out his recipe. So you see, I just cain't rightly give it to you."

I agreed he couldn't rightly give out that stolen recipe. With elaborate Texan hospitality he hastened to invite our return, for the owners were planning the addition of a large bar to be decorated with North American animals. The pièce de résistance would be two mountain lions attacking each other over the bar. Well, that should do it!

Having lost out on the hush puppies, slowly we followed the coastline of Texas, turning north to join Interstate 10, which hurried us into the mass of humanity called Houston. The following morning our host and hostess greeted us with the news that the blue norther had left Tulsa, blown through Dallas and arrived in Houston. All pipes were frozen. The massive city of Houston is at sea level, so pipes must be built into attics. Our southward adventure was beginning to make me feel like Nanook of the North. But coffee was brewing and hot orange rolls baking. Immediately I asked for the recipe.

Houston Orange Rolls

Makes 50 plain or filled rolls

Marian Hansen and Lynn Bailey began teaching breads and pastries as my protégés. To my delight and gratification, they were an instant success. They ventured into catering and were flooded with customers. Truly, these are rolls that literally melt in your mouth.

½ pound (2 sticks) butter, at room temperature
½ cup sugar
1 cup boiling water
2 packages active dry yeast

1 cup warm water
2 eggs, well beaten
½ teaspoon salt
7 cups flour
melted butter (optional)

Cream the butter and sugar in an electric mixer until light and fluffy. Add the boiling water and let cool until tepid.

While the butter mixture is cooling, combine the yeast and warm water, stirring until dissolved, and blend into the butter mixture with the eggs and salt. Gradually add the flour and beat thoroughly. This may be done in a heavy-duty mixer using the flat beater. Add no more than the 7 cups of flour. The dough will be quite soft, almost a batter. Place the dough in a lightly buttered bowl, cover with plastic wrap and a towel, and refrigerate overnight.

Plain Hot Rolls: Butter a baking sheet. The next morning remove dough from the refrigerator and turn out on a floured surface. Divide in 5 equal portions. While working with one portion, return the remaining dough to the refrigerator. Roll each piece into a 12-inch circle. With a dough scraper cut into 10 wedges. Roll from the wide end into a crescent, curving the ends like a croissant. Place rolls on the baking sheet. Let rise about 1½ hours, or until bubbles form under the skin. Preheat the oven to 400°F. Brush the rolls with melted butter, if desired. Bake 12 minutes, or until golden, and serve warm.

Hot Rolls with Orange Filling: Refrigerate the dough overnight and in the morning make the filling.

1⅓ sticks butter, at room
    temperature
1 pound confectioner's
    sugar
⅓ cup frozen orange juice
    concentrate
Grated rind of 1 large
    orange

Cream the butter and sugar in an electric mixer or a food processor until fluffy. Add the juice and rind. If using a food processor, give it two or three quick turns.

Line round or oblong pans with foil shiny side up and brush with melted butter.

Divide the cold dough in 5 equal portions. While working with one portion, return the remaining dough to the refrigerator. Sprinkle work surface and rolling pin with flour. Roll one piece of dough into a rectangle 10 inches long. Brush thinly with orange filling, using a rubber spatula. Roll up tightly from the long side, jelly-roll style. Cut into ten 1-inch slices. Place in the pans and cover. Repeat directions with 4 remaining pieces of dough. Let rise until doubled, about 1½–2 hours. Reserve the remaining filling to brush on the baked rolls.

Preheat the oven to 350°F. Bake the rolls about 20 minutes, or until a light gold color. While still warm, brush with the remaining filling. Serve warm. Leftover rolls can be frozen.

No-Knead Coffeecake

Makes 3 coffeecakes

Buttery and rich, this no-knead dough wrapped around a luscious pecan filling makes each bite melting perfection. Marian and Lynn often made these cakes for classes as well as for the many parties they catered. An excellent coffeecake to keep in your freezer.

Dough:

1 package active dry yeast
¼ cup warm water
2¼ cups flour
2 tablespoons sugar
1 teaspoon salt
¼ pound (1 stick) butter
¼ cup evaporated milk

1 egg
¼ cup currants or
   chopped raisins,
   marinated in 2
   tablespoons brandy for
   1 hour

Filling:

4 tablespoons butter
½ cup packed brown
   sugar

½ cup chopped pecans

Vanilla Glaze:

2 tablespoons butter

1 cup sifted confectioner's
  sugar

½ teaspoon vanilla

1 or 2 tablespoons
  evaporated milk

Combine the yeast and water in a small bowl, stirring until dissolved, and set aside. Into a mixing bowl or food processor bowl sift together the flour, sugar, and salt. Cut in the butter until mixture resembles cornmeal. Add the milk, egg, currants, and yeast mixture. Mix well by hand or with a few spins of a food processor. Wrap the dough loosely in plastic wrap. Chill at least 2 hours or, preferably, overnight.

To make the filling, cream the butter in a small bowl with an electric mixer. Add the brown sugar and beat until fluffy. Stir in the pecans, cover, and chill.

Line a baking sheet with aluminum foil shiny side up. Remove dough from refrigerator and divide into 3 equal portions. Refrigerate 2 pieces and roll the third on a lightly floured surface into a 12 × 6-inch rectangle. Spread with one third of the filling. Roll up from the long side, jelly-roll style. Seal the seams and ends. Bend into a crescent shape and place on the baking sheet. With kitchen scissors make cuts along the outside edge 1 inch apart and ½ inch into center. Repeat directions with remaining 2 portions of dough. Cover and let rise until light, about 45 minutes.

Preheat the oven to 350°F. Bake the crescents 20–25 minutes. Frost while warm with Vanilla Glaze.

Vanilla Glaze: In a small saucepan melt the butter and cook until golden. Add the sugar and vanilla and stir to blend. With a whisk stir in sufficient evaporated milk to make fairly thin spreading consistency.

T he plumber arrived, thawed the pipes, and left for two hundred more houses in distress. We braved the chill wet air of Houston for a special dinner arranged at Ninfa's Tacos al Carbon Restaurant, both for the warming, excellent food and to hear a remarkable American success story. Ninfa had opened a tiny tortilla factory on Navigation Boulevard close to the ship channel, a rough area of Houston. After the death of her husband, Ninfa soon discovered the tiny factory could not support a large, growing family. She opened a small restaurant serving simple Mexican food and slowly incorporated recipes inherited from her husband's Italian relatives. In time the sons graduated from college and assumed the responsibility of Ninfa's business, giving their mother leisure time for traveling abroad.

After a fascinating meal of *queso de chihuahua*, deep-fried pork with avocado and tomato slices, marinated grilled chicken, beef ribs with *salsa verde*, a special rice, beans and guacamole, we followed Richard, our host, into the kitchen. As I watched one cook frying *sopaipillas* in hot coconut oil, Richard explained, "You have to keep stirring them, that's the secret." A young Mexican woman rolled out *sopaipilla* dough and prepared a special *empanada* filled with bananas. By the time we returned to the table, there was our dessert, the hot *empanada* sprinkled with confectioner's sugar and cinnamon, and drizzled with honey.

Ninfa's Banana Empanada

Makes 1 empanada to serve 2–4

¼ portion *sopaipilla* dough, page 363	Chopped pecans
	Oil for deep frying
1 ripe banana, peeled and sliced	Confectioner's sugar
	Cinnamon
Raisins	Honey

Roll the *sopaipilla* dough into a 10-inch circle. Place the banana in the center and top with a few raisins and pecans. Fold the dough over the fruit, press the edges together firmly, and crimp with a fork to seal.

In a deep fryer heat enough oil to cover the *empanada* (about 3 inches) to 370°F. Use peanut, sunflower, coconut—any good light oil. It must be very hot, otherwise you will have a soggy *empanada*.

Scoop the *empanada* up with a dough scraper or wide spatula and lower into the oil. Fry the *empanada* on one side about 2–3 minutes, or until golden, and carefully flip over. In another 3–4 minutes the *empanada* should be golden. Drain on paper towels. Serve immediately sprinkled with confectioner's sugar, a little cinnamon, and a bit of honey.

Dallas

H ouston's weather continued its bizarre pattern. Now a northern route back to warm Tulsa was our goal. Twenty miles south of Dallas the highway changed to a solid, thick slab of ice. We skidded into an Alaskan Dallas. Trees were split down the center by heavy ice. Icicle-laden shrubbery was in shreds throughout the entire city. We took refuge in a hotel and called a friend to join us for dinner. After we found they were refrigerating food outside and moving plants inside, we decided to venture no farther. The hotel dining room was empty except for the two of us and a swarm of waiters. Service was superb—a lovely wine and hot soup with toasted and buttered whole wheat bread were immediately placed before us. The rest of the meal really did not matter.

Texas Multi-Grain Bread

Makes 2 loaves

To prepare this bread use the fine grains from Hereford County, Texas (see sources of supply), and mold into free-form loaves. Cook on a baking stone or heavy baking sheet and a thick, crunchy crust will be the happy result.

2½ cups warm water
2 packages active dry
   yeast
½ cup honey
2 cups triticale flour
3 cups stone-ground
   whole wheat flour

½ cup whole hulled millet
2 teaspoons salt
½ cup light oil
½ cup toasted sesame
   seeds
2 cups unbleached white
   flour

72

Combine the water and yeast in a large mixing bowl, stirring until dissolved. Add the honey, triticale flour, 2 cups of whole wheat flour, and the millet. Beat until smooth. Cover and set aside 30 minutes, or until light and bubbly.

Stir down the sponge and add the salt, oil, sesame seeds, and remaining whole wheat flour. Beat thoroughly. Gradually add sufficient white flour to form a soft, workable dough that pulls away from the sides of the bowl. Turn the dough out on a floured surface and knead 8–10 minutes. Place in a warm buttered bowl, turning to coat the top. Cover loosely with plastic wrap and a towel. Let rise until doubled, about 1 hour.

Butter 1 or 2 baking sheets. If you have a baking stone, butter only 1 sheet.

Punch down the dough, turn out on a floured surface, and divide in half. Knead each piece thoroughly, cover, and let rest 10 minutes. Form each into a round loaf. Place one on a baking sheet. If using a baking stone, leave the second loaf on the kneading board, otherwise place on another baking sheet. Cover both loaves and let rise 40 minutes.

Preheat the oven to 375°F. If you are using a baking stone, put it in the preheated oven 30 minutes, or follow the manufacturer's instructions. Slip a floured paddle or wide spatula under the risen loaf and transfer to the hot stone. Bake the loaves 40 minutes. Let cool on wire racks.

Note: I tested one loaf by placing it on a cold baking stone to rise and then into a cold oven. Turn the temperature to 375°F. and add 10–15 minutes to the baking time.

D allas is a vibrant, exciting city. If the city fathers want something to happen, they pitch in and see that it does, whether it be grand opera and Maria Callas, the Dallas Cowboys, or a symphony. Even people who never go to a performance of the Metropolitan Opera will pay to bring such cultural and sports events to their city.

Dallas history began in 1841 when a few pioneers established a tiny village on the Trinity River. Water was a big problem, but that didn't stop Dallas from becoming the financial, cultural, and garment center of the Southwest. (As late as the 30's, when Dallas was host to the Texas Centennial Exposition, the water was so horrid that even a good illegal Kentucky bourbon couldn't hide the taste!)

Elegant Hush Puppies

Makes about 20 hush puppies

*This prize-winning Texas State Fair recipe was
given to me after a student, Elizabeth Sands,
heard my hush puppy tale (page 66) in a class at
"Cooking with Amber" in Dallas. The recipe was
originated by Parker Folse, Jr., and he prepared
a truly elegant hush puppy.*

¼ cup flour
¾ cup cornmeal
2 teaspoons baking
   powder
½ teaspoon salt
1 heaping tablespoon
   freshly chopped parsley
1 heaping tablespoon
   chopped scallion
1 tablespoon chopped
   pimiento

2–3 tablespoons chopped
   shrimp or crab meat
¼ teaspoon cayenne
½ teaspoon garlic powder
1 egg
½ cup milk,
   approximately
Oil for deep frying
2 shrimp shells (optional)
1 garlic clove (optional)

In a mixing bowl combine the flour, cornmeal, baking powder, and salt and blend well. Combine the parsley, scallion, pimiento, and shrimp, stir well, and add to the cornmeal mixture. Add the cayenne, garlic powder, and egg. Gradually add sufficient milk to make a batter of the consistency to be molded with your hands or a spoon.

In a deep fryer heat 3–4 inches of cooking oil (I prefer peanut or safflower oil) to 365°F. To give these elegant hush puppies even more flavor, drop in the shrimp shells and garlic and boil 2–3 minutes. For molding the hush puppies, Elizabeth suggests using a pastry bag fitted with a #6 star tip. Fill the bag with the batter and swirl crest shapes into the hot oil. This prevents thickness in the center and overcooking of the thin ends. Or drop the hush puppies into the oil by the tablespoons. Cook 3–5 minutes, turning once, until golden brown. Drain on paper towels and serve hot with some Gulf shore hot boiled shrimp!

Lemon-Egg Braids

Makes 2 loaves

*For all my wonderful friends and relatives in
Dallas who have entertained me so royally, a
bread to complement a lovely seated dinner party.
Note at the end of the recipe that the loaves can
easily be turned into holiday breads for gifts.*

1½ cups warm water	8 large eggs, lightly
2 packages active dry	beaten
yeast	9–10 cups flour
½ cup sugar	1 egg beaten with 1
2½ teaspoons salt	tablespoon water for
½ cup melted butter	glaze
Juice and grated rind of 1	Sliced almonds (optional)
lemon	

Combine ½ cup of warm water and yeast in a small bowl, stirring until dissolved, and set aside. In a large mixing bowl combine 1 cup of warm water, sugar, salt, butter, lemon juice and rind, and eggs. Blend very well. Add the yeast mixture and 3 cups of flour. Beat until smooth. Gradually add sufficient flour to make a soft dough that pulls away from sides of the bowl. Turn out on a lightly floured surface and knead 8–10 minutes, or until smooth and satiny. Place the dough in a warm buttered bowl, turning to coat the top. Cover loosely with plastic wrap and a towel. Let rise until doubled, about 1½ hours.

Punch down the dough, turn out on a lightly floured surface, and divide in half. Knead each piece thoroughly, cover, and let rest 10–15 minutes. Butter 2 baking sheets. Divide each portion into 3 equal pieces. Roll each piece into a rope 16–18 inches long. Braid 3 ropes together following the instructions on page 36 and place on a baking sheet, pinching the ends together. Plump the braid; do not stretch the dough. Braid the 3 remaining ropes. Cover and let rise 1 hour.

Preheat the oven to 350°F. Brush the loaves with the glaze and decorate with almonds, if desired. Bake 30–35 minutes. Let braids cool on a wire rack.

Food-Processor Croissants

Makes about 16 croissants

Yes, Dotty, there is a way to make flaky croissants in your food processor! I knew there had to be a way to encourage that superb machine to insert butter into layers of dough for those who have the desire but not the time to make a classical croissant. Dotty Griffith, food editor of The Dallas Morning News, *challenged me and I took the bait. My volunteer associates worked hours with me to refine a recipe. The final testing took approximately five hours. I am pleased with the result.*

⅝ pound (2½ sticks)
   butter
1 package active dry yeast
⅓ cup warm water
   (100°F)
½ cup instant nonfat dry
   milk

1 teaspoon salt
1 tablespoon sugar
3½ cups bread flour
¾ cup ice water
1 egg beaten with 1
   tablespoon water for
   glaze

Line a baking sheet with plastic wrap. Cut the butter into ¼-inch slices and place in rows on the plastic wrap. Cover securely with more plastic wrap and place in freezer overnight.

Combine the yeast and the warm water in a small mixing bowl, stirring until dissolved, and set aside. In the bowl of a food processor place the dry milk, salt, sugar, and flour and pulse three times to blend. With the motor running add the yeast mixture through the feed tube. Have the ice water ready and start pouring through the tube as soon as all the yeast mixture has been added. The dough will mass into a ball; process to knead 30 seconds. If the dough seems dry, add more ice water by teaspoons, just to obtain a cohesive slightly damp dough.

Remove dough from bowl and flatten into a 12 × 8-inch rectangle. Dust lightly with flour and cover well with plastic wrap. Place dough in freezer 45 minutes. Remove dough from freezer and with a dough scraper divide into 3 equal portions. Rewrap 2 portions and refrigerate.

Cut the remaining piece of dough into 22–24 small pieces and place in bowl of processor. Remove one third of the butter from the freezer and throw on top of the dough. Begin pulsing the machine. You want the butter cut into small but still visible pieces. This is very important, for, if you overprocess the butter so that it is completely incorporated into the dough, the rolls will not have the layered, flaky texture characteristic of good croissants. Pulse about 30 times, watching the butter carefully. If there are still large pieces left, stir the dough and butter quickly with a spatula and pulse a few more times. The dough will not mass into a ball. When all the butter is cut into even bits, remove dough, press together quickly, wrap with plastic wrap, and refrigerate.

Remove the remaining portions of dough from the freezer one at a time and follow directions as before. To combine the three pieces of processed dough into one piece, flour hands and kneading surface. Although the dough will be quite stiff, knead together quickly. With a heavy rolling pin roll the dough into an 18 × 12-inch rectangle (you should be able to see pieces of butter). Fold into thirds from a short side, turn the dough so open edge faces you, and roll again into a rectangle. The turning and rolling should be done three times. If the butter becomes quite soft, wrap the dough and refrigerate 30 minutes. After the final turn wrap the dough and refrigerate 45 minutes.

Butter a baking sheet. Remove dough and divide in half lengthwise. Refrigerate one portion, covered. Roll the other half into a 24 × 6-inch rectangle. If you are fortunate enough to own or can borrow a

croissant cutter, use it. If not, cut triangles that are 5–6 inches wide at the base. Roll up each triangle loosely from the wide end, stretching the dough as you roll it. Place on the baking sheet, curving ends in the classic croissant fashion. Repeat procedure with remaining dough.

Chocolate Filled Croissants: Here is a little trick I learned for filled croissants. Make a ¼-inch slash in the center of wide side of triangle. Sprinkle chocolate bits (use a good extra bittersweet chocolate!)

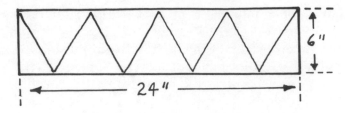

across the wide part of triangle just above the slash. Roll up from the wide side, lifting it up and over the chocolate. (The slit helps the dough fit better around the filling.) Place on buttered baking sheet and curve slightly. Or, if the croissants are too full, leave them straight.

CUT

Ham and Cheese Filled Croissants: These can be kept in the freezer and, with a salad, make a marvelous impromptu lunch. Purchase thinly sliced cooked ham and Swiss cheese from your best delicatessen. Place one slice of cheese across the triangle and top with slivers of ham. Roll up from the wide side, lifting it up and over the filling. Place on a buttered baking sheet and leave the points straight. Do not use any cheese other than Swiss; most of them melt, run all over the pan, and make the croissants stick.

Almond Filled Croissants: These will melt in your mouth! In the small bowl of an electric mixer beat 4 tablespoons of soft butter until creamy. Cut up ½ pound of almond paste and add to the butter, beating constantly. Add ½ cup confectioner's sugar, 1 egg, and 1 teaspoon grated lemon rind. Continue beating until smooth and fluffy. Refrigerate until thoroughly cooled. Spread about ¾ tablespoon over a triangle and sprinkle with sliced almonds. Roll up from the wide side, place on buttered baking sheet, and curve ends.

Cover croissants, plain or filled, and let rise 1½ hours.

Preheat the oven to 400°F. Brush each croissant lightly with the glaze. If desired, sprinkle sliced almonds over the almond filled croissants. Bake 12–15 minutes. Remove and enjoy!

H ot sunshine returned to melt the Dallas ice and we sloshed our way out on Interstate 35N back to lovely warm Tulsa. What a contrary adventure in looking for warm weather—it was good to get home!

MIDDLE AMERICA

MILEAGE—4,253 MILES

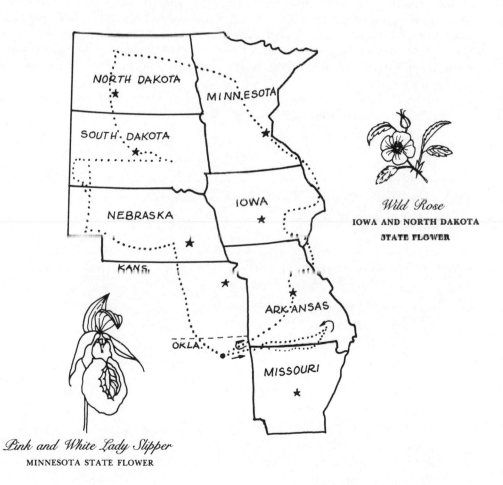

Wild Rose
IOWA AND NORTH DAKOTA
STATE FLOWER

Pink and White Lady Slipper
MINNESOTA STATE FLOWER

War Eagle, Arkansas

upped in the War Eagle Valley of northwestern Arkansas, in the center of the Ozark mountains, is a picturesque grist mill with the prettiest red-headed milleress in our country, Zoe Medlin Caywood. Not only does Zoe manage a grist mill three stories high, she is also a fine baker and is devoted to the milling of whole grains and life in her beloved Ozarks.

The War Eagle Mill has suffered many tragedies. The first mill, built in 1838, washed away in a flood. The mill was rebuilt but was destroyed to avoid its falling into the hands of the Union soldiers. A third mill burned in 1924. While building the fourth mill, Zoe's family found the original 1838 dam still intact and usable. Zoe pointed out a room underneath the mill where pigs had been allowed to pillage all the leavings that dropped from the grinding of all those grains—lucky pigs! An adjacent picnic ground was used by farmers and their families for camping after they made the long journey to the mill in horse-drawn wagons.

Many such mills were the hub of the rural community. It was common for horse trading, square dancing, and even a few weddings to take place at the mill site.

War Eagle Basic Sweet Dough

2 packages active dry
   yeast
½ cup warm water
1½ cups warm milk
¼ cup melted butter or
   margarine

½ cup packed brown
   sugar
1½ teaspoons salt
1 egg, lightly beaten
3 cups whole wheat flour
2–3 cups unbleached
   white flour

Combine the yeast and water in a small mixing bowl, stirring until dissolved, and set aside. In a large mixing bowl combine the milk, butter, sugar, salt, and egg and blend well. Add the yeast mixture and beat in the whole wheat flour. Beat 1–2 minutes in a heavy-duty mixer or vigorously by hand until the mixture is smooth. Cover and let rise 30 minutes, or until bubbly.

Stir down sponge and gradually add sufficient white flour to make a soft dough that pulls away from the sides of the bowl. Turn out on a surface lightly sprinkled with white flour. Knead about 10 minutes, or until smooth and satiny. Round into a ball and place in a warm bowl brushed with melted butter, turning to coat the top. Cover loosely with plastic wrap and a towel and let rise until doubled, about 1 hour. Punch down the dough, knead lightly, cover, and let rest 10 minutes. The dough is now ready to make into any of the following rolls and breads.

War Eagle Apple Coffee Ring

Makes 1 coffee ring

2 apples, peeled, cored, and diced
½ cup raisins, scalded, drained, and dried
½ cup packed brown sugar
2 teaspoons cinnamon
½ teaspoon nutmeg

¼ teaspoon allspice
1 recipe War Eagle Sweet Dough, preceding recipe
Melted butter
Confectioner's Icing, page 45 (optional)

Butter a baking sheet. Combine the apples, raisins, sugar, cinnamon, nutmeg, and allspice in a mixing bowl. Stir and mix very well. Roll the dough into a 20 × 10-inch rectangle. Brush lightly with melted butter to within ½ inch of the edges. Sprinkle the apple mixture over the dough. Roll up from the long side, jelly-roll style, and seal the seam. Place the roll seam side down on the baking sheet. Form a ring by inserting one of the ends into the other and pinching to seal tightly. With kitchen scissors make clips in the top of the ring at 1-inch intervals. Cover and let rise about 30–40 minutes, or until light.

Preheat the oven to 375°F. Bake the ring 25–30 minutes. Remove from oven and let cool 10–15 minutes on the baking sheet placed on a wire rack. Remove and frost with Confectioner's Icing, if desired.

Miniature Hot Cross Buns

Makes about 84 buns

These are delightful small rolls, a bit different than the usual Easter bun since they are made with whole wheat flour. Two bites and a roll has vanished! These buns store well in the freezer, but, if 84 are too many, cut the recipe in half.

1 recipe War Eagle
   sponge, page 82
1 teaspoon cinnamon
½ teaspoon cloves
½ teaspoon nutmeg

¾ cup currants, scalded,
   drained, and dried
½ cup candied lemon
   rind, diced
3 cups unbleached white
   flour, approximately

Lemon Glaze:
1 cup confectioner's sugar
2 teaspoons lemon juice

2 teaspoons water

At the end of the rising period for the sponge, stir in the spices, currants, and lemon rind. Gradually add sufficient flour to make a soft dough. Turn the dough out on a floured surface and knead until smooth, about 8–10 minutes. Place dough in a warm buttered bowl, turning to coat the top. Cover loosely with plastic wrap and a towel and let rise until doubled, about 1 hour.

Butter several baking sheets. Punch down the dough and knead lightly in the bowl. Pinch off pieces about 1 inch in diameter—the size of a walnut. Cup the dough in your hand and roll on counter top until smooth. Place on a baking sheet, cover, and let rise 45 minutes.

Preheat the oven to 375°F. Bake the rolls about 15 minutes, or until lightly golden.

Let the buns cool. Combine ingredients for Lemon Glaze, beating until smooth. With a knife or pastry bag form a cross over the bun with the glaze. These buns will keep well in the freezer if unglazed.

War Eagle Sweet Fortune Bread

Makes 1 large loaf

1 recipe War Eagle
   sponge, page 82
1 teaspoon allspice
¾ cup raisins, scalded,
   drained, and dried
½ cup finely chopped
   candied lemon or
   orange rind

½ cup chopped pecans
3 cups unbleached white
   flour, approximately
New penny, covered with
   aluminum foil

At the end of the rising period for the sponge, stir in the allspice, raisins, candied rind, and pecans and blend thoroughly. Gradually add sufficient flour to make a soft dough that pulls away from sides of the bowl. Turn the dough out on a floured surface and knead 8–10 minutes, or until smooth and resilient. Place in a warm buttered bowl, turning to coat the top. Cover loosely with plastic wrap and a towel and let rise until doubled, about 1 hour.

Butter a large baking sheet.

Punch down the dough, knead lightly, and shape into a large round loaf. Insert the covered penny deep into the loaf. Place on the baking sheet, cover, and let rise 30 minutes.

Preheat the oven to 375°F. Bake the loaf 40 minutes. Cover with foil during the last 10 minutes, if the loaf becomes too brown. Let loaf cool on a wire rack.

As I left War Eagle Mill, a late spring snow had covered the mountains, showing off vivid redbud trees in full bloom against the whiteness. No other cars were visible as the well-maintained road curved atop the Ozark world. A feeling of exhilaration enveloped me, I flipped a switch, listened to Maria Callas in *Tosca*, and followed the highway north for another journey.

The School of the Ozarks and Edwards Mill

N ear Hollister, Missouri, and Table Rock Lake, almost straight north of War Eagle, is the School of the Ozarks, established in 1906 for worthy students without sufficient means to pay for their education. A small school (one thousand two hundred students), but an active one. All the students work for their tuition on the campus. Through the help of private enterprises that financially assist the school, students have a choice of twenty-four areas of study in which to obtain degrees.

A complete grist mill has been built on the campus, with old-fashioned tools and lots of hand labor, through the generosity of one couple. The mill has a huge wheel, mill pond with ducks, and an exceptional museum. Demonstrations of how a variety of whole grains are ground is one of the many student projects. Following is an Edwards Mill recipe for your healthful pleasure.

Edwards Mill Cornmeal Pancakes

*The recipe for these exceptionally flavorful
cornmeal pancakes is designed for either 2–3
people or 4–6.*

2–3 people		4–6 people
¾ cup	yellow stone-ground cornmeal	1½ cups
⅛ cup	white flour	¼ cup
½ teaspoon	baking soda	1 teaspoon
½ teaspoon	sugar	1 teaspoon
½ teaspoon	salt	1 teaspoon
1 cup	buttermilk	2 cups
1 tablespoon	light oil	2 tablespoons
1	egg yolk, lightly beaten	2 yolks
1	egg white, stiffly beaten	2 whites

Combine the cornmeal, flour, soda, sugar, and salt in a mixing
bowl and blend well. In a separate bowl combine the buttermilk, oil, and
egg yolk. Add the buttermilk mixture to the dry ingredients, stirring
gently. Fold in the egg white. Let mixture stand 10 minutes before
cooking. Bake on a hot griddle brushed with a light oil or melted vegetable shortening. Use about ¼ cup for each pancake. Cook until bubbles
appear on top and bottom is light golden brown. Flip them over and
cook until the other side is golden. Serve immediately with maple syrup!

Note: One of my associates particularly enjoyed these pancakes,
which brought to mind the British West Indies where cornmeal is used
instead of wheat flour.

T ucked in narrow valleys, beside tumbling Ozark rivers and natural
springs, there are thirty-one old grist mills. Using the information in
a publication given to me by the School of the Ozarks, I determined to find as
many as possible. On country roads across southern Missouri and northern
Arkansas, I found a few empty buildings, useless now, that still had their huge
millstones. The ancient Aid-Hodgens Mill, over a hundred years old, with its
back against a mountain, is surrounded by trees. There is a long waterfall
pouring over a dam in front of the old red building—a perfect picture post-
card. I wished I could stay longer at Alley Springs, for the state park service
has made the grounds into lovely picnic areas. At the center is the brightly

painted and renovated old red mill, beside a natural spring through which flows 685 million gallons of cold, clear water daily. Magnificent watercress grew thickly around the edges of the pond. There were single leaves as large as the palm of my hand.

Luck was with me until I arrived in the tiny hamlet of Annapolis, close to the old Robinson Mill. Directions were given and I drove into the backwoods on a neglected dirt road, encouraged occasionally by a "Robinson" sign. Abruptly my road ended at a rushing stream. The creek bed looked fairly flat so I gunned my car and splattered through. There was hardly what anyone would call a road on the other side. Within half a mile, a mountain man stepped out from among the trees. I gasped and stopped. "Where's Robinson Mill?" I yelled. "Done burned to the ground but I'll be glad to show ya what's left." It seemed a better idea to figure out how to turn my car around in all those trees without getting stuck and ford back over that stream. I locked my doors, rolled up my window, waved gaily, carefully negotiated my turn, splashed back over the stream, and decided my Ozark mill experiences had ended.

Central Missouri

T wo months later I was sitting comfortably on the grounds of the Tan Tara Hotel, watching boats skim the lovely lake of the Ozarks, still mulling over those thirty-one grist mills to the south. Half the way between Kansas City and St. Louis, this sixty-year-old manmade lake is surrounded with beautiful homes, fine resorts, elegant restaurants, and well-maintained camping areas. In the spring redbud and dogwood create a fairyland, while the fall leaves are mellow and colorful around the irregular shoreline.

Fifty miles north my companion and I made a quick stop in Jefferson City, a small but pretty town. The state capitol building there has burned three times since 1821. The last architect of Missouri's capitol building must have taken his plans directly to Oklahoma; one can scarcely tell the two capitols apart. A few miles further north is busy Columbia, home of Missouri University, Stephens College for women, and of Viola Young.

Viola had retired from home extension work at the university, remarried, and with her new husband purchased a motor home to follow the Missouri football team. I've never seen a happier person—life beginning at sixty five! We talked breads for two hours and she shared recipes and wonderful advice.

Golden Sand Dollars

Makes 6 breads

*Charming, unusual small loaves of bread, easy to
make, and covered with toasted sesame seeds.*

1½ cups warm water
1 package active dry yeast
2 tablespoons instant dry
   milk
2 tablespoons sugar
2 teaspoons salt
2 tablespoons light oil

4–4½ cups flour
1 egg white beaten with 2
   teaspoons water for
   glaze
1 tablespoon or more
   toasted sesame seeds,
   see **Note**

Combine ½ cup of warm water with yeast in small bowl, stirring until dissolved, and set aside. In a large mixing bowl combine the milk, sugar, salt, oil, and the remaining cup of water. Stir in 1½ cups flour and beat thoroughly. Blend in the yeast mixture. Gradually add sufficient flour to make a soft, workable dough. Turn out on a lightly floured surface and knead for about 10 minutes, or until smooth and elastic. Round into a ball and place the dough in a warm buttered bowl, turning to coat the top. Cover loosely with plastic wrap and a towel and let rise until doubled, about 1 hour.

Punch down the dough and divide into 6 equal portions. Shape into balls, cover, and let rest 10 minutes. Butter two baking sheets. Roll balls into 5-inch circles and place on the baking sheets at least 2 inches apart. With your hand flatten each circle. Brush the tops with the glaze

and sprinkle evenly with sesame seeds. If you like, use more sesame seeds. Press the sesame seeds lightly into the dough. Cover with a light cloth and let rise until doubled, about 45 minutes.

Preheat the oven to 400°F.

With a floured spatula mark each loaf into 6 wedges. Bake 20 minutes, or until golden. Remove loaves to a wire rack and let cool.

Note: To toast sesame seeds, spread in a shallow pan and bake in a preheated 300°F oven 20–30 minutes, stirring occasionally. Watch carefully, as the seeds burn easily.

Hannibal and the President

W hile raising three sons, I read the adventures of Tom Sawyer and Huck Finn three times. A night in Mark Twain's Hannibal, Missouri, one of the most enchanting small towns in America, was a must on our journey. High on a bluff in a park overlooking Hannibal and the river, one can dream of the two boys rafting the mighty Mississippi. But, then, you see, two of my sons did canoe the complete length of the river—they made that dream come true.

As we entered the outskirts of Hannibal, banners were waving everywhere. To our consternation, all the hotels and motels were filled. The President of the United States with his cortege (plus the media) was arriving on the *Delta Queen* early the next morning. Finally at double price we ferreted out one room two blocks from the center of town.

Early the next morning we joined hundreds and hundreds of people, big strong farmers from Iowa, Illinois, and Missouri with their scrubbed, blue-eyed children. The sun was shining, there was a spirited gaiety exciting to everyone. Whether you approved of this particular President made no difference, as one stranger happily explained to me. "He's my President and I want to see him." Secret service men dripped from every small building, as did all the media with their trappings.

The *Delta Queen* came around the bend of the river, American flags flying, calliope playing, and high school bands on shore in full swing. People lined the walk from the river to the famous statue of Tom and Huck, about half a mile. We joined the thinnest part of the line and there I was, face to face with President Carter, scrunched between two unsmiling men who seemed to see everything. I wondered how the President withstood such smothering. But this was his day and the crowd cheered, for few Presidents have sailed down the Mississippi to visit Middle America.

Then, since there was no bread to research in this traffic jam, we left Hannibal before the President.

Nauvoo, Illinois

W e drove north along the river to Keokuk, which boasts the deepest lock on the river. Our destination was Nauvoo, in a lovely wooded area facing the Mississippi River, the Mormon town of Joseph Smith, who originated the religion and wrote the *Book of Mormon*. The grounds and houses are a beautifully preserved museum. Joseph Smith lived a short, active and violent life, was six feet two inches tall, weighed 245 pounds, and was killed at the age of thirty-nine in a political dispute.

On the grounds I discovered a mill that grinds hard-wheat flour, run by Carmen Outh and her family. To help her daughters through college, Carmen bakes and sells sixty-five loaves a day plus dozens of yummy cookies.

Nauvoo Whole Wheat Raisin Bread

Makes 2 loaves

Healthful and delicious—one of Carmen Outh's best breads.

¼ cup warm water	2½ teaspoons salt
2 packages active dry yeast	5 tablespoons melted butter
6 cups whole wheat flour, approximately	2 eggs
¼ cup instant dry milk	2 tablespoons honey
1 cup cold water	1 cup raisins, scalded, drained, and dried
½ cup sugar	

Combine the warm water and yeast in a small bowl, stirring until dissolved, and set aside. In a large mixing bowl combine 3 cups of whole wheat flour with the dry milk. Add the cold water, sugar, salt, and butter. Add the yeast mixture, eggs, and honey and beat well. Stir in the raisins. Gradually add sufficient whole wheat flour to form a soft dough. Turn out on a floured surface and knead until smooth and resilient, about 8 minutes. Round into a ball and place in a warm buttered bowl, turning to coat the top. Cover loosely with plastic wrap and a towel and let rise until doubled, about 2 hours.

Punch down the dough and divide in half. Shape each piece into a ball, cover, and let rest 20 minutes. Butter two 9-inch loaf pans. Shape the dough into loaves and place in the pans. Cover and let rise about 1 hour, or until tripled.

Preheat the oven to 350°F. Bake the loaves 45 minutes, or until lightly browned. Let cool on wire racks.

The Amana Colonies—Iowa

T he highway plunged through the rolling hills of Iowa, clad with acres and acres of magnificent tall, tasseled corn and low, bushy soybeans. Fascinated with such production, I wrote Iowa State University and received a letter from Mr. H. E. Thompson:

"We grow 14 million acres of corn, 8 million acres of soybeans, 1 million acres of oats, 100 thousand acres of wheat, 2½ million acres of hay, mostly alfalfa. Forty-five percent of the corn is utilized by livestock, 10% by industry, 35% is exported, and 15% has no place to go." Mind-boggling figures for just one state out of fifty.

In the center of this agricultural splendor are the seven Amana colonies. A splinter of the Lutheran church, formed in 1714 and ultimately faced with religious and political persecution, the Amana people moved across the Atlantic to an area close to Buffalo, New York. More immigrants swarmed to the area, and the group finally turned west and settled their famous colonies on the Iowa River.

Tha Amana communal way of life gradually disintegrated as the colonies ventured into successful businesses. A corporation was formed and the communal kitchens were closed. Buildings have been re-created in which tourists can see some of the "old-time way of life," from the making of superb German sausages to the spinning of wool. Family-style restaurants serve abundant well-cooked meals, but the breads I bought in bakeries lacked their old-time flavor until I found the Brumwell Mill.

Seven in One Bread

Makes 3 large or 4 regular loaves

*Eleanor Brumwell created the perfect bread to
show off the mill's excellent stone-ground flours.
When I made Eleanor's bread, the aroma of all
seven grains in one bowl was indeed soul
satisfying.*

2 packages active dry
  yeast
4 cups warm water
1 tablespoon salt
4 tablespoons honey
½ cup rolled wheat
  (wheat flakes), see **Note**
⅓ cup toasted wheat germ
¼ cup soy flour
⅓ cup rye flour
1¾ cups stone-ground
  whole wheat flour
⅓ cup cornmeal
4–5 cups unbleached
  white flour
¼ cup light oil

Combine yeast and water in a large mixing bowl, stirring until dissolved. Add the salt and honey and mix well. Add the rolled wheat, wheat germ, soy, rye, and whole wheat flours, and the cornmeal. Beat thoroughly. Add ½ cup of the unbleached white flour and the oil and stir. Gradually add sufficient white flour to form a workable dough that pulls away from sides of the bowl. Turn out on a floured surface and knead until smooth and elastic, about 8–10 minutes. Round into a ball and place in a warm greased bowl, turning to coat the top. Cover loosely with plastic wrap and a towel and let rise until doubled, about 1 hour. This is a lovely dough and despite so many whole grains has been well balanced to avoid a dense, heavy texture.

Punch down the dough, turn out on a lightly floured surface, and divide into either 3 or 4 portions. Knead each portion, cover, and let rest 10 minutes. Butter three 9-inch or four 8½-inch loaf pans. Mold the dough into loaves and place in the pans. Cover and let rise to tops of pans, about 45 minutes.

Preheat the oven to 375°F. Bake the loaves 45 minutes for the large loaves, 35 minutes for the smaller pans. Turn loaves out on wire racks to cool.

Note: If rolled wheat is not available, substitute pure bran.

Cedar Rapids, Iowa

D riving northeast from the Amana colonies, I now felt smothered in corn. Still more acres on either side of the road, so high nothing else was visible. Entering Cedar Rapids to find a small Czechoslovakian settlement was a relief after such overwhelming agriculture. The Bohemian district consists of only four blocks, but it has a most remarkable small museum with exquisite and elaborate Balkan costumes.

The bakery (there *had* to be one) was in the center of the four blocks, with a happy baker eager to talk. We ate *kolaches*, drank good coffee, and left with a special loaf of Bohemian rye bread fragrant with caraway seeds.

Bohemian Rye Bread

Makes 2 loaves

Although this is not Mr. Skyro's (the baker's) recipe, the flavor is similar—the chief difference is that he ground the caraway and I've left mine whole. Either way is fine.

2 packages active dry yeast	3 cups rye flour
2 cups warm water	1 cup bread flour
¼ cup light molasses	1½ tablespoons caraway
2 tablespoons light oil	seeds
2 teaspoons salt	4 cups white flour, approximately

Combine the yeast and water in a large mixing bowl, stirring until dissolved. Add the molasses, oil, and salt, blending well. Beat in the rye flour until mixture is smooth. Cover and let the sponge rise until light and doubled, about 45 minutes.

Stir in the bread flour and caraway seeds. Gradually add sufficient white flour to make a soft, workable dough. (Any dough with rye flour will be sticky.) Turn the dough out on a floured surface and knead until smooth and elastic, about 8–10 minutes. Round into a ball and place the dough in a warm buttered bowl, turning to coat the top. Cover loosely with plastic wrap and a towel and let rise until doubled, about 1 hour.

Punch down the dough, turn out on a lightly floured surface, and divide in half. Knead each piece thoroughly, cover, and let rest 10 minutes. Brush 2 baking sheets with melted butter. Shape the dough into round or baguette free-form loaves. Place on baking sheets, cover, and let rise until doubled, about 40 minutes.

Preheat the oven to 375°F. Slash the loaves with a razor blade and bake for 15 minutes. Reduce heat to 350°F and bake 20 minutes. The loaves may also be baked on a preheated baking stone (page 48).

Minnesota, Minneapolis and St. Paul

A fter a night in Dubuque in a delightful hotel perched high on a bluff overlooking the Mississippi River, we crossed to the Wisconsin side to drive the Great River Road. Our first stop was at the Villa Louis, a handsome home built by a colonel connected with the Astors and the fur trade. The house was designed for an *Upstairs, Downstairs* style of living. I was entranced by the immense kitchen containing a coal range with four ovens. What gay entertainments must have taken place over a hundred years ago, with boats stopping on the river at the edge of the sweeping green lawn.

Back across the Mississippi and into Minneapolis for two lovely days. Part of one day I got thoroughly lost in this beautiful, bustling city but fortunately ended up in an excellent French restaurant for lunch. As I left, I could see the city skyline and realized that I must have circled the whole thing. I made two interesting visits, one that took me through the magnificent Swedish Institute, filled with beautiful carved woodwork and walls. The other was a tour through the Betty Crocker kitchens, where I was fascinated by the portraits painted of her through the years. The first one was an artist's composite of home economists working for General Mills in 1936. My guide assured me that many people have been positive that they have met Betty Crocker. But she's a myth—and a stroke of genius.

Next stop was the Minnesota State Fair, which draws farmers, youthful contestants, and tourists from all the surrounding states and Canada. I followed the heavy traffic, crossed the Mississippi again (here a twelve-year-old boy could easily throw a silver dollar across the muddy stream) to St. Paul, and parked my car amongst a tremendous variety of trucks. Most of the streets were paved within the fair grounds, so walking was easy. And I walked the whole day alone, completely exhilarated. Around one corner would be trapeze artists and the next Ukranian dancers. Clowns abounded, hawkers sold tempting gadgets (all likely to fall apart when you got them back to your own kitchen), children were engulfed in cotton candy, a miniature train transported hundreds to the far corners of the fair, buildings contained innumerable exhibits, including breads, and the rich aroma of hundreds of farm animals permeated the air. Never have I seen a more exciting and diversified fair.

Later I contacted the Fair Board and through them met a superb breadmaker, Marjorie Johnson, a tiny woman with great energy who really knows what to do with bread dough and loves it.

Orange Bowknots

Makes about 40 rolls

Marjorie Johnson has won enough blue ribbons at the Minnesota Fair to fashion a royal evening gown for her four-foot-ten frame! Year after year she has won First Place and Sweepstakes Winner in several categories. Marjorie has been most generous in sharing some of her winning recipes.

1¼ cups warm water
2 packages active dry
   yeast
⅓ cup instant dry skim
   milk
½ cup melted vegetable
   shortening

⅓ cup sugar
1 teaspoon salt
2 eggs, well beaten
¼ cup orange juice
2 tablespoons grated
   orange rind
5–6 cups flour

Orange Icing:
2 tablespoons orange juice
1 teaspoon grated orange
   rind

1 cup confectioner's sugar

In a large mixing bowl combine the water and yeast, stirring until dissolved. Blend in the milk, shortening, sugar, salt, eggs, orange juice and rind, and 3 cups of flour. Beat well by hand or with the dough hook of a heavy-duty mixer. Gradually add sufficient flour to make a soft, workable dough that pulls away from sides of the bowl. Turn out on a lightly floured surface and knead until smooth and satiny, about 8 minutes. Round into a ball and place dough in a warm buttered bowl, turning to coat the top. Cover loosely with plastic wrap and a towel and let rise until doubled, abou 1 hour.

Punch the dough down, knead lightly, and let rest for 10 minutes. Butter a baking sheet. Roll the dough into a rectangle 10 inches long and ½ inch thick. Cut into strips 10 inches long and ¼ inch wide and tie each into a knot. Arrange on the baking sheet at least ¾ inch apart, cover, and let rise until doubled, about 20 minutes.

Preheat the oven to 400°F. Bake the bowknots 8–10 minutes. If you have a "hot" oven, lower temperature to 375°F. Place the rack in the center of the oven to avoid burning bottoms of rolls. Let rolls cool on wire racks. Blend the ingredients for the orange icing and brush over tops of the cooled rolls.

Streusel Coffeecake

Makes 2 coffeecakes

"Melt in your mouth" or "luscious" describes this First Place and Sweepstakes Winner that Marjorie has created. To top all this, the cake is easily and quickly prepared.

Dough:

¼ pound (1 stick) butter, at room temperature
1 cup sugar
2 eggs, well beaten
½ teaspoon salt
2 cups flour

1 teaspoon baking powder
1 teaspoon baking soda
1 cup buttermilk
1 teaspoon vanilla
1 teaspoon almond extract

Topping:

2 tablespoons melted
butter
½ cup packed brown
sugar

1 tablespoon flour
½ cup chopped nuts
½ cup canned coconut
flakes

Preheat the oven to 350°F. Brush the two 8-inch round pans with melted butter and dust with flour.

Cream the butter and sugar until fluffy. Add the eggs and beat well. Sift together the salt, flour, baking powder, and soda. Add the buttermilk and flavorings to the butter mixture, blend in the dry ingredients, and stir until smooth. Spread one quarter of the batter in each of the pans. Combine all the topping ingredients, mixing well with your hands or a pastry blender, and sprinkle half of it over the two coffeecakes. Divide the remaining batter between the pans and spread the rest of the topping over the cakes. Bake 25–30 minutes. Let cool in the pans or serve immediately.

Lake Itasca

N inety miles northwest of Minneapolis, we changed highways at Sauk Center and drove right through *Main Street*. The signs were twice as large as usual, white lettered on bright green, for we were in the Middle America hometown of Sinclair Lewis. Further north we turned into the state park at Lake Itasca, the source of the Mississippi River. Twenty years before this writing, we had launched two of our sons in their canoe on the tiny streamlet that issues from the lovely, shimmering lake. A simple sign stands beside the point where clear, sparkling water tumbles over rocks to begin the river. Nothing had changed, not even the lovely lodge built of logs surrounded by tall pines. So very quiet except for the songs of countless varieties of birds, this totally beautiful spot in our country is not seen by many people.

The tiny river winds out of sight through cattails and low trees, meandering north through farmland until it joins with Lake Bemidji. We had driven to Bemidji that year and waited three days to check our sons' progress up the river. Portaging over fences, turnstiles, and culverts turned out to be the most difficult aspects of their journey. I washed all their clothes (for the last time until Vicksburg one and a half months later) and watched them cast off across Lake Bemidji.

Bemidji

P aul Bunyan and his famous blue ox, Babe, are immortalized by statue on the Lake Bemidji waterfront. He was the "strongest, most durable, most proficient lumberjack ever to hone a double-bladed axe for his springtime shave" says the latest, truthful tourist brochure. Not much is known about his birth but he grew so big and so fast, it took a whole dairy to keep his bottle filled. Everywhere he stepped a lake was created, and I believe that, for Minnesota is filled with small, lovely lakes about the size of his shoes. Why, I was even told that as a grown man he used a pine tree for a toothpick!

Through a close friend I hit a real bread jackpot as big as Paul Bunyan, for Bemidji is the home of Americans with Swedish, Norwegian, and Danish ancestry. All are well known for their lovely coffeecakes and breads. I've much to share with you from this charming town with delightful people who welcomed me into their homes.

Danish Almond Rusks

Makes 18–56 rusks

A tiny, bubbly Danish lady, Helena Paulson, lives in a tiny house and served me the most delicious coffee I've ever tasted, with Danish rusks on a tiny tray. When she discovered my husband was patiently waiting in the car, she scurried around, quickly prepared another tiny tray, and darted outside to serve him.

Helena related that her father had lived in a great house in Denmark. A young woman was employed there as a maid and the two fell in love, much against the wishes of his father. They persisted in their love affair and finally the father said they could marry and he would give them passage to America, but the son would be disowned. Helena's parents came to the New World to live happily ever after. Helena married a Norwegian. Here is the recipe for her rusks, perfect to make in the food processor.

3 cups unsifted flour
¼ pound (1 stick) cold
    butter, cut into 8 pieces
1 cup sugar

1 cup ground blanched
    almonds
2 eggs
1 teaspoon baking soda
½ cup sour cream

Preheat the oven to 300°F. Butter a baking sheet.

Combine the flour and butter in a processor bowl with the steel blade. Whirl several times until well mixed and add the remaining ingredients. Process until the mixture forms into one lump. Remove to a lightly floured surface and knead lightly several times to incorporate all the little pieces of dough. If making by hand, use a pastry blender to cut the butter into the flour until well blended and add the remaining ingredients.

Divide the dough in 4 equal portions. Using your hands, form each piece in a roll 12–14 inches long. Place the rolls on the baking sheet and bake 45 minutes, or until golden brown. Lower the heat to 250°F. Remove the pan from the oven and slice the rolls into 1-inch pieces. Place the slices flat side down on the baking sheet and bake 20 minutes. Turn the pieces over and bake another 15–20 minutes. Turn off the oven and let the rusks cool on the baking sheet in the oven.

The rusks freeze exceptionally well, but will also stay fresh in a tin for 2–3 weeks. Excellent to have for an emergency serving, for they defrost in minutes.

An Old Danish Coffeecake

Makes 2 coffeecakes

This century-old recipe was originally made with part lard and part butter. I have tested and made it with all butter; the texture is creamy and lovely. The recipe calls for chopped dates; try to find prepared chopped sugared dates, as they are easier to handle.

Dough:

5–6 cups flour

¼ pound (1 stick) plus 7 tablespoons cold butter

½ cup sugar

1 teaspoon salt

1 package active dry yeast

½ cup warm water

1 cup warm milk

4 egg yolks, beaten

Filling:

6 egg whites

1 cup sugar

1 pound chopped dates

In a large mixing bowl combine 4 cups of the flour, the butter, sugar, and salt and with a pastry blender cut in the butter until the mixture resembles meal. Or combine and mix the ingredients in a food processor, transferring the mixture to a large bowl once the butter is cut in. Combine the yeast and water in a small mixing bowl, stirring until dissolved. Add the milk and egg yolks, combine with the flour mixture, and beat thoroughly. Gradually add sufficient flour to make a very soft dough. Knead on a lightly floured surface 5 minutes. Round into a ball and place the dough in a warm buttered bowl, turning to coat the top. Cover loosely with plastic wrap and a towel and let rise until doubled, about 2 hours.

To make the filling, beat the egg whites until fluffy. Slowly add the sugar, beating constantly until you can feel no granules of sugar when you rub the mixture between two fingers. Fold in the dates. If the dates are sticky, mix 1 tablespoon of sugar into them.

Butter well 2 Bundt pans.

Punch down the dough, turn out on a lightly floured surface, knead lightly, and divide in half. Roll one piece (keep the other portion covered) into a 22 × 9-inch rectangle. Spread half the filling down the center. Fold one long side of the dough to the center and fold the other side on top envelope style. Seal the seam and ends. Place in the pan seam side down. Repeat directions with remaining portion of dough. Cover and let rise 45 minutes.

Preheat the oven to 350°F. Bake the cakes 45 minutes. Turn them out on a rack to cool. The cake is delicious alone, but it can be glazed with Confectioner's Icing (page 45).

A regal lady in Bemidji of Swedish background, Anne Stennes, told me a magical story, the beginning of a Christmas tradition. A young Sicilian woman named Lucia became a devout Christian in 300 A.D. Lucia put her faith into action by feeding, loving, and caring for the poor. Lucia's fiancé, a pagan nobleman, attempted to force the girl to renounce her faith by submitting her to torture. She became revered as a saint by the early church.

One bitterly cold winter when Sweden suffered from famine, Santa Lucia appeared with food. She was dressed in a white robe and wore a crown of light. She became a symbol of light, the meaning of her name. St. Lucia's Day is celebrated on the shortest day of the old calendar, December 13, which opens the month of Christmas celebration in Sweden. The custom evolved for the eldest daughter, dressed in a white gown with a crown of candles, to serve saffron buns and coffee to each member of the family.

The local branch of the Swedish Institute in Bemidji each year elects a young woman who is then presented at a huge breakfast. She continues the old custom by serving the St. Lucia buns.

Swedish Christmas Buns

Makes 12 buns, 1 crown, 1 Joseph's Beard,
and 12 Christmas crosses

1 cup milk
½ teaspoon powdered
   saffron or saffron
   threads
¾ cup sugar
1 teaspoon salt
¼ pound (1 stick) butter,
   at room temperature
2 packages active dry
   yeast
¾ cup warm water

6–7 cups flour
2 eggs
½ cup raisins, scalded,
   drained, and dried plus
   48 raisins for
   decorating
½ cup ground blanched
   almonds
1 egg yolk beaten with 1
   tablespoon water for
   glaze

In a small saucepan heat the milk until just scalded. Remove from heat and add the saffron, sugar, salt, and butter, blending well. Let cool to lukewarm.

Combine the yeast and water in a large mixing bowl, stirring until dissolved. Blend in the milk mixture. Add 2½ cups of flour and beat until smooth. Add the eggs, ½ cup of raisins, and almonds. Gradually add sufficient flour to make a soft, workable dough that pulls away from sides of the bowl. Turn dough out on a lightly floured surface, cover, and let rest 10 minutes. Knead about 8 minutes, or until smooth and satiny. Round into a ball and place the dough in a warm buttered bowl, turning to coat the top. Cover loosely with plastic wrap and a towel and let rise until doubled, about 1 hour.

The dough may be divided in 4 portions and formed into the following shapes. Or make only the St. Lucia buns. They will all freeze well.

St. Lucia Buns: Butter 2 baking sheets. Divide one quarter of the dough into 6 portions. Cut each portion in half—you will have 12 pieces in all. Using your hands, roll each piece into a rope 10–12 inches long. Cross 2 ropes on a baking sheet and roll each end into a snail or curl, using the illustration as a guide. Press a large raisin in the center of each curl and brush the bun with the glaze. Repeat directions with remaining portions of dough. Cover and let rise about 50 minutes, or until light and puffy.

Preheat the oven to 400°F. Bake the buns 10 minutes, or until golden. Let buns cool on wire racks.

St. Lucia's Crown: Butter a baking sheet. Divide one quarter of the dough into 9 parts. Using your hands, roll each into a 15-inch rope. Twist 2 of the ropes together and arrange in a curve on the baking sheet. Curl the remaining 7 strands into snail-shaped buns and place

along the outside of the twisted curve, using the illustration as a guide. Let the "crown" rise, covered, 30 minutes.

Preheat the oven to 400°F. Brush the crown with the glaze and bake 25 minutes. Let cool on baking sheet set over a wire rack. This is an exceptionally pretty cake.

Joseph's Beard: Divide one quarter of the dough into 3 portions. Using your hands, roll each into an 18-inch rope. Arrange the ropes as follows, using the illustration as a guide. First rope: mold into a U shape, curling both ends upward, and place on a buttered baking sheet. Second rope: place immediately above the first rope, curling the ends up just above the first two curls. Third rope: arrange above the second rope and curl the ends above the second two curls. The beard is now complete! Cover and let rise 30 minutes.

Preheat the oven to 400°F. Brush the "beard" with the glaze and bake 25 minutes, or until golden. Let cool on baking sheet placed over a wire rack. (This prevents the "beard" from coming apart.)

Christmas Crosses: Butter 2 baking sheets. Divide one quarter of the dough into 12 portions. Using your hands, roll each into a rope 5–6 inches long. Place 2 ropes in shape of a cross on a buttered baking sheet. Repeat directions with remaining portions of dough. Cover and let rise 25 minutes.

Preheat the oven to 375°F. Brush the dough with the glaze and bake 15 minutes, or until golden. Let cool on wire racks.

Norwegian Sweet Bread

Makes 48 rolls and 4 breads

What a joy this bread is for Christmas. The recipe is for a large amount and may be divided to make sweet rolls or a traditional Norwegian Christmas bread. Make two or three recipes, and you will have gifts aplenty. The recipe was given to me by Gudrun Berg, a fine cook and a lovely hostess.

5 cups warm milk, or 3
   cups warm milk and 2
   cups warm water
2 packages active dry
   yeast

2 cups melted butter
1 cup sugar
6 eggs, lightly beaten
1 tablespoon salt
6 cups flour

Combine 3 cups of warm milk and yeast in a large mixing bowl, stirring until dissolved. Add the butter, 2 cups milk, sugar, eggs, and salt and blend thoroughly. Beat in 4 cups of flour. Add 2 more cups of flour and beat hard to mix completely. Do not be concerned if there are a few lumps; the dough should be like a thick pancake batter. Divide the batter between 2 bowls—there should be about 12 cups of the mixture.

CINNAMON ROLLS

1 teaspoon cardamom, or
   grated rind of 1 lemon
3 cups flour,
   approximately
½ cup melted butter
1 cup sugar

1 tablespoon cinnamon
Raisins, scalded, drained
   and dried (optional)
Confectioner's Icing, page
   45 (optional)

To half the prepared batter, add the cardamom or grated rind. Gradually add sufficient flour to make a soft dough. Turn out on a lightly floured surface and knead lightly about 5 minutes. Round into a ball, place in a warm greased bowl, turning to coat the top. Cover loosely with plastic wrap and a towel and let rise until doubled, about 1½ hours.

Punch down the dough, turn out on a floured surface, knead lightly, cover, and let rest 10 minutes. Butter 4 or 5 square or round 9-inch cake pans. Divide the dough into 4 portions and cover those not being worked on. Roll one piece into a 12 × 8-inch rectangle. Brush with melted butter to within ¼ inch of edges. Combine the sugar and cinnamon, mix well, and sprinkle one quarter over the melted butter. Add raisins, if desired, or none (if the kids pick them out). Roll up from the long side, jelly-roll style, and seal the seam. Slice into 1-inch rolls with a sharp knife. Place the rolls cut side down in pans ½ inch apart. Repeat with remaining portions of dough. Cover lightly and let rise about 45 minutes, or until puffy and touching.

Preheat the oven to 375°F (or to 350°F if you are using glass pans). Bake the rolls 20–25 minutes. Turn out on wire racks to cool. Frost, if desired, with Confectioner's Icing.

Norwegian Christmas Bread (JULE KAKE)

1 teaspoon cardamom
1 cup candied cherries
1 cup candied mixed fruit
1 cup golden raisins, scalded, drained, and dried

3 cups flour, approximately
1 egg beaten with 1 tablespoon water for glaze
Sliced almonds

Note: If you prefer not to use candied fruits, substitute 1 cup chopped almonds and increase the raisins to 1½ cups.

To the remaining half of the batter, add the cardamom, cherries, candied fruit, and raisins.

Proceed as directed in Cinnamon Rolls, adding the flour, kneading, and proofing.

Punch down the dough and divide into 4 portions. Knead each portion well, cover, and let rest 10 minutes. Butter 2 large or 4 small baking sheets. Smooth each piece of dough into a round loaf and place on a baking sheet. Cover and let rise about 1 hour.

Preheat the oven to 350°F. Brush each loaf with the glaze and press almonds over the top. Bake 45 minutes, or until golden brown. Remove loaves and let cool on wire racks.

Another adaptation of this marvelous dough is to divide it in 3 pieces. Each portion is then divided into 3 pieces, which are rolled into ropes and braided, making 3 beautiful Christmas braids which may be brushed with the glaze or frosted with Confectioner's Icing (page 45) after they are cool.

Abliskiver

Makes about 76 abliskiver

Margaret and Pete Boysen, my guides and hosts in Bemidji, shared a very old recipe from Peter's family. His mother Ellen came to the New World at the age of thirteen in 1895. In her family abliskiver was traditionally served on Christmas Eve, with prune purée in the center and rolled in granulated sugar. Helena (of the little house) said that abliskiver was served more often in her family for afternoon coffee and on birthdays, not filled with anything, just plain little cakes rolled in granulated sugar. Sometimes they were served for breakfast with butter, syrup, or jam, but she loved them best with hot chocolate. Occasionally her grandmother would fry eggs in the little cups of the pan as a special treat for the children. Abliskiver pans are available in kitchen specialty shops.

Dough:

1 package active dry yeast	4 eggs, separated
1 quart warm milk	1 teaspoon salt
¼ pound (1 stick) butter,	¼ teaspoon cardamom
at room temperature	5–6 cups flour
½ cup sugar	

Filling:

12-ounce package pitted	Sugar
prunes	1 teaspoon almond extract

In a small bowl combine the yeast with 1 cup of the milk, stirring until dissolved, and set aside. Cream the butter and sugar until light and fluffy. Add the beaten egg yolks, salt, and cardamom. Blend in the yeast mixture. Beat in sufficient flour to make a batter similar to thick pancake batter. Cover and let rise 2 hours. Stir the sponge and fold in the egg whites, first beaten softly stiff.

While the batter is proofing, make the filling. Pour hot water over the prunes, bring just to a boil, cover, and let cool. Drain prunes and purée in a food processor or blender with sugar to taste and the almond extract.

Place ½ teaspoon shortening in each cup of an *abliskiver* pan. Set the pan on a moderate burner and heat as you would a pancake grill. Pour in sufficient batter, about 2 tablespoons, to half fill each cup, add a scant teaspoonful of the prune purée, and top with just enough batter to cover the prunes. Using 2 teaspoons, turn the little cakes until evenly browned, about 5–10 minutes total cooking time for each batch. The cooking is a bit tricky—it takes a little practice on your part. Serve the cakes immediately.

Note: This large recipe can easily be cut in half. If you do so, use the entire package of yeast. *Abliskiver* may be filled with any preserves. They are delicious reheated and sprinkled with confectioner's sugar.

North Dakota

|E| ighty-five miles along the Old West Trail from Bemidji, the highway enters North Dakota at Grand Forks. We stopped for the night farther west at Devil's Lake. Now for some reason, I thought North Dakota would be flat, no lakes, all wheat, and maybe a little snow. I was wrong. The eastern portion of the state begins with soft, low, lushly green rolling hills and small lakes excavated by glaciers thousands of years ago. Fort Totten at the edge of Devil's Lake, a state park and museum, is exceptionally well cared for, with a magnificent parade ground in the center surrounded by handsome two-story officers' quarters. Forts are scattered over both North and South Dakota, for when the emigrants began surging through, the Sioux Indians objected strenuously. The federal government established forts to control the Indians and protect the constantly moving line of emigrants heading west.

On our journey, the gentle, rich land was filled with fields of sunflowers, wheat, and sugar beets. Sunflowers do not ripen simultaneously. The tall flower stands straight, with pods facing east to absorb the morning sun. Some, with heads held high, still had their ring of yellow petals, while in other fields the pods drooped, pregnant with seeds. Although North Dakota is second in America in production of wheat, I was stunned with these tremendous fields of sunflowers. Later I read that most are produced for their oil and are primarily exported to Europe. A small percentage of seed is grown for human and bird consumption. As we approached Bismarck, farther south, the yellow petals had disappeared and the heads were ready for harvesting. To me, the fields of sunflowers have more personality than fields of grain simply because each one is different. But, then, I was raised in wheat country.

The Capital of North Dakota

|P| opulation: 45,000. Bismarck, dominated by a handsome capital building, is strategically located on the historic and beautiful Missouri River. An excellent restaurant across the river and a pleasant motel presented us with a delightful evening in this prairie city.

Then I met Darlo Tufto and Judi Adams, attractive young home economists who in turn introduced me to two of the most important organizations in the state—the North Dakota Wheat Commission and the National Sunflower Association (North Dakota leads in the production of sunflowers). I left Bismarck ladened with fascinating material, recipes, and a sack of North Dakota Maid flour (excellent).

The following recipes are from the North Dakota Wheat Commission and the National Sunflower Association. Each had been carefully constructed and was in turn tested in my kitchen.

North Dakota
Wheat Germ Yogurt Bread

Makes 4 loaves

3½ cups whole wheat
   flour
¾ cup instant dry milk
2½ teaspoons salt
2 packages active dry
   yeast
2¾ cups warm water
1 cup plain yogurt

¼ cup honey
¼ cup molasses
2 tablespoons light oil
3½–4 cups bread flour
1 cup toasted wheat germ
1 cup bran
1 egg, beaten
Wheat germ for topping

In a large mixing bowl combine the whole wheat flour, dry milk, salt, and yeast. Combine the water, yogurt, honey, and molasses in a saucepan and heat to 115°–120°F. Add to the whole wheat flour mixture and beat hard with a rubber spatula until smooth. If using a heavy-duty mixer, beat 2 minutes. Add the oil and 2 cups of bread flour and beat until smooth. Blend in the wheat germ and bran. Add sufficient bread flour to make a soft dough that pulls away from sides of the bowl. Turn out on a lightly floured surface and knead for 5 minutes. Round into a ball and place in a warm buttered bowl, turning to coat the top. Cover and let rise until doubled, about 1 hour.

Punch down the dough and divide in 4 equal portions. Knead each portion, cover, and let rest 10 minutes. Butter 4 baking sheets. Divide one portion of dough into 3 equal pieces and roll each into 12-inch ropes. Form into a braid and place on a baking sheet. Repeat directions with remaining portions of dough. Cover and let rise until doubled, about 45 minutes.

Preheat the oven to 350°F. Brush the loaves with the egg, sprinkle with the wheat germ, and bake 30–35 minutes, or until a dark golden color. Let cool on racks.

Bread Sticks

Makes 20 bread sticks

A recipe for crisp bread sticks is a "must" for a bread file. This one is easy, and the recipe can easily be doubled.

1 package active dry yeast
⅔ cup warm water
1 tablespoon sugar
¼ cup light oil
1 teaspoon salt
2 cups bread flour, approximately

Oil to brush on the bread sticks
1 egg white beaten with 2 tablespoons water for glaze
Sesame seeds, poppy seeds, or coarse salt

Butter a large baking sheet.

In a large mixing bowl combine the yeast and water, stirring until dissolved. Add the sugar, oil, salt, and 1 cup of flour. Beat until smooth with a rubber spatula or for 1 minute in a heavy-duty mixer. Gradually add sufficient flour to make a soft, workable dough. Turn out on a lightly floured surface and knead until smooth and elastic. Roll the dough into a rectangle and with a dough scraper cut into 20 slices. Roll each portion into a pencil-like rope 8 inches long. Place 1 inch apart on the baking sheet, brush lightly with oil, cover, and let rise 20 minutes.

Preheat the oven to 350°F. Brush the glaze over the bread sticks and sprinkle with seeds or salt. Bake 25 minutes, or until golden brown. Let bread sticks cool on wire racks.

North Dakota Whole Wheat Rolls

Makes about 30 rolls

2 packages active dry
  yeast
2 cups warm water
½ cup instant dry milk
1 egg

⅓ cup melted butter or
  light oil
¼ cup sugar
1 teaspoon salt
3 cups bread flour
3 cups whole wheat flour

Butter thirty 2-inch muffin forms.

Combine the yeast and ½ cup warm water in a small bowl, stirring until dissolved, and set aside. In a large mixing bowl combine the dry milk, 1½ cups warm water, egg, butter, sugar, and salt and blend well. Stir in the yeast mixture. In another bowl combine the two flours, blending well. Beat 2 cups of the flour mixture into the liquid mixture. Gradually add enough flour to mixture to make a thick batter. If using a heavy-duty mixer, knead 5 minutes with the dough hook; if kneading by hand, 8–10 minutes. Divide dough among the muffin tins, filling them two thirds full. Cover and let rise until doubled, about 1 hour.

Preheat the oven to 400°F. Bake the rolls 20 minutes, or until golden brown. Let cool on racks. Freeze leftover rolls.

Sun 'n Cinn
  Coffee Braid

Makes 2 breads

*An elegant bread that is a delight to mold.
Directions are given at the end of the recipe for
toasting sunflower seeds.*

Dough:

2 packages active dry
  yeast
½ cup warm water
¾ cup warm milk
⅓ cup sugar

6 tablespoons melted
  butter
1 teaspoon salt
4 egg yolks, lightly beaten
4–4½ cups flour

Filling:

1½ cups toasted
  sunflower seeds,
  chopped

⅔ cups honey
2 teaspoons cinnamon

Confectioner's Icing, page
  45

Toasted sunflower seeds
Candied cherries

In a small mixing bowl combine the yeast and water, stirring to dissolve, and set aside. Blend the milk, sugar, butter, and salt in a mixing bowl. Add the egg yolks, stir in 1 cup of the flour, and add the yeast mixture. Gradually add sufficient flour to make a soft, workable dough that pulls away from sides of the bowl. Turn out on a floured surface, form dough in a ball, cover, and let rest 10 minutes. Knead 10 minutes, or until silky and elastic. Round into a ball and place the dough in a warm buttered bowl, turning to coat the top. Cover loosely with plastic wrap and a towel and let rise until doubled, about 1 hour.

Punch down the dough and divide in half. Knead each portion, cover, and let rest 10 minutes. Butter 2 baking sheets. Roll one piece of dough into a 12 × 9-inch rectangle. Cut into thirds lengthwise. Combine the sunflower seeds, honey, and cinnamon. Divide the filling in half. Using the drawings as a guide, spread one third of one portion

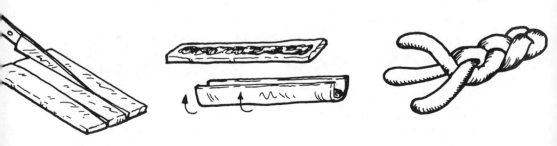

down the center of a strip of dough and repeat with the other 2 strips. Pinch the edges together firmly over the filling, creating a tube-like strip. Braid the three tubular strips together and place on a buttered baking sheet, pinching and tucking ends under. Do not stretch the loaf; plump the braid. Repeat directions with remaining portion of dough and filling. Cover and let rise until doubled, about 45 minutes.

Preheat the oven to 375°F. Bake the loaves 30 minutes, or until light golden. Remove from oven, let cool slightly on baking sheet, and remove to a wire rack. Frost the loaves with Confectioner's Icing, garnishing with extra sunflower seeds—and candied cherries for Christmas!

Toasted Sunflower Seeds: Place a single layer of raw, hulled sunflower seeds in a shallow pan in a preheated 300°F oven 30–40 minutes. Vary the length of time according to the brownness and crispness preferred. Stir occasionally.

Sunflower Seed Bread

Makes 3 loaves

A popular bread at many of my demonstrations—equally good heated for dinner or toasted for breakfast.

2 packages active dry yeast	6 cups flour, approximately
¼ cup warm water	2 eggs, lightly beaten
1 cup warm milk	Grated rind of 1 orange
6 tablespoons sugar	1 cup orange juice
2 teaspoons salt	1½ cups raw sunflower seeds
¼ cup melted butter	

Combine the yeast and water in a small bowl, stirring until dissolved, and set aside. In a large mixing bowl blend milk, sugar, salt, and butter. Add the yeast mixture. Beat in 2 cups of the flour. Add the eggs, grated rind, orange juice, and sunflower seeds. Gradually add sufficient flour to form a soft, workable dough that pulls away from sides of the bowl. Remove to a floured surface and knead 10–12 minutes. Round into a ball and place in a warm buttered bowl, turning to coat the top. Cover loosely with plastic wrap and a towel and let rise until doubled, about 1½ hours.

Punch down the dough, divide in 3 equal portions, knead lightly, cover, and let rest 10 minutes. Butter three 8-inch loaf pans. Form the dough into loaves and place in the pans. Cover and let rise until doubled, about 45–60 minutes.

Preheat the oven to 375°F. Bake the loaves 40 minutes. Turn out on wire racks to cool.

South Dakota

P ioneers arrived in the territory of South Dakota during the middle 1800's and pushed their plows into the rich soil without having to pull up a tree or clear a stone. Railroads were built and the buffalo slaughter brought the mighty Sioux to their knees. The nomadic plains culture passed into history.

Less than a million people live in either North or South Dakota. One can drive miles through exquisitely tailored farm land without seeing a tree, a farmhouse, or even a person except perhaps a farmer far off in the distance on some huge machine. From Bismarck we followed the Missouri River into South Dakota, a beautiful drive for the tamed river here is a long, slender lake.

Immigrants have introduced their own foods and cook everything from Irish stew to Chinese rice, but the foods native to the land are still plentiful. Deer, antelope, and buffalo appear on many local menus. So do fresh mountain trout, slab-sided walleye, and northern pike from the lake areas and goose; duck or pheasant suppers make chicken seem pallid.

Fortunately for the baking tradition of our country, the Czechoslovakians spread into every state of the union. In Mitchell, South Dakota, lives Helen Koupal, who has given me a beautiful Christmas bread recipe along with its traditional background in her family.

Bohemian Houska

Makes 1 large or 3 smaller loaves

Houska (it had a holiday name, vanoce) was always served on Christmas Eve, warm if possible, with butter and good coffee with country cream. There was a dish named "Kuba," made with barley, mushrooms, and garlic topped with butter, and a dish made of prunes, raisins, and peanuts simmered until tender and thickened a little with gingersnaps. On the table would be a very large bowl filled with polished red apples, oranges, and a bowl of mixed nuts. Helen follows this tradition of her parents from the old country. She prepares five houskas at Christmas, for she has three sons, their wives, thirteen grandchildren, and four great-grandchildren. At the time of this writing, Helen and her husband had celebrated their fifty-sixth anniversary. I shall treasure her letter, for it was written by a happy woman. And now for her delicious bread:

½ cup warm water
1 cup plus 1 teaspoon
   sugar
¼ teaspoon ginger
2 packages active dry
   yeast
½ cup warm heavy cream
1 cup warm milk
8½ cups flour,
   approximately
½ cup melted butter
2 teaspoons salt

3 eggs, lightly beaten
¼ teaspoon mace
Grated rind of 1 lemon
2 cups golden raisins,
   scalded, drained, and
   dried
½ cup chopped walnuts,
   almonds, or pecans
1 egg yolk mixed with 1
   tablespoon water for
   glaze
Sliced or slivered almonds

Combine the water, 1 teaspoon of sugar, ginger, and yeast in a small bowl, stirring until dissolved, and set aside. In a large mixing bowl combine the cream, milk (milk and cream may be heated together just to take off the chill), 1 cup of sugar, and 2 cups of flour. Beat well and blend in the yeast mixture. Add the butter, salt, eggs, mace, grated rind, raisins, and nuts. Gradually add sufficient flour to make a soft dough that pulls away from the sides of the bowl. Turn out on a lightly floured surface and knead 8–10 minutes, or until smooth and resilient. Round into a ball and place dough in a warm buttered bowl, turning to coat the top. Cover loosely with plastic wrap and a towel and let rise until doubled, about 1½–2 hours.

Punch down the dough, turn out on a board, and knead 2 minutes. Cut off one third of the dough, cover, and set aside. Divide the larger portion into thirds and knead each portion. Cover and let rest 10 minutes. Butter a baking sheet. Roll each of the three pieces into an 18-inch rope. Braid the ropes and place on the baking sheet. Tuck the ends under and plump the braids—do not stretch the dough. Divide the smaller portion into thirds and roll each piece into a 14-inch rope. Braid the 3 ropes, tuck the ends under, and plump the braid. Place this braid atop the large braid and press down lightly. Secure in several places with toothpicks, if necessary. Cover and let rise until almost doubled, about 1 hour.

Preheat the oven to 350°F.

Brush the bread thoroughly with the glaze, decorate with the almonds, pressing them lightly into the dough, and bake about 1 hour. During the last 25 minutes, cover the loaf with aluminum foil if the bread has browned too quickly. Remove and let cool on a wire rack.

Note: The dough may be divided in 3 portions. Divide each portion into 3 pieces and form 3 braids. Proceed as directed, baking the smaller loaves about 45 minutes.

T he city of Mitchell has one of the most astounding buildings in America—the Corn Palace. Topped with Russian domes and minarets, the whole building is decorated with columns and cornices and murals sculptured entirely in corn. Yes, real corn, of all colors, that produces a Byzantine effect like nothing else I can think of in America. We had detoured to Mitchell and now turned west to drive through the handsome capital of Pierre and then followed a long, straight highway to the Badlands National Park.

As we signed in to spend the night, a young Indian girl told us the concessions were leased by the Sioux tribe. That meant no spirits could be served or sold. To anyone raised in Oklahoma, that's never a problem, for long ago we learned that any night spent traveling in the United States could be in a dry county, precinct, or state. We settled in front of our tiny abode, sipped a light cocktail from our bar kit, and enjoyed a glorious sunset over the eerie formations of the badlands, cast in deep colors of lavender and rose. Not a bird, animal, or person was in sight, and all we could hear was the tiny tinkle of ice in our glasses. One of those rare evenings never to be forgotten.

Our dinner was a T-bone steak with instant mashed potatoes slathered with canned gravy. The steak was fine.

Corn Oysters

Makes about 48 corn oysters

This recipe was given to me by the South Dakota Department of Tourism Development and the Sioux Indian tribe and is quite different from the usual Indian fry bread. I love them served unadorned, to savor the corn flavor, but certainly the cakes may be topped with butter and maple syrup.

1 package frozen whole-
   kernel corn
⅔ cup flour
1 teaspoon baking powder
1 teaspoon salt

⅓ teaspoon pepper
3 eggs
1 tablespoon honey
¼ cup light oil

Place the corn in a small saucepan, cover, and cook slowly 10 minutes without adding water. (I use whole-kernel corn packaged in a plastic pouch and drop it into boiling water, following the directions on the package.)

Sift together the dry ingredients into a mixing bowl. Beat the eggs and honey until light and mix into the dry ingredients. Fold in the corn. Heat the oil in a skillet over moderate heat and drop the batter from a tablespoon into the hot oil. Brown cakes on both sides and serve immediately. The cakes cook quickly, so watch to see that they do not burn.

F ifty miles west of the badlands, out of the prairie, the Black Hills rise suddenly, covered with trees of an unexpectedly dark and vivid green. A long walkway to the Iron Mountain National Park headquarters is lined with the flags of the fifty states, each flagpole marked with a plaque giving the date of admission to the Union. Although the tremendous stone faces of the four Presidents were carved by human beings, the complete presentation is far more natural and thrilling than I expected. We left the park on the seventeen-mile Iron Mountain Road, which weaves through tunnels and over "pigtail" bridges and curves around and over the mountains. Thinking back, we realized the road was constructed so that the view of the four Presidents is framed over and over again by the landscape. The drive is a vivid, emotional experience.

We turned south toward Oklahoma, and at the edge of the Black Hills is Wind Cave National Park. I am a long time park buff, but I was not aware of this exquisite spot. The beautiful rolling hills are covered with tall, rich grasses. Soon we saw a herd of bison, pronghorn deer, and a prairie dog town, the population basking in the sun on its haunches and looking around completely unafraid.

Eighty-five miles through western Nebraska ranch country, without seeing a single town nor even a filling station, a joggle over to Interstate 80, and we were driving south through Kansas. Only one more night of steak and potatoes! Juicy broiled chicken, rice with pine nuts, and homemade bread would be our first menu back at home.

119

THE
OREGON TRAIL

MILEAGE—8,945 MILES

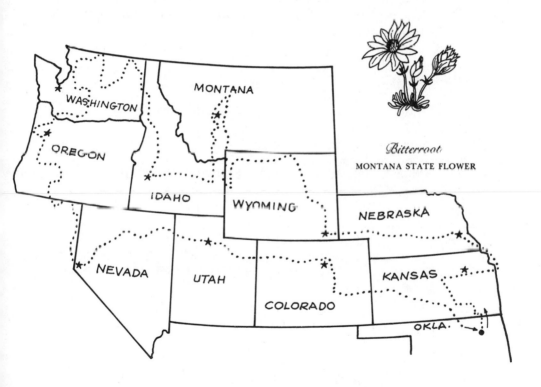

Bitterroot
MONTANA STATE FLOWER

Kansas

C lose to Leadville, Colorado, a tiny stream bubbles from natural springs deep within the Rocky Mountains to begin its course across eastern Colorado, receiving water from tributaries to become an important river as it enters west central Kansas. It is the Arkansas river, which curves through flat wheat fields, winds through the city of Wichita and the tiny hamlet of Oxford before entering Oklahoma. At Oxford the river is so narrow I could have thrown a pebble to the other shore, but it is also deep and swift and has kept an ancient grist mill working more than one hundred years. From the flour-covered miller words flowed per second as fast as the water of the river. The mill and river are his life. He filled my arms with sacks of flour and both hands with postcards. As we left I was still trying to catch up with the last paragraph he had spoken.

Hillsboro

H heading due north into Mennonite country, we discovered the small city of Hillsboro where an unusually large sod house has been turned into an excellent museum. Most sod houses consisted of one room, but this one boasts five and contains exciting artifacts brought from Russia when Mennonites immigrated to the New World. They also brought the "red wheat" that has made Kansas number one in the production of high-protein wheat. A gentle, elderly curator had me pitch buffalo chips (dried!) into an ancient Russian stove containing an oven, a well to make lard, and room at the top to smoke meats. Exquisite dresses and a Russian bear coat were displayed among the many fascinating possessions these people carried across the ocean. After finding out the purpose of my journey, Mr. Jost, the curator, promised two Mennonite recipes from his wife.

Mennonite Whole Wheat Bread

Makes 3 loaves

Mrs. Jost has designed an easily made whole grain bread with an excellent flavor, especially fine for a beginning baker.

3 cups warm water
2 packages active dry
  yeast
2 tablespoons molasses
3 cups stone-ground
  whole wheat flour

2 tablespoons melted lard
  or vegetable shortening
2 teaspoons salt
4–5 cups unbleached
  white flour

Combine the water, yeast, and molasses in a large mixing bowl, stirring until dissolved. Beat in the whole wheat flour to make a smooth batter. Cover and set aside 30 minutes, or until light and bubbly.

Stir down the sponge and add the lard and salt. Gradually add sufficient white flour to make a soft, workable dough that pulls away from sides of the bowl. Turn the dough out on a floured surface and knead until smooth and elastic, about 8–10 minutes. Round into a ball and place in a warm bowl brushed with melted lard or shortening, turning to coat the top. Cover loosely with plastic wrap and a towel and let rise until doubled, about 1 hour.

Punch down the dough, turn out on a lightly floured surface, and divide into 3 equal portions. Knead each thoroughly, cover, and let rest 10 minutes. Brush three 8½-inch loaf pans with melted shortening. Mold the dough into loaves and place in the pans. Cover and let rise until just curved over tops of pans.

Preheat the oven to 375°F. Bake the loaves 35–40 minutes, or until golden brown. Turn loaves out on a wire rack to cool.

Zwiebach

Makes about 62 rolls

Zwiebach means double. The commercial "zwiebach" for children is cooked twice; baked, sliced into pieces, returned to the oven, and finished at a low temperature until dry. But this is not what it means to the Mennonites. Their zwiebach is a perky double roll when finished. Even if only half the recipe is made, use the entire ½ cup of cream.

1 cup warm water	½ cup melted butter
2 packages active dry	¼ cup sugar
yeast	1½ teaspoons salt
3 cups warm milk	12½ cups flour,
½ cup warm heavy cream	approximately
½ cup melted lard or	
vegetable shortening	

In a large mixing bowl combine the water and yeast, stirring until dissolved. Blend in the milk, cream, lard, butter, sugar, and salt. Beat in 4 cups of flour to make a smooth batter. Gradually add sufficient flour to make a soft, workable dough that pulls away from sides of the bowl. Turn dough out on a lightly floured surface and knead 5 minutes, or until smooth and satiny. Round into a ball and place in a warm bowl brushed with melted shortening, turning to coat the top. Cover loosely with plastic wrap and a towel and let rise until doubled, about 1 hour. Punch down the dough, knead in the bowl, re-cover, and let rise again. (The second rising will make a better textured roll but it is not absolutely necessary.)

Brush 2 baking sheets with melted shortening.

Punch down the dough and knead lightly in the bowl. Pinch off small pieces about 1½ inches in diameter. Roll into smooth balls by cupping your hand over a piece of dough and rotating rapidly on an unfloured surface. Place these small balls 1 inch apart on the baking sheet. Pinch off slightly smaller pieces, form into smooth balls, and place on top of the larger ones. Press balls together lightly. Cover and let rise until almost doubled, about 30 minutes.

Preheat the oven to 400°F. Bake the rolls 15 minutes, or until light golden in color. Do not let rolls bake too long, as they burn easily on the bottom. Serve immediately or let cool, package, label, and freeze.

McPherson, Abilene, and Manhattan

F orty miles west of Hillsboro, we stopped in McPherson to have lunch and discovered the Wall-Rogalsky Milling Company and its friendly, knowledgeable public relations expert, Les Mason. We left with a 25-pound sack of excellent flour slung over my husband's shoulder, recipes, and several well-written booklets on Kansas wheat and flour. Through Les Mason I have selected two recipes, each quite different, from innovative Kansas cooks.

Quick Pecan-Topped Coffeecake

Makes 1 coffeecake

A luscious, nut-topped batter yeast cake, well designed by Mrs. Percy Shogren of Lindsborg. The cake may be prepared by machine or beaten by hand.

Topping:

⅓ cup melted butter
¼ cup packed brown
   sugar

1 tablespoon light corn
   syrup
½ cup coarsely chopped
   pecans

Dough:

¾ cup warm water
1 package active dry yeast
½ cup sugar

1 egg, lightly beaten
¼ cup melted butter
1 teaspoon salt
2½ cups flour

Brush the bottom of a Bundt pan with melted butter.

To make the topping, combine the butter, brown sugar, syrup, and pecans. Spread evenly over the bottom of the pan.

In a mixing bowl combine the water and yeast, stirring until dissolved.

Blend in the sugar, egg, butter, and salt. Stir in half the flour. Beat by hand until smooth or in a heavy-duty mixer with the flat beater for 2 minutes at medium speed. Add the remaining flour and beat 2 minutes more, or until smooth and glossy; this is the only kneading. Drop by spoonfuls on the topping. Cover and let rise until doubled, about 1–1½ hours.

Preheat the oven to 375°F. Bake the coffeecake 35 minutes. Turn out immediately on a wire rack placed over foil to catch drippings.

Karowei

Makes 3 karowei

*A Swiss-German Mennonite wedding in the early
1900's without these* karowei *was unthinkable,
according to Elizabeth Wedell. Frosted and
decorated with corn candy or decorating sprinkles,*
karowei *is still a favorite of Elizabeth's
grandchildren for any occasion. The original
recipe was enormous: I have divided it in half for
easier handling.* Karowei *dough must rise three
times before it is molded and left to rise before
baking, so allow yourself plenty of time to make it.*

1½ cups warm water	3 eggs, beaten
1 package active dry yeast	1 teaspoon salt
8½ cups flour, approximately	Confectioner's Icing, page 45
¾ cup heavy cream	Decorative candies
5 tablespoons butter	(optional)
1½ cups sugar	

Combine the water and yeast in a large mixing bowl, stirring until dissolved. Beat in 2 cups of flour to make a smooth batter. Cover and set aside 30 minutes, or until light and bubbly.

In a saucepan heat the cream, butter, and sugar to 115°F. Blend ingredients well and add to the sponge. Beat in the eggs, salt, and 1 cup of flour. Gradually add sufficient flour to make a soft, workable dough that pulls away from sides of the bowl. Turn out on a lightly floured surface and knead 10 minutes, or until smooth and satiny. Round into a ball and place the dough in a warm buttered bowl, turning to coat the top. Cover loosely with plastic wrap and a towel and let rise until doubled, about 1½ hours. Punch the dough down, knead lightly in the bowl, re-cover, and let rise again 1½ hours. Punch down the dough, knead lightly in the bowl, cover again, and let rise 1¼ hours.

Butter three 8-inch cake pans. Punch down the dough, turn out on a lightly floured surface, and knead lightly. Divide into 3 portions, round each into a smooth ball, and place in the cake tins. Cover and let rise until doubled, about 1½ hours.

Preheat the oven to 375°F. Bake the *karowei* 25–30 minutes. Let cakes cool on a wire rack and, while still warm, frost with Confectioner's Icing. Sprinkle decorating candies on top, if desired.

Note: Sliced, unfrosted cake makes a lovely, light, crisp, and fragrant toast.

C ontinuing north, the highway crosses the Old Santa Fe Trail, which opened the Southwest to settlement and trade with the Mexicans. On picturesque Smokey Hill River, at the edge of Lindsborg, a mill has been completely restored to perfect order. It is a fascinating, complicated mill with chutes running in all directions in the three story building and has an excellent museum. The setting among huge trees is a perfect picnic ground, which I am certain was a camping area for farmers when they came to have their grain ground.

We could easily have enjoyed two full days in Abilene, the town that houses the Dwight D. Eisenhower center—the family home, museum, library, and burial chapel. Abilene was the end of the famous Chisholm Trail over which thousands of cattle were driven every year from Texas to the railroad center here in the late 1860's.

Besides Eisenhower family history, Abilene has Lena Benson. In 1926 Lena clerked in a store and wanted nothing to do with cooking or kitchens. Fate had other plans. During August of that year, Lena paid $5.00 to have her horoscope read, which informed her she should be serving food to the public. Lena joined her brother in a restaurant venture, but, as she says, he got the "heebie-jeebies" and she bought him out. Lena retired in 1974 after forty-seven and a half years of serving food to the public. Her fame spread all over the state of Kansas. Her most important customer was President Eisenhower, on a birthday. Lena's secret is that she loves people and her food was consistently superb.

Lena's Cornmeal Rolls

Makes about 60 rolls

2 cups milk
⅔ cup white or yellow
   cornmeal
½ cup sugar
¼ pound (1 stick) butter
   or margarine
1½ teaspoons salt

2 packages active dry
   yeast
½ cup warm water
2 eggs, lightly beaten
7 cups flour,
   approximately
Melted butter

Measure milk into a saucepan and over moderate heat slowly add the cornmeal. Stir constantly with a whisk until mixture is thick. Add the sugar, butter, and salt and stir until dissolved. Transfer to a mixing bowl and let cool to lukewarm.

In a small bowl combine the yeast and water, stirring until dissolved. Add the yeast mixture and eggs to the cornmeal mixture, blending well. Gradually add sufficient flour to make a soft dough. Turn out on a lightly floured surface and knead lightly, about 4–5 minutes, adding as little flour as possible. Place the dough in a warm buttered bowl, turning to coat the top. Cover loosely with plastic wrap and a towel and let rise until doubled, about 1 hour.

Butter four 9-inch round cake tins. Punch down the dough and form into pan rolls (page 43). Brush the tops with melted butter and let rise until doubled and light, about 1 hour.

Preheat the oven to 350°F. Bake the rolls 15–20 minutes. Serve hot.

Note: Cornmeal rolls freeze well before baking. Form into rolls, place in buttered pans, cover securely with plastic wrap, and freeze. Remove from the freezer 3 hours before baking.

Lena's Icebox Rolls

Makes about 100 rolls

1 package active dry yeast	1 cup cool water
½ cup warm water	2 eggs, lightly beaten
1 cup boiling water	½ cup sugar
2 teaspoons salt	8–9 cups flour
½ cup vegetable shortening or butter (1 stick)	Melted butter

In a small mixing bowl combine the yeast and warm water, stirring until dissolved. In a large mixing bowl combine the boiling water, salt, and shortening, stirring until dissolved. Add the cup of cool water to the hot-water mixture, stirring until lukewarm. Add the yeast mixture and blend in the eggs and sugar. Beat in 3 cups of flour until mixture is smooth. Gradually add sufficient flour to make a soft, workable dough. Knead lightly in the bowl until the dough is smooth. The dough is now ready to shape into desired rolls (pages 42–44). Place on buttered baking sheets and brush with melted butter. Cover and let rise until doubled, about 1–1 ½ hours.

Preheat the oven to 350°F. Bake rolls about 15 minutes, or until golden.

Note: The dough may be covered in a bowl with plastic wrap and towel, then refrigerated to use as desired. Baked rolls freeze well.

K ansas is a neat state—literally. Highways are well maintained, rest islands are manicured, large and comfortable, with shaded picnic areas. Small towns have stately old homes built at the turn of the century, with well-kept lawns and huge trees. Although there are no mountains in Kansas, it is not completely flat. From Kansas City, at eight hundred feet above sea level, the land gradually rises until at the western border the elevation reaches four thousand feet. Traveling east from Abilene, the steeply rolling Flint Hills are filled with magnificent grasses, which make them splendid ranch country. At Manhattan begins the huge complex of universities and trade schools that extends through Lawrence, home of the University of Kansas on a handsome, hilly campus, and on into Kansas City, Kansas, and Kansas City, Missouri, both located at the confluence of the Missouri and Kansas rivers. In Manhattan, the American Institute of Baking provides complete courses for experienced and beginning bakers. Its research departments provide information on every aspect of home or commercial baking and can respond to questions from around the world.

Kansas City

D uring the early nineteenth century, the area of trees and grass near the two big rivers now called Kansas City was a sparsely populated Indian settlement. In 1846 the Wyandot Indians, a civilized tribe forced out of its home in Ohio, founded a small village here that ultimately became the geographical center of the continental United States. As railroads headed west, Kansas City developed into a shipping center for grains and cattle from all the Western states. The city today has unsurpassed capacity for grain storage and unbelievably extensive stockyards.

In the midst of this exciting city lives a lively young Junior Leaguer of German ancestry, Linda Davis, born and raised in Abilene. Energetic and attractive, Linda teaches cooking and does demonstration programs. Linda has shared many recipes with me; some will appear later in the book, but here are two of my favorites.

Food-Processor Apple Kuchen

Makes 1 large or 2 smaller kuchens

Dough:

1 package active dry yeast
¼ cup warm water
2½ cups flour
⅓ cup instant dry skim milk

¼ cup sugar
1 teaspoon salt
4 tablespoons cold butter
1 large egg
¼–½ cup cold water

Filling:

3 cups peeled, cored, and thinly sliced cooking apples
1 tablespoon lemon juice
½ cup sugar

2 tablespoons flour
1 teaspoon cinnamon
2 tablespoons butter
1 egg
½ cup heavy cream

Combine the yeast and warm water in a small mixing bowl, stirring until dissolved. Combine the flour, dry milk, sugar, and salt in bowl of food processor. Cut in the butter with either the steel or plastic blade. Add yeast mixture and egg and process 10 seconds. With the motor running, slowly add enough cold water to form a ball of dough. As soon as the ball has formed, stop pouring in water—you may not need the entire ½ cup. Process 30–40 seconds. Remove dough and lightly knead by hand a few times. Round into a ball and place in a warm buttered bowl, turning to coat the top. Cover loosely with plastic wrap and a towel and let rise until doubled, about 1 hour.

Generously butter a 10-inch spring-form pan, or a 3 × 9-inch baking pan, or two 8-inch cake tins. Punch down the dough and pat into the pan or pans. If using a spring-form pan, pat the dough 1½ inches up the sides.

Toss the apples with lemon juice and arrange over the dough in a pretty, symmetrical design. Combine the sugar, flour, and cinnamon and cut in the butter. Sprinkle sugar mixture over the apples. Cover the *kuchen* and let rise until doubled, about 1 hour.

Preheat the oven to 350°F. Bake the *kuchen* 20 minutes if it is molded in the spring-form pan; 15 minutes for the large baking pan; and 10–15 minutes in the cake pans. Beat the egg and cream together and spoon over the apples. Return to the oven and bake 15 minutes, or until the custard is set. Serve warm.

Note: This unusually delicious *kuchen*, made so easily in a food processor, may also be made with fresh peaches or Italian plums.

Linda's Christmas Crescents (FROZEN KRANTS)

Makes 3 crescents

Dough:

4 cups flour
1 teaspoon salt
1 cup milk
1 tablespoon sugar

½ pound (2 sticks) butter, at room temperature
1 package active dry yeast
3 egg yolks, at room temperature

Filling:

3 egg whites, at room temperature
½ cup granulated sugar
3 teaspoons cinnamon
¾ cup packed brown sugar
1½ cups finely chopped pecans, walnuts, or almonds

1 cup flaked coconut
1½ cups raisins, scalded, drained, and dried
Confectioner's Icing, page 45

Combine the flour and salt in a large mixing bowl. In a small saucepan heat the milk, sugar, and butter to 115°F, stir to dissolve, and let cool to lukewarm. Add the yeast, stirring until dissolved. Beat the egg yolks and add to the flour with the milk mixture. Beat thoroughly, preferably with a dough hook, and place in a buttered bowl, turning to coat the top. Cover securely with plastic wrap and a towel and refrigerate overnight.

The next morning, beat the egg whites until softly stiff. Slowly add the granulated sugar, beating constantly to make a soft meringue. Combine the cinnamon and brown sugar. Fold the brown sugar mixture, nuts, coconut, and raisins into the meringue.

Butter 3 baking sheets. Remove dough from refrigerator and divide into 3 portions. Roll one portion (keep other two covered with plastic wrap) into an 18 × 12-inch rectangle. Spread one third of the filling over the dough to within 1 inch of edges. Roll up from long side and seal seam and ends. Place on a baking sheet and curve into a crescent.

Repeat directions with remaining portions of dough. Cover and let rise 2 hours.

Preheat the oven to 375°F. Bake the crescents 20 minutes. Frost lightly with Confectioner's Icing while warm.

T he Plaza of Kansas City was the first suburban shopping area built in the United States. Today it is still one of the most beautiful commercial shopping centers in the Midwest. Kansas City produced another early institution that housewives loved—Wolferman's markets. They were the "Silver Palate" of the thirties and forties, with branches in other cities as far away as Tulsa. During World War II, they were the only markets that had paper bags! They sold beautiful meats, fresh produce, and elegant canned foods. Their outstanding bakery had the finest of English muffins. Wolferman's as a market does not exist now, but the grandson and his wife, Fred and Kristie Wolferman, have opened their own Original English Muffin Company.

English Muffins

Makes 20–25 muffins

No recipe has ever been available for a Wolferman's English muffin, but after eating tons of them, and several testings, I finally made one of the most satisfactory homemade English muffins I've tasted. A trick to obtaining the correct texture, with many holes to hold all the butter when the muffins are toasted, is to add baking soda and egg whites.

2 packages active dry
   yeast
2 cups warm water
2 teaspoons salt
7–8 cups bread flour,
   approximately

1 teaspoon baking soda
   dissolved in 2
   tablespoons water
3 egg whites, at room
   temperature
White cornmeal

Combine the yeast and water in a large mixing bowl, stirring until dissolved. Add the salt and 3 cups of flour and beat until smooth. Blend in the dissolved baking soda thoroughly. Beat the egg whites until softly stiff and fold into the batter. Gradually add sufficient flour to make a soft, workable dough that pulls away from sides of the bowl. Turn out on a floured surface and knead about 5 minutes. Round dough into a ball and place in a warm bowl brushed with melted shortening or butter, turning to coat the top. Cover loosely with plastic wrap and a towel and let rise until doubled, about 1 hour.

Punch down the dough, knead lightly, cover, and let rest 10 minutes. Roll the dough out ⅜ inch thick—between ¼ and ½ inch. Cut out muffins with a 3-inch round biscuit cutter. Sprinkle a sheet of wax paper with white cornmeal. Place muffins on the paper and sprinkle tops with more cornmeal. Cover and let rise 45 minutes.

Bake the muffins on an ungreased griddle over moderate heat, about 8 minutes for each side. It may take longer; keep a close check to see that they do not burn. Remove the wire racks and cool, then split with a fork, toast, and serve with loads of butter and strawberry jam. Freeze any leftover muffins.

Lincoln, Nebraska

"T he Tower of the Plains," the Nebraska state capitol building is outstanding. No other capitol that I have seen has been as carefully designed to reflect the history of the state, its pioneer movement, and its agriculture. Exquisite mosaics in black and white Belgian marble depict the Spirit of the Soil, Vegetation, and Animal Life. The Four Seasons are beautifully represented by signs of the zodiac in the rotunda dome. Surprising small details are tucked in corners (a wonderful carved buffalo head), and one room has a unique ceiling of native walnut carved in a corn and acorn motif. A colorful mosaic of Indians on horseback in full war dress is dashingly exciting high in the tower. The Senate Chamber is splendidly luxurious. (Nebraska is the only state with a unicameral system—only one legislative chamber—which has been highly successful.) Atop all this magnificence, perched on the tower, is the "Sower of Grains," a statue that can be seen for miles.

Graduated steps in a setting of flower beds and elegant fountains lead to the capitol building. In a handsome office building on our right, I found the Nebraska Wheat Board. To my relief, I was heartily welcomed, for there is one thing all Nebraskans have in common—a fierce loyalty to their university football team, and each year one of their toughest competitors happens to be the University of Oklahoma. But I was ladened with excellent material and recipes.

The Wheat Board later gave me permission to use the following three recipes. The first is an unusually fragrant fruit bread and the other two use bulgur wheat.

Buttermilk Fruit Bread

Makes 3 loaves

2 packages active dry
  yeast
1 cup warm water
1 cup warm buttermilk
⅓ cup sugar
1½ teaspoons salt
2 teaspoons cinnamon
½ cup melted butter
3 eggs, lightly beaten

3 cups stone-ground
  whole wheat flour
1½ cups chopped candied
  fruit
½ cup golden raisins,
  scalded, drained, and
  dried
2–3 cups white flour

In a small bowl combine the yeast and water, stirring until dissolved, and set aside. Combine the buttermilk (do not worry if it curdles), sugar, salt, cinnamon, and butter in a large mixing bowl and blend well. Add the eggs and yeast mixture. Beat in the whole wheat flour to make a smooth batter. Add the fruit and raisins and 1 cup of white flour. Gradually add sufficient flour to make a soft, moist dough that pulls away from sides of the bowl. Turn out on a lightly floured board and knead 10 minutes, or until smooth and resilient. Round dough into a ball and place in a warm buttered bowl, turning to coat the top. Cover loosely with plastic wrap and a towel and let rise until doubled, about 1 hour.

Punch down the dough and divide into 3 portions. Knead each, cover, and let rest 10 minutes. Butter three 8-inch loaf pans. Mold dough into loaves and place in the loaf pans. Cover and let rise to tops of pans, about 1 hour.

Preheat the oven to 375°F. Bake the loaves 35–40 minutes. Let loaves cool on wire racks.

Reconstituting Bulgur Wheat

Makes about 3 cups reconstituted bulgur wheat

What is bulgur wheat? Bulgur is precooked, cracked wheat made with either a hard red winter, hard red spring, or western white wheat. High in fiber, nutritious, and happily inexpensive, bulgur has no preservatives or additives. It is a versatile form of wheat, which can be eaten alone, mixed with fruits, vegetables, salads, and used in main dishes and breads. Bulgur has been around a long time; it is an ancient food used for centuries by Armenians and the Arabic peoples of the Middle East.

1 cup dry bulgur wheat
½ teaspoon salt
1¾ cups boiling water

Add bulgur and salt to boiling water. Stir and cover the saucepan. Cook over low heat about 20 minutes. Remove from burner and let stand covered 5–10 minutes. Do not lift the lid while bulgur is cooking; it does not need to be stirred. Bulgur will continue to expand after the cooking time as long as moisture is available. The reconstituted bulgur may be used immediately or cooled and refrigerated.

Whole Wheat Bulgur Bread

Makes 2 loaves

1 cup reconstituted
    bulgur wheat,
    preceding recipe
2 tablespoons molasses
2 tablespoons honey

2 teaspoons salt
¼ cup vegetable
    shortening or butter
    (½ stick)
3 cups whole wheat flour

2 packages active dry
  yeast
2¼ cups warm water
  (115°F)
¼ cup cornmeal

1 cup oatmeal or rolled
  oats
3 cups white flour,
  approximately

In a large mixing bowl combine the bulgur, molasses, honey, salt, shortening, 2 cups of whole wheat flour, and the yeast. Add the warm water and mix thoroughly. If using a heavy-duty mixer, beat 2 minutes. Add the remaining whole wheat flour, cornmeal, and oatmeal and mix well. Gradually add sufficient white flour to make a soft, workable dough. Turn out on a floured surface and knead 8–10 minutes. Round the dough into a ball and place in a warm buttered bowl, turning to coat the top. Cover loosely with plastic wrap and a towel and let rise until doubled, about 1 hour. This is a lively dough—a pleasure to work.

Punch down the dough, knead lightly in the bowl, and let rise a second time, about 45 minutes.

Punch down the dough again, turn out on a lightly floured surface, and divide in half. Knead each portion, cover, and let rest 10 minutes. Butter two 8½-inch pans. Mold the dough into loaves and place in the pans. Cover and let rise until just curved over tops of pans, about 1 hour.

Preheat the oven to 375°F. Bake the loaves 45 minutes, or until golden. Let loaves cool on wire racks.

Bulgur Honey Bread

Makes 3 loaves

1 cup reconstituted
  bulgur wheat, page 25
3 cups boiling water
½ cup honey
2 tablespoons light oil
2 teaspoons salt

2 packages active dry
  yeast
½ cup warm water
6–7 cups unbleached
  white flour

Combine the bulgur, boiling water, honey, oil, and salt in a large mixing bowl. Stir to blend well and let cool to lukewarm.

Combine the yeast and warm water, stirring until dissolved, and add to the bulgur mixture. Beat in 3 cups of flour to form a smooth batter. Gradually add sufficient flour to make a soft, workable dough. Turn out on a lightly floured surface and knead until smooth and elastic, about 5 minutes. Round dough into a ball and place in a warm buttered bowl, turning to coat the top. Cover loosely with plastic wrap and a towel and let rise until doubled, about 1½ hours.

Punch down the dough and divide into 3 portions. Knead each, cover, and let rest 10 minutes. Butter three 8½-inch loaf pans. Mold the dough into loaves and place in the pans. Cover and let rise until curved over edges of pans, about 1 hour.

Preheat the oven to 350°F. Bake the loaves 35 minutes. Let cool on wire racks.

Interstate 80

A portion of the Oregon Trail has vanished, to become a segment of the great truck artery that connects New York City to San Francisco. Here its new name is Interstate 80. But within the state of Nebraska there are many opportunities for travelers to trace the westward movement of emigrants and pioneers from the eastern seaboard. Following the Oregon Trail and Pony Express route, we stopped to see a museum that has a complete sod house inside the museum building, Bill Cody's handsome ranch home, and the ruins of Fort Kearney. After a pause to spend the night in the city of Kearney and relish one of the finest steaks I've tasted (must be that Nebraska air!), we were ready to tackle the "trail" again. The Sutherland rest area by the highway is to me one of the most thrilling pioneer memorials. In a huge grassy area, 150-year-old wheel ruts have been protected and symbolic iron wheel rims stand secured to them, representing the sturdy wagons. Later we walked through a tiny Pony Express station made of adobe brick, and drove on through flat plains with magnificent lush crops of corn and wheat. These gave way to rolling hills, then to a few bluffs and arroyos, and we left Interstate 80 at Cheyenne.

Cheyenne, Wyoming

T he capitol building has a classic gold dome that glitters in the bright sunshine. The total population of Wyoming is about the same as that of metropolitan Tulsa. To our delight, our hotel had an extraordinarily fine dining room serving rack of lamb with all the embellishments and superb medallions of beef. A rye roll, crescent shaped, was served, but the chef would not part with his recipe so I've created one for you that will match his expertise.

Rye Crescent Rolls

Makes 32–40 rolls

2 packages active dry
   yeast
½ cup warm water
12-ounce can beer
2 tablespoons molasses
2 teaspoons salt
⅓ cup light oil
3 cups rye flour
1 tablespoon caraway
   seeds (optional)

2–3 cups white flour
Melted butter
1 egg white beaten with 1
   tablespoon water for
   glaze
Coarse (kosher) salt,
   caraway seeds, or fennel
   seeds

Combine the yeast and water in a large mixing bowl, stirring until dissolved. In a saucepan heat the beer, molasses, salt, and oil until warm, about 110°F. Blend into the yeast mixture. Beat in the rye flour and caraway seeds, if desired. Gradually add sufficient white flour to form a soft dough that pulls away from sides of the bowl. Turn out on a floured surface and knead until smooth and elastic, about 8 minutes. Round into a ball and place in a warm bowl brushed with melted butter, turning to coat the top. Cover loosely with plastic wrap and a towel and let rise until doubled, about 1 hour.

Butter 2 baking sheets. Punch down the dough, turn out on a lightly floured surface, and knead lightly. Divide into 4 equal portions. Roll one portion (cover remaining pieces) into a 10-inch circle. Cut into either 8 or 10 wedges. Roll each triangle from the base toward the tip, stretching as you roll, and place tip side down on a baking sheet. Curve into a crescent shape. Repeat directions with remaining portions of dough, leaving ¾ inch between the crescents. Cover and let rise until doubled, about 1 hour.

Preheat the oven to 400°F. Brush the crescents with melted butter for plain rolls. Or brush with the glaze and sprinkle with salt or seeds. Bake 15 minutes. Serve immediately. These rolls do not freeze well, but, if there are any left, split and toast for breakfast.

I nterstate 25 North curves through the center of Wyoming, partially following the old Oregon Trail. We drove through miles of handsome, rugged ranch country bordered on the west by mountains. An isolated storm moving over them crackled with vivid streaks of lightning. Ranch land is replaced by tremendous oil fields, with tanks painted blue and white occasionally elaborated with stars and stripes. Then the Teapot Dome appears; the huge rock formerly did have the shape of a teapot, until a devastating storm wrecked the spout. What an odd symbol it is for the great oil scandal of the Harding administration. When we parked for the night in Buffalo, our car was surrounded by muddy pickup trucks (most inhabited by huge dogs), whose owners all wore cowboy hats and handsome, hand-tooled high-heeled boots. The population of Wyoming may be less than a million, but this outdoor society makes up for lack of size with its tremendous energy.

The next morning's drive was through the rugged, magnificent Big Horn Mountains, across flat plains into Cody, and finally through a fascinating, narrow winding canyon with seven miles of construction on the roadway and no protective railing—one false jiggle and off into the wild blue yonder! We spent two wonderful days and nights in Yellowstone National Park, which never changes. My husband had been there the summer of 1923 and I in 1963. But roads are better now and camp grounds larger; in the new motels and the handsome old hotel—more people. A traffic jam means an animal is posing, and travelers with every description of camera stumble and scramble over rocks attempting to get the perfect photograph of that bull elk with full antlers standing in a clear mountain stream.

We settled into Jackson just south of the Tetons for four lovely days and there I found good bread.

Oatmeal Sunflower Millet Bread

Makes 2 loaves

In the last letter I received from Laurel Wicks, she said she had temporarily abandoned Jackson for warmer climates, to cook on a yacht in the Caribbean. Laurel had owned a successful bakery in Jackson, sold it, and was determined to write the great American novel. I found her a delightful, free-wheeling young woman and certainly a superb cook.

2½ cups warm water
½ cup safflower oil
½ cup honey or molasses
3 packages active dry
   yeast
6–7 cups whole wheat
   flour

2 teaspoons salt
½ cup rolled oats
¼ cup millet flour
¼ cup raw sunflower
   seeds

Measure into a large mixing bowl the water, oil, and honey. Stir with a rubber spatula until dissolved. Sprinkle in the yeast and stir until dissolved. Cover and let stand 20 minutes, or until the mixture is bubbly. When the yeast has become foamy, beat in 4 cups of flour to form a smooth batter. Cover and let rest in a warm place 30 minutes.

Stir down the batter and add the salt, oats, millet flour, and sunflower seeds. Blend the mixture well and gradually add sufficient flour to form a soft dough that pulls away from sides of the bowl. The dough should be moist but not sticky. Turn out on a floured surface and knead until smooth and resilient, about 10 minutes. Round into a ball and place in a warm buttered bowl, turning to coat the top. Cover loosely with plastic wrap and a towel and let rise until doubled, about 1 hour.

Punch down the dough and divide in half. Knead each thoroughly, cover, and let rest 10 minutes. Butter two 9-inch loaf pans. Form the dough into loaves and place in the pans. Cover and let rise until just curved over tops of pans.

Preheat the oven to 350°F. Bake the loaves 40 minutes, or until golden brown. Let cool on wire racks.

Sourdough Cinnamon Rolls

Makes about 18 large or 30 small rolls

Tourists and natives in the Jackson Hole area, which includes the exquisite Teton Mountain Range, love sourdough breads, particularly when turned into sweet rolls and a luscious lemon bread that I tested.

Dough:

1 package active dry yeast
1 cup warm water
½ cup sugar
2 teaspoons salt
½ cup melted butter

2 cups sourdough starter,
    pages 183 and 185
5 cups flour,
    approximately

Filling:

1 cup packed brown sugar
1 cup finely chopped
    pecans

2 teaspoons cinnamon
½ teaspoon nutmeg
½ cup melted butter

Confectioner's Icing, page 45

Combine the yeast and water in a large mixing bowl, stirring until dissolved. Blend in the sugar, salt, and butter. Stir in the sourdough starter and 2 cups of flour and beat until smooth. Gradually add sufficient flour to make a soft, workable dough. Turn out on a floured surface and knead until smooth and elastic, about 10 minutes. Cover with a towel and let rest while preparing the filling.

Combine and mix well the brown sugar, pecans, cinnamon, nutmeg, and butter.

Butter 2 baking sheets.

Divide the dough in half. Roll 1 piece into a 15 × 9-inch rectangle. Spread half the filling over the dough to within ½-inch of edges. To make very large rolls, roll up from the short side, jelly-roll style, and seal the seam. Slice into 1-inch rolls and place cut side up on a baking sheet. Repeat with remaining portion of dough. Cover and let rise until doubled, about 1½ hours. For smaller rolls, roll up the rectangle from the long side, seal the seam, and slice into 1-inch rolls. Proceed as directed. Cover and let rise 1 hour.

Preheat the oven to 375°F. Bake the rolls 20–25 minutes, or until light golden brown. Remove rolls to wire racks and frost with Confectioner's Icing made with your choice of flavoring.

Lemon Sourdough Bread

Makes 1 loaf

After consuming a hefty sandwich on thick sourdough bread at one of the popular spots in Jackson Hole, I discovered they served a sourdough lemon bread. That was indeed intriguing, for the bread was moist, with the lemon flavor intermingling beautifully with sourdough. Right there I decided to take a favorite lemon bread, remove the buttermilk, and substitute sourdough!

¼ pound (1 stick) butter, at room temperature
1 cup sugar
Grated rind of 1 lemon
2 eggs
2½ cups flour
½ teaspoon salt
¾ teaspoon baking soda

⅓ cup lemon juice
⅓ cup water
1 cup sourdough starter made with white flour, page 185
Confectioner's Icing made with lemon juice, page 45

Preheat the oven to 350°F. Butter a 9-inch loaf pan.

Cream the butter and sugar with grated rind until light and fluffy. Add the eggs one at a time, beating well after each addition.

Combine the flour, salt, and baking soda. In a small bowl, combine the lemon juice and water. Add the dry ingredients to the butter mixture alternately with lemon mixture, beating until fluffy. Fold in the sourdough starter until batter is smooth. Pour into the loaf pan and bake 1 hour, or until bread tests done. Leave the bread in the pan and place on a wire rack 10 minutes. Turn out and brush with the Confectioner's Icing while warm. Quick bread is much easier to slice after it has cooled.

Montana

A fter studying the map (carefully!), we drove north, back through the Tetons into Yellowstone, stopped to watch Old Faithful spout once again, and crossed into Montana. Our first stop was the beautiful campus of Montana State University at Bozeman, carpeted with luscious green lawns and shaded with tremendous trees.

A relaxed two-hour session with Dr. Charles McQuire produced much information on the problems of breadmaking and the growing of wheat in the west.

Dr. McQuire, after many years with The Pillsbury Company, retired to do research on the improvement of protein count in wheat and to study strains that can withstand severe winters and conditions of insufficient moisture. Two fascinating facts: seventy to seventy-five percent of Montana's wheat is exported to the Orient; and Pillsbury has increased the amount of whole wheat flour it mills forty times in the past few years. The last fact is most encouraging, for I have found in all my journeys that people love the whole grain breads and care about more natural foods.

Helena, the Hutterites, and Scobey

W andering the grounds around the capitol in Helena, I was fortunate to meet Joseph Lundberg, who guided me about the capitol building. He also gave me a marvelous recipe from Governor Ted Schwinden and told me about the Hutterite Colony north of Cascade, Montana. My visit with the Hutterites was a special adventure, which is told at the beginning of this book.

Wheaten Muffins

Makes 30 muffins or 24 muffins and 1 small loaf

Governor Schwinden has created a superior muffin, a bit different than most, excellent hot out of the oven served either plain or slathered with fresh butter. The recipe produces quite a few muffins. I poured the last of the batter into a small 6 × 2-inch loaf pan that made a wonderful little bread to tuck in the freezer. Try leftover muffins sliced and toasted with blackberry jelly and cream cheese for breakfast—a wonderful combination on those earthy muffins.

¼ pound (1 stick) butter or vegetable shortening, at room temperature
1 cup sugar
2 large eggs (about ½ cup)
2 cups unbleached white flour

2 teaspoons salt
2 tablespoons baking powder
2 cups whole wheat flour, preferably stone ground
2 cups milk

Preheat oven to 425°F. Butter well 30 muffin tins, or 24 muffin tins and a 6 inch loaf pan.

Cream the butter and sugar in the bowl of an electric mixer, or by hand, until light and fluffy. Add the eggs, one at a time, beating thoroughly. Sift together the white flour, salt, baking powder, and whole wheat flour. Add one quarter of the dry mixture to the butter mixture and stir quickly with rubber spatula. Add one third of the milk and again stir quickly. Alternate adding dry ingredients with the milk, stirring very quickly after each addition. Fill the muffin tins about two thirds full. Bake muffins 20–25 minutes. Bake a small loaf at 375°F for 25–30 minutes.

F ifty miles north of Helena, we left Interstate 15 at Cascade. Lunch at the one café in town had been a piping hot bowl of soup and an excellent BLT for the total sum of $4.90 for the two of us—including two glasses of milk! then we plunged into the wheat fields and found the "bomb" and the Hutterites (page 144). From a recipe originally calling for one hundred pounds of flour I calculated down and tested to get to a working recipe that makes a good family loaf.

It is fascinating to compare this bread with others that have great similarity in their construction. Look at Sophie's Pueblo Bread (page 379), Puerto Rican Bread (page 433), and Cuban Bread (page 439). The reason for this is that they all have a common origin, the method of breakmaking first brought to our continent by Jesuit priests.

Hutterite Bread

Makes 2 large or 3 smaller loaves

3 packages active dry
  yeast
3 cups warm water
¼ cup sugar

¼ cup melted lard
1 tablespoon salt
6½ cups bread flour,
  approximately

Combine the yeast and water in a large mixing bowl, stirring until dissolved. Stir in the sugar and set aside 15 minutes, or until bubbly. Add the lard and salt. Beat in 4 cups of flour to form a smooth batter. Gradually add sufficient flour to make a soft, workable dough. Turn out on a floured board and knead 10–15 minutes. Round into a ball and place in a warm bowl brushed with melted lard or vegetable shortening, turning to coat the top. Cover loosely with plastic wrap and a towel and let rise until doubled, about 1½ hours.

Punch down the dough and divide in half. Knead each portion, cover, and let rest 10 minutes. Brush two 9-inch loaf pans with melted lard or spray with nonstick vegetable spray. Form the dough into loaves and place in the pans. Cover and let rise until well rounded over edges of pans.

Preheat oven to 400°F. Bake the loaves about 40 minutes. Turn loaves out on wire racks to cool.

Note: Vegetable shortening may be substituted for lard, although the latter does give a marvelous crust. The two portions of dough make large, high loaves. The dough may be divided into 3 portions for 8½ × 4 ½ × 2½-inch pans and baked 35 minutes.

T en miles south of the Canadian border and two hundred miles northeast of my Hutterite colony is the tiny town of Scobey, where Alvin Russtebakke lives and owns and runs the Great Grains Milling Company. I've not been to Scobey nor met Alvin, but through letters, the telephone, and our shared interests we have become great friends. He and his two sons mill some of the finest whole wheat flour I've worked with. Alvin says no one comes to Scobey unless they have to, but the mail goes through, so I receive flour promptly from him when I need it. I've tried many of Alvin's recipes and find them all to be well designed—and certainly healthy! Here are three; if you are looking for flavorful whole grain breads and sweet rolls, these are for you. The recipes should be made only with the best stone ground whole wheat flour available.

Whole Wheat
Overnight Potato Rolls

Makes 60 Rolls

1 package active dry yeast	2 eggs
1½ cups warm water	1 cup lukewarm mashed
½ cup packed brown	or riced potatoes
sugar	5 cups stone-ground
¼ cup light oil, or melted	whole wheat flour
vegetable shortening or	
butter	

Combine the yeast and water in a large mixing bowl, stirring until dissolved. Add the sugar, oil, eggs, and potatoes, blending well. Beat in 2 cups of flour to form a smooth batter. Gradually add sufficient flour to make a soft, workable dough. Always be careful when adding whole wheat flour; the dough can easily become too dry. Turn out on a lightly floured surface and knead until smooth and elastic, about 10 minutes. Shape into a ball and place in a buttered (but not warmed) bowl, turning to coat the top. Cover securely with plastic wrap and a heavy towel. Refrigerate overnight.

The dough will keep well 4–5 days. When ready to bake, remove dough from refrigerator and shape into desired rolls (pages 42–44).

Place on buttered baking sheet. Cover and let rise for about 1½ hours, or until light. Brush with melted butter, if desired. Bake in a preheated 375°F oven 15 minutes, or until lightly browned. Serve immediately.

Great Grains Cinnamon Rolls

Makes 18 rolls

½ Whole Wheat Potato
  Roll dough, preceding
  recipe
Melted butter
½ cup packed brown
  sugar
1 tablespoon cinnamon

¾ cup raisins, scalded,
  drained, and dried
  (optional)
Confectioner's Icing made
  with orange or lemon
  juice, page 45 (optional)

Butter a baking sheet or 2 cake tins.

Roll the dough into an 18 × 9-inch rectangle and brush with melted butter to within ½ inch of edges. Combine the sugar and cinnamon and add the raisins, if desired. Sprinkle over the dough, roll up from the long side, jelly-roll style, and seal the seam. Cut into 1-inch slices and place ½ inch apart on the baking sheet or in cake tins. Cover and let rise 1½ hours, until the rolls are light and touch each other.

Preheat oven to 375°F. Bake rolls 20–25 minutes. The rolls are delicious without icing, but, if desired, frost with Confectioner's Icing while warm.

Pecan Rolls

Makes 18 rolls

Topping:

4 tablespoons butter
¼ cup packed brown
   sugar

2 tablespoons light corn
   syrup
½ cup pecan halves

Dough:

½ Whole Wheat
   Overnight Potato Roll
   dough, page 147
Melted butter

½ cup packed brown
   sugar
1 tablespoon cinnamon

Melt the butter in a saucepan, stir in the sugar and syrup, and cook until dissolved. Pour into a 13 × 9 × 2-inch baking pan and sprinkle pecans on top. Prepare the roll as described in Great Grains Cinnamon Rolls and place slices ½ inch apart on top of the sugar mixture. Cover and let rise 1½ hours.

Preheat the oven to 375°F. Bake the rolls 25 minutes, or until lightly browned. Invert pan over a tray to allow the topping to drizzle through the rolls. Yum, yum!

A|fter the intriguing Hutterite adventure, we turned south again to go up into mountains for a two-night rest at the famed Chet Huntley Lodge. This gave me time to type my notes and reflect on our travels into "Big Sky" country—Yellowstone, the Tetons, and Jackson Hole country—some of the most splendid, exhilarating areas of the United States. Our National Park Service accomplishes miracles in protecting wildlife and forests and giving millions of people each year a chance to enjoy areas from the seashores of Maine to the volcanoes of Hawaii.

Idaho

P|ioneers passed through Idaho territory as fast as the oxen would go, for there was nothing but desert, jagged mountains, and swift, difficult rivers. Idaho territory was neglected until it was found that the soil is rich in minerals and with irrigation would grow the richest of crops. Water flows from two main sources, the unusually large number of beautiful rivers that receive water from the snows of the mountains and the tremendous quantities of water trapped in the lava underground.

We came into Idaho in the eastern zone, at Idaho Falls. We had lunch at a restaurant beside the awesome, fast Snake River tumbling over huge rocks, with a magnificent Mormon temple in the background. Our lunch—Idaho potato soup with the skin left on and a baked Russet potato dripping with melting butter. We would soon be in potato field country, so now was the time to look for potato breads. The ideas for these two came from the tourist bureau in the capitol building at Boise.

Idaho Potato Bread

Makes 3 loaves

Both the Idaho Potato Bread and Country Bread have been tested with Russet baking potatoes. Usually 2 to 3 medium potatoes will produce 2 cups of riced potatoes and water. If you do not have a ricer, mash potatoes using a minimum of potato water. Be certain there are no lumps. Instant potato flakes may be substituted for riced potatoes to make potato water.

1 cup warm potato water
   (see following recipe)
2 packages active dry
   yeast
2 tablespoons honey
6–7 cups unbleached
   white flour
1 cup warm milk

½ cup melted butter
2 eggs, lightly beaten
1 cup riced potatoes
2 teaspoons salt
2 tablespoons honey
Grated rind of 1 lemon
   (optional)
2 cups bread flour

Combine the potato water, yeast, and honey in a small mixing bowl, stirring until dissolved. Beat in 1 cup of unbleached flour until a smooth batter is formed. Cover and set aside 30 minutes, or until light and bubbly.

In a large mixing bowl blend the milk, butter, eggs, potatoes, salt, honey, and grated rind. Add the sponge and stir well. Beat in the bread flour until smooth. Gradually add sufficient unbleached flour to form a soft, workable dough that pulls away from sides of the bowl. Turn dough out on a floured surface and knead 8–10 minutes, or until smooth and elastic. Round into a ball and place in a warm buttered bowl, turning to coat the top. Cover loosely with plastic wrap and a towel and let rise until doubled, about 1 hour.

Butter three 8½-inch loaf pans. Punch down the dough, turn out on a lightly floured board, and knead lightly. Divide into 3 equal portions. Mold 2 regular loaves and place in pans. Cut off one third of the dough from the third portion and set aside. Divide the large piece into 3 portions, roll into 12-inch ropes, and braid. Plump the braid and tuck into the third prepared pan. Divide the smaller portion into 3 pieces and roll into 14-inch ropes. Braid and place atop the large braid, tucking ends under the larger braid. Cover and allow loaves to rise just to edges of pan.

Preheat oven to 350°F. Bake the loaves 30–35 minutes. Let cool on wire racks.

Idaho Country Bread

Makes 2 loaves

2 cups warm potato water
2 packages active dry
  yeast
2 teaspoons salt
3 tablespoons melted
  vegetable shortening or
  lard
⅓ cup light molasses or
  honey
2 cups riced potatoes

3 cups stone-ground
  whole wheat flour
2½ cups unbleached
  white flour,
  approximately
1 egg white beaten with 1
  tablespoon water for
  glaze
Fennel or caraway seeds

Potato Water: Place 2 large or 3 medium potatoes, peeled and diced, in a saucepan and cover well with water. You will need 2 cups of potato water after the potatoes have cooked. Bring the potatoes to a boil and cook until very tender. Drain the potato water and let cool to 100°–105°F. Rice the potatoes and reserve.

Combine the potato water with the yeast, stirring until dissolved. Add the salt, shortening, molasses, and potatoes, stirring well. Beat the whole wheat flour to form a smooth mixture. Gradually add sufficient white flour to make a soft, workable dough that pulls away from sides of the bowl. Turn dough out on a floured surface and knead 8–10 minutes, or until smooth and elastic. Round into a ball and place in a warm bowl brushed with melted shortening, turning to coat the top. Cover loosely with plastic wrap and a towel and let rise until doubled, about 1 hour.

Lightly brush a baking sheet with melted shortening or spray with nonstick vegetable spray. Punch down the dough, turn out on a lightly floured surface, and divide in half. Knead each and round into smooth balls. Place on the baking sheet, cover, and let rise 30 minutes. A most active dough. Make crisscross slashes with a razor, brush with the glaze, and sprinkle with seeds.

Preheat the oven to 375°F. Bake loaves 35–40 minutes, or until dark brown. Remove loaves from oven and let cool on wire racks.

T wo extinct volcanoes stand like sentinels on the flat plain northwest of Pocatello, awesome landmarks that guided thousands of pioneers traveling west. Suddenly there was a warning of "No gas available for 50 miles" on our route to Sun Valley, where we arrived safely and spent the night at the Sun Valley Lodge. Built in 1937, its halls are lined with huge, nostalgic photographs of movie stars of the golden age of Hollywood.

The northern route from Sun Valley goes through the Sawtooth Mountains, with peaks eight thousand feet high. The highway follows the Salmon River, which ultimately flows into the Columbia, through stunning, rugged scenery and on to high, lushly green meadows filled with woolly cattle and cowboys on horseback. Tall poles along the highway indicate the boundaries for plowing winter snows. We passed Hell Roaring and Fourth of July creeks, and our highway changed to the Ponderosa Pine Scenic Route. For eighty miles we drove a twisting, winding road through the dense pine forests, and all at once came out into open country, where thousands of sheep were grazing, watched by a Basque sheepherder and his dogs. Then into Idaho City, to have lunch at Calamity Jane's, where the split-pea soup was thick enough to eat with a fork. I felt as though I had driven through a western movie.

Heading down into the valley around Boise, the capital, we went through lush areas of wheat fields running up the mountainsides and sugar beet and sunflower fields. As far as one can see, water from the irrigation systems twists into the air. In the southern part of the state, potatoes had recently been harvested, for hundred-pound sacks lay in neat rows in the fields, waiting to be shipped or stored in the long, low sheds that are partially buried and topped with sod sprouting long grasses. By this time, I had fallen in love with the state of Idaho, for I had not expected such grandeur, such lush crops, and such splendid resorts other than the famous Sun Valley.

Highway 95 cuts north through fields of onions, more sugar beets, garlic, peas, then peach, apricot, pear, and cherry orchards, and into lentil country. Ninety-five percent of the lentils produced in the United States come from the area around Moscow, which is in both Idaho and Washington states. The gentleman in charge of the lentil commission has his desk and chair on the state line between the two states, so no one will be offended. During the decade of the 70's, lentil production rose from 5,000 acres to 530,000. Several people attempted to find lentil flour for me, without success. I gave up on trying to do a lentil-flour bread—a waste of effort with an ingredient so difficult to find.

We entered the Nez Percé Reservation, and there came an awkward moment followed by some fascinating information. Through my research, I knew the Indians make a bread with a camas root bulb. At the reservation's headquarters, we stopped to get information. Two heavy-set young Indian women looked at each other, shrugged, and one of them disappeared. Soon she returned with a flat statement. "We don't give out that kind of information." I retreated hastily, disappointed. But two miles further, we found a tiny, lovely spot, the Nez Percé National Historical Park. A young ranger, Steve Hyndman, brought out a camas bulb for me to see and feel. Small and purplish in color, it looks like an ordinary flower bulb. Steve promised me the recipe for camas bread, and even though camas root is not available, it is fascinating to read exactly how the women of the tribe make their bread.

Camas Bread

C amas closely resembles a plant known as "death camas," which is highly poisonous. The camas root bulb used by the Nez Percé Indians is an entirely different plant. The following "recipe" is quoted from Ranger Steve Hyndman's letter to me.

Camas bulbs are dug in the early and middle summer season. It is best to remove the black outer layers immediately upon digging.

Cooking the bulbs: A pit is dug in the morning some eighteen inches in depth and perhaps five feet in diameter. A layer of very hot stones is placed on the bottom of the pit. Over the stones place a layer of green meadow grass with a little water sprinkled over it, followed by a layer of green alder leaves. (The alder provides flavor.) The camas bulbs are placed in white flour sacks and laid evenly over the leaves. Burlap sacks are used as cover, and a layer of about six inches of earth spread over all.

At nightfall, a rather large fire of wood is built over the pit and allowed to burn out. This process is repeated the next night. The morning of the third day (after two days and two nights), the pit is opened and bulbs checked. (They are almost always done. If not, more fire is placed on top for another day.) The bulbs are removed and some are placed in jars while still hot. Others are allowed to cool and are eaten then, or later. Modern refrigeration will let one keep cooked bulbs indefinitely. Or, they can be allowed to dry and will, in this manner, also keep indefinitely. Sometimes the bulbs get overcooked into a dark brown, glue-like mass. A gruel can be made from this for immediate consumption, or sun-dried loaves made of it for future use.

In the days before refrigeration and "canning" in glass jars, the Nez Percé people prepared camas into loaves. This was done by taking the hot fresh bulbs and mashing them into a kind of dough which was formed into loaves with the fingers. These loaves or cakes were then cooked some more, in order to seal the outside, after which they were allowed to cool and were dried in the sun or over a campfire. These dried cakes were stored for future use, keeping fit to eat for several months.

The State of Washington

D espite the Great Depression, the building of the Grand Coulee Dam was begun in 1934 and finished in 1941. It created a lake that extends north beyond the Canadian border, while another section turns south to Coulee City. We drove in a great circle through fertile valleys that stretch south and west to Ellensburg, Ephrata, and Wenatchee (the apple center), and north to Omak and the border. The orchards were laden with green and red apples, pears, nectarines, and peaches. The trees become so burdened with fruit that the branches have to be propped up with boards. Huge pen stocks out of the dam feed water into tunnels and canals and distribute it to over six thousand farm units. Never have I seen so many apples; the production is simply incredible. Needless to say, there has to be an apple bread here.

Apple-Sunflower Bread

Makes 1 loaf

A quick bread, perfect for preparing in a food processor. The aroma while it bakes is tantalizing!

2 cups flour
1 teaspoon baking powder
1 teaspoon baking soda
1 teaspoon cinnamon
2 medium apples, peeled
  and cored

¼ pound (1 stick) butter,
  at room temperature
¾ cup sugar
Grated rind of 1 lemon
2 eggs
½ teaspoon vanilla
½ cup sunflower seeds

Preheat the oven to 350°F. Butter well a 9-inch loaf pan.

Sift the flour, baking powder, soda, and cinnamon together. Grate the apples in a food processor and transfer to a small bowl. Insert the steel or plastic blade. Add the butter and sugar to the processor bowl and whirl several times until creamy. Add the rind, eggs, and vanilla, pulsing 3 times to blend well. Blend in the apples. Add the dry ingredients, whirling 30 seconds to make a smooth batter. Pour the sunflower seeds through the funnel, pulse 3 times, or until well distributed. Spread the batter in the loaf pan and bake 50 minutes, or until the bread tests done. Turn out on a wire rack to cool. As with all quick breads, slicing will be easier if left alone 24 hours.

We continued our loop north toward the North Cascades National Park and turned off on a gravel road that winds nine miles up a mountain to the Sun Lodge. Dining atop this mountain with its view of the Cascade Range and the excellent food made this one of those rare and perfect evenings. At breakfast there was a rainbow shining constantly before us, half a melon piled with fresh fruit, and hot apple cider stirred with a cinnamon stick. My husband had to drag me off that mountain.

Carrot Mountain Bread

Makes 3 loaves

2 packages active dry yeast	¼ cup honey or light molasses
2 cups warm water	½ cup light oil
5–6 cups stone-ground whole wheat flour	2 cups grated carrots
	2 tablespoons poppy seeds
	2 teaspoons salt

Combine the yeast and water in a mixing bowl, stirring until dissolved. Add 2 cups of flour and the honey, beating until smooth. Cover and set aside 1 hour.

Stir the sponge and add the oil, carrots, poppy seeds, and salt, blending well. Slowly add sufficient flour to form a soft dough that pulls away from sides of the bowl. Turn out on a lightly floured surface and knead about 8 minutes, or until smooth and elastic. Round into a ball and place in a warm bowl brushed with melted butter or vegetable shortening, turning to coat the top. Cover loosely with plastic wrap and a towel and let rise until doubled, about 1 hour.

Punch down the dough and divide into 3 equal portions. Knead each piece, cover, and let rest 10 minutes. Butter three 8½-inch loaf pans. Form the dough into loaves and place in the pans. Cover and let rise to tops of pans, about 45 minutes.

Preheat the oven to 375°F. Bake the loaves 35 minutes, or until light brown. Let loaves cool on wire racks.

I n the North Cascades park we passed Cutthroat Creek, Liberty Bell Mountain, Ross Dam, which has created a sea-green lake, and drove into a narrow defile labeled "GORGE" with a dramatic waterfall plunging down the mountain. Huge trucks lumbered past, burdened with enormous logs. The mountains were swathed in clouds and we splashed through the intermittent rain to arrive, finally, in the beautiful city of Seattle, built on high bluffs, with majestic trees everywhere and the magnificent bay clad with islands below.

I found Gail Worstman, a bubbly young woman devoted to natural foods, through a feature story on breads in a local newspaper. Gail guided us through a *dim sum* lunch and took us to a bakery to watch thousands of hamburger buns being made for a holiday weekend. At Gail's instigation, the bakery was featuring a whole grain bread. My friendship with Gail has continued and we would later meet again on the island of Kauai. After I had asked questions of everyone I met, including a hairdresser and a food editor, I came to the conclusion that all of Seattle loves homemade whole grain breads. Dining at a swinging young restaurant, The Sunlight, close to the University of Washington campus, we had a wholesome lentil soup and what else, a whole wheat bread. Later, I was inspired to design this recipe.

Sesame-Sunflower Bread

Makes 4 loaves

Sponge:

2 packages active dry yeast	1 cup warm water
	1 cup unbleached white flour

2 cups warm water	½ cup toasted sesame seeds
1 cup instant dry skim milk	¾ cup sunflower seeds
½ cup honey or light molasses	1 cup rye flour
¼ cup safflower oil	2 cups stone-ground whole wheat flour
2 teaspoons salt	3½ cups unbleached white flour
½ cup toasted wheat germ	
¼ cup soy or millet flour	

To make the sponge, combine the yeast and water in a bowl, stirring until dissolved. Beat in the flour until smooth. Cover with a towel and set aside 30 minutes, or until light and bubbly.

In a large mixing bowl combine the water, dry milk, honey, oil, salt, wheat germ, soy flour, and sesame and sunflower seeds. Blend well. Stir down the sponge and add to the honey mixture with the rye flour. Beat until smooth. Blend in the whole wheat flour. Gradually add sufficient white flour to make a soft, workable dough that pulls away from sides of the bowl. Turn out on a floured surface and knead until smooth and elastic, about 8–10 minutes. Round into a ball and place dough in warm bowl brushed with melted butter or vegetable shortening, turning to coat the top. Cover loosely with plastic wrap and a towel and let rise until doubled, about 1½ hours.

Turn the dough out and divide into 4 equal portions. Knead each, cover, and let rest 10 minutes. Butter four 8-inch loaf pans. Form the dough into loaves and place in the pans. Cover and let rise to tops of pans, about 1 hour.

Preheat the oven to 375°F. Bake the loaves about 40 minutes. Turn loaves out on wire racks to cool.

Ruthless White Bread

Makes 3 loaves

In Seattle lives a splendid cook, Ruth Morgan. A great collector of recipes, she loves to share them, but her friends declare that her recipes are demanding and have nicknamed them all "Ruthless." Ruthless White Bread has been a slow creation of Ruth's for several years. One of the secrets is to use as little flour as possible. Rub butter on your hands while kneading.

1½ cups scalded milk
4 teaspoons salt
¼ cup plus 1 teaspoon
   sugar
½ cup cold water
2 packages active dry
   yeast

1 cup warm water
¼ cup melted butter
6 cups unbleached white
   flour, approximately
Melted butter (optional)

In a large mixing bowl combine the milk, salt, and ¼ cup of sugar, stirring until dissolved. Add the cold water and let cool to lukewarm.

Combine the yeast and the warm water in a bowl, add the teaspoon of sugar, and stir until dissolved. Add yeast mixture to the milk mixture and blend in the butter. Beat in 3 cups of flour to make a smooth mixture. Gradually add sufficient flour to make a soft, workable dough that pulls away from sides of the bowl. Turn out on a floured surface and knead until smooth and silky, about 8–10 minutes. Round into a ball and place in a warm buttered bowl, turning to coat the top. Cover loosely with plastic wrap and a towel and let rise until doubled, about 1 hour.

Punch down the dough and divide into 3 portions. Knead each portion, cover, and let rest 10–15 minutes. Butter three 8½-inch loaf pans. Form the dough into loaves and place in the pans. Cover with a damp towel and let rise until near tops of pans.

Preheat the oven to 400°F. Bake the loaves 30 minutes. Let cool on wire racks. Brush tops of loaves with melted butter, if desired.

Mount Rainier National Park

A s our highway entered a canyon bordered with tall pines that leads to the entrance of the park, a sign popped up—GROWLY BEAR BAKERY. Soon there was a second sign—GROWLY BEAR BAKERY AND BEARTIQUE, with an arrow pointing to the left, though we could see nothing but forest beyond.

We drove for half a mile and there was a tiny building. Inside were the beautiful aroma of fresh bread and Susan Lundstad, the creator of the adorable sweet dough Growly Bear in the following recipe. She makes other goodies that I looked at longingly—a fresh huckleberry pie, assorted cookies, huge cinnamon buns, a marvelous variety of breads, and meat pies. But the bear captivated me and here he is.

Growly Bear

Makes 3 little bears

Not long after I returned home to my kitchen and conquered the bear, my youngest son and his wife produced a handsome baby boy. Mike baked twenty-five little bears to distribute instead of the tradition-worn cigar.

1 recipe Basic Sweet
   Dough, page 432
9 raisins

1 egg beaten with 1
   tablespoon water for
   glaze
Tiny American flag

Divide the risen dough into 3 portions. Work with only 1 piece at a time; cover the other 2 portions. Butter one 19 × 13-inch and one smaller baking sheet, or 3 small baking sheets.

Cut off one quarter of 1 portion of dough. Set aside smaller piece. Divide the large piece of dough in half. Form 1 piece into a rough triangle, about 5 inches across the base and 6 inches long, for the body and place on a baking sheet. Round the second piece into a ball for the head. Press to elongate the ball to make fat cheeks. Fit this part, about 2½ inches high, atop the base of the rough triangle, using the illustration as a guide. Divide the small portion of dough into 5 pieces. Roll 4 of them into balls and set in place for the paws—hands and feet. Cut two long slivers of dough off the fifth piece, about 1 inch long and ½ inch wide. Curve both slivers and place at the top of the head for ears. Shape the final piece into a pointed nose. Make an indentation in center of head and press the nose into dough pointed side up. Press in 2 large raisins for eyes and 1 for the belly button. Brush well with the glaze.

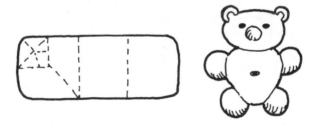

Repeat directions with remaining two portions of dough. Cover and let rise 45 minutes–1 hour, or until light and puffy.

Preheat the oven to 350°F. Brush the bears thoroughly with the glaze so the pieces will remain stuck together! Bake about 20–25 minutes, or until deep golden brown. Remove from oven and let cool on baking sheet. Do not move bears until they are cool. Stick a tiny American flag in one paw. Any child under 80 will love one of these bears.

Note: At Christmas I have inserted a tiny candy cane in his paw and dribbled a bit of icing with decorative candies on top. He loves that.

L uckily we obtained a room for two nights at the Paradise Inn, now a Historical Building. The original enormous lobby is graced by huge fireplaces at each end and has tremendous logs for cross beams. "Flying-buttress" logs outside protect the lodge when it is almost buried in snow during the winters. We had not yet seen Mount Rainier—in fact I had no idea where it was, for the entire landscape was obscured by clouds. The next morning bright sunshine poured into our room and outside was that magnificent snow-capped mountain in our backyard. I was so overwhelmed by such majestic beauty, so close, that breakfast seemed beside the point until some blueberry muffins were served by our handsome young waiter. I inquired, he returned with a note, and I ended up in the kitchen with Jodi Hartely, age twenty and six feet tall. Jodi is devoted to national parks and outdoor sports. She learned the baking trade from her father and grandfather, and it enables her to work in many national park lodges.

Mount Rainier Blueberry Muffins

Makes 24 muffins

2½ cups unbleached
   white flour
1 cup bran cereal
¼ teaspoon salt
2 teaspoons baking
   powder
½ teaspoon baking soda
2 cups buttermilk

1 egg, beaten
½ cup light molasses
¼ cup melted butter
1 cup blueberries, fresh or
   frozen, lightly floured
1 cup raisins, scalded,
   drained, and dried
   (optional)

Preheat the oven to 400°F. Butter well twenty-four 2½-inch muffin tins.

In a large mixing bowl combine the flour, bran, salt, baking powder, and soda. In a smaller bowl blend the buttermilk, egg, molasses, and butter. Add the buttermilk mixture to the flour mixture with a rubber spatula. Mix quickly so that all ingredients are barely wet. Fold in the blueberries and raisins, if desired. Fill muffin tins two thirds full. Bake 20–25 minutes. Serve immediately.

A forty-mile drive through deep tree-lined canyons took us to the other side of Mount Rainier. On both sides of the mountain, walks covered with wild mountain flowers lead right up to the glaciers. After another breakfast of Jodi's blueberry muffins, we drove off to Yakima, through more orchards on all sides, into Ellensburg, one of the rodeo centers of the west. As we left Ellensburg, we thought there had been a light snow—in the summer? We stopped the car to finger the "snow," and realized it was the fine gray pumice ash from Mount St. Helens.

Mount St. Helens and Portland, Oregon

O n the north side of the historic Columbia River, the highway curves around tree-clad bluffs, and suddenly an opening gave us our first view of the incredible gray devastation of Mount St. Helens. Within an hour we were in a small single-engine plane with a pilot who had climbed the mountain fifteen times. Three days before our arrival, the mountain had erupted again and plumes of smoke still rose from the crater. Slowly we circled the volcano and saw the huge cone glowing red in the center of the massive opening. Spirit Lake was jammed with fallen trees and a wide swath of wreckage down the Toutle River was the color of mud. Enormous Caterpillar tractors hung stranded on the edge of ridges now completely devoid of trees. Millions of them were scattered below like matchsticks over the ugly gray wasteland. No wonder that inland shipping had ceased when the catastrophe occurred, for the debris from the Toutle River had clogged the mouth of the Columbia.

Reluctantly we left Mount St. Helens and drove thoughtfully into Portland, the beautiful city on the Willamette River. The territories of Washington and Oregon rewarded the pioneers who settled there for the rich farm land, fishing, mining, and seemingly unlimited game for hunting. Even now people migrate here because of the natural beauty and outdoor life and to have access to the many wilderness areas that remain. Fresh fish, exceptional vegetables, luscious berries of all kinds, and fruits from the great orchards are the pride of the region, and so are good breads. After five sunshiny days in Portland, I had some lovely recipes to share.

Millet Bread

Makes 4 loaves

A bread, created in Seattle, which passed from Hermia Llewllyn to Betty McGrath to Dinal Tillotson to Karen Parker, who took it to Portland. Judy Bell inherited it next and mailed it back over the Oregon Trail to Mary Gubser. Flax seeds are available in health food stores; they are soft and can easily be ground into flaxmeal with a blender or Magic Mill. An especially fine recipe.

1 cup oatmeal
½ cup flaxmeal
½ cup toasted wheat germ
1 cup whole hulled millet
½ cup sunflower seeds
2 tablespoons light oil
2 teaspoons salt
3½ cups very hot water
¼ cup light molasses

¼ cup honey
2 packages active dry
  yeast
½ cup warm water
4 cups stone-ground
  whole wheat flour
2–3 cups unbleached
  white flour

In a large mixing bowl combine the oatmeal, flaxmeal, wheat germ, millet, sunflower seeds, oil, salt, and hot water (very hot tap water is fine). Add the molasses and honey and stir to blend.

In a small bowl combine the yeast and warm water, stirring until dissolved. When the whole grain mixture has cooled to lukewarm, add the yeast mixture. Beat in the whole wheat flour. Add sufficient white flour to make a soft, workable dough that pulls away from sides of the bowl. Turn out on a lightly floured suface (use white flour) and knead until smooth and elastic, about 8 minutes. If the dough is sticky, add white flour to kneading surface and hands while kneading. Round into a ball and place in a warm buttered bowl, turning to coat the top. Cover loosely with plastic wrap and a towel and let rise until doubled, about 1 hour.

Punch down the dough and divide into 4 portions. Knead each, cover, and let rest 10 minutes. Butter four 8½-inch loaf pans. Mold the dough into loaves and place in the pans. Cover and let rise to tops of pans.

Preheat the oven to 350°F. Bake the loaves 35 minutes, or until dark golden brown. Turn loaves out and let cool on wire racks.

Danish Kringle

Makes 2 kringles

Although the kringle is as Danish as Copenhagen, this luscious coffeecake originated in Vienna. The classic kringle uses fine pastry layered with sweet butter and may be filled with almond paste or fruit. My Portland Connection has devised a simpler version, easy to prepare, which freezes beautifully.

Dough:
2 cups sifted flour
½ teaspoon salt
1 tablespoon sugar
¼ pound (1 stick) cold butter, cut into 8 pieces

1 package active dry yeast
¼ cup warm water
¼ cup cold milk
1 egg, beaten

Filling:
¾ cup crushed zwieback
6-ounce can almond paste
1 egg

½ cup melted butter
½ teaspoon almond extract

Resift the flour with salt and sugar. Place the mixture in bowl of food processor, add the butter, and pulse 5 times. Combine the yeast and water in a bowl, stirring until dissolved. Add to processor bowl. Pour in the milk and egg and pulse 6 times to blend. Scrape dough out onto a floured surface and knead 2 or 3 times. Round into a ball, pat with flour, wrap in plastic wrap, and refrigerate overnight.

To make the filling, crush the zwieback in food processor bowl. Add the almond paste and pulse 3 times. Add the egg, butter, and almond extract and process until well mixed. Transfer the filling to a bowl, cover with plastic wrap, and refrigerate overnight.

The next morning, remove dough and filling from the refrigerator. If possible, remove the filling earlier as it is quite stiff and will be easier to spread if allowed to soften. Butter a large baking sheet. Divide dough in half and return 1 portion, covered, to the refrigerator. Roll the first piece into a 16 × 8-inch rectangle. This is a very tender dough; use plenty of flour on the counter and rolling pin. Spread half the filling in a 3-inch strip down the center of the rectangle. Fold 1 of the long sides over the filling, completely enclosing it. Fold over the other long side to form an envelope. Seal the long edge and the ends with moist fingers. You now have a rectangle about 16 × 4 inches.

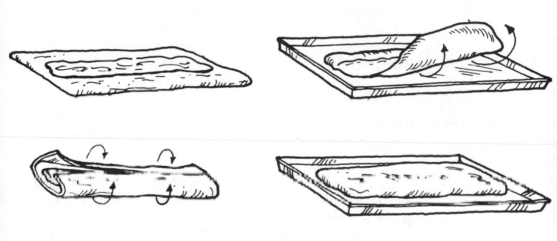

Gently place the rectangle seam side down on the baking sheet. Repeat directions with the second piece of dough. Cover and let rise 1 hour.

Preheat the oven to 375°F. Bake the kringles 25 minutes, or until golden brown. Remove from baking sheet and let cool on wire racks. The cakes may be wrapped and frozen, if desired.

Optional: A thin Confectioner's Icing (page 45) may be dribbled over the kringles just before serving, a final touch usually added by the donor of this recipe. I found the cake delicious served as is.

Christmas: Frost with Confectioner's Icing (page 45) and decorate with whole almonds.

Filbert Bread

Makes 2 loaves

*Filberts grow prolifically in Oregon. I mentioned
this to my Portland Connection and soon she
created a fascinating bread. Toast the filberts in a
preheated 300°F oven until dark golden brown.
Remove, place in a terry cloth towel, and rub
briskly to remove skins. Do not worry if all the
skin is not removed, for the bits left will add
color to the bread.*

2½ cups warm water
2 packages active dry
    yeast
1 tablespoon honey
4 cups unbleached white
    flour
1 cup toasted filberts,
    finely ground

2 teaspoons salt
2 tablespoons light oil
2 cups stone-ground
    whole wheat flour
1 egg white beaten with 1
    tablespoon water for
    glaze

Combine the water, yeast, and honey in a large mixing bowl, stirring until dissolved. Beat in the white flour to make a smooth batter. Cover and let proof 3 hours.

Stir down the sponge and blend in the filberts, salt, and oil. Gradually add sufficient whole wheat flour to make a soft dough that pulls away from sides of the bowl. Turn out on a floured surface (use white flour) and knead until smooth and elastic, about 8–10 minutes. If the dough is sticky, sprinkle white flour on kneading surface and hands. Round dough into a ball and place in a warm bowl brushed with melted butter or vegetable shortening, turning to coat the top. Cover loosely with plastic wrap and a towel and let rise until doubled, about 1 hour.

Punch down the dough and divide in half. Knead each, cover, and let rest 10 minutes. Spray a baking sheet with nonstick vegetable spray. Form one portion of dough into a long baguette (page 39) and the other into a round loaf. Place on the baking sheet, cover, and let rise about 45 minutes.

Preheat the oven to 375°F. Slash both loaves, brush with the glaze, and bake 30–35 minutes. Remove and let cool on wire racks.

Note: For an excellent crust, try baking the loaves on a baking stone.

Judy's Lime-Pistachio Rolls

Makes 60 rolls

No longer do we have to depend upon the countries of the Middle East for pistachios. Now they are easy to obtain from the San Joaquin Valley. I could visualize and almost taste a delicious pistachio roll. Again I turned to my Portland Connection and together we have created an enchanting roll.

Dough:
2 packages active dry
    yeast
½ cup warm water
¼ cup sugar
1 teaspoon salt
1 cup warm milk

1 cup melted butter
2 egg yolks
2 cups bread flour
3 cups all-purpose flour,
    approximately

Filling:
1 cup plus 6 tablespoons
    sugar
Grated rind of 3 large
    limes
¾ teaspoon nutmeg
⅜ pound (1½ sticks)
    butter, at room
    temperature

4½ tablespoons fresh lime
    juice
1 cup toasted salted
    pistachios, coarsely
    chopped

Combine the yeast and water in a bowl, stirring until dissolved, and set aside. In a large mixing bowl combine the sugar, salt, milk, and butter, blending well. Beat the egg yolks and add to milk mixture with yeast mixture. Beat in the bread flour until smooth. Gradually add sufficient all-purpose flour to make a soft, workable dough. Turn out on a floured surface and knead until smooth and silky. Round into a ball and place in a warm buttered bowl, turning to coat the top. Cover loosely with plastic wrap and a towel and let rise until doubled, about 1½ hours.

Prepare the filling while dough is proofing. In a small mixing bowl combine 1 cup of sugar, grated rind, and nutmeg and blend well. In a separate bowl cream the butter with 6 tablespoons of sugar and add the lime juice.

Divide the dough in 4 portions. Knead each lightly, cover, and let rest 10 minutes. Butter five 9-inch cake tins. Roll one portion of dough (keeping the rest covered) into a 15 × 8-inch rectangle. Spread one quarter of the butter mixture over the rectangle to within ½ inch of edges. Sprinkle one quarter of the pistachios on top. Spread one quarter of the sugar mixture on top of the nuts, spreading gently with your hand. Roll up from the long side, jelly-roll style, sealing the seam. Slice into 1-inch rolls and place 13 rolls cut side up ½ inch apart in each cake tin. Repeat directions with remaining portions of dough, filling mixtures, and pistachios. Cover and let rise about 1 hour, or until the rolls are light and puffy and touch each other.

Preheat the oven to 350°F. Bake the rolls about 25 minutes. Turn out on wire racks to cool.

Note: These rolls are devastatingly delicious and actually need no frosting, but they could be brushed lightly with a thin Confectioner's Icing (page 45) flavored with lime juice. The rolls may be frozen before they are frosted.

Otis, Oregon

A fter an early breakfast in downtown Portland with a swinging young food reporter dressed in embroidered blue jeans, we left the city on Interstate 5, then changed to state highways heading for the coast. By noon, I was starving and luckily we found a crossroads restaurant freshly painted canary yellow, a favorite color of mine. It had to be good! The dining room had surprising, comfortable touches—magazine racks filled with children's books and newspapers—and an unhurried, pleasant waitress. We had an excellent salad, an unusual oyster stew, and homemade bread that was amazingly good.

To find the powder room, I maneuvered through the kitchen, where a lone woman was manning everything, and into another room with a big table topped with a batch of bread dough waiting to be kneaded. Lace curtains decorated the spotless bathroom, which displayed an antique sign—Hamburg 10¢; Tuna Fish 15¢. My return through the kitchen started a conversation. "That's a marvelous bread you make; any possibility of obtaining the recipe?" She dashed into a small back room and returned with two pages of dimly printed paper. "Here, you can have it—do what you want with my recipe. But be sure to throw in some cooked oatmeal—anything the kids leave over from breakfast—throw it in!" Then Virginia Morgan showed me her store of flours—excellent unbleached white, a good whole wheat, soy, millet, all were at hand to use on her mixing table. As I left, Virginia called, "Don't forget the oatmeal!"

Virginia's Basic Bread

Makes 3 loaves

Virginia Morgan has created a bread with multiple suggestions for additions and substitutions. I give you her basic recipe first and at the end many ideas for different adaptations. Texture and flavor will vary with choices of ingredients. Be inventive, but, remember, Virginia said too many different things in one batch can muddy the taste, and I agree. From her basic dough she has made English muffins, cinnamon rolls, bagels, hot rolls and—as Virginia says—what have you.

2 cups warm liquid—
water with ½ cup
instant dry milk, sweet
milk, buttermilk, warm
yogurt, potato water, or
whatever you have!

2 tablespoons honey,
brown sugar, or
molasses

2 packages active dry
yeast

2–3 cups stone-ground
whole wheat flour

2 teaspoons salt

2 tablespoons melted
shortening, lard,
margarine, butter, or
safflower oil

3–4 cups unbleached
white flour

Combine the liquid, honey, and yeast in a mixing bowl, stirring until dissolved. Beat in 2 cups of whole wheat flour. If the batter is not very stiff (it should be like a thick cake batter), add the last cup of whole wheat flour. Cover with a towel and let proof 1 hour. The batter will become light, bubbly, and double in bulk.

Stir down the sponge and blend in the salt and shortening. At this point you may add any of the suggested flours, seeds, or wheat germ, as described at the end of the recipe. For example, my first experiment was to add 1 cup of cooked oatmeal (left over from breakfast) and ½ cup each of wheat germ and soy flour. After selected additions, gradually add sufficient white flour to make a soft, workable dough that pulls away from sides of the bowl. Turn out on a lightly floured surface and knead until smooth and elastic, about 8 minutes. Round into a ball and place in a warm bowl brushed with melted shortening or margarine, turning to coat the top. Cover loosely with plastic wrap and a towel and let rise until doubled, about 1 hour.

Punch down the dough, turn out on a lightly floured surface, and divide into 3 portions. Knead, cover, and let rest 10 minutes. Brush three 8½-inch loaf pans with melted shortening. Form the dough into loaves and place in the pans. Cover and let rise until just rounded over tops of pans.

Preheat the oven to 400°F. Bake the loaves 30 minutes. Turn out on wire racks to cool.

Variations

Additions to make: 1 cup cooked soy grits, oatmeal, or any leftover cereal. Nice not to waste anything!

More additions: ½ cup ground sunflower seeds (whirl in food processor)

½ cup cooked potatoes, mashed or sieved

¼-½ cup toasted wheat germ

1 cup bran, either a cereal or unadulterated bran

Substitutions: ½ cup soy or millet flour for white flour

2 cups rye flour for 1 cup each whole wheat and white flour

With the rye flour substitution, throw in the grated rind of 1 large orange.

A night on the Oregon coast at the Sea Otter Crest Inn, with the Pacific Ocean pounding on rocks far below the high cliff, was a short respite to reflect the distance we had driven and to wonder if we would have had the guts of those pioneers for whom such a trip took long, dreary months instead of days.

We left the coast to drive through rolling country to Corvallis and Oregon State University. Fortunately, classes had not begun. Professors were relaxed and available and we had a long chat with Dr. Kronstadt, a world authority on grains, particularly wheat. Excitedly, he told us that verification had arrived, from a farm close to the Canadian border. An experimental crop had yielded 185 bushels of wheat per acre—an utterly incredible production. Dr. Kronstadt had just returned from China and explained that China is attempting to raise wheat in order to introduce more breads into the Chinese diet. Dr. Kronstadt gave me handsome stalks of both wheat and triticale. Cattle is number one in the state of Oregon and wheat number two, but its agriculture also has great variety—from wild berries to fruit to rabbits.

After heading south on Interstate 5 again, we detoured to Crater Lake, one of the loveliest of mountain lakes, left by the last receding glaciers. Medford was then a stop for three nights, for six miles away is the small city of Ashland where some of the finest Shakespearian plays I've seen are produced. To our consternation, the valley in which both Ashland and Medford are located was engulfed with smoke from a mountain forest fire. An army of fire trucks, ambulances, helicopters, and small airplanes swarmed over the area. Smoke was so thick for the first Shakespeare play that we could hardly see the actors. But I was more worried about Harry and David's (Fruit-of-the-Month) pear trees.

After crossing the state line into northern California, it's a long day's drive to Lake Tahoe. Mount Shasta is on the way, and we turned off on a state highway to see the extinct volcano at Lassen National Park. There are few people in this part of California for the country is all desert and mountains. There would be no breads to look for until Nevada.

Winnemucca, Nevada

T he discovery of gold and silver brought people to this dry land. By 1864 Nevada was a state of the Union. The Comstock Lode near Virginia City almost alone paid the cost of the Union military during the Civil War. Even though the veins of silver are nearly depleted, Virginia City has tapped another source of income—tourists. It's fun to tramp the boardwalks, visit with the talkative shopkeepers, and look at the flamboyant homes that lucky miners built.

From Virginia City to Winnemucca is 165 miles of desert and dry mountains. We arrived at five, I called the Winnemucca Hotel and found we could dine there Basque-style at six.

Many Basques flooded into Nevada and Idaho during the mining boom, and when that industry declined, they turned to what they knew best, sheep raising. The Basques are independent, colorful people from the Pyrenees in northern Spain, although they are of different stock than the Spanish. Their native language is unique, and no one yet is certain how it evolved. They settled in Nevada and Idaho and later in California. There is an active department in both teaching and research on Basque culture at the University of Nevada in Reno.

Originally, the Winnemucca Hotel and other similar establishments served the sheepherders as a place to sleep and eat. The men often played a game called "mus" and drank wine from skin bottles. Dinner was and still is served family style. Go with a huge appetite, for the amount of food is overwhelming and everything is delicious. After a huge pot of soup, salad, and several other courses, I thought we had finished, when a huge platter of sizzling hot, enormous steaks were served. I ate every bite, including my share of sheepherder's bread.

Our host, Miquel Olana, explained in great detail how a sheepherder used to prepare his bread. In the morning, a hole was dug in the ground and lined with glowing embers. The bread dough was mixed and placed in a big iron pot, covered tightly, and placed in the hole. The pot was covered with twigs, more embers, and dirt. Then off for a long day of watching three thousand sheep; back at camp that night, a warm pot of bread would be ready. Through Miquel I met Marilyn Jayo of Elko, who in turn put me in touch with a Basque woman in California who has shared her recipe for Basque bread.

Sheepherder's Basque Bread (EUSKALDUN OGIA)

Makes 1 loaf

Odette Echevery of San Francisco has given me a carefully detailed explanation of the preparation of Basque bread. For your convenience and mine, the bread is baked in a nice, modern oven. If you want to dig a hole in your backyard, please do, but I've not tested that method!

3 cups hot water
¼ pound (1 stick) butter
   or margarine
½ cup sugar
2½ teaspoons salt

2 packages active dry
   yeast
9 cups flour,
   approximately
Light oil

Note: A heavy 4-quart cast-iron Dutch oven (with lid) that has been well seasoned will hold all the dough and give the bread an authentic appearance.

Combine the hot water (it need not be boiling), butter, sugar, and salt in a large mixing bowl. Stir until ingredients are dissolved and let cool to lukewarm, about 100°F. When the mixture has cooled, sprinkle in the yeast, stirring until dissolved. Cover and let proof 15 minutes, or until mixture begins to bubble. Beat in 4 cups of flour until mixture is smooth. Gradually add sufficient flour to make a workable dough that pulls away from sides of the bowl. Turn out on floured surface and knead 10 minutes, or until smooth and elastic. Round into a ball and place the dough in a warm bowl brushed with light oil, turning to coat top. Cover loosely with plastic wrap and a towel and let rise until doubled, about 45–60 minutes.

Brush a heavy 4-quart Dutch oven with oil. Cut a piece of aluminum foil to fit the bottom and brush with oil. Punch down the dough and knead lightly on a floured surface. Round into a ball, place in prepared Dutch oven, and press down, pushing the dough to fill the bottom of the pot. Brush the underside of the lid with oil and place atop the Dutch oven. Let the bread rise until it pushes the lid up ½ inch, about 1 hour and 20 minutes. The time can vary; set a timer and watch carefully toward the end of proofing period.

Preheat the oven to 375°F. Bake the bread 15 minutes. Remove the lid and bake 40–45 minutes more. If the top becomes too brown, cover with aluminum foil during the last 15 minutes. Remove from oven and turn bread out on a wire rack to cool. This is a very large loaf; some assistance in handling the heavy pan and bread may be needed. An excellent bread for a family gathering. It will have a design on top from the lid of the Dutch oven.

Salt Lake City

A cross the desert below the barren mountains, through Emigrant Pass (6,777 feet) and past Doby Summit, we arrived in Elko, Nevada, the center for Euzkalkunak, the Basque organization that sponsors the National Basque Festival each Fourth of July. More desert mountain passes took us finally to the Great Salt Desert and Salt Lake. It is 365 miles from Winnemucca to Salt Lake City, and the last 128 of them are flat and white with salt.

Then, a burst of beauty! The setting of Salt Lake City, framed with snow-capped mountains. Handsome highways lead to the center of the city, which is beautifully planned with wide streets, easy parking, and flowers everywhere. Temple Square is the heart of Mormon society. Here is the Mormon Temple, begun in 1853 and completed in 1893, at a cost of $4,000,000. The Tabernacle seats 6,500 and a visitor's center provides complete information. Close by is the Bee Hive House, the official residence of Brigham Young, and Lion House, the home for his wives and children.

Lion House

L ion House, built in 1855, reflected Brigham Young's New England background. It still contains some of the many household items, such as rugs, draperies, and furniture, that he imported from England. The huge dining area was the gathering place to which President Young summoned his family with a bell (which is still there) for prayers and meals. Statues of two lions at the front door gave the building its name. Lion House has been through several transformations since Brigham Young's death and is now a restaurant serving church employees, business people, and others with membership cards. Each day carts of food are transported to the General Authorities of the church. Michael Larson, the manager of Lion House, has generously shared favorite recipes from his kitchen.

Lion House Dinner Rolls

Makes about 60 rolls

2 packages active dry
  yeast
2 cups warm water
⅓ cup sugar
⅓ cup melted butter or
  vegetable shortening

2½ teaspoons salt
⅔ cup instant dry skim
  milk
5–6 cups flour
1 egg
Melted butter

Combine yeast and water in a large mixing bowl, stirring until dissolved, and let stand 5 minutes. Add the sugar, butter, salt, dry milk, 2 cups of flour, and the egg. Beat the mixture either by machine or with a rubber spatula until smooth. Add 2 cups more of flour, one at a time, and beat until smooth. Add 1 cup more of flour, ½ cup at a time, until well mixed. Turn the dough out on a floured surface and knead until smooth and elastic. Round into a ball and place in a warm buttered bowl, turning to coat the top. Cover loosely with plastic wrap and a towel and let rise until tripled, about 1 hour.

Brush 3 large baking sheets with melted butter. Punch down the dough and turn out on a lightly floured surface. Use the last of the flour, as needed, for rolling and molding the dough. (Do not use any more flour if the dough is moist but not sticky.) Cover dough and let rest 10 minutes. Mold dough into desired shapes (pages 42–44). Place rolls on baking sheet and brush surface of rolls with melted butter. Cover and let rise until light, about 1–1½ hours.

Preheat the oven to 400°F. Bake the rolls 12–15 minutes.

Note: The entire process may be done either by hand or machine. It takes thorough beating and kneading to develop the gluten in the dough. Soft dough makes lighter, more tender rolls. This small version of the Lion House recipe makes a dough that can be handled easily. Any soft dough can be managed more easily if proofed overnight in the refrigerator and then rolled and shaped. Always add flour gradually to keep the dough as soft as can be handled. All this wonderful advice comes from the Lion House cooks.

Lion House Orange Rolls

Makes 26 rolls

1 recipe Lion House
    Dinner Roll dough,
    preceding recipe
4 tablespoons butter, at
    room temperature

½ cup sugar
1 tablespoon fresh orange
    juice
1 teaspoon grated orange
    rind

Orange Glaze:

1½ cups confectioner's
    sugar
3 tablespoons fresh
    orange juice

1 teaspoon grated orange
    rind

Butter 3 jelly-roll pans. When the dough is ready for molding after the first rising, punch down the dough and divide in half. Roll each half into a 13 × 9-inch rectangle. Spread the rectangles with the butter to within ¼ inch of edges. Combine the sugar, orange juice, and grated rind. Spread the mixture over the butter. Roll up from the long side, jelly-roll style. Seal the seams. Cut with a sharp knife or dental floss into 1-inch slices. Twist each slice like a corkscrew and stretch them as you

place them on the baking sheets ¾ inch apart. Cover and let rise until double in bulk, about 1 hour.

    Preheat the oven to 350°F. Bake the rolls about 20 minutes, or until nicely browned. Remove rolls and let cool on wire racks. Combine ingredients for the glaze, whisking until smooth. Frost rolls while warm. (Freeze rolls without frosting.)

Lion House Whole Wheat Bread

Makes 2 loaves

1 package active dry yeast
3 cups warm water
1 cup white flour
1 cup oatmeal or rolled
  oats
1½ teaspoons salt
¼ cup light molasses

6 tablespoons instant dry
  skim milk
6 tablespoons melted
  butter or vegetable
  shortening
5–6 cups whole wheat
  flour

Combine the yeast and water in a large mixing bowl, stirring until dissolved. Add the white flour, oatmeal, salt, molasses, dry milk, and butter and blend well. Gradually add sufficient whole wheat flour to form a soft, workable dough that pulls away from sides of the bowl. Turn dough out on a floured surface (use white flour) and knead about 8 minutes by hand or 5 minutes with a dough hook on a heavy-duty mixer. Round into a ball and place in a warm buttered bowl, turning to coat top. Cover loosely with plastic wrap and a towel and let rise until doubled, about 1 hour.

Punch down the dough, turn out on a floured surface, and divide in half. Knead each lightly, cover, and let rest 10 minutes. Butter two 8½-inch loaf pans. Form the dough into loaves and place in the pans. Cover and let rise until doubled, or just curved over edges of pans.

Preheat the oven to 400°F. Bake the loaves 15 minutes. Reduce heat to 350°F and bake 40 minutes more. Turn loaves out on wire racks to cool.

We attended an evening concert to hear the magnificent Mormon Tabernacle Choir, accompanied by its unexcelled pipe organ, walked through the lovely tree-shaded campus of the state university, and had dinner at a charming place far off in a narrow canyon. We left on Highway 40 for northern Colorado for the last lap of the journey—through the Rocky Mountains to the national park at Estes, south to Denver and Colorado Springs, with a stop to drive just once more to Pike's Peak and spend a quiet night at the elegant old hotel, The Broadmoor. And, finally, we crossed a corner of New Mexico and were back home in Oklahoma, our car filled with sacks of good flour and my journals filled with recipes and memories of the Oregon Trail.

ALASKA!

MILEAGE—10,622 MILES

Forget-me-not
ALASKA STATE FLOWER

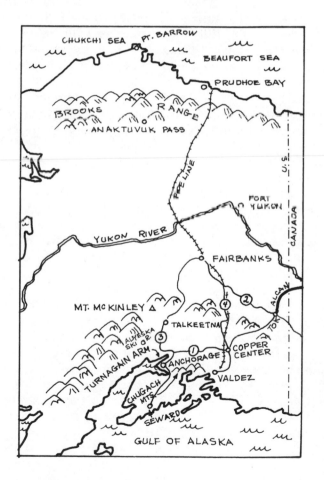

Juneau

U nited Airlines Flight 519 ascended into a clear, blue sky, banking around an amazingly fog-free San Francisco to set a northern course. Within minutes Mount Shasta sparkled in the early morning light. Slowly the complete Cascade Range of mountain peaks and forests unfolded below like a *National Geographic* relief map. Diamond Peak, Mount Hood, mounts Washington and Jefferson, and the great Willamette and Columbia rivers made a dramatic backdrop for the unbelievable devastation of Mount St. Helens. Eight months had gone by since we had driven through this rugged beauty. Now an inner excitement told me this new journey was to be an exceptional one.

A change of planes in Seattle to Alaskan Airways and we headed northeast for Juneau. A cloud cover made the plane seem suspended motionless in space, then snowy peaks jutted through the haze and we slowly descended. Excitedly I waited for the first sight of tiny Juneau nestled by the sea on the side of a mountain. Mendenhall Glacier glistened blue and white to our left. Far above the small capital city was the 1200-square-mile ice field that feeds neighboring glaciers as well as Mendenhall. Quickly we found this was a do-it-yourself airport. We grabbed bags and a taxi and logged our first nine miles in Alaska to Juneau.

Juneau is divided into three parts—tourism, the federal government, and the state government. There is a paved main street and a waterfront street. The Red Dog Saloon never closes. The atmosphere is sawdust on the floor and belly up to the bar with the tourists. By air and sea the Gastineau Channel waterfront handles as much traffic as Juneau does by land. Tiny seaplanes are constantly landing and taking off and one or two cruise ships appear each day. Five blocks away is the Governor's Mansion, a stately, white Southern home complete with tall pillars, totem pole, and a tiny lawn of exquisite grass. Across the street is the capitol building and the library. Two blocks farther on is Uncle Sam's eight-story residence. In the midst of all this walkable "downtown" dwells a small bakery and restaurant called The Fiddlehead. And there I tasted some of the finest food in the state.

Debbie Marshall, one of the four owners, is an attractive young blonde devoted to the preparation of excellent food. Anyone who settles in Alaska also has to love the great outdoors, for there is more than enough of it. (Some of its glaciers are so huge that just one of them could completely cover the state of Delaware.) The four young partners of The Fiddlehead have a creative and cooperative philosophy and they meet the Juneau community need for a congenial restaurant. Their imaginative cookery reflects the new ecological awareness in nutrition, and their concept is successful, for they boast a staff of thirty, the café is always crowded, and their marvelous breads in the bakery vanish by noon each day. Debbie has shared two of their most popular recipes. I have tested them in my kitchen and now here they are for you.

Sunflower-Millet Bread

Makes 2 loaves

2 packages active dry
  yeast
2 cups warm water
¼ cup honey
½ cup sunflower seeds

½ cup whole hulled millet
4 cups whole wheat flour,
  approximately
3 tablespoons light oil
1½ teaspoons salt

In a large mixing bowl combine the yeast and water, stirring until dissolved. Blend in the honey, seeds, and millet. Beat in 2 cups flour until smooth. Cover the bowl with a towel and let proof about 30 minutes, or until the mixture becomes a light, bubbly sponge.

Stir down the sponge and blend in the oil and salt. Gradually add sufficient flour to make a soft, workable dough that pulls away from sides of the bowl. Turn the dough out on a lightly floured surface and knead until smooth and resilient. Cover with a towel and let rest 30 minutes.

Butter two 8½-inch loaf pans. Divide dough in half, shape into loaves, and place in the pans. Cover and let rise 1 hour.

Preheat the oven to 350°F. Bake the loaves about 40 minutes, or until golden brown. Remove from pans and let cool on wire racks.

Honey-Butter-Oatmeal Bread

Makes 2 loaves

For this bread, use rolled oats—not the instant kind that vanishes in a cup of water.

2 packages active dry
  yeast
¼ cup warm water
2 cups warm buttermilk
⅓ cup honey

1⅓ cups rolled oats
5 cups unbleached white
  flour, approximately
1½ teaspoons salt
¼ cup melted butter

Combine the yeast and water in a small bowl, stirring until dissolved. In a large mixing bowl combine the buttermilk, honey, and the yeast mixture and blend well. Add the oats and 1 cup of flour. Beat the mixture thoroughly—100 strokes if you are in good condition! If using a heavy mixer, beat 1 minute with the flat beater. Cover bowl with a towel and let proof 30 minutes, or until the mixture becomes a bubbly sponge.

Blend in the salt and butter. Gradually add sufficient flour to make a soft dough that pulls away from sides of the bowl. Turn out on a lightly floured surface and knead about 10 minutes, or until smooth and satiny.

Divide dough in half. Round each piece into a smooth ball, cover, and let rest 30 minutes.

Butter two 8½-inch loaf pans. Shape the dough into loaves and place in the pans. Cover and let rise 30 minutes.

Preheat the oven to 325°F. Bake the loaves 45 minutes. turn out on wire racks to cool.

Z igzagging up the hill from the Governor's Mansion, the crooked streets (not very walkable at all) lead to the House of Wickersham and Ruth Allman. Judge Wickersham built this house, with its magnificent view overlooking Juneau and the constant movement on the waterfront at the turn of the century. The judge was an avid collector and prominent in politics. For thirty years he advocated statehood for Alaska, basing his ideas on the history of the admission to the Union of my own home state of Oklahoma in 1907. Ruth Allman, the judge's niece, is an Alaskan historian, curator of this museum home filled with Alaskan memorabilia, and a well-known authority on sourdough cookery. With flair, Ruth serves flaming sourdough waffles to the tourist groups that come here twice a day. After a delightful visit, I left with much new knowledge of Alaskan sourdough cuisine and Alaskan humor.

Sourdough Starters and Breads

F our thousand years ago, somewhere along the Nile River, leavening for bread was discovered. Flat cakes of millet, wheat, and barley, cooked on hot stones between layers of camel dung or on sticks, had been the primitive bread for centuries, until a little beer slopped into bread dough under the warm Egyptian sun created a whole new approach to breadmaking. All this is recorded on walls of temples and tombs. An Egyptologist in central Egypt, Shafid Farik, once showed me many murals and hieroglyphics that explained in detail the processes of planting, tilling, reaping, and preparing bread. Dr. Farik and I climbed a desert hill to a tiny village where loaves of bread were rising under the hot sun in the center courtyard—covered with flies. The women throwing straw into an oven resembled the paintings on the temple walls. They were dressed in long black robes and wore black lace head-bands across their foreheads. Several giggling women pushed me closer to feel the heat of the oven. It seemed as though I had stepped back two thousand years in time.

For centuries sourdough was the only leavening until commercial yeast was introduced in the nineteenth century. Sourdough faded in popularity until gold was discovered in Alaska. At the University of Alaska, I learned that "To those who lived alone or in small groups of three or four—mining, trapping, or homesteading—sourdough became the basis of their 'staff of life.' Bread could not be made without it." Alaskan miners became known as "sourdough miners."

In the early days, supplies were ordered once a year. The trappers and miners carefully organized their lists of supplies needed for the annual ship-ment. Unusual formation of ice and heavy wind or seas could delay the passage of the supply ship. From the ship all these orders were transferred to small boats, river steamers, dog sleds, or backpacks to reach their destinations. An avalanche or a quick thaw could drag a whole team of dogs and laden sled under the ice into swift, cold water. And there could sink dogs, sled, and sup-plies for a year. Alaska was, and still is, a rugged place.

But there is nothing difficult about maintaining a sourdough starter. If an old miner in the icy mountains could keep one active, you can easily do the same in a modern kitchen. Following are two sourdough starters. Both have been tested and retested and replenished to my satisfaction. There are more starters in other sections of this book.

Ruth Allman's Sourdough Starter

Makes about 1 quart starter

2 cups thick potato water
2 tablespoons sugar
2 cups flour

Potato Water: Peel 2 medium potatoes and cut into large cubes. Place in a saucepan, cover with 3 cups of tap water, bring to a boil, and cook rapidly until the potatoes are very tender, about 20–25 minutes. Put the potatoes and water through a sieve over a bowl, using a wooden spoon to mash tthe potatoes through. Or pass the potatoes and their cooking water through a potato ricer. There should be about 2 cups of thick potato water. If there is more, use all of it.

The best container for a sourdough starter is a straight-sided ceramic crock (about 5½ × 5 inches) with a lid. A plastic or glass container may be used, but no metal of any kind; sourdough and metal create an undesirable chemical reaction. Combine the potato water, sugar, and flour in the crock and beat until smooth. If there are lumps, let the starter sit 10–15 minutes and beat again. Label the crock with the name of the starter and the date. Cover with a piece of doubled cheesecloth but not the lid. Place crock in a cozy corner overnight.

How long does it take a sourdough starter to become "ripe"? According to Ruth it can take three days to one year. To begin, try forty-eight hours. Stir the sponge occasionally; the mixture will rise and fall, then settle to a light simmering bubble when it is ready. The starter should have a clean, fresh, sour aroma. After two days, place the lid over the cheesecloth and refrigerate. The starter is now ready for breadmaking at your convenience. The longer a starter is kept and activated, the stronger it will become—and the better bread it will make.

To Replenish: Each time some of the starter is used, add an equal amount of warm water and flour to what remains—if possible, 2 cups of each if there is enough room in the jar. If the container seems too full, place it in a sink while it "works." I've had it boil right over, down the sides of the crock and all over the counter—so watch it! If the starter seems thin, add extra flour, if too thick, add warm water. When you have leftover potato water, by all means use it in the starter. While the

184

starter works, the mixture does thin. It should be the consistency of thick pancake batter.

If the starter is not used regularly, stir thoroughly once a week, because liquid will form at the top of it. "Beewack" is the name of this starter liquid. After the Alaskans found it could be made so easily, they made barrels of the stuff, waited until the solids sank to the bottom, and gathered around with tin cups to imbibe this malodorous liquid. Ruth Allman warns that Beewack is never bottled—only a fool would carry a live bomb.

University of Alaska Sourdough Starter

Makes 1 quart starter

2 cups warm water
1 package active dry yeast
2 cups flour

Measure the water into a ceramic, glass, or plastic container. Sprinkle with the yeast and stir until dissolved. Beat in the flour until the mixture is smooth. If there are lumps, let the starter rest 10 minutes and beat again. Cover with a piece of doubled cheesecloth and place in a warm corner overnight. The sponge or starter is now ready to use. If it seems too thick, thin with a little water. If too thin, add ½–1 cup more flour and beat well. Label with date and name of starter.

Sourdough Waffles

Makes 10–12 waffles

Flapjacks and sourdough biscuits were the main breads of the sourdough miner or trapper. There was no place for a waffle iron in a backpack, but when women arrived with more gear they often used a waffle iron heated on hot coals.

2 cups sourdough starter, preceding recipes
3 tablespoons light oil
1 tablespoon sugar

1 egg
1 teaspoon salt
1 tablespoon warm water
1 teaspoon baking soda

Measure the sourdough starter into a mixing bowl. Add the oil, sugar, egg, and salt and beat well.

"Combine the tablespoon of warm water and baking soda in a jigger glass, stirring with the little finger."—Ruth Allman. A most practical method, but if no jigger glass is available, try a small bowl. Fold the soda mixture gently into the sourdough mixture just before cooking. As the soda is folded in, the batter becomes thicker, doubles in volume with bubbles, and makes happy little sounds.

Bake immediately following the directions that come with your waffle iron. Directions from my waffle iron: Heat iron until the light goes out. Pour 1 cup of waffle batter over the hot waffle iron, close, and cook until the light goes out. Sourdough waffles are not as crisp as regular waffles, but they have a marvelous flavor and are very filling.

Crisper waffle: Use the same ingredients, but add 1 more egg. Separate eggs and add the yolks to the batter. Beat the egg whites until softly stiff and fold into the batter after the soda mixture.

Flaming Sourdough Waffles

Serves 1

*A very special recipe created by Ruth Allman for
the celebration of Alaskan statehood and raising of
the forty-ninth star. Try these—they are
delicious!*

1 slab Seward's Icebox
  (1 scoop ice cream)
1 section prepared
  Sourdough Waffle,
  preceding recipe

Alaskan wild strawberries
  (defrosted strawberries
  are fine)
1 sugar cube
Lemon extract

Place the ice cream atop the waffle and douse with a portion of
strawberries. Dip chunk of Glacier Ice (sugar cube) into Firewater
(lemon extract) holding the cube with tongs. Have a lighted candle
ready and flame the sugar cube over the candle. Place atop the ice
cream while flaming and serve immediately.

Alaskan Sourdough Bread

Makes 2 loaves

*To achieve a true sourdough bread is a day-long
project. No commercial yeast is used in this
recipe. There is nothing difficult about the
procedure, but there are long rising periods. Plan
ahead and you can grocery shop, visit your
beautician, or read a favorite novel during the
proofing periods. Now, let's look at the recipe.*

2 cups sourdough starter,
   pages 183 and 185
1 cup warm potato water
1 tablespoon sugar

¼ cup light oil
2 teaspoons salt
4–5 cups bread flour
Melted butter

If you have leftover potato water from making the starter, use it. Otherwise add 2 tablespoons of instant potato flakes to 1 cup of warm water, stirring until dissolved.

In a large mixing bowl combine the sourdough starter, potato water, sugar, oil, and salt. Beat in 2 cups of the bread flour until mixture is smooth. Cover with a heavy towel and let proof 2–3 hours, until the sponge is light and bubbly. If there is time to proof 3 hours, the resulting dough will be more active.

Gradually add sufficient flour to make a soft dough. Turn out on a floured surface and knead 10–12 minutes. If using a heavy-duty mixer with a dough hook, knead at medium speed 10 minutes. Finish by hand-kneading 3 minutes. Add sprinklings of flour, but be careful as a sourdough seems to inhale flour. Place dough in a warm greased bowl, turning to coat the top. Cover loosely with plastic wrap and a towel and let rise at least 2 hours, 3 if possible.

Spray a baking sheet with nonstick vegetable spray. Punch down the dough and divide in half. Knead each piece thoroughly. Mold into 2 long baguette loaves, or form 1 portion into a round loaf. Place on the baking sheet, cover, and let rise until light, about 1½–2 hours.

Preheat the oven to 425°F.

Slash the loaves with a razor or a very sharp knife. Brush with melted butter and bake 10 minutes. Reduce oven temperature to 375°F and bake 30 minutes more, or until a deep golden brown. Serve immediately or let cool on wire racks.

Note: Try baking a round loaf on a heated baking stone (see page 48) using the same temperatures—the result is excellent. If bread flour is not available, use a good unbleached white flour, which has the higher protein count necessary for good proofing.

Skagway and Sitka

O ur flight to Skagway in a single-engine Piper plane with a knowledgeable bush pilot was a stunning one-hour trip following the inland waterway. Glaciers spread in every direction over the landscape. "That's whar the gold was," explained our pilot waving to the left. The Chilkat Mountains stood out against the sky, their jagged peaks white with snow that never melts. At the end of the long inlet is the tiny town (eight hundred souls), cradled between two mountains. This was the spot where prospectors had gathered, for the harbor was deep enough for passenger and supply ships.

But Sitka was my real goal, for there the Russians had settled, making it their prosperous Alaskan capital during the heyday of the fur trade. It was in Sitka that the United States took possession of Alaska after Seward's "ridiculous purchase of this northern icebox."

Arrangements were made for a flight to Sitka. The following day we were airborne, but the clouds became very heavy and after thirty minutes we turned back to Juneau. The next day, undaunted, we tried again. Skagway Airlines (with the cancan girl on the tail of its planes) was certain it could fly us through. Our perky little plane started off on the same route; indeed, by now, we were beginning to recognize islands and the correct way for the plane to turn. What a magnificent sight the intricate waterways are as they unfold into lovely lakes dotted with green, pine-clad islands. Within fifteen minutes of Sitka, clouds began to form again, and our young pilot became intent and quiet. He looked at me, shook his head, banked the plane toward Juneau. I could have cried. But we did have four hours of beautiful flying all through those exquisite waterways.

Russian Kulich

Makes 4 loaves

Through Margaret and Jack Calvin, owners of the Old Harbor Press at Sitka, I received this recipe created by Sasha Kashevaroff, who wrote this about Russian Easter bread: "During the last week of Lent the Russian housewife devotes great care to the making of her kulich, *for on its quality depends her rating as a cook. The bread is not eaten until after the Easter midnight service. During the three days of open house after Easter, there is always a decorated* kulich *on the dining table."*
You will need four 1-pound coffee tins for molding the loaves.

2½ cups warm milk
1 package active dry yeast
⅓ cup melted butter
⅓ teaspoon salt
1 cup sugar
9 cups flour,
   approximately
3 egg yolks, beaten
2 eggs, beaten

1 teaspoon vanilla or
   lemon extract, or 3
   drops oil of roses (see
   Sources of Supply)
½ cup raisins, scalded,
   drained, and dried
½ cup chopped almonds
Confectioner's Icing, page
   45
Decorative candies

Combine the milk and yeast in a large mixing bowl, stirring until dissolved. Blend in the butter, salt, and sugar. Add 4 cups of the flour and beat until smooth. Cover, set aside, and let rise 2 hours.

Stir the sponge and add the egg yolks and whole eggs, choice of flavoring, raisins, and almonds. Gradually add sufficient flour to make a soft, workable dough that pulls away from sides of the bowl. Turn the dough out on a lightly floured surface and knead about 8 minutes, or until smooth and resilient. Place in a warm buttered bowl, turning to coat the top. Cover loosely with plastic wrap and a towel and let rise until doubled, about 1 hour.

Turn the dough out and divide into 4 equal portions. Knead each piece, round into balls, cover, and let rest 10 minutes. To mold the classical round, tall loaves, use four 1-pound coffee tins. Spray them with a nonstick vegetable spray and brush with melted butter. Don't forget to brush the top edges. Drop the portions of dough into the tins. Cover and let rise to within ½ inch of the tops.

Preheat the oven to 350°F. Place the loaves on a lower rack; they will mushroom high, and if placed in center of oven will rise to the top of the oven and stick to it. Bake 30–40 minutes. The loaves should slide out of the tins easily. Let cool on wire racks.

The loaves may be frosted with Confectioner's Icing and sprinkled with tiny candies. If serving the *kulich* soon after removing from the oven, frost right away. If not, wait until you are ready to serve before frosting. Use one decorated loaf as an Easter centerpiece surrounded by colored Easter eggs. The breads freeze well without the icing.

Glacier Bay National Park

Our party of twenty stood on a high rocky island in a glacial lake only a few hundred yards from two glaciers. The nearest one glistened blue under the midnight sun and we could hear the thrilling sound of booms and cracks deep within this mammoth piece of ice. Icebergs "calved" into the water, and occasionally a small avalanche cascaded down the glacier. A waterfall gushed tons of water far back inside the glacier. There were hundreds of northern birds (including darling little puffins) and seals sunning themselves and diving into the icy waters.

Back aboard the Glacier Bay boat, a hot midnight snack was waiting for us before we turned in in our small but comfortable stateroom for six short hours of sleep. To get to Glacier Bay National Park, we had flown over more jagged, ice-covered peaks to an old military runway, bused over nine rough unpaved roads, past homesteaders' settlements with no television, no telephone, no indoor plumbing. The Glacier Bay boat is not known for its cuisine, so bread was forgotten for this trip, but cruising that glacial lake under the midnight sun was one of our most thrilling adventures in Alaska.

Anchorage

The time had come to leave Juneau for Anchorage, the largest city in the state. Fortunately the sun was shining and the air was sparkling clear as we flew over the Chugach Mountains. An absolutely breathtaking panorama spread below us. The enormous glaciers all join each other, intertwined rivers of ice topped by the hundreds of square miles of ice fields that feed them. The pilot pointed out one particular glacier, the largest in Alaska, where surely New Hampshire, Vermont, and Rhode Island all could be lost.

Anchorage is a well planned Western city with a population of 250,000. Within two hours I found The Bread Factory, a sophisticated hippie restaurant and bakery that serves excellent food and an unusually fine whole wheat bread in a relaxed, efficient atmosphere. Kent Hindmarsh, the young baker, finished with his chores, sat with us as we ate a delicious lentil soup and quiche. Kent was raised on a ranch in Colorado. He volunteered immediately to give me his own favorite bread recipe, and I fished out my trusty notebook. "Three handfuls of oats." I looked at his hands and mentally calculated how much he could grab at one time. "Oh, yes, a handful of cornmeal, too." Back in my own kitchen, I began measuring Kent's recipe. I grabbed a big handful of oats—one cup. And so it went, until I arrived at this recipe.

Kent's Ranch Bread

Makes 3 loaves

2 packages active dry
yeast
2¼ cups warm water
13-ounce can evaporated
milk
3 tablespoons sugar or
honey

2 cups oatmeal or rolled
oats
2 teaspoons salt
¼ cup light oil
½ cup cornmeal
2 cups whole wheat flour
3 cups unbleached white
flour, approximately

Combine the yeast and ¼ cup warm water in a small bowl, stirring until dissolved. In a large mixing bowl blend the remaining 2 cups of water, milk, sugar, and oatmeal. Add the yeast mixture, stir well, and cover. Let the sponge proof about 30 minutes.

Stir down the sponge and add the salt, oil, cornmeal, and whole wheat flour. Beat until fairly smooth. Gradually add sufficient white flour to form a soft dough that pulls away from sides of the bowl. Turn out on a floured surface and knead 8–10 minutes. Round into a ball and place in a warm buttered bowl, turning to coat the top. Cover loosely with plastic wrap and a towel and let rise about 1 hour, or until doubled in bulk. This dough is active and puffs quickly.

Punch down the dough and divide into 3 equal portions. Knead each piece, cover, and let rest 10 minutes. Butter three 8½-inch loaf pans. Form the dough into loaves and place in the pans. Cover and let rise until just curved over tops of pans, about 30 minutes.

Preheat the oven to 375°F. Bake the loaves 35 minutes, or until golden. Turn loaves out on wire racks to cool.

Turnagain Arm is a deep, narrow inlet between two low mountains north of Anchorage. Captain Cook ventured into this treacherous body of water, hoping it would lead to the St. Lawrence River. At the end of the "arm," the adventurous captain had to turn his ship around—hence the name. Alaskans are descriptive and practical about place names.

Forty miles north of Anchorage, beyond Turnagain Arm, is the Alyeska ski resort, where an interesting sourdough bread is made that I had heard about. Twelve of those forty miles were under construction, but we were assured we would have no difficulty. If I had known what was ahead of us, I would have brought a complete history of Alaska to keep me occupied. Two long waiting periods amidst fifty other cars were our first hurdles. Then to our consternation, a sign—DETOUR. To where? There was a mountain on one side of the highway, railroad tracks below on the other side, and still farther below a fast bore tide surging up Turnagain Arm. Slowly the long line of cars began to disappear down the embankment to the railroad track. For two very long miles we actually rode the rails, with that icy water boiling by on my side of the car. Back to our broken highway and a few more yards to face a second detour. All the cars wiggled along the rails for another two miles, a very slippery ride indeed.

A superb bacon, lettuce, and tomato sandwich on sourdough whole wheat bread plus a bowl of piping hot vegetable soup containing chunks of tofu restored our confidence. We did have to go back over that highway—there was no other way. This time we waited a full hour at a point where blasting had been done, but we became absorbed in watching five men, dangling from long ropes tied to something up on the mountain, swinging back and forth chipping at loose rocks. Then we rode those slippery rails again, but this time the frigid tide was on my husband's side of the car.

Arctic Cracked Wheat Sourdough Bread

Makes 3 loaves

WHOLE WHEAT SOURDOUGH STARTER

2 cups warm water	2 cups stone-ground
2 tablespoons honey	whole wheat flour

Combine the water and honey in a crock. (As with other sourdough starters, use no metal, only ceramic, glass, or plastic containers.) Stir until honey is dissolved. Beat in the flour until the mixture is smooth. Cover with a doubled piece of cheesecloth and set aside in a warm, cozy corner until the sponge becomes bubbly. Let the sponge "work" two days. If the container can handle more sponge, add 2 cups more of warm water and 2 cups of whole wheat flour. Beat thoroughly, cover with the cheesecloth, and let it proof again overnight. Stir thoroughly, replace the cheesecloth, and top with a lid. Do not close tightly, as the starter needs a little air—otherwise it may bubble all over the refrigerator. The sourdough starter is now ready to use.

THE BREAD

2 cups whole wheat
  sourdough starter
1 cup cracked wheat
2 tablespoons honey

1 cup warm water
1 cup unbleached white
  flour

2 cups warm water
1 package active dry yeast
½ cup instant dry skim
  milk
½ cup light oil or melted
  butter

2 teaspoons salt
¼ cup honey or molasses
½ cup toasted wheat germ
5–6 cups unbleached
  white or bread flour
2 cups whole wheat flour

In the evening in a large mixing bowl combine the sourdough starter, cracked wheat, 2 tablespoons honey, 1 cup warm water, and 1 cup white flour. Stir until well blended, cover with plastic wrap and a towel, and let stand overnight.

The next morning in a large mixing bowl combine the 2 cups of warm water and yeast, stirring until dissolved. Add the dry milk, oil, salt, honey, wheat germ, and 1 cup of white flour. Beat well and add the sponge. Gradually add all of the whole wheat flour and sufficient white flour to make a soft, workable dough that pulls away from sides of the bowl. Turn out on a floured surface and knead about 10 minutes, or until smooth and resilient. Round into a ball, place dough in a warm buttered bowl, turning to coat the top, and cover loosely with plastic wrap and a towel. Let rise until doubled, about 1–1½ hours.

Punch down the dough and divide into 3 portions. Knead each piece, cover, and let rest 10 minutes. Form into loaves: baguette, round, or 8½-inch loaves. Brush baking sheets or loaf pans with melted butter. The dough is unusually active for a sourdough and proofs quickly. Cover loaves and let rise until almost doubled, about 45–60 minutes.

Preheat the oven to 375°F. Slash the loaves with a razor and bake the free-form loaves 30–35 minutes and the pan loaves 40 minutes. Remove loaves and let cool on wire racks.

Fairbanks

ust above the Arctic Circle in the Brooks Range south of Point Barrow is the tiny village of Anaktuvuk Pass. In 1962, our eldest son
had lived with the Simon Paneak family while preparing an anthropological
study of the Nunamuit Eskimos, the last nomadic group in Alaska. Evolyn
Melville and her husband flew to Anaktuvuk Pass to make a one-day health
survey for the government while he was there. As a result of their meeting, I
knew one person in the state of Alaska by correspondence. I wrote Evolyn
asking advice on researching bread in her state, and to my delight, she offered
to be our guide for ten days on an automobile trip of interior Alaska (the parts
of it with roads!). I accepted by return mail. This turned out to be an adventure and a rare opportunity to understand our forty-ninth state.

We flew to Fairbanks to meet Evolyn and within two days we were on
Alaskan Highway 3. It's lumpy. All Alaskan highways are lumpy, but that's not
the fault of the road builders. Dig into the ground two feet and the ground is
frozen—permafrost. In Vermont highways have the heaves, in Alaska, bumps.
I forgot all the lumps and bumps listening to our guide who had sixty-one
years of experience of Alaskan life. We learned it is an open, friendly, still
pioneer society. When she was not too certain where we were, she stopped the
car, stepped out to hail the first car, truck, RV, or jeep and asked. Evolyn
talked to everyone whether she knew them or not, and there was always this
open, friendly response. By the time we returned to Fairbanks, I was convinced
we had met everyone in Alaska.

We passed Mount McKinley, cloaked in clouds. Our destination the first
night was a minuscule town, Talkeetna. The two blocks of unpaved main street
had three log houses, one garage, a very small museum, and THE ROADHOUSE.
A roadhouse, any Alaska roadhouse, is a motel with a run-down-the-hall
bathroom. Our room had two beds, linoleum floor, one table, and one light
suspended in the center of the ceiling. I took off for that bathroom and
bumped into a big, burly truck driver stalking the hall barefoot, clad in a bath-
robe. Everyone gathered in the kitchen, where you could sit on high stools and
have a drink, or breakfast, or perhaps a beef stew with homemade bread. Evolyn and her husband had once owned and managed a roadhouse in Fort
Yukon on the Yukon River, not far from the Canadian border. There had to
be a roadhouse bread and Evolyn shared her recipe. It is an excellent basic
white bread that can also be made into cinnamon rolls.

Roadhouse Bread

Makes 4 loaves

Along with caring for three small children,
Evolyn had manned the roadhouse kitchen,
cooking for construction workers, truck drivers,
miners—all men with huge appetites. At least
eight to sixteen loaves of bread were made each
day. Together we redesigned the recipe to smaller
proportions. The texture is unusually good and
the bread is adaptable to a variety of moldings.

1 quart warm water
¼ cup sugar
¼ cup instant potato
  flakes
2 packages active dry
  yeast
1 tablespoon salt

2 tablespoons melted
  shortening or light oil
½ cup instant dry skim
  milk
10½ cups flour,
  approximately

Combine water, sugar, potato flakes, and yeast in a large mixing bowl, stirring until dissolved. Blend in the salt (this can be reduced to 2 teaspoons or eliminated for those on a no-salt diet), shortening, and dry milk. Beat in 4 cups of flour until mixture is fairly smooth and gradually add sufficient flour to make a soft dough that pulls away from sides of the bowl. Turn dough out on a lightly floured surface and knead until smooth and satiny, at least 10 minutes—this dough is a pleasure to knead. The dough may be prepared in a heavy-duty mixer with a dough hook, but finish kneading by hand for at least 3 minutes. Round into a ball and place the dough in a warm bowl brushed with melted shortening, turning to coat the top. Cover lightly with plastic wrap and a towel and let rise until doubled, about 1 hour.

Punch down the dough and divide into 4 equal portions. Knead each piece lightly, cover, and let rest 10–15 minutes.

Regular 8-inch Loaves: Brush four 8½-inch loaf pans with melted shortening. Shape the dough into loaves and place in the pans. Cover and let rise until rounded over tops of pans, about 45 minutes. Preheat the oven to 375°F. Bake the loaves 30–35 minutes, or until golden brown. Remove loaves from the oven and turn out on wire racks to cool. If a soft crust is desired, brush tops of loaves with melted butter.

Roadhouse Braid: Butter a baking sheet. Divide one portion of dough in 3 equal pieces. Roll each into a 14-inch rope. Braid the three ropes, tuck the ends under, and place on the baking sheet. Plump the braid. Cover and let rise 45 minutes. Preheat the oven to 375°F. Bake the loaf 30 minutes. Let cool on a wire rack.

Cottage Loaf: You will need melted butter, sesame seeds, and 1 egg beaten with 1 tablespoon water for glaze.

Brush a 1-quart soufflé dish with melted butter. Sprinkle heavily with sesame seeds. Cut one quarter off one portion of dough and set aside. Form the larger piece into a round ball and place in prepared dish. Cup the smaller piece of dough in your hand and quickly rotate on a surface until it forms a smooth ball. Make an indentation in the center of the larger portion of dough and place the little ball on top. Dust your forefinger with flour and stick down through both balls of dough to the bottom of the soufflé dish. (Pull finger out!) Cover and let rise 30–35 minutes. Brush top of loaf with the glaze and sprinkle heavily with sesame seeds.

Preheat the oven to 375°F. Bake the loaf 35 minutes. Remove soufflé dish to a rack and let cool 10 minutes. Unmold bread and let cool on rack.

Alaskan Cinnamon Bread: I met a number of Alaskan women who prepared cinnamon bread just a bit differently than we in the "lower Forty-eight."

You will need melted butter, brown sugar, cinnamon, and white sugar.

Butter an 8-inch loaf pan. Roll 1 portion of dough into a 12 × 9-inch rectangle. Brush with melted butter to within ¼ inch of the edges. Spread lightly with brown sugar and sprinkle with cinnamon—as much as you like. (I'm a heavy cinnamon sprinkler!) Then sprinkle lightly with white sugar. Roll up from the short end, jelly-roll style, and seal the seam and ends. Place seam side down in the loaf pan. Pat into shape and tuck under all around. Puncture the loaf 6 times down the center with a toothpick to help release air. Cover and let rise to top of pan, about 45 minutes.

Preheat the oven to 350°F. Bake the loaf 35 minutes. Let cool on a wire rack and frost with Confectioner's Icing (page 45). The Alaskans never have time for frosting because the loaf is consumed immediately.

Buckwheat Bread

Makes 4 loaves

*A dark, intriguing bread that has a flavor of both
the Old and New Worlds, this is another soul-
satisfying recipe from our pioneer friend Evolyn.*

1½ cups cracked wheat
2½ teaspoons salt
¼ cup light oil
1½ cups hot water
3 cups warm water
   (100°F)
¼ cup sugar
¼ cup instant potato
   flakes

2 packages active dry
   yeast
5–6 cups bread flour
1 cup instant dry skim
   milk
½ cup toasted wheat germ
3 cups buckwheat flour
2 cups stone-ground
   whole wheat flour

Combine the cracked wheat, salt, oil, and hot water. Stir ingredients to blend and let cool to lukewarm.

In a large mixing bowl blend together the warm water, sugar, instant potatoes, and yeast. Let stand 15 minutes, or until the mixture begins to bubble. Combine the cracked wheat mixture with the yeast mixture. Add 2 cups of bread flour and stir well. Cover and let proof about 20–30 minutes. When the sponge is bubbly, add the dry milk and wheat germ. Measure in the buckwheat flour and beat until smooth. Add the whole wheat flour and beat thoroughly. Gradually add sufficient bread flour to make a soft dough that pulls away from sides of the bowl. The dough will be quite dark in color because of the buckwheat. Turn out on a lightly floured surface (use bread flour) and knead until smooth and resilient, about 8–10 minutes. A most responsive dough—you will enjoy the kneading. Round into a ball and place in a warm buttered bowl, turning to coat the top. Cover loosely with plastic wrap and a towel and let rise until doubled, about 45–60 minutes.

Punch down the dough and divide into 4 equal portions. Knead each portion, cover, and let rest 10 minutes. Butter four 8½-inch loaf pans. Form the dough into loaves and place in the pans. Cover and let rise until curved over tops of pans, about 30 minutes.

Preheat the oven to 350°F. Bake the loaves 35 minutes, or until dark, crusty brown. Turn out and let cool on wire racks. If a softer crust is preferred, brush loaves while hot with melted butter.

T he following morning the sky was a spotless blue and brilliant sunshine flooded the rugged landscape. And there, in the distance, stood Mount McKinley in all its ice-covered glory, with snow-covered peaks ranged on either side. My husband had disappeared, but suddenly reappeared, grabbed my arm, and propelled me into a small building to meet a bush pilot who would not only fly us close to Mount McKinley but would land us on a glacier. Before I knew it, we were strapped in a tiny plane, flying high over green meadows toward Mount McKinley. When we reached the mountains, glacier after glacier sparkled below us in the sun, clear blue-green water showing through the ice holes.

Clump, clump, clump—the sound of landing skis moving into place. Down we flew onto our glacier. The plane slid in several directions and the pilot yelled that he was maneuvering it to a level spot for take-off later. Whatever he wanted to do was fine with me—I was thrilled, overwhelmed, and one solid goose bump. The motor stopped, and there was not a sound. The pilot reached in front of me and opened the door. As I stepped down toward the ice, I thought that surely I should say something great—like "one step for mankind." I couldn't think of a thing and that is rare for me. Here we were at eight thousand feet, with the top of Mount McKinley right behind us. I sat on the glacier, walked on the glacier, kicked at it, breathed the clear air, and just felt happy.

Our pilot announced the take-off would be rough. We slid rapidly and bumpily over the ice. Suddenly we were airborne and my heart resumed its normal beat. The return flight was through a long pass between high mountain peaks. Between two mountains the pilot banked so close, I felt I could reach out and grab a piece of ice. Farther on he dipped the plane low over a lush, green meadow so we could see the moose grazing and the beaver dams that appear everywhere in the intricate waterways created by the melting of the glaciers. Our adventure of one and a half hours was over and the plane gently landed on the gravel runway. I shall not ever forget a single detail.

In 1900, the rich soil in the Matanuska Valley close to Anchorage was discovered. The area was opened for homesteading and later, during the Great Depression, homesteaders sent back tales and photographs of fifty-pound cabbages, enormous radishes, and other fantastically bizarre vegetables that might be grown in the short summers with twenty-four-hour sunlight. But homesteading was not successful. The farms were too small and the frigid winters too difficult.

June and Clyde Oberg, devoted Mormons, purchased an old homestead farm in the Matanuska Valley twenty-five years ago. Through the hard work of the entire family, the farm has become a showplace. It has a small, picturesque lake, magnificent vegetable and flower gardens, exquisite green grass, and a large rambling farmhouse connected to the barns for easy handling of cattle in the winter. The Mormons have a way of turning any barren land—whether desert or frozen ground—into a thing of beauty.

At June's invitation, I spent a morning watching the family produce a beef stew, fresh salad from the garden, fresh homemade rhubarb pie, cinnamon rolls, and a superb whole wheat bread that would be served to the tour groups that stop here daily. I punched the bread and washed dishes. By eleven the stew was bubbling, the cinnamon rolls cooling, and the bread baking. I wandered outside just in time to greet two passenger cars filled with Colombian travelers from South America. They stopped for coffee and ate all our cinnamon rolls! The bread was out of the oven, the pies finished, the stew ready when a tour bus parked in front of the farmhouse. I ate like a farmhand—after all I had been in June's kitchen since 7:30 A.M. watching and working. When I returned to my own kitchen, I successfully used June's recipe for whole wheat bread, with the aid of my Magic Mill to grind the wheat (which must be used immediately), to make beautiful brown loaves.

June Oberg's Freshly Ground Whole Wheat Bread

Makes 4 loaves

To simulate June's freshly ground whole wheat flour, purchase stone-ground whole wheat flour. Measure the amount needed and place in a 300°F oven until the flour is warm. Then make the bread immediately.

2 packages active dry yeast
3½ cups warm water
½ cup instant potato flakes
2 teaspoons salt
⅓ cup sugar

½ cup light oil or melted butter
7 cups freshly ground whole wheat flour, approximately
3 cups unbleached white flour

Combine the yeast and water in a large mixing bowl, stirring until dissolved. Add the instant potatoes, salt, sugar, and oil. Beat in 4 cups of whole wheat flour until smooth. Add the remaining whole wheat flour and sufficient white flour to make a soft workable dough that pulls away from sides of the bowl. Turn out on a lightly floured surface and knead 8–10 minutes, or until smooth and resilient. Round into a ball and place in a warm buttered bowl, turning to coat the top. Cover loosely with plastic wrap and a towel and let rise until doubled, about 1 hour. A most receptive dough that rises fast—particularly if you are fortunate enough to have freshly ground whole wheat.

Punch down the dough, turn out on floured surface, and knead. Divide into 4 equal portions, knead each piece, cover, and let rest 10 minutes. Butter four 8½-inch loaf pans. Mold the dough into loaves and place in the pans. Cover and let rise until curved over tops of pans, about 40 minutes.

Preheat the oven to 350°F. Bake the loaves 30 minutes, or until dark, golden brown. Let loaves cool on wire racks.

Valdez, the Pipeline, and Delta Junction

S outh of the Oberg farm to Valdez (pronounced Valdeez), the highway bumped constantly up and down because, according to our guide, of permafrost. We were penetrating the Chugach Mountains, where gold mining has been replaced by the oil industry. The bright shiny pipeline constantly reappears, crossing a river, winding over a hill, around a mountain, through a mountain. Waterfalls gushing dirty glacial waters drop from high above. Valdez is at the end of the pipeline, the only port in Alaska that is open the year round. There we saw the magnificent sculpture representing the men who built the pipeline and stood on a rocky embankment only a quarter mile from the dirty glacier that had receded in the violent and devastating earthquake of 1964. Close by, salmon were swimming up a rushing stream to spawn.

After a restful night in a real motel, we went back the next morning over the Richardson highway to join Highway Number 1. As we sped down the highway, lumping and bumping along, Evolyn waved to everyone—truck drivers, tour buses, pickup trucks, RVs, and passenger cars. It was as though she belonged to a secret society, and she does—that of the Alaskan pioneers. We stopped overnight at the Copper Center Roadhouse, now named an Historic Building. The area was a supply center for the early miners. We turned off the highway to have lunch in Sourdough. There had to be a town named Sourdough somewhere! And in Sourdough is The Sourdough Roadhouse, built in 1903, a perfect spot for lunch, if a bit primitive. The bathrooms were privies—

blue doors for boys, pink for girls; now, how is one to tell the difference during the long dark winter? A bronze plaque labeled this building as an historic house, too, but I had a feeling the state would have to prop it up before long.

While my companions stoked up on sourdough pancakes and fresh rhubarb pie, I went into the kitchen and met Pam McLean, the cook. Pam proudly displayed four huge jars full of sourdough starter seventy years old. Pam had tried living in the "lower forty-eight" but returned to Alaska with a husband and two children, not to live in Anchorage or Fairbanks, but in the bush. No indoor plumbing, no running water. "Oh, sure, I have running water—I run to the river, fill a pail, and run back." She gave me her recipe for sourdough pancakes in very large quantities.

Sourdough Pancakes

Makes about 8 medium pancakes

Pancakes or waffles made with sourdough have a soft texture that belies their earthy, filling qualities. This is a scaled-down version of Pam's recipe. Serve immediately with butter and maple syrup.

1 cup sourdough starter, pages 183 and 185
1 cup water
1 cup flour
¼ cup instant dry skim milk

2 tablespoons sugar
1 teaspoon salt
2 tablespoons light oil
¼ teaspoon baking soda dissolved in 2 teaspoons water

Combine all ingredients except the dissolved baking soda. Blend thoroughly with a rubber spatula. The batter will keep for several days. It may be made the night before and cooked the next morning for breakfast, or may be made immediately before baking. Most batters do thicken a little, but stirring just before cooking will remedy that.

When ready to serve, add the dissolved baking soda, folding it in carefully. Cook the pancakes on a hot griddle brushed with oil or vegetable shortening. Bake on one side until golden and then flip and bake on the other side. The pancakes may be made in any desired size.

We left a bunch of bananas that we had bought in Valdez with Pam. Fruit is difficult for her to obtain and she was eager to make a banana cream pie. I wouldn't have minded staying overnight to have a piece of that pie, except for those wild colored privies out back. A return to Highway 1 took us to the Tok cut-off.

Two very wide gravel highways meet at Tok—Alaskan Highway 1 and the Alcan. There was a great air of excitement at the junction, where there is only a lodge, motel, restaurant, gift store, and an information service. Amidst swirling dust RVs, vans, and campers of every description were arriving. People milled around and yelled greetings to highway friends. This is where the American and Canadian highways first meet in Alaska, and all these people had been driving hundreds of miles in the wilderness; finally to arrive in Alaska was a great accomplishment. Creating more dust and activity, a two-elephant circus had pitched its tent and the whole tribe of Athabascan Indians had turned out to see it. A long line of people stomped down the tall weeds, waiting to buy tickets.

The following morning the circus was gone, leaving nothing but broken weeds and a mud hole, but we were to meet again. Construction on Highway 2 filled the rippled, washboard roadbed with dust. Finally we reached blacktop pavement and entered the Delta Junction area.

There I met a Viking god—they grow them big and solid in Alaska. Scott Hollembaek, stripped to the waist, was working in a two-story seed warehouse built by his father Barney and brother Eric. The three of them sell more seeds of all kinds than anyone in Alaska. They are clearing hundreds and hundreds of acres of virgin soil to grow wheat and barley. Scott showed me a field of experimental grains which they hope will adapt easily to the short growing season. "Send one of your books to my mother, Ileen—she loves to make bread." By correspondence Ileen and I have become "bread" friends. She is a marvelous cook and I love her breads.

Honey-Egg Bread

Makes 4 loaves

1 quart warm potato
  water, page 184
2 packages active dry
  yeast
½ cup honey
½ cup light oil
1 tablespoon salt

10–11 cups bread flour
3 large eggs, lightly
  beaten
1 egg mixed with 1
  tablespoon water for
  glaze (optional)
Sesame seeds (optional)

If you have no leftover potato water, dissolve 6 tablespoons instant potato flakes in 1 quart of warm water and beat with a whisk to blend.

Combine the potato water and yeast in a large mixing bowl, stirring until dissolved. Add the honey, oil, and salt and beat in 4 cups of flour until smooth. Cover and let stand 20–30 minutes, or until light and bubbly.

Stir down the sponge and add the eggs. Gradually add sufficient flour to make a soft, workable dough that pulls away from sides of the bowl. Turn out on a floured surface and knead 8–10 minutes, adding more flour if necessary. Round into a ball and place the dough in a warm buttered bowl, turning to coat the top. Cover loosely with plastic wrap and a towel and let rise 1–1½ hours, or until doubled in bulk. Punch down the dough, knead lightly in the bowl, re-cover, and let rise a second time, about 45 minutes.

Turn dough out on a lightly floured surface and divide into 4 equal portions. Knead each piece thoroughly, cover, and let rest 10–15 minutes. Butter four 8½-inch loaf pans. Form the dough into loaves and place in the pans. Cover and let rise until curved over tops of pans.

Preheat the oven to 350°F.

If a shiny crust is desired, brush tops of loaves with the glaze and sprinkle with sesame seeds. Bake 40–45 minutes, or until golden. Remove loaves and let cool on wire racks.

Ileen's Brown Bread

Makes 4 loaves

"My bucket of dark flour has everything in it, whole wheat, rye, and steel-cut oats. I just got tired of having three containers around." I decided to give that idea a try. I mixed all three together and made four terrific loaves of bread.

1 quart warm potato
   water, page 184
6 cups stone-ground
   whole wheat flour
4 cups stone-ground rye
   flour
2 cups steel-cut oatmeal
2 packages active dry
   yeast

½ cup light oil
½ cup molasses
1 tablespoon salt
3 large eggs, beaten
1 egg mixed with 1
   tablespoon water for
   glaze
Sesame seeds or wheat
   germ

If you have no leftover potato water, dissolve 6 tablespoons instant potato flakes in 1 quart of warm water and beat with a whisk to blend.

Combine the whole wheat and rye flours with the oatmeal in a large bowl. Combine the yeast and the potato water in a large mixing bowl, stirring until dissolved. Add the oil, molasses, and salt. Beat in 4 cups of the flour mixture until smooth. Cover and let proof 20–30 minutes, or until light and bubbly.

Stir down the sponge and add the eggs. Gradually add sufficient flour mixture to make a soft, workable dough that pulls away from sides of the bowl. Turn out on a floured surface and knead 8–10 minutes, or until smooth and resilient. Place the dough in a warm buttered bowl, turning to coat the top. Cover loosely with plastic wrap and a towel and let rise until doubled, about 1–1½ hours.

Punch down the dough and turn out on a lightly floured surface. Divide into 4 equal portions. Knead each piece, cover, and let rest 10–15 minutes. Butter four 8½-inch loaf pans. Form the dough into loaves and place in the pans. Form the dough into loaves and place in the pans. Cover and let rise until just curved over tops of pans, about 30–40 minutes.

Preheat the oven to 350°F. Brush the loaves with the glaze and sprinkle with sesame seeds or wheat germ. Bake about 45 minutes. Let loaves cool on wire racks.

Point Barrow

W hat would be your reaction if you were flown to the northernmost city in the United States (population 2,800) and discovered a Mexican restaurant named Pepe's with six Mexican cooks and a tall, handsome female owner/manager with long blonde hair? "Only in America!" is all you can say. We had walked three foggy blocks from the airport to the center of town and the Top of the World Hotel, with Pepe's next door. I was freezing, despite layers of clothes—slack suit, wool sweater, a light topcoat. That topcoat was the mistake. What I desperately needed was an Eskimo summer parka made of bright padded prints with a fur-lined hood. But after a cup of steaming tea in the coffee shop at Pepe's we were ready to tackel Point Barrow.

Following the suggestion of a local government employee, we boarded the city bus (same model as in Detroit) and rode all over town, watching the Eskimos get on and greet each other with stoic faces but much handshaking. The complete round cost us five cents each as senior citizens; everyone else except babies tucked in the backs of parkas paid fifty cents. We passed the city hall, a three-story building containing a supermarket, prefab homes surrounded by rusty snowmobiles, several two-story apartment buildings, and the cold, cold Arctic ocean with a few floating icebergs. What a change the oil wells have made. Those prefabs have replaced tundra huts that not so long ago were made of driftwood, moss, and rocks.

Eagerly we returned to Pepe's for lunch. Bread soup, drip beef sandwiches, and guacamole salad were served expertly by a Mexican waiter in a lovely dining room filled with colorful Mexican artifacts. I could hardly believe we were where we were. Fran Tate, the owner, came to Point Barrow as an architectural engineer and switched professions to start this amazing restaurant at the top of the world. Fran gave us a taste of caribou (stringy), bear (strong), frozen fish (very fishy), and an Alaskan doughnut (not bad).

Uqsrukuaqtaq (ESKIMO DOUGHNUTS)

Makes about 25 doughnuts

*Mrs. Noah (Molly) Itta generously gave her
recipe to Fran Tate for me to use in my book. I
have tested her recipe and the doughnuts are light
and delicious, especially when fresh and hot.
Please note the final instructions for cooking!*

3½ cups warm water
4½ tablespoons sugar
2 packages active dry
   yeast
1½ teaspoons salt
½ cup melted lard or oil

10 cups flour,
   approximately
Oil for deep frying
Confectioner's sugar
   (optional)

Combine ½ cup of warm water, 1½ tablespoons sugar, and yeast in a small bowl, stirring until dissolved. In a large mixing bowl combine 3 cups of warm water. 3 tablespoons sugar, salt, and lard. Blend in the yeast mixture. Beat in 4 cups of flour to make a smooth batter. Gradually add sufficient flour to make a soft, workable dough. Knead on a floured surface about 5 minutes. Round into a ball, cover with a bowl or a heavy towel, and let rise 30 minutes.

Roll out the dough about ½ inch thick. Cut with a doughnut cutter, or use a 2-inch biscuit cutter and punch a hole in the center of each piece. Cover and let rise 25 minutes.

Fry in any kind of fat or oil. Seal, whale, or caribou fat that has been ground or hammered and boiled into oil may also be used. Now, since those ingredients are not readily available in the "lower forty-eight," I suggest peanut, safflower, or sunflower oil. Heat 3 inches of oil to 370°F. Fry the doughnuts about 3 at a time until golden on both sides. Drain on paper towels. Molly did not suggest this, but a sprinkling of confectioner's sugar over the hot doughnuts is yummy. Molly does say that this batch makes about 25 doughnuts, depending on how big your cutter is.

A|t five o'clock we returned to the airport via the local taxi, driven by two very young Eskimos absorbed in loud radio music. The plane filled with oil field workers returning to Prudhoe Bay after fun and games in Point Barrow. Twice we circled for a landing through heavy mist. The pilot announced he would try once more and then fly on to Fairbanks. Down we flew again very gently through the mist. Suddenly everyone (except the workers, who were fast asleep) saw the bright pipeline streaking across the tundra, but the weather closed in and we flew on to Fairbanks. Our one-day trip was a great adventure and I had a recipe I never expected.

Our busy guide Evolyn had arranged for me to meet Marguerite Stetson at the University of Alaska in Fairbanks. Many of my questions were answered and I was given a number of wonderful recipes and pamphlets. I have chosen and tested several of the best.

Whole Wheat Barley Bread

Makes 2 loaves

2 packages active dry yeast	2 teaspoons salt
2½ cups warm water	⅓ cup instant dry skim milk
3 tablespoons sugar	2 cups whole wheat flour
3 tablespoons melted butter	1 cup barley flour
	3–4 cups bread flour

Combine the yeast and ½ cup warm water in a small bowl, stirring until dissolved, and set aside. In a large mixing bowl combine 2 cups of warm water, the sugar, butter, salt, and dry milk and blend well. Add the yeast mixture and beat in the whole wheat and barley flours until fairly smooth. Gradually add sufficient bread flour to form a soft dough that pulls away from sides of the bowl. Turn the dough out on a floured surface and knead until smooth and resilient, about 8–10 minutes. Round into a ball and place in a warm buttered bowl, turning to coat the top. Cover loosely with plastic wrap and a towel and let rise until doubled, about 1 hour.

Butter two 8½-inch loaf pans. Punch down the dough and shape in 2 loaves. Place in the pans, cover, and let rise until just curved over tops of pans.

Preheat the oven to 375°F. Bake the loaves 30–35 minutes, or until golden. Let cool on wire racks.

Sour Cream Blueberry Bread

The Home Extension Service at the University of Alaska has done extensive research on the use of wild berries in Alaska. Everything from rose hips to wild blueberries has been canned, make into jams and jellies, and used in salads and bread.
I have to hide this one from my husband. The bread is luscious, like a fresh cake.

4 cups sifted flour
2 teaspoons baking soda
1 teaspoon salt
½ pound (2 sticks) butter, at room temperature
2 cups sugar
4 eggs

2 cups ripe mashed bananas (about 3 large bananas)
1 cup sour cream
2 cups blueberries or lingenberries, fresh or frozen
1 cup chopped pecans

Sift the flour, baking soda, and salt together. Set aside. Cream the butter and sugar until light and fluffy in an electric mixer. Add the eggs, bananas, and sour cream and blend well. Gradually add the flour mixture, beating until the batter is smooth. Stir in the berries and pecans with a rubber spatula.

Preheat oven to 350°F. Butter the pans.

This recipe makes a lot of batter. Following are directions for baking in pans of various sizes.

Five 7-inch loaf pans: bake 40–50 minutes, *or*

Two 9-inch loaf pans plus one 7-inch loaf pan: bake the large pans 1 hour and 5 minutes; the small pan 40–50 minutes, *or*

One 10-inch tube pan (angel food cake tin): bake 1 hour and 10 minutes plus one 7-inch loaf pan: bake 40–50 minutes.

Check the breads with a cake tester. The cooking time in Alaska was longer than the testing time in my own kitchen. I am certain it has something to do with the atmosphere, because it just never gets quite that cold in Oklahoma!

Apple-Blueberry Muffins

Makes 12 muffins

This irresistible recipe makes muffins that are just as delicious as they sound. The recipe won a blue ribbon at the Tanana Valley Fair in Fairbanks. If there are any left, split and toast for breakfast.

1½ cups sifted flour
2 teaspoons baking
   powder
½ teaspoon salt
½ cup sugar
1 egg
1 cup milk

¼ cup light oil
½ teaspoon cinnamon
1 cup fresh peeled and
   grated apple
¾ cup blueberries,
   Alaskan if possible,
   fresh or frozen

Preheat the oven to 425°F. Butter twelve 2½-inch muffin tins.

Sift the flour, baking powder, salt, and sugar into a mixing bowl. In another bowl beat the egg until frothy and blend well with the milk and oil. Make a hole in the center of the dry ingredients and pour in the milk mixture. With a rubber spatula stir just until the flour mixture is wet. Fold in the cinnamon and fruit. Fill muffin tin cups two thirds full and bake 25 minutes.

E volyn shared our last two days in Fairbanks, showing us the Tanana State Fair and the herd of musk-ox kept by the University of Alaska. (They can become pets, they are so gentle.) We did a little shopping and watched the same two-elephant circus parade through town. We feasted on our last fresh salmon and finally got aboard our plane for home. As we flew toward Anchorage, there again was Mount McKinley in all its pristine beauty. For thirty minutes we had our final magnificent view of the entire range of mountains that rises so suddenly out of the tundra. It had been an amazing journey.

THE OHIO VALLEY

MILEAGE—4,185 MILES

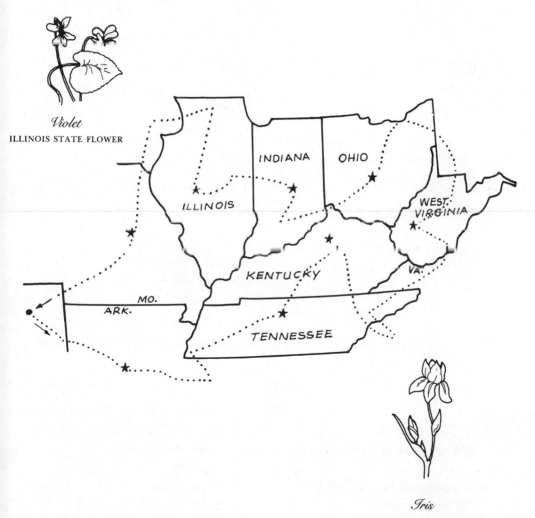

Violet
ILLINOIS STATE FLOWER

Iris
TENNESSEE STATE FLOWER

Arkansas and Mississippi

Brilliant fuchsia redbud and white dogwood bloomed in the hollows of the rugged Ozark hills turning this first day of a new journey into a fairyland of springtime landscapes. We were looking for blueberry farms. Arkansas agriculturists have built a new industry, extending the market season for luscious blueberries well beyond that of the Maine and Michigan suppliers. As our route turned south to Fort Smith, an idea for a coffeecake formed in my mind. I jotted a few notes and this is the result.

Blueberry Coffeecake

Makes 1 loaf

A cake that may be served warm or at room temperature or may be frozen for future use. Frozen or fresh blueberries may be used.

FILLING

½ cup packed brown
   sugar
⅓ cup sifted flour
2 teaspoons cinnamon

4 tablespoons butter, at
   room temperature
Grated rind of 1 lemon

Combine all ingredients and blend with a pastry blender or fingertips until crumbly.

BATTER

3 cups sifted flour
2 teaspoons baking
   powder
1 teaspoon baking soda
½ teaspoon salt

⅜ pound (1½ sticks)
   butter, at room
   temperature
1½ cups sugar
Grated rind of 1 lemon

3 eggs
1 cup sour cream
2 tablespoons lemon juice

2 cups fresh or frozen
blueberries
Confectioner's sugar

Preheat the oven to 350°F. Thoroughly butter a Bundt pan.

Resift flour with baking powder, soda, and salt. Set aside. In a mixing bowl cream the butter, sugar, and grated rind until light and fluffy. Add the eggs one at a time, beating thoroughly after each addition. Add flour mixture alternately with the sour cream, beating well after each addition. Use a rubber spatula to scrape down the sides. Blend in the lemon juice and blueberries. Continue folding in the berries until mixture is smooth and creamy. Pour two thirds of the batter into the pan. Sprinkle the filling over the batter. Top with remaining batter. Bake 50 minutes if you used fresh blueberries in the filling, 1 hour for frozen berries, or until cake tests done. Let cake cool in pan on wire rack 10–15 minutes. Turn out on a serving tray and sieve confectioner's sugar over top.

To freeze: Do not sprinkle top with sugar. Let cake cool completely. Wrap in foil, label, slip into a plastic bag, and freeze. When ready to serve, let defrost and reheat in foil.

W hile we were curving south to Fort Smith, one of my volunteer associates, Dora Malone, and her husband, Jim, mounted on handsome matching twin motorcycles, wearing red checked shirts and those NASA-type helmets, were curving across northern Arkansas (All roads in Arkansas curve one way or another.) Swerving abruptly into the tiny hamlet of Green Forest, Dora spotted a bakery called The Gingerbreadman. Off came the helmets and in Dora went to meet Klaus Kupfersberger—one could hardly find a more German name in the heart of Berlin. His heavy accent was no problem to Dora, who was raised in a German family. Using her excellent German and her American charm, Dora extracted a delicious coffeecake recipe, which she wrote down and tucked into the saddle of her motorcycle.

Apricot-Chocolate Coffeecake

Makes 2 coffeecakes

Although Mr. Kupfersberger has chocolate in the cake's title, cocoa is used. The cake is unusually fine and shows his excellent training in Germany.

Dough:

1 package active dry yeast	½ teaspoon salt
¼ cup warm water	1 tablespoon grated
¾ cup warm milk	orange rind
½ cup melted butter	3 eggs, lightly beaten
6 tablespoons sugar	4½ cups flour

Topping:

½ cup sugar	1 teaspoon cinnamon
2 tablespoons	2 tablespoons butter
unsweetened cocoa	1 cup apricot jam
¼ cup flour	1 cup chopped nuts

In a small bowl combine the yeast and water, stirring until dissolved. In a large mixing bowl combine the milk, butter, sugar, salt, grated rind, and eggs, blending well. Add the yeast mixture with 1 cup of flour and beat until smooth. Cover and let rise until bubbly, about 30 minutes.

Stir down the sponge and gradually add sufficient flour to make a soft, workable dough. Turn out on a lightly floured surface and knead 10 minutes, or until smooth and elastic. Round into a ball and place in a warm buttered bowl, turning to coat the top. Cover loosely with plastic wrap and a towel and let rise until doubled, about 1 hour.

To make the topping, combine the sugar, cocoa, flour, and cinnamon. Cut in the butter until well mixed and crumbly—a streusel type of topping.

Butter 2 baking sheets. Punch down the dough, turn out on a lightly floured surface, and knead lightly. Divide in half. Roll 1 portion (keeping the other covered) into a 14 × 10-inch rectangle. Roll up from the long side, jelly-roll style, and seal the seam and one of the ends.

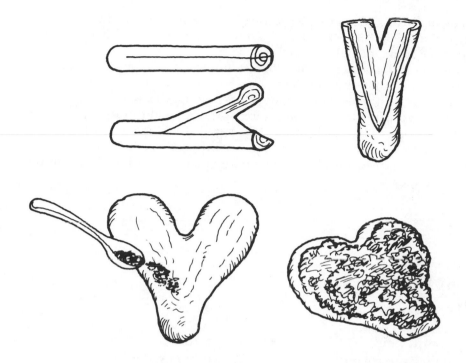

Using the illustrations as a guide, with a sharp knife or dough scraper, beginning at the open end, make a cut down the length of the roll, cutting all the way through to the bottom for the first 2 or 3 inches and then cutting only to the center for the rest of the cut. Stop cutting about an inch from the sealed end. Spread the dough into a heart shape and place on a baking sheet. With a rubber spatula spread half the jam over the dough. Sprinkle half the topping and nuts over the jam. Repeat directions with second portion of dough. Cover with a light towel and let rise 20 minutes.

Preheat the oven to 350°F. Bake the coffeecakes 20–25 minutes. Remove cakes and let cool on wire racks or serve warm.

B efore the War Between the States, Cherokee Indians moved from the eastern seaboard into the territory of Arkansas. Battles raged with the Osage Indians, but, through the assistance of the Choctaw tribe from Kentucky, the Cherokees established agrarian settlements and their own courts of law. The Civil War destroyed their way of life, as hordes of horse thieves, bandits, and fugitives swarmed into the rugged hill country. Help came when "Hanging Judge" Parker was appointed federal Judge at Fort Smith. A man of great energy, knowledge of the law, and understanding of the Indian, he brought law and order to the turbulent frontier of western Arkansas and the

Indian territory of Oklahoma. We stopped at Council Oaks, where under a magnificent tree, the Cherokee signed a final treaty with the federal government and moved on into Oklahoma Territory.

Little Rock, dominated by the white-columned state capitol building with its unusually handsome bronze doors, sits high on the bluffs bordering the Arkansas River. Ten miles east of Little Rock, the Ozarks fade into the Delta Highlands, a vast agricultural empire. Rice, soybeans, and cotton now reign in flat, sweeping fields that reach to the Mississippi River and south into Louisiana. As we drove over an elevated highway through rice fields and swamps filled with cypress trees, I made a mental note to have a rice bread here in the book. The recipe uses brown rice.

Brown Rice Bread

Makes 2 loaves

6–7 cups flour
½ cup white cornmeal
2½ teaspoons salt
¼ teaspoon baking soda
2 packages active dry
   yeast
2 cups warm water

¼ cup melted butter
½ cup honey
2 cups cooked brown rice
   (cooked until very
   tender), at room
   temperature
Melted butter

Combine 2 cups of the flour, cornmeal, salt, and baking soda in a mixing bowl. Set aside. In a large bowl combine the yeast and water, stirring until dissolved. Add the butter and honey. Beat in the flour mixture to make a smooth batter. Add the rice. Gradually stir in sufficient flour to make a soft, workable dough. Turn out on a lightly floured surface and knead until smooth and elastic, about 10 minutes. Round into a ball and place in a warm buttered bowl, turning to coat the top. Cover loosely with plastic wrap and a towel and let rise until doubled, about 1 hour.

Punch down the dough, turn out on a lightly floured surface, and divide in half. Knead each for 1 minute, cover, and let rest 15 minutes. One loaf may be molded into a round and placed in a buttered 8-inch cake tin. The remaining portion can be formed into a regular loaf and placed in a buttered 8½-inch loaf pan. Brush each loaf with melted butter, cover, and let rise until doubled, about 45–60 minutes.

Preheat the oven to 375°F. Bake loaves about 35–40 minutes. Remove loaves to a wire rack and brush with more melted butter. When cool, this evenly textured bread is good for sandwiches.

W‌e crossed the Mississippi River at Helena and drove into the rolling hills of northern Mississippi. A stop at the lovely campus of "Ole Miss," the state university in Oxford, gave me a chance to meet the Dean of Home Economics, Dr. Jean Kincaid, and Mary Sue Pettleton, a professor. Mississippians love quick Southern breads, hot rolls, and coffeecakes and now use zucchini in their recipes, for it is grown extensively in the state. With our propensity for huge agricultural projects, we could easily feed the whole world on Mississippi zucchini and black-eyed peas!

Bishop's Bread

Makes 2 coffeecakes

From Louisiana and Mississippi to the eastern coast, I have found this coffeecake or bread to be a favorite, but could never find the origin of the name. Perhaps the bishop was an overnight guest in a Methodist parsonage, and the preacher's wife had to whip up something special for breakfast. Dr. Kincaid related that many such coffeecakes are also often used as desserts in the south, warm from the oven.

2½ cups flour
2 cups packed dark brown
   sugar
¼ pound (1 stick) butter
¼ teaspoon salt
½ cup milk

1 cup sour cream
½ teaspoon baking soda
1 egg, beaten
1 teaspoon baking powder
1 teaspoon cinnamon

Preheat the oven to 350°F. Butter well two 8-inch cake tins.

Combine the flour, sugar, butter, and salt, mixing with a pastry blender or in a food processor. Reserve ⅔ cup of the mixture for the topping. Combine the milk and sour cream in a mixing bowl and blend in the baking soda. Add the flour mixture, egg, and baking powder. Stir and mix well until the batter is thick and creamy. Divide the batter between the cake tins. Add the cinnamon to reserved topping mixture and sprinkle half over the top of each cake. Bake 30 minutes. Serve warm.

Tennessee and Kentucky

O ne night in Memphis, we savored Creole cuisine at Justine's, a restaurant with a fifty-year reputation for fine food, and we drove to Nashville to glimpse the handsome capitol overlooking the city and took a fascinating tour through the historic white-pillared home of President Andrew Jackson. Later, our chosen route would turn back into Tennessee, but now we took the highway through rolling farm lands of Kentucky.

North and east of Bowling Green, exquisite farms are enclosed with the famous black fencing and handsome, meticulously groomed horses nibble on the Kentucky bluegrass. Majestic homes on the hilltops all look like replicas of Mount Vernon, complete with tall, white-columned porticos.

Determined to visit every national park possible, we drove to the entrance of Mammoth Cave National Park. The drive from the visitor's entrance to the beginning of the cave tour was long and winding, through exquisitely manicured grounds. Even the rabbits looked well groomed! The drive was better than the cave tour, which I kept comparing to the three hours of Carlsbad Caverns in New Mexico—a most exciting experience, bats and all. Misty rain was falling as we left the park and drove to the Cumberland Parkway, then turned north to Shakertown and the Inn at Pleasant Hill, for one of our most interesting experiences.

Shakertown, Kentucky

M other Ann Lee, one of eight children born to an illiterate blacksmith, married an alcoholic and bore four children, all of whom died. Leaving her depressing life, she joined the small religious group of celibates who founded the Shaker religion. She became a fervent, aggressive leader and immigrated from England to the American Colonies in 1774. Under her guidance, the Shakers became highly organized, dedicated to a strict, rather primitive religion honoring simplicity, humility, and charity in common ownership. They believed that human passions had to be overcome to prevent war, murder, envy, and jealousy in this world. Shaker colonies spread from the New England states to Kentucky. Their hope for survival was adoption of children. Their main source of income was the growing and selling of excellent seeds in great variety.

The Shaker name comes from their religious service. Men and women formed lines facing each other. Another group sang, and slowly the two standing groups started to dance. The singing became faster, and as the two lines continued to dance, they began to shake. The description of Shaker services reminds me of the southern Holy Rollers I saw in tent meetings as a child.

Despite their innovative productivity, the Shakers declined; at this writing there are only two members known to be left. A number of Shaker museums are scattered over the eastern states, but Pleasant Hill is the only one that is also an inn. We arrived in a cold downpour of rain and were quickly guided to our room, Number 1 in the Ministry building. Furnished with high twin beds, two Shaker rockers, and a perfectly made chest of drawers, it had the familiar walnut board on all four walls, with plain hooks spaced two feet apart. We hung our dripping coats on the hooks, settled into our rockers for a small libation, and stared at an incongruous television set that certainly did not fit in here. But there was a complete modern bath, definitely a lovely addition.

The dining room, popular locally (there was a long waiting line), is in the administration building, which has perfectly carved twin winding staircases, one for each sex. Dinner was outstanding American food, with excellent fresh vegetables and Shaker lemon pie, the filling prepared with a whole lemon chopped into fine pieces.

Through Ann Voorhiis, manager of the inn, I met Elizabeth Kremer, the shining light of the kitchen and dining room. Elizabeth, a pretty older woman, a little shaky but not a Shaker, lives in an elegant upstairs apartment just above those pristine staircases. Elizabeth told me the Shakers cooked whatever was available in any region where they lived. Vegetables were grown and canned, and they made everything themselves, from bottles to cradles. Elizabeth has researched Shaker foods and was most kind to share two recipes. Both are excellent.

Shaker Spicy Gingerbread

Makes 1 gingerbread

2½ cups flour
1½ teaspoons baking soda
¼ teaspoon cloves
1 teaspoon cinnamon
1 teaspoon ginger
¾ teaspoon salt
½ cup shortening

½ cup sugar
1 egg
1 cup dark molasses
1 cup hot water
½ cup raisins, scalded,
   drained, and dried
   (optional)

Preheat the oven to 350°F. Spray a 12 × 7½ × 2-inch baking pan with nonstick vegetable spray and brush with melted shortening or butter.

Sift the flour, soda, spices, and salt together. In a large mixing bowl beat the shortening and sugar until creamy. Add the egg and beat in the molasses. Slowly mix in the flour mixture alternately with the water. If desired, add the raisins—an afterthought that Elizabeth thinks is delicious. Pour batter into the pan and bake about 35 minutes, or until firm in the center. Remove and let cool in the pan or serve immediately.

Shaker Wheaten Bread

Makes 2 loaves

1 package active dry yeast
1 cup warm water
1 cup warm milk
2 teaspoons salt
3 tablespoons butter

4 tablespoons honey or
   maple syrup
2 cups white flour
3 cups whole wheat flour
Melted shortening or
   butter

Combine the yeast and ¼ cup warm water in a small bowl, stirring until dissolved, and set aside. Combine milk, salt, butter, honey, and ¾ cup warm water in a large mixing bowl, blending well. Add the yeast mixture and beat in the white flour to make a smooth batter. Gradually add sufficient whole wheat flour to make a workable dough that pulls away from sides of the bowl. Turn out on a lightly floured surface (use white flour) and knead about 8 minutes, or until smooth and elastic. Round into a ball and place in a warm bowl brushed with melted shortening or butter, turning to coat the top. Cover loosely with plastic wrap and a towel and let rise until doubled, about 1 hour and 45 minutes.

Punch down the dough, turn out on a lightly floured surface, and divide in half. Cover and let rest 10 minutes. Butter two 8½-inch loaf pans. Shape the dough into loaves and place in the pans. Cover and let rise until just rounded over edge of pans, about 1 hour and 15 minutes.

Preheat the oven to 350°F. Brush tops of loaves with melted shortening and bake about 50 minutes. Remove loaves and let cool on wire racks.

Danville, Kentucky

A t the suggestion of the staff at Pleasant Hill, we drove to Harrodsburg for lunch at the Beaumont Inn. Originally a private home, it still has many of its original furnishings and elegant antiques. Huge rooms, high ceilings, a great carved, curving staircase—these are of a period in our history we will not see the likes of again.

We finished the short drive to Danville to meet, as arranged for us by the Shaker Inn, a lady named Miss Frances Green, a tall elderly black woman of at least eighty who had a box of beaten biscuits prepared for me. Miss Frances told me any recipe could be used, because the only secret ingredient is "beating." How long? She was a little vague but intimated that most people are not willing to beat long enough for blisters to pop on the dough. Nevertheless, Miss Frances said, she had a dream of making beaten biscuits as popular as Chinese food!

Beaten Biscuits

Makes 36–40 biscuits

We all have dreams and frustrations, and this recipe can certainly help work off the latter. The name beaten biscuits means exactly what it says— beat, beat, and beat the dough until those blisters do appear. However, experimenting with both my heavy-duty mixer and food processor, I was able to cut the beating time considerably.

7 cups flour	½ teaspoon baking
¾ cup lard	powder
2 teaspoons salt	1½ cups water
2 teaspoons sugar	

Combine the flour, lard, salt, sugar, and baking powder in the large mixing bowl of a heavy-duty mixer. Beat with the dough hook until ingredients are well blended. Add the water, knead until ingredients are pulled together, and knead 2 minutes more. Divide the dough into thirds and place one portion in food processor bowl. Pulse 1 minute and remove dough. Repeat with remaining 2 portions of dough. Return all the dough to mixer bowl and knead with dough hook 2 minutes more. After this workout on both machines, the dough is ready for hand-beating.

Divide dough in half for easier handling. Begin beating with a rolling pin, the side of a hammer, meat cleaver, or any similar instrument. Beat the dough until your arm is tired. I found that covering the dough with plastic wrap and resting is fine for both you and the dough. Keep beating until blisters appear on the dough; about 15 minutes should produce a couple of blisters. Dough that is made entirely by hand is usually beaten 30–45 minutes.

Roll out the dough ½ inch thick and with a cookie cutter or small biscuit cutter cut into 1½-inch rounds. Prick the tops twice with a fork and place on ungreased baking sheets.

Miss Frances bakes her biscuits in a preheated 350°F oven for 40 minutes. I prefer to bake them at 400°F for about 20 minutes, or until light and creamy in color. The biscuits keep for weeks in a jar and freeze very well. They are delicious hot and when cold, split as a base for appetizers.

Berea, Kentucky

O ur route led us through more lovely horse farms with huge barns painted black and sporting brilliantly contrasting white doors. Then the bluegrass faded into rolling hills, quiet and densely covered with tall stately trees. At Berea is the lovely Berea College campus, built for Appalachian hill people who had had little chance for formal education. The college was established first as a trade school; students have an opportunity to work and are offered a curriculum that ranges from hotel management to weaving and music.

Facing the campus is Boone Tavern, a part of Berea College operated and managed by Miriam R. Pride. Miriam relates that for many years Richard T. Hougen was manager of the hotel and is responsible for developing the recipes that have made Boone Tavern famous. Originally rooms were heated with coal and the cooking was done on wood-burning ranges. Now the kitchens have the finest equipment and adjoin a large, carpeted, and very popular dining room where superb American food is served. Miriam has given me two of Mr. Hougen's innovative recipes, with his permission.

Black Forest Coffeecake

Makes 1 large coffeecake

Excellent with creamy scrambled eggs for breakfast or even as a light dessert for dinner.

2 cups sifted flour
1 teaspoon salt
4 teaspoons baking
  powder
¼ pound (1 stick) butter,
  at room temperature
1 cup sugar
2 beaten eggs, at room
  temperature

1 cup milk
2 tart apples, cored,
  peeled, and thinly sliced
½ cup brown sugar
⅛ teaspoon nutmeg
⅛ teaspoon cloves
Confectioner's sugar
  (optional)

Preheat the oven to 350°F. Butter well a 13 × 9-inch baking pan.

Resift the flour with the salt and baking powder and set aside. Cream the butter and sugar until light and fluffy. Add the eggs and stir well. Add the flour mixture alternately with the milk, beginning and ending with the flour mixture. Beat thoroughly and pour into the pan. Place the apple slices in rows across the top of the batter and press them down lightly to keep them in place.

Combine the brown sugar with the nutmeg and cloves, mixing well, and sprinkle over the apples. Bake about 40–45 minutes. Sprinkle with confectioner's sugar, if desired. Serve hot or at room temperature.

Peanut Rolls

Makes 24 rolls

Crunchy with peanuts, these rolls are lightly textured, excellent for an informal dinner party.

1 package active dry yeast	2 eggs, beaten
¼ cup warm water	4½ cups flour,
1 cup warm milk	approximately
¼ cup melted butter	1 cup chopped raw
¼ cup sugar	peanuts, toasted 30
1 teaspoon salt	minutes in a 250°F oven

Combine the yeast and water in a small bowl, stirring until dissolved, and set aside. In a large mixing bowl combine the milk, butter, sugar, salt, and eggs. Add 1 cup of the flour and the yeast mixture and stir well. Blend in the peanuts. Gradually add sufficient flour to make a soft dough. Turn out on a lightly floured surface and knead 2–3 minutes. Place in a warm buttered bowl, turning to coat the top. Cover loosely with plastic wrap and a towel and let rise until doubled, about 2 hours.

Butter 24 muffin tins. Rub a little butter on your hands and pinch off small bits of dough about the size of a walnut. Place 3 balls in each muffin cup. Cover and let rise until doubled, about 45 minutes.

Preheat the oven to 375°F. Bake rolls 15 minutes. Leftover rolls taste wonderful, sliced and toasted slowly in a 225°F oven until golden and crisp.

The University of Tennessee at Knoxville

R eba Hendren, a most remarkably organized woman, is assistant professor of health and nutrition at the University of Tennessee and is much involved in the Home Extension Service. Reba informed me that every land grant university has a Home Extension Service to assist people of the state in all aspects of cooking and to teach and help the young 4H groups. Through Reba I was able to obtain recipes for Tennessee breads and good information on nutrition. I am most grateful to Reba and have selected for you my favorite among her recipes.

Angel Potato Biscuits

Makes about 30 biscuits

Reba has added another dimension to Angel Biscuits, a popular refrigerator roll. Mashed or riced potatoes give her rolls a marvelous airy quality and a crisp crust—delicious!

2 packages active dry
  yeast
¼ cup warm water
1½ cups warm buttermilk
1 cup riced or mashed
  potatoes
5 cups flour,
  approximately

¼ cup sugar
¾ teaspoon baking soda
1 tablespoon baking
  powder
1 teaspoon salt
1 cup vegetable
  shortening

Combine yeast and water in a small bowl, stirring until dissolved. In a large mixing bowl blend the buttermilk with yeast mixture and slowly beat in the potatoes until smooth.

In a separate mixing bowl combine 4 cups of the flour, sugar, baking soda, baking powder, and salt. Cut shortening into flour mixture with a pastry blender or whirl mixture in a food processor. If using a processor, return flour mixture to mixing bowl. Stir potato mixture into flour mixture, adding enough of the final cup of flour to make a workable dough. Turn out on a floured surface and knead until light and elastic, about 5–8 minutes. Place the dough in a bowl brushed with melted shortening or butter, turning to coat top. Cover with plastic wrap and a towel and refrigerate 1 hour.

Butter 2 large baking sheets. Turn dough out on a floured surface and pat or roll to desired thickness—½ inch makes a nice biscuit. Cut with a 2-inch biscuit cutter and place on baking sheet. Cover and let rise until doubled, about 1 hour.

Preheat the oven to 450°F. Bake the rolls 15–18 minutes.

Note: The dough will keep in refrigerator 2–3 days.

Christmas Stollen

Makes 3 loaves

½ cup warm water
2 packages active dry
 yeast
¾ cup warm milk
½ cup sugar
1 teaspoon salt
⅔ cup melted butter or
 margarine
3 eggs

1 tablespoon grated
 lemon rind
6–7 cups flour
⅔ cup blanched almonds,
 chopped
¾ cup mixed candied
 fruit, chopped
⅔ cup golden raisins,
 scalded, drained, and
 dried

Combine water and yeast in a small bowl, stirring until dissolved. In a large mixing bowl blend the milk, sugar, salt, and butter. Stir in eggs, lemon rind, and yeast mixture. Beat in 2½ cups flour to make a smooth batter. Gradually add sufficient flour to make a soft, workable dough that pulls away from sides of the bowl. Turn dough out on a lightly floured surface and knead until smooth and elastic, about 10 minutes. Place in a warm buttered bowl, turning to coat the top. Cover loosely with plastic wrap and a towel and let rise until doubled, about 1–1½ hours.

Combine almonds, fruit, and raisins. Punch down the dough, pat it out flat, and place the almond and fruit mixture in the center. Bring the edges together and begin kneading to distribute the mixture. If the fruit mixture tends to stay in one spot, cover dough, let rest 10 minutes, and continue kneading quickly.

Butter 3 baking sheets. Divide dough into 3 equal portions. Roll each piece into a 12 × 8-inch oval. Using the illustrations as a guide,

fold in half lengthwise so that top portion does not quite reach the bottom edge. Place on prepared baking sheets, cover, and let rise until doubled, about 45–60 minutes.

Preheat the oven to 375°F. Bake the *stollen* 25–30 minutes, or until golden brown.

To Decorate: Prepare an icing with 1 cup Confectioner's sugar, ¼ teaspoon vanilla, and sufficient milk to make a spreadable consistency. Frost the cakes while warm. They may be decorated with whole blanched almonds, candied cherries (they stick better if cut in half), or colorful candied fruits.

Stollen tastes even better a few days after it is made; wrap well so that the bread does not dry out. *Stollen* also freezes well.

Basic Biscuits

Makes about 10–12 biscuits

Biscuits are as Southern as the Confederate flag and every restaurant or housewife in the South has a slightly different version. Reba Hendren not only has devised an excellent biscuit but also, using the same dough, an innovative quick sweet roll to serve for breakfast or unexpected coffee hour.

2 cups flour	⅓ cup vegetable
4 teaspoons baking	shortening
powder	⅔ cup milk
¾ teaspoon salt	

Preheat the oven to 450°F. Butter a baking sheet.

Sift together flour, baking powder, and salt into a shallow bowl. Cut in the shortening with a pastry blender until mixture resembles coarse cornmeal. Stir in milk. Pile dough on a lightly floured board and with floured hands knead the dough 10–12 strokes. Pat or roll out the dough ½ inch thick. For plain biscuits, use a biscuit cutter of any desired size; 2 inches is the usual size. Place on baking sheet and bake about 15 minutes.

Biscuit Cheese Tea Rolls

Makes 12 rolls

8-ounce package cream cheese, at room temperature	¼–½ cup chopped pecans
	⅓ cup raisins, scalded, drained, and dried
½ cup packed brown sugar	1 recipe Basic Biscuit dough, preceding
¾ teaspoon vanilla	recipe

Preheat the oven to 425°F. Butter a 9-inch cake tin.

Combine cream cheese, brown sugar, and vanilla. Add the pecans and raisins. If the mixture is too stiff to spread, add a small amount of honey.

Roll the biscuit dough into a 14 × 10-inch rectangle and spread with the cheese mixture. Roll up from the long side, jelly-roll style. Seal the seam. Cut into 12 rounds and place cut side down in the cake tin. Bake until light and golden, about 15 minutes. Serve immediately.

D riving southeast from Knoxville toward Gatlinburg, we stopped for lunch at a small roadside café and were rewarded with a bowl of soup filled with fresh vegetables and a piece of Kentucky Derby pie that was pure caloric intake—a thin flaky crust, a filling thick with chocolate chips topped with a walnut crust, served hot. The landscape changed to steep hill country and then to low mountains as we entered the Great Smoky National Park. Gatlinburg, at one main entrance of the park, is built along a beautiful mountain river. It is a one-street town, lined with motels and garish shops selling anything from antiques (very expensive) to cotton candy. We stopped for a night's rest and then drove on into the Appalachian highlands. The park's aim is to maintain the mountain forest as it was when Tennessee became the sixteenth state in 1796. June and July are the most dramatic months, when rhododendron cover the mountainsides—a sublime time for hikers and canoeists. A long, winding drive took us into Hominy, and I was not certain at this point whether we were in Tennessee or North Carolina. But lunch in Asheville with the Sunday crowd at The Burning Steak was fried chicken and corn bread—we were certainly in the South.

West Virginia

N o other state in the Union, not even Maine, has more intriguing, irregular boundaries. A slender panhandle pierces into Pennsylvania, three counties jut into Maryland and Virginia, the western line follows the Ohio River, allotting all the islands to West Virginia—what a time the sixth graders have learning to draw their state! Further, the topography is all up and down, in other words, rugged, and certainly beautiful.

We entered the state close to White Sulphur Springs to spend a night at the famous Greenbrier. Two years before, I took a week-long series of cooking lessons here while blizzards raged outside; what great fun to be caught again in this luxurious inn during a beautiful snowstorm. From the Greenbrier we drove slowly toward the capital, Charleston. West Virginia is a state of great contrasts. In the coal mining regions the houses are built right down to the highway and then straight up the hillsides. Huge coal chutes built on high trestles cross the road overhead and unload coal into open gondola cars on the other side. Other roads wind beside beautiful rivers, some with treacherous rapids excellent for the daring canoeist. Close to historic areas where battles of the War Between the States were fought there are often old inns to spend the night.

But we pressed on to meet the Wick clan in South Charleston. Faye Wick had introduced herself to me by a letter, from the jungles of Indonesia where she was living in a compound one hundred miles from anyplace. She had taught her Indonesian cook to make bread from my first book, *Mary's Bread Basket*. I kept in touch with Faye as she traveled to odd parts of the world and finally we met in California. When Bechtel gives her husband a holiday, the Wicks make tribal visits to West Virginia.

Cat Head Biscuits

Makes about 7 biscuits

Nancy Wick of South Charleston provided this recipe, handed down from her grandmother, who ran Ma Shaffer's Boarding House on Third Avenue in Charleston from 1920 to 1945. I am a good biscuit maker, but these are tops.

2 cups flour	2 teaspoons salt
1 tablespoon baking powder	2 tablespoons light oil
⅛ teaspoon baking soda	¾ cup buttermilk

Preheat the oven to 400°F. Butter a baking sheet.

Combine the flour, baking powder, soda, and salt in a shallow mixing bowl. Make a well in the center. Pour in the oil and buttermilk. Stir quickly until well mixed and turn out on a floured surface. Knead lightly with floured hands and pat out ½ inch thick. Cut with a 3-inch cutter. Nancy's grandmother used a large empty evaporated milk can for a cutter. Place biscuits on baking sheet and bake about 12 minutes.

T he West Virginia Department of Agriculture, under the direction of Commissioner Gus R. Douglass, does outstanding research, particularly with corn. It is a grain that has figured in our history since Governor William Bradford declared the first Thanksgiving holiday after the corn harvest of 1621. Corn was a staple that sustained the pioneers on their move westward. Our revolutionary soldiers and those of the Civil War were often issued parched corn to eat. West Virginia now produces five to six million bushels of corn each year. With magnificent rivers and swift mountain streams to power the grist mills, in West Virginia the grinding of corn and other grains became a part of the state's first social as well as agricultural life.

Corn Kernel Corn Bread

Makes 1 corn bread

1 cup flour	1 cup milk
1 cup cornmeal	3 tablespoons melted
4 teaspoons baking	margarine
powder	1 cup frozen yellow
1 teaspoon salt	cream-style corn,
¼ cup sugar	cooked according to
2 eggs, well beaten	package instructions

Preheat the oven to 450°F. Brush a 9-inch square baking pan with melted shortening.

Combine dry ingredients in a mixing bowl, stirring to blend well. In a separate bowl combine the eggs, milk, margarine, and corn. Add all at once to the dry ingredients, mixing quickly and thoroughly. Pour batter into the pan and bake about 30 minutes, or until bread tests done. Serve hot.

Corn Light Bread

Makes 1 loaf

*Tired of whole wheat, rye, and white breads?
Then try this Corn Light Bread with a cake-like
texture. And you do not have to wait until the
bread cools—it's best right out of the oven. If
there is any left, try toasting it for breakfast.*

2 cups cornmeal
1 cup flour
½ cup sugar
1 teaspoon baking soda

1 teaspoon salt
2 cups buttermilk
3 tablespoons light oil

Preheat the oven to 375°F. Butter a 9-inch loaf pan.

Combine the dry ingredients in a mixing bowl, blending well. Measure the buttermilk into a separate bowl and add the oil. Add the buttermilk mixture to the dry ingredients and stir to blend well. Pour batter into the loaf pan and let stand 10 minutes.

Bake 35–40 minutes, or until the loaf pulls away from sides of the pan and is a lovely golden color. Remove from oven and let cool 5 minutes in the pan. Turn out and serve immediately.

Molasses Yeast Bread

Makes 3 loaves

*The aroma of this bread as it bakes conjures up to
me visions of the beautiful hills of West Virginia.
I loved it both hot out of the oven and toasted the
following morning.*

1½ cups boiling water
1 cup rolled oats
⅓ cup vegetable
   shortening
2 packages active dry
   yeast
½ cup warm water

½ cup molasses
2 eggs, lightly beaten
2 teaspoons salt
6½ cups unbleached
   white flour,
   approximately

Combine the boiling water and oats in a large mixing bowl. Stir well and add the shortening. Set aside until shortening is melted. In a small bowl combine the yeast and warm water, stirring until dissolved. Stir the molasses, eggs, and salt into the oats mixture. Add the yeast mixture and 3 cups of flour and beat until batter is smooth. Gradually add sufficient flour to make a soft, workable dough that pulls away from sides of the bowl. Turn out on a floured surface and knead until smooth and elastic, about 8 minutes. Round into a ball and place in a warm bowl brushed with melted shortening, turning to coat top. Cover loosely with plastic wrap and a towel and let rise until doubled, about 1 hour.

Punch down the dough and turn out on lightly floured surface. Divide into 3 equal portions, knead each lightly, cover, and let rest 10 minutes.

Butter three 8½-inch loaf pans. Shape dough into loaves and place in pans. Cover and let rise to tops of pans, about 45 minutes.

Preheat the oven to 350°F. Bake loaves 40 minutes. Turn out on wire racks to cool.

Ohio and Indiana

O n a quiet Sunday morning we drove north on Interstate 79 through a mountainous area of West Virginia, past many lovely state parks and forests and into southern Pennsylvania. I was eager to drive through the city of Pittsburgh when there would be little traffic, for the dramatic setting of this great industrial city is something to see. The original settlement was on a point of land where the Allegheny and Monongahela rivers meet to form the Ohio River. Driving slowly, we tried to picture the battles here between the French and the English. More than thirty years later, when the Indians finally were subdued by the famous "Mad Anthony" Wayne in 1795, the Ohio Valley was opened for rapid settlement. Ohio, an Iroquois word meaning "great river," became a state in 1803.

After a quick visit to Oberlin University and a night at a resort hotel by

Lake Erie, we took a circuitous drive through beautiful farming country to the capital, Columbus. A talk with the food editor on a local paper suggested that Ohioans prefer just plain white and whole wheat breads, except in the ethnic areas of the larger cities. But, in an attempt to find an old grist mill, we found something else, the Amish. When there are horse droppings along the side of the road and no electric wires going into the houses, there you will find the strict, gentle Amish. The Amish village of Sugar Creek is a center for Swiss cheese; Charm is a tiny hamlet nestled in a hillside; Walnut Creek is another colorful town. In the countryside, we saw two young Amish women selling pies and sticky buns from their front yard. One was very pregnant and wore the traditional straight pins meticulously aligned down the front of her plain dress. Despite the fact that in one small town we saw a group of black-clad men with black hats sitting on a bench eating ice cream cones and one Amish woman in a supermarket with a TV dinner in her basket, the Amish tradition is very strong. After some research, I came up with two entrancing Amish coffeecakes.

Amish Fruit-Topped Coffeecake

Makes 1 coffeecake

A very pretty upside-down cake. With a little imagination you can make it look almost like a stained glass window.

Topping:

2 tablespoons melted
  butter
3 tablespoons sugar

6 cooked dried apricot
  halves
6 cooked dried prune
  halves

Batter:

1½ cups sifted flour
2 teaspoons baking
  powder
½ teaspoon salt
½ cup sugar

1 egg, beaten
½ cup milk
3 tablespoons melted
  butter

Preheat the oven to 350°F. Brush an 8-inch square baking pan with melted butter.

To make the topping, spread the butter over bottom of pan. Sprinkle with the sugar and arrange apricot and prune halves alternately in rows on top of the sugar.

In a mixing bowl sift together the flour, baking powder, salt, and sugar. Combine the egg, milk, and butter in a separate bowl. Make a well in dry ingredients and add milk mixture, stirring to make a smooth batter. Carefully pour over the fruit. Bake about 35 minutes. Let cool slightly in pan and invert on serving tray. Serve warm.

Sugarplum Plucket Ring

Makes 1 coffeecake

Lydia and Annie Beiler, my Amish friends in Pennsylvania, told me they call a bubble or pull-apart loaf Plucket bread. The name is so descriptive, I could not resist the following recipe.

Dough:

1 package active dry yeast
¼ cup warm water
½ cup milk, scalded
⅓ cup sugar

⅓ cup vegetable shortening
1 teaspoon salt
3–4 cups flour
2 eggs, beaten

½ cup melted butter
¾ cup sugar
1 teaspoon cinnamon
½ cup whole blanched almonds

½ cup candied cherries (optional)
⅓ cup dark corn syrup

Combine yeast and water in a small bowl, stirring to dissolve, and set aside. In a large mixing bowl blend the milk, sugar, shortening, and salt. Let cool to lukewarm. Add the yeast mixture and 2 cups of flour, beating until smooth. Stir in the eggs. Gradually add sufficient flour to make a soft dough. Mix thoroughly, turn out on a lightly floured surface, and knead lightly 2–3 minutes. Round into a ball and place in a warm buttered bowl, turning to coat top. Cover loosely with plastic wrap and a towel and let rise until doubled, about 1 hour.

Punch down the dough, turn out, knead lightly, cover, and let rest 10 minutes. Butter well a 10-inch tube pan. Place the melted butter in a small bowl. Mix the ¾ cup of sugar with cinnamon in a separate bowl. With a dough scraper cut off pieces of dough the size of a walnut. Dip a piece in the butter, then in the cinnamon sugar, and arrange in the tube pan. When one layer is finished, sprinkle with almonds and cherries, if desired. Repeat directions for two more layers. Mix the corn syrup with any butter that is left and sprinkle over the cake. Cover and let rise about 45 minutes, or until doubled but not to the top of pan—or the balls will fall out into the oven!

Preheat the oven to 350°F. Bake the ring 40 minutes. Remove pan to a wire rack and let cool 15 minutes. Invert cake on serving tray large enough to catch drippings. To serve, pull the coffeecake apart with 2 forks. The cake can be cooled, wrapped, and frozen.

R eceding glaciers thousands of years ago left flat, rich, and deep soil throughout both Ohio and Indiana. I have read that Ohio has a greater variety of trees than any other state and, indeed, trees were large and lushly green everywhere as we drove south toward Lebanon to dine and spend a night in the historic Golden Lamb Inn. The following Sunday morning, we drove to the Ohio River on the southern border between Ohio and Kentucky. The Queen City, Cincinnati, built on high bluffs overlooking the river, has a do-it-yourself tour. Charming golden and orange crowns are posted throughout the city. With little traffic to bother us, we followed the crowns from slums to elegant mansions, to the river where the *Mississippi* and *Delta Queen* dock, to middle-class and blue-collar neighborhoods, to the University of Cincinnati, and to beautiful parks on high bluffs with views overlooking the city. We left for Indiana before church was out.

Spring Mill State Park

I have tucked in a special file a list called "Places to Return To." Spring Mill State Park in southern Indiana is tops on that list. The moss-covered ruins of an old grist mill were discovered there and cleaned and completely restored. An exceptionally long sluice box extends from the mill into the side of a hill to convey the sparkling clear water that turns the enormous wheel for grinding the grain. A large portion of the two-story mill house has been turned into a museum. A crowd of schoolchildren were asking the miller questions. He was particularly proud of the fan-light windows over all the doors. A re-created frontier trading post has been built around the mill, with free-standing log houses furnished as they would have been when the early settlers lived in them and people weaving, working in leather, cooking—it is all extremely well done.

The park contains one hundred acres of virgin woodland with magnificent specimens of the white oak and tulip poplar of this area. Beautiful picnic grounds, caves, lakes, a great variety of birds (even geese), and a handsome inn complete this small paradise. A whole grain bread would be a most appropriate addition.

Whole Wheat Batter Bread

Makes 1 large or 2 small loaves

The aroma of healthful whole wheat and honey is wonderful. This is a bread quick to make for a picnic at Spring Mill State Park.

2 packages active dry
   yeast
¾ cup warm water
1 cup warm milk
¾ cup melted butter
½ cup honey

2 teaspoons salt
3 eggs, lightly beaten
1½ cups whole wheat
   flour
4½ cups unbleached
   white flour

Combine the yeast and water in a bowl, stirring until dissolved, and set aside. In a large mixing bowl combine the milk, butter, honey, salt, and eggs, blending well. Add the yeast mixture and whole wheat flour, beating until smooth. Gradually add the white flour, beating thoroughly until batter is smooth. Using the flat beater on a heavy duty mixer, beat 3 minutes. Cover bowl loosely with plastic wrap and a towel and let rise 1 hour.

Brush a 3-quart casserole or two 1½-quart casseroles with melted butter. Slap the dough down with your hand or a rubber spatula and beat 30 seconds. Pour batter into casseroles, cover, and let rise until ½ inch from top, about 30 minutes.

Preheat oven to 375°F. With kitchen scissors cut a 4-inch cross ½ inch deep into top of each bread. Bake about 45–50 minutes for a large loaf, 40 minutes for smaller loaves. Remove breads and let cool on wire racks.

W ith Lake Michigan and sand dunes on its northern border, broad flat plains in the center that produce rich crops of corn and soybeans, the Ohio River on the south open for water traffic to the Gulf of Mexico, Indiana is as American as apple pie. The capital, Indianapolis, has the advantage of being in the center of the state. It is famous for its Motor Speedway, but I was more fascinated with the elaborate statuary of American soldiers and sailors, representing all our wars, that stands, inappropriately, in the busy downtown, overwhelmed by tall buildings. As we drove back through elegant farms on our way to Illinois, a simple white bread began to take shape in my mind—a bread from which a variety of cinnamon breads that all Americans love could be made.

Indiana Basic White Bread

Makes 3 loaves

4 packages active dry
  yeast
½ cup warm water
2¼ cups warm milk or
  potato water, page 184

2½ teaspoons salt
3 tablespoons sugar
¼ cup melted butter
7–8 cups unbleached
  white flour

In a small bowl combine the yeast and water, stirring until dissolved, and set aside. Combine milk, salt, sugar, and butter in a large mixing bowl. Blend well and add the yeast mixture. Beat in 3 cups of flour and gradually add sufficient flour to make a soft, workable dough that pulls away from sides of the bowl. Turn out on a lightly floured surface and knead until smooth and resilient, about 10 minutes. Round into a ball and place in a warm buttered bowl, turning to coat the top. Cover loosely with plastic wrap and a towel and let rise until doubled, about 45 minutes.

Knead down, re-cover, and let rise again, about 30 minutes.

Turn dough out on a floured surface and divide into 3 equal portions. Knead each, cover, and let rest 10–15 minutes. Butter three 8-inch loaf pans. Shape dough into loaves and place in pans. Cover and let rise to tops of pans.

Preheat the oven to 400°F. Bake loaves about 35 minutes. Turn loaves out on wire racks to cool.

Double Cinnamon Swirl

Makes 2 loaves

You will need: ½ to ¾ cup Cinnamon Sugar (page 46) and some melted butter. I prefer to make two loaves at the same time so that one can rest while I work on the other. Butter two 8-inch loaf pans.

At end of second rising, roll one third of the Indiana Basic White Bread dough into a 12 × 8-inch rectangle. Roll out second portion of dough in same manner. Sprinkle each portion with cinnamon sugar to within ½ inch of edges. Roll up from the short side, jelly roll style. Seal seams and ends. (Use no melted butter during the first rolling.) Cover and let rest 10 minutes. Give dough a quarter turn so that narrow end faces you. Roll again into 12 × 8-inch rectangle and brush lightly with melted butter. Sprinkle again with cinnamon sugar to within ½ inch of edges. Roll up from short side and seal seam and ends. While one loaf is resting, work on the other. When both are finished, place in loaf pans. Cover and let rise to tops of pans, about 1 hour.

Preheat the oven to 350°F. Bake loaves 30–35 minutes. Remove from pans and let cool on wire racks.

Illinois

I have crisscrossed the state of Illinois on many journeys, but this time we entered from a different direction and rambled through the center. From Champaign and Urbana, we drove south to the tiny towns of Arthur and Arcola, the Illinois Amish center. It was the Amish Sunday and many were riding in their large, handsome family buggies, dressed in black and crisp white. Beautiful children peeped over the sides, the fathers and mothers sat straight and prim, and the gorgeous, fast-trotting horses whipped the carriages briskly down the road. I never cease to admire the great integrity of the Amish.

Following a country road west, we came to Griggsville, a town known for its "motels" for purple martins. Martins are champion bug eaters, and here, close to the Mississippi, mosquitoes were a problem. To attract these gregarious birds, the main street is now lined with martin houses; the center one can hold five hundred birds. Then, going north in a roundabout way we reached the Dickson Mounds. Ohio, Indiana, and Illinois are Indian mound states, where superb burial grounds have been carefully preserved. A handsome building has been constructed at the Dickson site. One room surrounds a large portion of the burial ground, where the skeletons and artifacts have been left as they were found. The schoolchildren on tour were completely silent, which is most unusual. It is an awesome sight, absorbing and magnificently presented.

Then off we went into the corn and soybean country of Illinois, one of our flattest states, with rich, deep soil. We drove into Dixon, once the home of President Ronald Reagan, and there was no doubt about that fact, for an archway across Main Street announced it in glowing neon lights. Here I made contact with some excellent breadmakers.

Swedish Coffee Bread

Makes 4 loaves

This is a fine old family recipe given to me by Evelyn and Francis Bangston in Dixon. She and her husband enjoy preparing bread together and became interested in breadmaking simply because they wanted to eat good bread.

4 cups scalded milk
½ pound (2 sticks) butter
2 eggs, well beaten
1 teaspoon salt

2 teaspoons cardamom
2 packages active dry
 yeast
¼ cup warm water

12 cups flour, approximately	1 egg beaten with 1 tablespoon water for glaze
	Cinnamon Sugar, page 46

In a large mixing bowl combine the milk and butter, stir to dissolve butter, and let cool to lukewarm. Add the eggs, salt, and cardamom. Combine the yeast and water in a bowl, stirring until dissolved. Add to the milk mixture. Beat in 4 cups of flour to make a smooth batter. Gradually add sufficient flour to make a soft, workable dough that pulls away from sides of the bowl. If this is too much dough to knead at one time, divide in half and cover 1 piece. Knead each portion thoroughly and form into 1 piece for a final kneading. Place the dough in a warm buttered bowl, turning to coat the top. Cover loosely with plastic wrap and a towel and let rise until doubled, about 1 hour.

Punch down the dough, turn out on floured surface, cover, and let rest 10 minutes. Butter four 8½-inch loaf pans. Divide dough into 4 equal portions, form into loaves, and place in pans. Or the dough may be formed into 4 free-standing braided loaves. Divide 1 portion into 3 parts. Roll each piece into a rope 14–16 inches long. Braid, plump, and place on a buttered baking sheet. Repeat for remaining portions of dough. Cover loaves and let rise 1 hour.

Preheat the oven to 350°F. Brush the loaves with the glaze and dust lightly with cinnamon sugar. Bake 30 minutes. Let loaves cool on wire racks.

F or years I have been using a wide assortment of flours from Elam's in Broadview, Illinois (see Sources of Supply). Then by telephone and letter, I met Stanley Roy, the moving force of this well-known mill and distributor. Stanley has generously given me a wide choice of recipes and I've chosen two of my favorites.

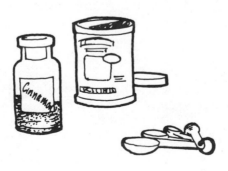

Four Grains Bread

Makes 2 loaves

1 cup stone-ground yellow cornmeal	2 packages active dry yeast
1 cup scalded milk	1 cup raisins, scalded, drained, and dried
¾ cup boiling water	
4 tablespoons butter, at room temperature	1 cup buckwheat flour
	1 cup stone-ground whole wheat flour
½ cup molasses	
2 tablespoons brown sugar	3 cups unbleached white flour with wheat germ (see **Note**)
2 teaspoons salt	
⅓ cup warm water	

In a large mixing bowl stir the cornmeal into milk and boiling water, mix well, and let stand 20 minutes. Beat in the butter, molasses, brown sugar, and salt. Combine the warm water and yeast, stirring until dissolved. Add yeast mixture, raisins, and buckwheat and whole wheat flours to cornmeal mixture, beating until smooth. Gradually add sufficient white flour to make a workable dough. Place on floured surface (use white flour) and knead until smooth and elastic, about 7 minutes. Place in a warm buttered bowl, turning to coat top. Cover loosely with plastic wrap and a towel and let rise until doubled, 1 hour.

Punch down the dough, knead, cover, and let rest 10 minutes. Butter two 8½-inch loaf pans. Divide dough in half, form into loaves, and place in pans. Cover and let rise until doubled, about 45 minutes.

Preheat the oven to 375°F. Bake loaves about 40 minutes. Let loaves cool on wire racks.

Note: Elam's has a superb white flour with wheat germ. It is available in health food stores and through my Sources of Supply (page 483).

Prune and Nut Whole Wheat Bread

Makes 1 loaf

2½ cups stone-ground
  whole wheat flour
1 cup packed brown sugar
2½ teaspoons baking
  powder
1 teaspoon salt
½ teaspoon baking soda

1 cup chopped pitted
  prunes
1 cup finely chopped
  pecans
1 cup milk
½ cup light cooking oil
1 egg

Preheat the oven to 350°F. Spray a 9-inch loaf pan with nonstick vegetable spray and brush with melted butter.

In a large mixing bowl combine the flour, sugar, baking powder, salt, and baking soda and blend well. Stir in prunes and pecans. In a separate bowl combine the milk, oil, and egg. Add the liquid mixture to dry ingredients, stirring just long enough to moisten thoroughly. Spoon into the pan. Bake 1 hour. Remove from oven and let cool in pan 10 minutes. Remove to a wire rack. The bread will slice better the next day.

M y final recipe from this journey comes from Burr Ridge, Illinois, in the environs of Chicago. The bread is not only outstanding in quality and flavor but also has a delightful story. Rovena Hrochova was born in Tregon, Czechoslovakia, in 1900. She lives now in Burr Ridge with a daughter who has patiently and meticulously watched her mother go through the complete process of making this bread over and over, for Rovena speaks little English and cooks through instinct, touch, and feel. Getting the recipe down on paper has been a major feat. Rovena Hrochová is happy to share it with all my readers.

Czechoslovakian Christmas Bread

Makes 1 large or 2 smaller loaves

Both butter and lard are used. Rovena Hrochová says that it is possible to use all butter, but the bread will not be quite as moist and will become stale faster. The bread can be called houska, *the everyday term;* vanocka (vanoce *in Bohemian) is its Christmas holiday name.*

1¼ cups warm water
1 cup plus 1 tablespoon
  sugar
2 packages active dry
  yeast
1¼ cups evaporated milk
¼ pound butter (1 stick),
  at room temperature
¼ pound lard, at room
  temperature
3 egg yolks
1 egg
Grated rind of 1 lemon
1 teaspoon vanilla

8 cups flour,
  approximately
2½ teaspoons salt
1 cup golden raisins,
  scalded, drained, and
  dried
½ cup coarsely chopped
  almonds
1 egg white beaten with 1
  tablespoon water for
  glaze
Sliced or slivered
  blanched almonds
  (optional)

In a large mixing bowl combine the warm water, 1 tablespoon sugar, and yeast, stirring until dissolved, and add milk. Set aside. Cream the butter and lard in bowl of electric mixer. Add 1 cup sugar, egg yolks, and whole egg and beat until light and lemon colored. Add the grated rind and vanilla and stir into the yeast mixture. Beat in 3 cups of flour and salt until the batter is smooth. Add the raisins and almonds. Gradually add sufficient flour to form a soft dough. Turn out on a lightly floured surface and knead until smooth, about 8 minutes. Round into a ball and place in a warm buttered bowl, turning to coat the top. Cover loosely with plastic wrap and a towel and let rise until doubled, about 1½ hours.

Punch down the dough, turn out on a lightly floured surface, and knead lightly. Mold into either 1 large elaborate braid or two smaller loaves.

One Magnificent Braid: Butter a large baking sheet. Divide the dough into 8 equal portions. Roll each into 18-inch ropes. Braid 4 ropes together (page 37) and place on baking sheet. Brush the braid with the glaze. Braid 3 ropes together, plump the braids, and place atop the 4-plait braid, pressing down lightly. Brush with glaze. Divide the last piece of dough in half. Roll into smooth 10-inch ropes and twist together (page 35). Place atop the first two braids, pressing lightly. Brush the entire braid with glaze. Rovena suggests sprinkling either sliced or slivered untoasted almonds over top of braid. Cover and let rise 30–45 minutes.

Preheat the oven to 350°F. Bake braid 45 minutes. Remove from oven and let cool on baking sheet 15 minutes. With two spatulas carefully remove the braid to a wire rack.

Two Braids: Butter 2 baking sheets. Divide dough into 6 equal portions. Roll into 16-inch ropes. Braid 3 ropes, plump, and place on baking sheet. Repeat with remaining 3 portions. Brush loaves with glaze and let rise 45 minutes. Bake in a preheated 350°F oven 35–40 minutes, or until golden brown. These braids may also be decorated with a sprinkling of almonds, if desired.

COLORADO
TO CALIFORNIA

MILEAGE—5,803 MILES

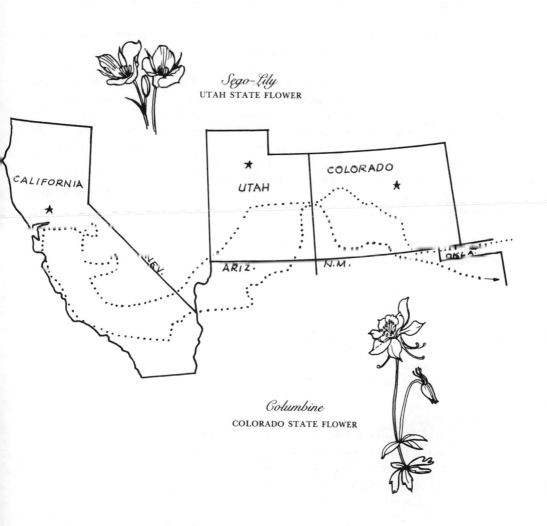

Sego-Lily
UTAH STATE FLOWER

CALIFORNIA

UTAH

COLORADO

ARIZ.

N.M.

OKLA.

Columbine
COLORADO STATE FLOWER

Colorado, the Rocky Mountain State

My favorite route into Colorado is through the panhandle of Oklahoma, across northern New Mexico to join Interstate 25 north to Pueblo, hopefully during the season for Rocky Ford cantaloupe, one of the finest melons in all the Americas. The Rocky Mountains rise abruptly out of the high plains, and a turn west to Canon City and Salida winds into the center of these magnificent mountains, with a stop to gaze into the narrow, awesome Royal Gorge. Finally our route leads to Independence Pass, on a high, narrow road over twelve thousand feet above sea level, which is open only during the summer months. The highway from Pueblo to the Pass follows the infant Arkansas River, which grows rapidly as it tumbles over rocks and through canyons.

Independence Pass leads to Aspen, one of the most charming small cities in the land. Originally a wealthy mining center and now both a sports area and cultural center, the town blossoms with fascinating people. The snow is deep in the winter, golden aspen surround the city during October, and a tent-covered symphony is in residence for the summer. Aspen boasts many manicured turn-of-the-century homes, and two of my grandsons live there.

Aspen also has Crystal Glenn, born in Nebraska and now a resident of Aspen for twenty-five years. Crystal teaches "frontier cooking" classes through the Colorado Mountain College extension courses. She has had much exposure to novice cooks and the problems of baking bread here. At this altitude, bread requires less rising time and can become dry and crumbly. Also, during winter months, most homes are maintained at cool temperatures, while people layer on more clothes. Bread dough likes to be cozy too! Crystal has devised several breads for a high-altitude baking and cool homes. These she has most generously shared with me.

Whole Wheat Camp Bread Mix

Makes enough for 8 regular or
15 miniature loaves

Crystal Glenn has created an excellent bread mix
for campers, with directions for proofing at high
and lower altitudes. The mixture will keep for 2
months at high altitude, stored in tightly covered
plastic containers.

5 pounds whole wheat
flour
1 pound gluten flour
¾ cup sugar
4 tablespoons salt

2 cups instant nonfat dry
milk
1 cup melted vegetable
shortening or oil

Combine all ingredients except the shortening. Divide the mixture into 4 portions. Place 1 portion in the large bowl of an electric mixer and blend in ¼ cup of shortening with the flat beater, beating until the mixture looks and feels like coarse flour. Repeat directions for the 3 remaining portions.

If you do not have a heavy-duty mixer, add the shortening at the time you make the bread, as instructed in the following recipe.

Whole Wheat Camp Bread

Makes 2 loaves

2 cups hot water (120°F)
¼ cup melted vegetable
shortening or oil (omit
if shortening has
already been added to
bread mix)

5½ cups Whole Wheat
Camp Bread Mix,
approximately,
preceding recipe
1 package active dry yeast
½ cup warm water
1 teaspoon sugar

In a large mixing bowl combine the hot water with the shortening, if necessary, and add sufficient bread mix to make a batter, about 2 cups. In a small bowl combine the yeast, warm water, and sugar, stirring until dissolved. Add to the batter, stir well, and gradually beat in sufficient bread mix to form a workable dough. Knead 5 minutes, cover, and let rest 5 minutes. Knead briefly. Cover and let rise 20 minutes at high altitude, 40 minutes at a lower level. Shape dough and place in well-oiled baking utensils—Dutch ovens, foil pans, a rock oven, or two 8½-inch loaf pans. Bake at 375°F 30 minutes, or until done. Test loaf by tapping for a hollow sound.

Fried Cakes: Pinch off small pieces of dough, shape into flat tortilla cakes, and fry in hot fat. Crystal's grandchildren love eating this with cheese.

High-Altitude Pumpernickel Bread

Makes 2 loaves

Crystal Glenn's method of combining whole grain flours at eight thousand feet results in an outstanding bread. By following her instructions, the bread is quickly made; the secret is to keep ingredients warm and cozy so the yeast can work properly and happily high in the mountains.

2 cups very hot tap water	1 egg
3 tablespoons plus 1 teaspoon molasses or sorghum	2 packages active dry yeast
2 teaspoons instant coffee or Postum (for color)	½ cup warm water
1 tablespoon salt	2 cups rye flour
3 tablespoons butter or light oil	1 cup whole wheat flour
	1 cup gluten flour
	3½–4 cups unbleached white flour

Combine the hot water, 2 tablespoons molasses, coffee, salt, butter, and egg. Mix well and let mixture cool to 115°F. Combine the yeast and warm water, add 1 teaspoon of molasses, and stir until dissolved. Add to coffee mixture. Beat in rye and whole wheat flours until smooth. Cover and let proof 30 minutes.

Stir down the sponge and add the gluten flour. Gradually add sufficient white flour to form a soft, workable dough. (Crystal suggests that, if desired, 1 cup more whole wheat or rye flour may be substituted.) Turn out on a lightly floured surface (use white flour) and knead 5 minutes. Cover and let dough rest 5 minutes. Knead again 3–4 minutes.

Place the dough in a warm buttered bowl, cover with a towel, and let rise 20 minutes in a 100°F oven.

Butter two 8½-inch loaf pans. Punch down the dough, turn out, and knead about 2 minutes. Shape into 2 loaves and place in pans. Return to the 100°F oven and let rise 20 minutes. Raise oven temperature to 375°F and bake the loaves about 35 minutes. Remove loaves from pans and let cool on wire racks.

Suggestions: A pan of hot water placed in the oven underneath the rising dough helps speed the process. Crystal (and I, also) enjoy baking whole grain breads on a ceramic sheet or a baking stone, available in all good kitchen stores and from catalogs. If using a baking stone for this bread, place the formed loaves directly on the stone for the last rising in the oven and the baking.

Fast Basic Bread

Makes 3 loaves

A bread especially programmed for beginners. The process works well in cool climates and has been tested at sea level by Crystal Glenn. I've made the bread successfully at seven hundred feet.

2 cups hot tap water (120°F)	1 tablespoon salt
	¼ cup honey or molasses
6–7 cups unbleached white flour	2 packages active dry yeast
1 egg	½ cup warm water
3 tablespoons light oil	1 teaspoon honey

Measure the hot water into a large mixing bowl and add enough flour to make a batter, about 3 cups. Stir in the egg, oil, salt, and honey or molasses. Beat until smooth, cover, and set aside.

Combine the yeast and warm water in a bowl, stirring until dissolved. Add honey and 2 tablespoons flour, beat well, and let stand until bubbly, about 10–15 minutes. Add to the batter and beat thoroughly. Gradually add sufficient flour to make a workable dough. Turn out on a floured surface and knead until smooth and elastic, about 8 minutes. Let rise in a warm spot—Crystal likes an oven preheated to 100°F and then turned off. Place in a warm bowl brushed with melted butter, turning to coat the top. Cover loosely with plastic wrap and a towel and let rise in oven 20 minutes. If there is time, punch down the dough, and let rise again 20 minutes to produce a smoother texture.

Butter three 8½-inch loaf pans. Divide the dough into thirds, form into loaves, and place in the pans. Place pans in a 100°F oven to rise for 30 minutes. Raise temperature to 375°F and bake loaves 40–45 minutes. The bread will be well browned with a hard crust.

High-Altitude Popovers

Makes about 12 popovers

In higher altitudes, popovers sometimes do not "pop." Heavy iron popover pans are available at kitchen and hardware stores and produce outstanding popovers.

3 eggs, at room
   temperature
½ teaspoon salt
1 tablespoon melted
   vegetable shortening or
   light oil

1 cup slightly warmed
   milk (100°F)
¾ cup flour

Preheat the oven to 475°F. Brush a heavy popover pan with melted shortening and place in the oven.

Combine the eggs, salt, and shortening, beating well. Add the milk and flour. Stir just until smooth. Pour into pan, filling each cup two thirds full. Bake 15 minutes. Reduce temperature to 350°F and bake 25 minutes. As the popovers are removed from the oven, steam will escape from the hollow centers, which are now ready to receive lots of butter and homemade jelly!

Note: Regular 2-inch muffin tins may also be used and heated a short time, if desired. Also custard cups, especially those made of pottery, are excellent. Place these in a pan so they will be easier to handle.

Nick's Whole Wheat Pancakes

Makes about 12 pancakes

On one visit to Aspen, we walked in for breakfast to find young five-year-old Steven's face happily smeared with beaten egg whites. His daddy was preparing breakfast pancakes that were to become my favorite.

1 cup stone-ground whole wheat flour	1 cup milk
	4 eggs, separated

Combine the flour and milk in a mixing bowl, stirring until smooth. Add the egg yolks and blend well. Beat the egg whites until softly stiff. Fold into the batter. Use ¼ cup batter for each pancake and bake on a hot griddle brushed with a light oil or vegetable shortening. An electric skillet is excellent—set temperature at 340°F, add a little oil, and wipe out any excess.

Try adding 1 cup fresh or frozen blueberries, or 1 cup coarsely chopped pecans, or, my daughter-in-law's favorite, sliced bananas. Serve hot with maple syrup.

F|ur traders and mountain men first opened Colorado, followed by the military and then the prospectors when gold and silver were discovered in 1858. Colorado became a territory in 1861 and was declared the "Centennial State" in 1876. Interstate 70 cuts through the center of the state. Choices of drives southward lead to the Gread Sand Dunes National Monument, Black Canyon of the Gunnison, or to the southwest corner, Mesa Verde National Park, where some of the largest and best preserved cliff dwellings in the world have been discovered.

On this journey, we continued west to Grand Junction on the western slope of the Rocky Mountains and into the small city of Moab, Utah, to stop for two nights. Moab is between two national parks, Arches and Canyonlands, neither of which has been developed. A primitive five-mile hike in Arches to the Double-O arch led us up over enormous boulders and down into scrub brush; slipping and sliding, you are guided by little piles of rocks placed at strategic intervals by park rangers. After a quick look at the Double-O, it was a long five miles back again! Canyonlands doesn't even have little piles of rocks, so we chartered a small plane. The pilot flew us into the canyons for a swift view of ancient cliff dwellings and to see the confluence of the Green and Colorado rivers. This wilderness was the locale for many of Zane Grey's novels and headquarters for Butch Cassidy and assorted other outlaws. This kind of sightseeing makes for a very hearty appetite. We found a hippie café in Moab where freshly stone-ground whole wheat bread was used for sandwiches.

Whole Wheat Raisin Bread

Makes 3 loaves

A bread made completely with whole wheat and packed with raisins. If you like even more raisins, add another cup; or try using currants. Your bread will have a better texture if you use a finely ground whole wheat flour.

3 cups warm water
3 packages active dry
   yeast
½ cup honey
5–6 cups stone-ground
   whole wheat flour

1 cup unprocessed bran
   (miller's bran)
¼ cup melted butter or
   safflower oil
2½ teaspoons salt
4 cups raisins, scalded,
   drained, and dried

In a large mixing bowl combine the water and yeast with ¼ cup of the honey, stirring until dissolved. Beat in 3 cups of flour to make a smooth batter. Cover and let proof 30 minutes.

Stir down the sponge and add the bran, butter, salt, raisins, and remaining honey. Gradually add sufficient flour to form a soft, work-able dough. Turn out on floured surface and knead until smooth and elastic, about 8 minutes. Place in a warm buttered bowl, turning to coat the top. Cover loosely with plastic wrap and a towel and let rise until doubled, about 1 hour.

Punch down the dough and divide into 3 equal portions. Knead each, cover, and let rest 10 minutes. Butter three 8½-inch loaf pans. Form the dough into loaves and place in pans. Cover and let rise to tops of pans, about 30 minutes.

Preheat the oven to 350°F. Bake loaves 35–40 minutes. Let loaves cool on wire racks.

Eastern Utah and Northern Arizona

I n the West you can never drive precisely from point A to point B. Vast spaces with rugged mountains and deserts require detours of hundreds of extra miles to reach a desired destination. But those tremendous areas are worth every mile, for the scenery changes constantly and is over-whelmingly beautiful and dramatic.

South of Moab, a highway leads through desert country to Mexican Hat. Just before this tiny hamlet is a turnoff to Muley Point, recently renamed Goosenecks State Reserve. A narrow, gravel switchback road rises to the top of a mesa with a breathtaking view fifty miles in three directions—to Monument Valley and the Navajo nation, and, straight down, to the San Juan River that snakes in serpentine curves through a deep, narrow canyon. Behind you lie thousands of acres of ranch land and wilderness.

After Mexican Hat, perched on the steep bank of the treacherous San Juan River, the single road leads into the Navajo nation. We spent the night at Kayenta, the entrance to Monument Valley, composed of a Holiday Inn, an Indian school, and a trading post. Eighty percent of the time no one can go into the valley because of the treacherous winds. We continued on the single lane highway that crosses through the Navajo country, where each Indian fam-ily now has a prefabricated house, a Ford or Chevy pickup, and sheep. Many of the older men still wear black hats and long plaited hair. We stopped at a trading post to buy a drink—Coke, that is, for no liquor is allowed on a reser-vation. Indians greeted each other, ignoring us. Bolts of colorful velvets and satins were stacked to the ceiling. A refrigerator case was filled with odd cuts of meat.

We left for a drive of another hundred miles to Tuba City, a small trad-ing center, and found a tiny café. Fry bread was made here. My husband walked over to a soft ice cream machine and pumped swirls of ice cream over his hot bread. I thought the Indians would crack up laughing. Apparently they found fry bread à la mode hilarious. See Navajo Fry Bread (page 381)—and try it!

California

W e spent one night in the elegant old El Tovar on the rim of the Grand Canyon, the twelfth time we have stood here in awe of such unbelievable, majestic beauty. After a quick drive through green forests and into the back door of Flagstaff, we headed west to California. Our destination was the Los Angeles area, to stay in Pasadena and at Malibu Beach.

Excellent breads blossom in this state, where fresh fruits, vegetables, and whole grains are so popular. Within a short time, I met a charming young reporter, Lanny Williams of the *San Pedro News Pilot*. San Pedro has an unusual number of ethnic bakeries clustered together.

Lanny introduced me first to a small Italian grocery store with merchandise stacked so high the old-fashioned cash register was almost hidden. Two older Italian women dressed in that black, black material they always seem to find somewhere chatted volubly in Italian. We explored Mundo's for Mexican breads of every description, a Norwegian baker with Nordic specialties beautifully prepared, and Joseph's, where the croissants were luscious. But I was most intrigued by a Dalmatian bakery that produced a whole wheat French bread as well as many other delicacies. I talked to the baker, a handsome man with fiery black eyes.

The next morning Lanny called to suggest I read the morning *Los Angeles Times*. A bomb had killed two men at midnight in front of the Dalmatian bakery. Actually, the police thought the bomb was intended for the baker. Croatian émigrés blamed the Yugoslavian secret police for the attack. The baker was safe at present, as it was evidently the men who made the bomb who were obliterated. An unpleasant story. I hoped the fiery-eyed baker would be able to go on working in peace.

Pan Dulce

Makes 12 buns

Mexican sweet buns, a popular sweet roll everyone enjoys. Children love them with hot chocolate.

Dough:

1 package active dry yeast
1 cup warm water
¾ cup plus 1 tablespoon
   sugar
5 cups flour

1 teaspoon salt
2 tablespoons butter, at
   room temperature
3 eggs, well beaten

Topping:

1 cup sugar
1 cup vegetable
   shortening or butter, at
   room temperature
¼ teaspoon salt

1 teaspoon cinnamon or
   cocoa
1 egg
⅔ cup sifted flour

Combine the yeast, water, and 1 tablespoon of sugar in a mixing bowl, stirring until dissolved. Beat in 1½ cups of flour and the salt to make a smooth batter. Cover and let proof until light and bubbly, about 45 minutes.

Cream the butter and ¾ cup sugar in bowl of an electric mixer until fluffy. Add the eggs and the sponge, blending well. Stir in sufficient flour to make a soft dough. Knead lightly in the bowl, cover loosely with plastic wrap and a towel, and let rise until doubled, about 1 hour.

To make the topping, cream the sugar, shortening, salt, and cinnamon and beat in the egg. (If desired, cream the sugar and shortening alone, divide the mixture in half, and add cinnamon to one half and cocoa to the other. In this case, use 2 egg yolks instead of 1 whole egg, one yolk for each mixture.) Add the flour and stir until a crumbly mixture is formed. Set aside.

Butter a large baking sheet. Punch down the dough, turn out on a floured surface, and divide into 12 equal portions. Form each into a round bun by cupping with one hand and rotating rapidly. Place buns on the sheet and press down to make flat rolls about 4 inches in diameter. Spread topping on each bun with your hands, pressing down lightly on the dough. Cover and let rise until doubled, about 30 minutes.

Preheat the oven to 400°F. Bake the buns 10–15 minutes. Let cool on racks.

Whole Wheat Tunnel Coffeecake

Makes 1 coffeecake

Californians enjoy innovative whole grain breads and a few sweets as well. This combines both. My students added Tunnel to the name, for sometimes a small one appears in the center, though none of the filling is lost.

Dough:

2 packages active dry
   yeast
¼ cup warm water
4 eggs
1 cup sour cream
½ cup honey

½ teaspoon salt
½ pound (2 sticks) butter
Grated rind of 1 orange
3 cups whole wheat flour
2 cups white flour,
   approximately

Filling:

¼ cup California golden
   raisins
¼ cup chopped candied
   orange peel

½ pound cream cheese, at
   room temperature
½ cup sugar
2 eggs
1 teaspoon orange extract

Topping:

1½ cups orange
   marmalade

2 teaspoons lemon juice
Confectioner's sugar

Combine the yeast and water in a bowl, stirring until dissolved. In a large mixing bowl combine the eggs, sour cream, honey, salt, butter, and grated rind. Add the yeast mixture. Beat in the whole wheat flour to make a smooth batter. Gradually add sufficient white flour to make a soft, workable dough that pulls away from sides of the bowl. Turn out on a floured surface and knead 5–8 minutes, adding small amounts of flour if needed. Place dough in a warm buttered bowl, turning to coat the top. Cover loosely with plastic wrap and a towel and let rise until doubled, about 1½–2 hours.

While the dough is rising, prepare the filling. Combine the raisins and orange peel in a small bowl and set aside. In the small bowl of an electric mixer beat the cream cheese and sugar until smooth and fluffy. Blend in the eggs and orange extract. Beat 1–2 minutes. Set aside.

Punch down the dough, knead lightly, cover, and let rest 10 minutes. Brush a 3-quart ring mold with melted butter. (Neither a Bundt pan nor an angel food cake pan is large enough for this cake.) Sprinkle a large surface with flour. Roll dough into a circle 24–26 inches in diameter. Fold in half and place over one half of the mold. Unfold the dough and carefully fit it into bottom of mold, covering the hole in the center and leaving 1–2 inches of dough hanging over the outer rim of

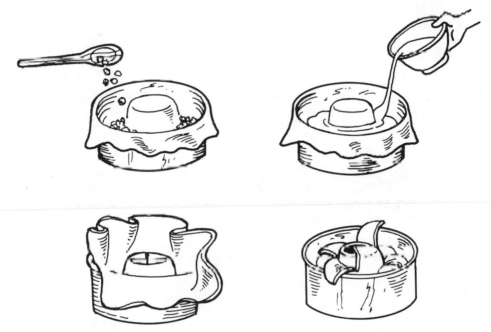

the mold. If you bread the dough, pinch it together firmly. Sprinkle the reserved raisins and orange peel on the bottom. Pour the cheese mixture on top of the fruit. Lift overlapping dough over the filling and begin to pleat the dough, turning the mold as you go. As you fold, the dough will automatically cover both the filling and the hole in the center of the mold. Press the dough over the mold in the center and with a pair of scissors cut a cross in the central hole. Fold each triangle back over the folds of dough. Cover and let rise 30 minutes, or until dough comes to within ¼ inch of the top.

Preheat the oven to 350°F. Bake the coffeecake 40 minutes. Remove from oven and let cool in pan on a wire rack 10 minutes. Turn out on rack to finish cooling. The cake may now be frozen and finished later.

Presentation: Invert the cake on a round serving tray with a shallow rim. The bottom of the cake becomes the top! Combine the marmalade and lemon juice in a saucepan and heat until bubbly, stirring to keep the mixture from burning. Spoon over the cake, letting it run down the sides. Let cool and sieve confectioner's sugar over the top. An elegant addition to a brunch.

Challah

Makes 2 loaves

In one of the San Pedro Jewish bakeries, I became fascinated with a challah spiral, or snail formation, baked to a very dark brown that was unusually beautiful. Here with my own recipe for challah, I also give directions for two braidings that are most charming. The classical braiding of a challah transforms the everyday bread into a special one for the Sabbath.

2 packages active dry
    yeast
2½ cups warm water
½ cup sugar
½ cup light vegetable oil
2 teaspoons salt
3 eggs, beaten

2 cups raisins, scalded,
    drained, and dried
    (optional)
9 cups unbleached white
    flour, approximately
1 large egg beaten with 1
    tablespoon water for
    glaze
Poppy or sesame seeds

Combine yeast and water in a large mixing bowl, stirring until dissolved. Add the sugar, oil, salt, eggs, and raisins, if desired. Beat in 3 cups of flour to make a smooth batter. Gradually add sufficient flour to make a soft, workable dough that pulls away from sides of bowl. Turn out on a lightly floured surface and knead 8–10 minutes, until smooth and satiny. Place the dough in a warm bowl brushed lightly with oil, turning to coat the top. Cover loosely with plastic wrap and a towel and let rise until doubled, about 1–1½ hours.

Punch down the dough, divide in half, knead each piece, cover, and let rest 10 minutes. The dough is now ready to mold into several shapes.

Spiral or Snail Challah: This shape works well when raisins have been added to dough. Roll 1 portion of dough into a long smooth rope 33–36 inches long. Twist loosely into a snail shape and place on a baking sheet sprayed with nonstick vegetable spray. (Nonstick vegetable spray is kosher. Check the can; the new ones will have been marked K.) Repeat directions with second portion of dough. Cover and let rise until doubled, about 1 hour.

Preheat the oven to 350°F. Brush loaves with the glaze, let glaze set 2–3 minutes, and brush a second time. Sprinkle with seeds. Bake 30 minutes. Let loaves cool on wire racks.

If you wish the loaves to be a very dark brown, do not sprinkle with seeds. Bake 20 minutes and brush again with glaze. Seeds may be sprinkled on at this time. Return loaves to oven and bake 10 minutes more.

Classic Four-Strand Braid: Divide 1 portion of dough into 4 equal pieces. Roll the pieces into ropes 13–14 inches long; the ropes should be thick in the center and tapered at the ends. Using the illustrations as a guide, arrange the ropes in the shape of a cross, with the 4 tips overlapping in the center. Pinch these tips together to seal. Lift up the ends of

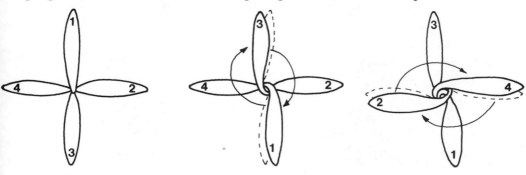

the 2 vertical strands and cross them over each other. Then lift up the second 2 strands—the horizontal ropes—and cross them over. Continue crisscrossing opposite strands of dough until they are all braided. Pinch the ends to seal. Place the loaf on a baking sheet that has been sprayed with nonstick vegetable spray or sprinkled with a little cornmeal.

Classic Eight-Strand Braid: Divide 1 portion of dough into 8 pieces. Roll each into a rope 12–14 inches long. Using the illustrations as a guide, place the 8 ropes side by side and pinch together at the top.

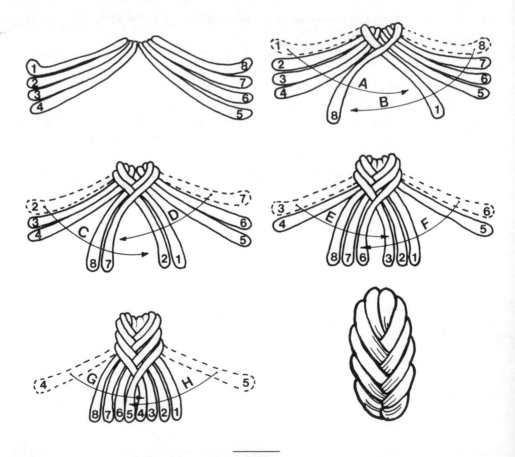

Move 4 strands to the left and 4 strands to the right. Bring the rope on the far left over to the center. Bring the rope on the far right over to the center, covering the first strand braided. Continue bringing each outside rope to the center, alternating sides as you braid. Keep the top pinched together. When you reach the ends of the strands, stretch the ropes to make them long enough to tuck into the braid. (This braiding reminds me of the way young girls braid their hair—quite lovely.) Place the loaf on a baking sheet, as described above.

Cover the braids and let rise 45 minutes.

Preheat the oven to 350°F. Brush the loaves twice with glaze and bake 20 minutes. Brush with glaze again and sprinkle with seeds, if desired. Bake 10–15 minutes more, or until very dark brown. Let cool on racks.

Whole Wheat Baguettes

Makes 3 loaves

From Palm Springs and San Diego, north to San Francisco and Portland, Oregon, the most popular breads are sourdough, pita, croissants, unusual whole grains, and whole wheat baguettes. This whole wheat baguette recipe of mine is dedicated to my Dalmatian baker, who I hope is safe and whole.

2 packages active dry yeast	2 tablespoons light oil
2 cups warm water	3 cups stone-ground whole wheat flour
1½ tablespoons sugar	3½ cups unbleached white flour
2 teaspoons salt	

Combine the yeast, water, and sugar in a large mixing bowl, stirring until dissolved. Add the salt, oil, and whole wheat flour and beat until smooth. If using a heavy-duty mixer, beat 3 minutes. Gradually add sufficient white flour to make a soft, workable dough that pulls away from sides of the bowl. Turn out on a lightly floured surface and knead 10–15 minutes by hand or 8 minutes on a machine. If you tire during the hand-kneading, cover and let dough and your arms rest. Place dough in a warm bowl lightly brushed with oil, turning to coat top. Cover loosely with plastic wrap and a towel and let rise until doubled, about 1 hour.

Punch down the dough and divide into 3 equal portions. Knead each, cover, and let rest 10 minutes. Form into long baguette loaves (page 39). Place loaves on a baking sheet sprinkled with cornmeal. Slash loaves and cover with a light towel. Place pan in a cold oven on middle rack. Place a pan with boiling water on lower rack, close oven door, and let rise 20 minutes. Remove towel. Heat oven to 400°F and bake the loaves 45–50 minutes. Remove loaves and let cool on wire racks.

L eaving Los Angeles, we stopped in Malibu Beach to wander through J. Paul Getty's museum, remembering vividly the time we met Mr. Getty in his English castle. An exquisite lunch had been served to four of us by the kind of impeccable butler who can happen only in England or in the movies! After two nights with a good friend close to the beach at Malibu, we continued north on the Pacific Ocean drive. A stop to take all the tours of the Hearst castle at San Simeon required lunch to restore us. Avoiding the fast-food vending machines, we walked across the highway and down a dirt road to a delightful small restaurant where the following bread would be right at home. I have a nose for good food!

Multi-Grain Walnut Bread

Makes 4 loaves

1 cup rolled oats
2 cups boiling water
2 teaspoons salt
¼ cup light molasses
4 tablespoons butter
2 packages active dry
 yeast

1¼ cups warm water
1 cup rye flour
1 cup whole wheat flour
½ cup toasted wheat germ
⅓ cup unprocessed bran
 (miller's bran)

½ cup stone-ground
  cornmeal
1 cup ground walnuts

6 cups unbleached white
  flour, approximately

Combine oats and boiling water in a mixing bowl, add salt, molasses, and butter, stir thoroughly, and let cool to lukewarm.

In a separate small bowl combine the yeast and warm water, stirring until dissolved. Add to the oatmeal mixture, blending well. Stir in the rye and whole wheat flours, wheat germ, bran, and cornmeal, beating until smooth. Add the walnuts and sufficient white flour to make a soft, workable dough that pulls away from sides of the bowl. Turn out on a lightly floured surface (use white flour) and knead until smooth and resilient, about 8 minutes. Place dough in a warm buttered bowl, turning to coat top. Cover loosely with plastic wrap and a towel and let rise until doubled, about 1½ hours.

Punch down the dough, turn out on lightly floured surface, and divide into 4 portions. Knead each, cover, and let rest 10 minutes. Butter four 8½-inch loaf pans. Form dough into loaves and place in pans. Cover and let rise to tops of pans, about 1 hour.

Preheat the oven to 375°F. Bake the loaves 35–40 minutes. Remove loaves and let cool on wire racks.

A fter a night in the lodge at Big Sur, we drove through Monterey, took the Seventeen Mile Drive around the peninsula, and saw the great artichoke area at the end of the drive. And then it was on to wonderful San Francisco, where we ate no less than fifteen meals! What abundance—the beautiful wines to the north, the ranches that provide excellent lamb, the fresh, fresh fish, and every vegetable that can be grown available from the land to the south.

The French have invaded the United States and established—not forts—but bakeries across our nation. Tiny, excellent bakeries are to be found in the Midwest, Alaska, Hawaii, and all the way back to Boston. But the Italians are not far behind. In bakeries such as Il Fornaio in San Francisco, Italians are introducing fascinating and unusual breads that are completely different from those of the French. This is a good thing, for the San Francisco sourdough breads have slipped a notch and the small, wonderful sourdough bakeries are almost gone. Most of the sourdoughs are now mass produced and taste as though someone had stuck a needle in the loaf to inject it with prefabricated sour flavor.

Before leaving San Francisco, I checked at the main library concerning ethnic groups. The city contains 2,334,928 whites, 142,570 Chinese, 98,394 Filipinos, 4,687 Hawaiians, and 189,742 Mexicans. There are Aleuts, Eskimos,

Guamians, American Indians, and 391,162 blacks. This fascinating mixture in such a small area makes it a unique city that San Franciscans love. Our last trip was just before the cable cars were to be removed for renovation, and bouquets of balloons were tied to the top of each car. Even waiting to catch a ride is an adventure, for usually there is sidewalk entertainment; we were treated to a black female preacher and to a dancer on roller skates. Here are breads that suit the style of this international American city.

San Francisco Sourdough Bread

Makes 2 loaves

Americans are still enamored with the mystique of the San Franciscans' daily bread. Most of us do not have their water, nor the soft, cool atmosphere, nor their wonderful ovens. But the bread is fun to try, and a very good one with a similar texture can be accomplished with a little patience. Use any of the sourdough starters described on pages 183, 185, and 310.

1 cup sourdough starter	2 tablespoons light oil
1½ cups warm water	2 tablespoons sugar
5 cups bread flour, approximately	½ teaspoon baking soda
1 teaspoon salt	Melted butter
	Cornmeal (optional)

Combine the starter, water, and 2 cups of flour in a ceramic mixing bowl and beat until smooth. Cover loosely with plastic wrap and a towel and set aside in a cozy corner 24–48 hours, stirring occasionally. The longer you leave the sponge the more biting a flavor your bread will have. (If you have no ceramic bowls, use glass or plastic, but metal should never be used with sourdough.)

Stir the sponge and add the salt, oil, and sugar. Mix the baking soda with 1 cup of flour and add to the sponge. Gradually add sufficient flour to make a workable dough. Turn out on a lightly floured surface

and knead 10–15 minutes, sprinkling flour on kneading board and hands as needed. Sourdough has a tendency to inhale flour. Place dough in a warm buttered bowl, cover loosely, and let rise until doubled, about 2 hours.

Punch down the dough, turn out on a floured surface, and divide in half. Form into baguettes (page 39), using black metal baguette pans to hold the shape as sourdough tends to spread out, not up. Brush baguette pans with melted butter and sprinkle with cornmeal. Cover loaves and let rise until doubled, about 1–1½ hours.

Preheat the oven to 375°F. Cut long deep slashes in the breads with a sharp razor blade and brush with melted butter. Bake 40–45 minutes.

Or form 2 round loaves and place in buttered 9-inch cake tins sprinkled with cornmeal. Cover and let rise 1–1½ hours, or until doubled. Slash a tick-tack-toe grid on the tops and bake in preheated 375°F oven 35–40 minutes. Or place round loaves directly on a cold baking stone lightly sprinkled with cornmeal. Place in cold oven and turn temperature to 400°F. Brush with butter and bake 1 hour.

Pita Bread

Makes 12 pita loaves

Pita is another bread that has swept the country. We Americans have found this flat bread, which the Arabs have used for centuries in the Middle East, to be most adaptable to our relaxed living style—a whole new idea for making sandwiches. Here is an excellent recipe.

1 package active dry yeast
2 tablespoons honey
2 teaspoons salt
2 cups warm water
½ cup soy flour

2 cups whole wheat flour
1½ cups unbleached
white flour,
approximately

Combine the yeast, honey, salt, and water in a large mixing bowl, stirring until dissolved. Stir in the soy and whole wheat flours to make a smooth batter. Gradually add sufficient white flour to form a workable dough. Turn out on floured surface (use white flour) and knead until smooth and elastic. Round into a ball and place in warm bowl lightly brushed with melted butter, turning to coat the top. Cover loosely with plastic wrap and a towel and let rise until doubled, about 1½ hours.

Punch down the dough and knead lightly. Divide into 12 equal portions. Cup each piece in your hand and rotate rapidly to form a ball. Cover and let rest 15 minutes.

Preheat oven to 450°F and set the baking rack at the lowest level.

Spray a baking sheet with nonstick vegetable spray. Arrange towels in a large container, such as a roaster. Roll out 2 of the balls to about 6 inches in diameter and ¼ inch thick. Place on the sheet and bake for about 6 minutes, or until puffed and brown on the bottom. Do not allow to burn! Place in the prepared roaster and cover with a towel. Repeat directions with remaining portions of dough.

Keep covered, as the pitas dry quickly. They may be cooled and frozen.

An American Pizza

Makes one 12-inch pizza

As we wandered up and down the hills of San Francisco, grabbed a cable car when there was room, I spotted many fascinating pizzas. I found that my youngest son, an intrepid cook, had devised a pizza with Sicilian zip and flavor that is a complete meal for six to eight people.

DOUGH

1 cup warm water
1 package active dry yeast

3 tablespoons olive oil
3 cups flour,
    approximately

Combine the water and yeast in a large mixing bowl, stirring until dissolved. Add the oil and sufficient flour to make a soft dough. Knead on a floured surface 5 minutes or by machine 3 minutes. Place dough in a warm oiled bowl, turning to coat top. Cover loosely with plastic wrap and a towel and let rise until doubled, about 1½ hours.

TOMATO SAUCE

While dough is proofing, prepare the sauce. Use fresh tomatoes if possible, but imported canned plum tomatoes will do very well.

3 tablespoons olive oil
⅔ cup chopped onion
5 cloves garlic, finely
    chopped

Three 14-ounce cans
    imported plum
    tomatoes, or 6 cups
    peeled, seeded, and
    chopped fresh tomatoes
1 tablespoon dried
    orégano
Freshly ground black
    pepper

Pour oil into a large saucepan. Sauté onions over medium heat until limp, about 7–10 minutes. Add the garlic and sauté 1 minute. (Mike insists the garlic be chopped finely by hand—and knife.) If using canned tomatoes, remove seeds, and chop tomatoes. Add tomatoes to the saucepan with orégano and pepper. If using fresh tomatoes, add ½ teaspoon salt. (For canned tomatoes no salt is needed.) Bring mixture to a boil and reduce to a thick sauce, stirring frequently to prevent it from burning. The sauce must boil rapidly about 30 minutes, or until it begins to thicken. Lower heat to prevent scorching and let sauce simmer about 15 minutes, or until thick enough to spread without being absorbed by the dough.

THE FINISHED PIZZA

½ pound grated
  provolone
½ pound grated
  mozzarella
1 pound Italian sausage

Cornmeal
3-ounce can sliced
  mushrooms (optional)
2.2-ounce can sliced black
  olives (optional)

To achieve a really fine pizza, arrange enough bricks to hold the pizza pan (12 inches in diameter) on floor of gas oven or on lowest rack of electric oven and let heat 1 hour at 450°F.

Combine the two cheeses. Remove the sausage skin and crumble the meat into a skillet. Sauté until cooked, about 15 minutes, stirring to break up the larger pieces. Drain on paper towels. By now the tomato sauce should be thick enough to mound on a spoon. If so, you are ready to put all these goodies together.

Roll the dough out slightly larger than the pizza pan. Sprinkle the pan with cornmeal. Pick up dough carefully and place on the pan. Cut off any skirt of dough hanging over edge. Spread tomato sauce over the dough. Cover with the cheeses. Top that with the sausage and, if desired, sprinkle with mushrooms and olives. Place immediately atop the bricks and bake 20 minutes. The pizza should be hot and bubbly. Let cool 5 minutes. Now, that will surely stick to the ribs!

Yosemite, Fresno, and King's Canyon

E asily accessible, Yosemite National Park becomes jammed with vacationers during the summer. Despite elbow to elbow people, the rugged, magnificent beauty created by the glaciers and bordered by the high Sierras is still overwhelming. Gossip in the laundry house had it that ultimately it will be necessary to make a reservation to enter the park. Two days of drives and walks led to large appetites. To my delight we found a small café whose specialty was a long whole wheat sandwich thickly layered with cheeses, a pickled something or other, and thin slices of ham packed into the third level. Purchase was made by the inch. One inch took care of me for hours.

Whole Wheat Bran Sandwich Bread

Makes 1 loaf

To make a loaf that slices easily, use a finely ground whole wheat flour.

¾ cup warm water
3 packages active dry
  yeast
1 cup warm milk
2 eggs, beaten
⅓ cup honey
⅓ cup melted butter
2 tablespoons sugar
1 tablespoon salt

½ cup unprocessed bran
  (miller's bran)
½ cup toasted wheat germ
2 tablespoons cracked
  wheat
2 cups stone-ground
  whole wheat flour
2–3 cups white flour

Combine water and yeast in a mixing bowl, stirring until dissolved. Add the milk, eggs, honey, butter, sugar, salt, bran, wheat germ, and cracked wheat and blend well. Beat in the whole wheat flour to make a smooth batter. Cover and let rest 15 minutes. Gradually add sufficient white flour to make a workable dough. Turn out on a floured surface and knead 10 minutes, or until smooth and elastic. Place in a warm buttered bowl, turning to coat the top. Cover loosely with plastic wrap and a towel and let rise until doubled, about 1 hour.

Punch down the dough, cover, and let rest 10 minutes. Brush a 16 × 4 × 4-inch sandwich bread pan (pullman pan) with melted butter.

Brush bottom of lid with butter. Pat and press the dough into the pan. Push lid on pan and let dough rise to within ½ inch of top, about 45 minutes.

Preheat the oven to 375°F. Bake the loaf 30 minutes. Remove the lid and bake 10 minutes more. Turn loaf out on wire rack to cool.

To use as a sandwich bread, let the bread cool thoroughly and do not use it until the following day; the bread will be easier to slice then.

F lanked by two great national parks, with a background of austere, rough mountains, Fresno is centered in the most fertile valley of our country. On this journey, we crisscrossed the Sacramento and San Joaquin valleys, absorbed in the panorama of field after field of broccoli and cauliflower, fruit orchards, hundreds of nut trees, carrots, beans, melons, every fruit and vegetable imaginable. We stopped to purchase a box of huge freshly picked bing cherries, washed and refrigerated, ready to eat. The gray, sandy soil of the valley, so rich in minerals, touched with the magic wand of water, has been a source of riches greater than Sutter's gold mine. People from an amazing variety of nations have been attracted to the Fresno area, creating a city with an energy that one can sense immediately.

Gazair Saghatelian, born in the back of an Armenian bake shop, immigrated to the New World in 1917 and established a bakery in Fresno. The bakery was continued by the eldest son, and now the youngest daughter, Janet, is president and owner. A variety of breads are produced, but the exciting one is *lavosch*. It is distributed in all fifty states. Several fine restaurants where I have dined served fresh, crisp *lavosch,* using a beautifully folded white napkin as a receptacle. I met Janet after asking a waiter how to find the source of this "cracker bread." By letter, by phone, and in her home, Janet has shown me extraordinary, warm Armenian hospitality.

What great fun it was to watch the preparation of *lavosch* on the huge machine at The Valley Bakery, a young, agile baker jumping all over the thing like a veritable Superman. *Lavosch* is fun to make at home, too, and is without a doubt the best nibbling bread I've encountered.

Armenian Lavosch

Makes 12 loaves

The bread keeps for a long time in plastic bags and can be refreshed quickly in the oven if necessary.

2 packages active dry
  yeast
2½ cups warm water
3 tablespoons sugar
1 teaspoon salt
⅔ cup melted butter
3 cups whole wheat flour

¼ cup toasted wheat germ
3 cups flour,
  approximately
1 egg lightly beaten with
  ¼ cup water for glaze
Sesame seeds

In a large mixing bowl combine the yeast and water, stirring until dissolved. Blend in the sugar, salt, and butter. Beat in the whole wheat flour and wheat germ to make a smooth batter. Gradually add sufficient white flour to make a soft, workable dough that pulls away from sides of the bowl. Turn dough out on a floured surface and knead until smooth and elastic, about 8–10 minutes. Place dough in a warm buttered bowl, turning to coat the top. Cover loosely with plastic wrap and a towel and let rise until doubled, about 1–1½ hours.

Punch down the dough, knead lightly, and divide into 12 equal pieces. Shape each piece into a smooth ball and place 1 inch apart on a lightly floured counter. Cover loosely with plastic wrap and a towel and let rest 35 minutes.

Arrange one baking rack at the bottom level of the oven and another rack at top level. Preheat oven to 400°F.

On a lightly floured surface roll 1 ball of dough at a time into a circle 10–12 inches in diameter. It should be paper thin. Pick up the circle carefully with dough scraper and transfer to an ungreased heavy baking sheet. Do not worry if it does not hold a perfect round shape. Brush the round lightly with the glaze and sprinkle with sesame seeds. Prick surface several times with a fork and place on lowest rack of oven. Bake 4 minutes, and quickly transfer to upper rack for 4–6 minutes more. Total baking time will be 8–10 minutes. When it is done, the bread will be a bit puffed and golden brown.

While the first bread is baking, roll out another piece of dough, so that as you transfer one bread to the top baking rack, you can pop in the next on the bottom rack. If you have 2 ovens, the process will be even faster. Just keep rolling and popping breads into the oven and soon all will be baked. Pile them on a rack to cool and store in plastic bags.

Note: *Lavosch* can be made with all white flour. Eliminate the wheat germ but if possible use an unbleached white flour.

Armenian Pideh

Makes 3 loaves

A fun bread, easy to prepare. It looks like a flying saucer!

2 packages active dry
  yeast
2¼ cups warm water
1 cup instant dry skim
  milk
3 tablespoons sugar
1½ teaspoons salt

3 tablespoons melted
  butter
5–6 cups unbleached
  white flour
1 egg lightly beaten with 1
  tablespoon water for
  glaze
Sesame seeds

Combine the yeast and water in a large mixing bowl, stirring until dissolved. Blend in the dry milk, sugar, salt, and butter. Beat in 2 cups of flour to make a smooth batter. Gradually add sufficient flour to make a soft, workable dough that pulls away from sides of the bowl. Turn dough out on a lightly floured surface and knead until smooth and elastic, about 10 minutes. Place dough in a warm buttered bowl, turning to coat top. Cover loosely with plastic wrap and a towel and let rise until doubled, about 1½ hours.

Punch down the dough, knead lightly, cover, and let rest 10 minutes. Divide dough into 4 portions. Divide 1 portion into 3 pieces, set aside, and cover. Brush 3 baking sheets with melted butter. Pat out one large portion of dough into a 10-inch circle on a baking sheet. If dough pulls back, cover and let it rest 10 minutes. Make a 3-inch hole in center of the circle by pulling dough back with fingers. Form a smooth round bun with 1 small portion of dough and place in the hole. Repeat direc-

tions with 2 remaining portions of dough. Cover each loaf with plastic wrap and refrigerate 2–6 hours. Remove breads and gently pull off plastic wrap. Let stand 15 minutes at room temperature.

Preheat the oven to 350°F. Brush breads with the glaze and sprinkle heavily with sesame seeds. Bake 30 minutes, or until golden brown. Let cool on wire racks or serve hot.

W e crossed the rich valley again, this time going through fields of raisin grapes. The valley has a great similarity to old Armenia. I remember driving through the countryside there, in a rickety bus over dirt roads, through similar rich vineyards. No wonder so many Armenians settled in the Fresno area. Our next drive was over the low rolling foothills of the Sierras into Kings Canyon and Sequoia national parks, which were quieter and more peaceful than Yosemite. I loved the long walks among the giant sequoia trees, the largest of all growing things.

California Health Bread

Makes 4 loaves

Before leaving California, I must include a sprouting bread.

2 packages active dry
   yeast
½ cup warm water
2 cups warm buttermilk
½ cup honey
½ cup safflower oil
¼ cup toasted wheat germ

1 cup unprocessed bran
   (miller's bran)
¼ cup millet flour
1 cup wheat or alfalfa
   sprouts
2 eggs, lightly beaten
7–8 cups unbleached
   white flour

Combine the yeast and water in a large mixing bowl, stirring until dissolved. Blend in the buttermilk, honey, oil, wheat germ, bran, millet flour, sprouts, and eggs. Beat in 3 cups of flour to make a smooth batter. Gradually add sufficient flour to make a soft, workable dough that pulls away from sides of the bowl. Turn out on a lightly floured surface and knead until smooth and resilient, about 8 minutes. Place dough in a warm buttered bowl, turning to coat top. Cover loosely with plastic wrap and a towel and let rise until doubled, about 1–1½ hours.

Punch down the dough and divide into 4 portions. Knead each, cover, and let rest 10 minutes. Butter four 8-inch loaf pans. Shape dough into loaves and place in pans. Cover and let rise to tops of pans, about 1 hour.

Preheat the oven to 375°F. Bake loaves 40 minutes, and let cool on wire racks.

Zion National Park

T o leave California "scenically" presented difficulties. The only way to go over those mountains would be by backpacking, which is not my thing. So from Sequoia we turned back to the fertile valley and drove on to Bakersfield and through a landscape of grungy oil fields. But I grew up among oil fields, so from the high Sierras back to civilization was not too much of a shock. Then the only way to arrive at Zion was through Las Vegas, picking up Interstate 15 and driving through hot desert until we entered Utah.

Zion is the jewel of national parks, a spectacular multicolored gorge with the Virgin River swirling through the center. For three days each year for fifteen years we have walked the paths and driven the high drives behind the park, occasionally getting lost.

Our motel has always been the Driftwood Lodge, with a room facing the red rocks of the park. I met Lois Matthews, a devoted Mormon and a marvelous breadmaker, at the lodge. Through the years, Lois and I have become friends and she has invited me into her portion of the motel kitchen. Her whole wheat bread is a simple one, great for sandwiches. I've named it after the river that created Zion Park.

Virgin Whole Wheat Bread

Makes 3 loaves

1 cup warm water
¼ cup sugar
3 packages active dry
  yeast
2 cups warm milk
½ cup honey

¼ cup melted butter
2½ teaspoons salt
2 eggs, lightly beaten
2 cups white flour
7 cups whole wheat flour,
  approximately

In a small bowl combine the water, sugar, and yeast, stirring until dissolved. In a large mixing bowl combine the milk, honey, butter, salt, and eggs. Add the yeast mixture and white flour and stir until smooth. Gradually add sufficient whole wheat flour to make a soft dough that pulls away from sides of the bowl. Remove dough to a lightly floured surface and knead 8–10 minutes, or until smooth and elastic. Round into a ball and place in a warm buttered bowl, turning to coat the top. Cover loosely with plastic wrap and a towel and let rise until doubled, about 1 hour.

Punch down the dough, turn out on a floured surface, knead lightly, cover, and let rest 10 minutes. Butter three 8½-inch loaf pans. Divide dough into 3 portions, shape into loaves, and place in pans. Cover and let rise until slightly curved over top of pans, about 45 minutes.

Preheat the oven to 375°F. Bake loaves 40 minutes. Let cool on wire racks.

Swirling Virgin

Makes 2 loaves

1 cup packed brown sugar
1 tablespoon cinnamon
Grated rind of 1 orange
⅔ recipe Virgin Whole
   Wheat Bread dough,
   preceding recipe

½ cup golden raisins
   (optional)
Confectioner's Icing made
   with orange juice, page
   45 (optional)

In a small bowl combine the brown sugar, cinnamon, and grated rind.

Butter three 8-inch loaf pans. At the end of the first rising of the bread dough cut off one third and use for a regular 8-inch loaf. Divide the remaining two thirds of the dough in half. Roll one piece into a 14 × 9-inch rectangle. Brush with melted butter to within ½ inch of edges and sprinkle with half the sugar mixture. If you like, scatter with half the raisins. Roll up from narrow end, jelly-roll style. Seal seam and ends. Place seam side down in a loaf pan. Repeat directions for a second loaf. Cover and let rise until slightly curved over top of pans, about 45 minutes.

Preheat the oven to 375°F. Bake loaves 35–40 minutes. The loaves may be frosted with Confectioner's Icing.

Crossing eastern Utah on a four-lane highway with no services for over one hundred miles, we reentered Colorado. Dropping south to Durango and across a portion of New Mexico, we arrived back home in Oklahoma. Each journey is so different, but all of them bring unusual breads and delightful new friends. The national parks on this journey are memorable, but I think also of the vast agricultural system that would be so unbelievable to the Armenian farmers in their faraway country by the Caspian Sea.

THE
ORIGINAL THIRTEEN

MILEAGE—9,435 MILES

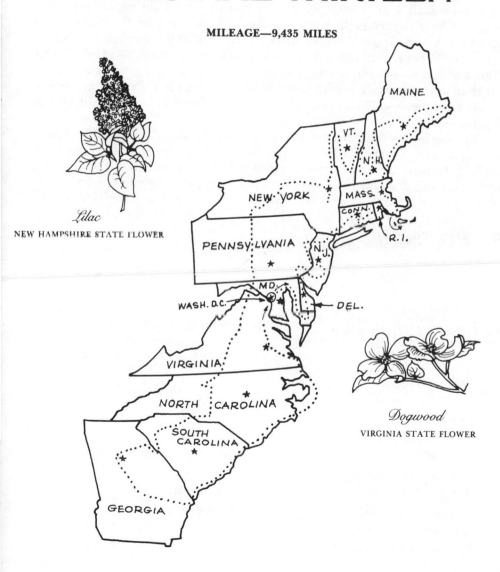

Lilac

NEW HAMPSHIRE STATE FLOWER

Dogwood

VIRGINIA STATE FLOWER

Washington, D.C.

T here is no lovelier spot in our nation to begin an American historical journey then Washington, D.C., our exciting capital, the center of the western world, where one is free to explore the White House, view the Declaration of Independence, enjoy exquisitely planted gardens, and dine in choice restaurants of almost any nationality.

Never shall I forget the comparison with the Russian capital on a day when our long dreary flight from Moscow, aboard an "Aeroflop" plane had landed on American soil at Dulles Airport. Our group immediately jumped to its feet and cheered at top voice. The curving drive through green, lushly planted Virginia, with the famous monuments in the distance, was more beautiful than any countryside we had seen in the Soviet Union. Besides, at the end of our drive there would be two beautiful granddaughters waiting with warm hugs for us.

But back to breads. A most intriguing Middle Eastern coffeecake recipe was given to me by my Washington daughter-in-law, who was born in Beirut. In 1895, Annie's father was carried out of a Turkish province of the Ottoman Empire during a massacre of the Armenians. Eighty years later, Annie was forced to carry her ten-month-old daughter out of war-torn Beirut. History hardly changes. More happily, neither do some of the world's enchanting breads. Let's take a look.

Annie's Middle Eastern Coffeecake

Makes 2 coffeecakes

Dough:
2 packages active dry
   yeast
¼ cup warm water
4 eggs
1 cup warm milk
2 tablespoons sugar
2 tablespoons melted
   butter

½ teaspoon salt
5 cups unbleached white
   flour
Melted butter
2 cups grated Gruyère

Topping:
2 cups sugar
1 cup water

Combine the yeast and water in a small bowl, stirring until dissolved. Whisk the eggs in a large mixing bowl. Add the milk, sugar, butter, and salt and blend well. Add the yeast mixture and beat in 2 cups of flour to make a smooth batter. Gradually add sufficient flour to make a soft, workable dough. Turn out on a lightly floured surface and knead until smooth and satiny, about 8 minutes. Round into a ball and place dough in a warm buttered bowl, turning to coat the top. Cover lightly with plastic wrap and a towel and let rise until doubled, about 1 hour.

Punch down the dough and turn out on a lightly floured surface. Roll into a large rectangle. Brush with melted butter to within ½ inch of the edges. Fold the dough over in thirds and pinch the edges together. Cover and let rest 15 minutes. Butter two 11- or 12-inch deep pie dishes or cake tins. (Deep glass pie plates work very well.) Divide dough into 4 equal portions. Roll 1 portion into an 11-inch circle and place in one of the pans. Sprinkle with 1 cup of the cheese. Roll out a second portion of dough into an 11-inch circle and cover the filled circle. Repeat directions with remaining portions of dough. Cover and let rise 1 hour.

Preheat the oven to 350°F. Bake the cakes until golden brown, about 35 minutes. Prepare the syrup topping while the cake is baking. Combine the sugar and water in a saucepan, bring to a boil, and stir until dissolved. Let boil 1 minute. Remove cakes from the oven and, if you plan to serve immediately, pour the boiling syrup over them. Allow 15 minutes for the syrup to soak in and serve warm.

The cakes taste best served fresh from the oven smothered in the hot syrup. If the cakes have cooled, reheat them 15–20 minutes in a preheated 350°F oven, add the syrup, and serve. Do not freeze the cakes.

Manaeesh

Makes 3 loaves

*I became enamored of this bread during a journey
to Beirut for Christmas of 1974. Helen Yeni-
Komshian (Annie's mother), born in Turkey, fled
with her family to Cypress during the Armenian
holocaust of 1915 and married an Armenian
doctor. She lived in Beirut for fifty years until she
was forced to leave during the third year of
Lebanon's civil war, abandoning two beautiful
homes, and came to live in the United States.
Helen is an extraordinarily fine cook and has
helped me with several ideas. This is an exotic,
pungent bread, most delicious eaten hot from the
oven, although it is quite good at room
temperature.*

Dough:

2 cups warm water

1 package active dry yeast

⅓ cup instant nonfat dry
   milk

⅓ cup light oil

2 tablespoons sugar

1 teaspoon salt

5–6 cups flour

Topping:

¾ cup *zataar,* following
   recipe

Olive oil

Sesame seeds

Combine the water and yeast in a large mixing bowl, stirring until
dissolved. Blend in the dry milk, oil (do not use olive oil), sugar, and
salt. Beat in 3 cups of flour until batter is smooth. Gradually add sufficient flour to make a soft, workable dough that pulls away from sides of
the bowl. Turn out on a lightly floured surface and knead until smooth
and silky, about 5 minutes. Oil your hands if dough tends to be sticky
while kneading. Round into a ball and place the dough in a warm bowl
brushed lightly with oil. Cover loosely with plastic wrap and a towel and
let rise until doubled, about 1 hour.

Punch down the dough, knead lightly, cover, and let rest 10 minutes. Lightly brush three 12 × 7-inch baking pans with oil. Divide dough into 3 equal portions. Roll1 piece into a 12 × 7-inch rectangle. Place in pan, pour 1 tablespoon olive oil over the dough, and spread with fingertips. Press oil into the dough until it is completely absorbed. Repeat directions with remaining portions of dough. Cover and let rise until doubled, about 30 minutes.

Mix ¾ cup *zataar* with sufficient olive oil to make a spreadable paste. Add the oil, slowly mixing with a fork. Taste and add sesame seeds for flavor. I love the flavor of sesame and usually add 3–4 tablespoons. Spread one third of this mixture over each pan of dough. Again, press and spread mixture with fingertips until the dough is drenched with *zataar*. Place the *manaeesh* in a cold oven and turn the temperature to 400°F. Bake until breads are puffed and lightly browned, about 25 minutes.

Zataar

Makes about 2 cups zataar

Zataar *is a mixture of thyme, sumac, and sesame seeds. Zataar may be made as described here or purchased at import stores. Sumac is a Middle Eastern spice also available at import stores (see Sources of Supply).*

1 cup dried leaf thyme	½ cup toasted sesame
½ cup sumac	seeds

Combine the three ingredients in a glass or plastic container. Sesame seeds counteract the bitterness of thyme; taste and add more seeds if desired. *Zataar* must be refrigerated.

Ka'ak (SESAME BREAD RINGS)

Makes 6 rings

Annie frequently purchases ka'ak rings for my enjoyment. Not many cities have Middle Eastern bakeries, so I've devised a recipe for six delicious small rings covered with sesame seeds.

2 packages active dry
    yeast
½ cup warm water
1 cup warm milk
½ cup melted butter
3 eggs, beaten
1 teaspoon salt
2 teaspoons sugar

1 teaspoon *mahleb*
    (see **Note**)
5–6 cups flour
1 cup sesame seeds,
    approximately
1 egg beaten with 1
    tablespoon water for
    glaze

Combine the yeast and water in a small bowl, stirring until dissolved. In a large mixing bowl combine the milk, butter, eggs, salt, sugar, and *mahleb*. Add the yeast mixture and 2 cups of flour, beating until the batter is smooth. Gradually add sufficient flour to make a soft, workable dough that pulls away from sides of the bowl. Turn dough out on a lightly floured surface and knead 5–8 minutes, until smooth and elastic. Round into a ball and place in a warm buttered bowl, turning to coat the top. Cover loosely with plastic wrap and a towel and let rise until doubled, about 1 hour.

Butter 2 large baking sheets. Punch down the dough, knead lightly, and divide into 6 equal portions. Roll 1 portion into a rope 19–20 inches long. Join the ends together, pinch to seal, and shape into a ring. Sprinkle sesame seeds on a plate or pan and dip the ring into the seeds, pressing lightly to cover bottom. Place seed side down on a baking sheet. Repeat directions with remaining portions of dough. Brush tops of rings with the glaze and sprinkle heavily with sesame seeds. Let rise 20 minutes.

Preheat the oven to 350°F. Bake the rings 25 minutes. For a crisper crust, spray the rings with water twice while baking. Remove and let cool on wire racks.

Note: *Mahleb* is a tiny, hard cherry seed that, when used crushed, gives bread a delicious flavor and aroma. Available in import stores (see Sources of Supply).

I was asked to leave my coat and purse with my husband, given a sharpened pencil and a pad of paper, and the gate to the rare books library at the Library of Congress was opened for me. Several books I requested were placed in front of me, and I felt as though I were on hallowed ground. It was an exhilarating experience to open the first American cookbook. The title: *American Cookery, by Amelia Simmons, an American Orphan,* pubished in Troy, New York, 1808. Miss Simmons penned this explanation, that the book was written for the modern American woman who was disadvantaged and had no training, especially orphans. She related a short history of cooking, with this final point: "When man past [sic] from vegetable to animal diet and fed on Flesh, Fowls, and Fish, then seasonings grew necessary." Salt was the first seasoning, and she gave a quote from the Bible to prove the point. In the back of the book were fold-out pages with table diagrams for parties of all seasons.

From Washington, D.C., and the labyrinths of the Library of Congress our journey into the thirteen original states began. Appointments dictated a northern route first.

Maryland

The bravery of Maryland troops during the Revolution gave the state its nickname, the Old Line State. Despite the small size of Maryland, the topography ranges from mountains in the extreme west, flowing into a plateau, to flatlands around Chesapeake Bay and along the Atlantic coast. Maryland declared independence July 3, 1776.

Most breads in Maryland are Southern and it was here I felt certain I would find beaten biscuits, but those I discovered in Kentucky. Fortunately I made contact with Marie Gunby, born in Delaware and married to a doctor who had been raised in a Maryland Methodist parsonage. That gave the good doctor and me much in common. The doctor's mother, an adroit minister's wife, was a fine cook and Marie inherited many of her recipes. Marie conjectures that the following recipe is seventy-five years old.

Maryland Hot Rolls

Makes about 60 rolls

¼ pound (1 stick) plus 2 tablespoons butter
½ cup sugar
1½ teaspoons salt
1 cup hot riced or mashed potatoes

1½ cups hot potato water, page 184
2 packages active dry yeast
¼ cup warm water
2 eggs, lightly beaten
7–8 cups flour

Combine butter, sugar, and salt in a large mixing bowl. Add the potatoes and potato water, stirring well to blend. Let cool to lukewarm.

Combine the yeast and warm water in a small bowl, stirring until dissolved, and add to the potato mixture with the eggs. Stir in 3 cups of flour to make a smooth batter. Gradually add sufficient flour to make a soft dough that pulls away from sides of the bowl. Potatoes do make a sticky dough, but be careful not to add too much flour; the less flour, the more tender the rolls. Turn dough out on a lightly floured surface and knead until smooth and satiny, about 10 minutes. Place dough in a warm buttered bowl, turning to coat top. Cover loosely with plastic wrap and a towel and let rise until doubled, about 1–1½ hours. If there is time, punch down the dough, knead in the bowl, re-cover, and let rise a second time, about 45 minutes.

The dough makes exceptionally fine cloverleaf rolls, but any molding may be used from pages 42–44. Cover the rolls and let rise until puffy, about 1 hour.

Preheat the oven to 350°F. Brush the rolls with melted butter, if desired, and bake 12 to 15 minutes. Serve hot.

Note: The rolls may be molded, placed on baking sheets, covered with plastic wrap, and frozen. Remove 3 hours before serving to allow time for the rolls to thaw and rise. Proceed as directed. Marie also makes cinnamon rolls with this dough, using Cinnamon Sugar (page 46), nuts, and raisins. They can be rolled, cut, and placed in muffin tins sprinkled with brown sugar for a simple sticky bun.

Spoon Bread

Serves 6–8 people

In 1913 "Mom" Gunby purchased a spoon bread recipe from the Star Villa Hotel in Cape May, New Jersey, for the total sum of $5.00. Marie mailed the recipe to me, plus another one that had a penciled notation, "delicious." I tried both. The $5.00 recipe separated into custard on top and a thick heavy layer of cornmeal at the bottom; the directions merely stated after the ingredients, "Mix and cook in a moderate oven." I threw the whole thing out and tried the "delicious" one. An absolutely perfect cornmeal soufflé!

2 cups milk	2 teaspoons sugar
1 cup cornmeal	1 teaspoon salt
1 tablespoon butter	4 eggs, separated

Preheat the oven to 350°F.

In a large saucepan scald the milk. Slowly stir in the cornmeal, beating constantly with a whisk. Continue stirring over medium heat until the mixture thickens. Remove from heat and add the butter, sugar, and salt, stirring until dissolved. Transfer the mixture to a mixing bowl. Often there is some residue of cornmeal on the bottom of the pot; scrape that into the bowl and whisk until smooth. Add the egg yolks, one at a time, beating after each addition. Beat the egg whites until softly stiff. Fold into the cornmeal mixture carefully and thoroughly. Pour mixture into an unbuttered 2½ quart soufflé dish. Place dish in a shallow pan containing 1 inch of hot water and bake about 30 minutes. Serve immediately with lots of butter and strawberry preserves. If there is any left, reheat the next morning and top with a poached egg.

Delaware

W hen we left Washington, D.C., on our journey through the Original Thirteen, the cherry blossoms were in full bloom—surely a good omen. We headed north to Baltimore for a quick survey of the enormous, busy shopping arcade built on the bay side, south to Annapolis for a drive around the grounds of our handsome Naval Academy, and across the bay into Delaware.

Delaware may be small in size, but it has three counties and boasts an exciting, rich history that began in 1609. The Dutch and Swedish settlers fussed at each other for some years, with the Dutch finally assuming control, and then they were overcome by the British. Towns and river were named and renamed. William Penn landed at New Castle on October 27, 1682. Mr. Penn and Lord Baltimore of Maryland disputed a long time over who owned what. Baltimore claimed all of Delaware as well as Maryland—politicians were greedy even back in those days. But Delaware prevailed and was the first state to announce its independence on July 2, 1776. And, because the area had long had problems with pirates, there were trained soldiers and officers available here to General Washington. A day's walk around New Castle, completely renovated, provides a marvelous sense of what an eighteenth-century city was like. George Washington attended a wedding here, but apparently didn't have time to sleep, although the old boy seems to have slept just about everywhere else.

Covered bridges, a steam train, beautiful beaches, handsome farms, an occasional black Amish buggy on the roads, a legal center in the capitol at Dover, lovely fresh fish and crab, some of the finest museums filled with Americana, Delaware has all of these.

Whole Wheat Currant Muffins

Makes 12 muffins

In 1785 Oliver Evans invented an automatic flour-milling machine that revolutionized the industry and opened Delaware ports for the shipping of tons of flour. We found a restaurant tucked on a side street in Dover that served a delicious whole grain muffin. This is my version.

1 cup whole wheat flour
1 cup white flour
2 teaspoons baking
  powder
½ teaspoon salt
2 tablespoons honey

1 cup milk
1 egg
¼ cup melted butter
½ cup currants
½ cup chopped pecans

Preheat the oven to 400°F. Butter twelve 2-inch muffin tins.

Combine the dry ingredients in a mixing bowl, stirring to blend. In a separate bowl blend the honey, milk, egg, and butter. Stir the milk mixture all at once into the dry ingredients and combine until just wet. Fold in the currants and pecans. Fill the muffin tins two thirds full. Bake 20–25 minutes. Serve warm.

Delaware Twelfth Night Coffeecake

Makes 1 coffeecake

Although there is no bread indigenous just to Delaware, a recipe was sent to me by a young lady in the state's tourist bureau. I found that I could easily turn it into a quick coffeecake with a secret nut hidden in it for good luck.

3 cups sifted flour
2 teaspoons baking
  powder
1 teaspoon baking soda
½ teaspoon salt
1 teaspoon nutmeg
1 tablespoon ginger
½ teaspoon mace
½ pound (2 sticks) butter,
  at room temperature

2 cups sugar
3 eggs, at room
  temperature
1 cup sour cream
1 whole nut (pecan,
  walnut, or almond)
Confectioner's Icing made
  with vanilla or lemon
  juice, page 45
Decorating candies

Preheat the oven to 350°F. Generously butter a Bundt pan.

Sift the flour, baking powder, soda, salt, nutmeg, ginger, and mace and set aside. In bowl of an electric mixer cream the butter and sugar until light and fluffy. Beat in the eggs one at a time. Add the dry ingredients alternately with the sour cream, beating well after each addition, and beat until the batter is creamy. With a rubber spatula stir in the nut. Pour batter into the pan and bake 45 minutes, or until cake tests done. Remove from oven and turn out on a wire rack to cool. Frost when ready to serve with Confectioner's Icing. Sprinkle with decorating candies.

New Jersey

E ven though New Jersey is the most urbanized state in the Union, it still is known as the Garden State. A charming and informative letter from James Justin, a specialist in soil and crops, gave me an interesting summary. The acreage in northeastern New Jersey, adjoining New York and close to Philadelphia, is all houses, industry, and asphalt. Between these two metropolitan areas is the "garden" of fruits and vegetables. Everything from the New Jersey Lily (asparagus) to *bok choy* grows in the rich soil in the center of the state. Seventy different vegetables are cultivated. The largest single crop is soybeans, followed by field corn, wheat, oats, barley, and rye. Farmers have learned to produce top yields in their small area through the assistance of the New Jersey Agricultural Experiment Station.

Besides all this wealth of agriculture, such a small state has a beautiful shore lined with resorts, a mountainous area in the north, and tremendous highways providing fast transportation in every direction. Let's look into several recipes of great variety.

Goat Cheese Dilly Bread

Makes 2 loaves

New Jersey is still the leader in dairy goats, and no buts about that! This fact comes from Mary Anne McGovern of the New Jersey Department of Agriculture. Goat's milk is nature's naturally homogenized milk, easy to digest. The bread recipe is excellent.

1 package active dry yeast	1 teaspoon salt
¼ cup warm water	2 teaspoons dill seeds
1 cup soft fresh goat cheese	1 tablespoon grated onion
2 tablespoons sugar	1 egg
1 tablespoon melted butter	2½ cups flour
	¼ teaspoon baking soda

Combine the yeast and water in a small bowl, stirring until dissolved. Set aside. Gently heat the goat cheese in a saucepan until lukewarm. In a large mixing bowl combine the cheese, sugar, butter, salt, dill seeds, onion, and egg and beat until well blended. Add the yeast mixture, flour, and baking soda and mix thoroughly, either with the flat beater of a heavy-duty mixer or by hand with a rubber spatula. This is the only kneading, so beat hard and thoroughly. Place the dough in a warm buttered bowl, cover loosely with plastic wrap and a towel, and let rise until doubled, about 1 hour.

Divide dough in half and place in 2 buttered 1-quart soufflé dishes. Cover and let rise 40 minutes.

Preheat the oven to 350°F. Bake the loaves 40–45 minutes. Turn breads out on a wire rack to cool.

D uring the summer season, leave the six-lane super highways of New Jersey for quiet country lanes to enjoy the roadside markets stacked with handsome vegetables and boxes and boxes of fresh blueberries. New Jersey is one of the leaders in production of that seductive little berry and third in production of cranberries. What could be more American than blueberries and cranberries (and a cranberry bog called Hog Wallow!)? In New Jersey markets there will always be perfect zucchini. Mary Anne McGovern has created an unusual, healthful zucchini bread made with whole wheat flour.

Zucchini Whole Wheat Bread

Makes 2 loaves

1½ cups packed brown
  sugar
5 cups whole wheat flour
1 teaspoon salt
1 teaspoon cinnamon
1 teaspoon baking soda
½ cup honey
2 eggs, beaten

1 cup light oil
2 teaspoons vanilla
3 cups shredded raw
  zucchini
⅓ cup chopped nuts
½ cup raisins, scalded,
  drained, and dried

Preheat the oven to 350°F. Generously butter two 9-inch loaf pans. Combine the sugar, flour, salt, cinnamon, and baking soda and mix well. In a separate bowl blend the honey, eggs, oil, vanilla, zucchini, nuts, and raisins. Add the dry ingredients to the liquid ingredients and beat well; this will be a thick batter. Pour into loaf pans and bake 1 hour. Test with a cake tester for doneness. Let breads remain in pans 10 minutes when removed from the oven. Turn out on wire racks to cool.

Blueberry Cornsticks

Makes 18 cornsticks or 48 miniature muffins

And now for New Jersey blueberries! Jean Byrne, the wife of a former New Jersey governor and mother of a large family, is especially interested in health through good nutrition. Jean particularly enjoys using fruits, vegetables, and whole grains. I was sent her menu and recipes for a complete family Thanksgiving dinner and in it found blueberry cornsticks. In testing the cornsticks, I found that the batter makes superb miniature muffins. Two of my grandsons popped them away in one bite!

1 cup yellow or white
  cornmeal
1 cup sifted flour
3 tablespoons sugar
4 teaspoons baking
  powder
½ teaspoon salt
1 egg

¼ cup melted butter
1 cup milk
1 tablespoon flour mixed
  with 1 tablespoon sugar
½–1 cup fresh
  blueberries, washed,
  drained, and left to dry,
  or frozen blueberries

Preheat the oven to 425°F. Brush 2 cornstick pans with melted shortening or butter and heat 5 minutes in the oven.

Sift together the cornmeal, flour, sugar, baking powder, and salt into a mixing bowl. Combine the egg, butter, and milk. Add all at once to the cornmeal mixture and beat until smooth, about 1 minute. Combine the flour and sugar mixture with the blueberries, shaking the fruit until lightly coated. Gently fold the blueberries into the batter until well distributed. Pour the batter into the heated pans and bake 15–20 minutes, or until lightly golden.

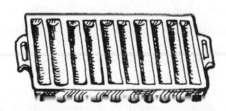

Miniature Blueberry Muffins: Brush two 24-mold muffin tins with melted butter, distribute the batter and bake at the same temperature 20 minutes. Serve hot.

At the suggestion of Mary Anne McGovern at the Department of Agriculture, I contacted Myrtle Ruch of the North American Blueberry Council in Marmora, New Jersey. Within forty-eight hours my desk was innundated with information and recipes. This I loved, as there are always blueberries in my freezer because this fruit native to North America is so versatile. The Indians were well aware of this when they offered dried berries to the Pilgrims. I tried a number of the recipes and have chosen two old classics with a new twist. Through the graciousness of the North American Blueberry Council, here are an outstanding muffin and a Sally Lunn.

Blueberry Streusel Muffins

Makes 12 muffins

*One of the finest blueberry muffins I've made—
like eating a piece of cake.*

Streusel-Walnut Topping:

2 tablespoons butter or
   margarine

2 tablespoons brown
   sugar
¼ teaspoon cinnamon
¼ cup chopped walnuts

Batter:

1½ cups flour
2 teaspoons baking
   powder
½ teaspoon salt
4 tablespoons butter or
   margarine, at room
   temperature

½ cup sugar
1 egg
1 teaspoon vanilla
½ cup milk
1½ cups fresh or frozen
   blueberries

To make the topping, melt the butter in a small saucepan. Remove from heat, stir in the sugar, cinnamon, and walnuts, and set aside.

Preheat the oven to 400°F. Generously butter twelve 2½-inch muffin tins.

Sift the flour, baking powder, and salt on a sheet of wax paper. In a large mixing bowl cream the butter and sugar until fluffy. Beat in the egg and vanilla. Stir in the flour mixture alternately with the milk. Fold in the blueberries until well distributed. (Frozen blueberries may be used without defrosting.) Spoon batter into muffin tins and sprinkle with topping. Bake about 20 minutes, or until tops spring back when lightly pressed with fingertip. Serve hot or let cool on a wire rack.

Blueberry Sally Lunn

Makes 1 loaf

Dough:

3½ cups flour, approximately

⅓ cup sugar

1 teaspoon salt

1 package active dry yeast

½ cup milk

½ cup water

¼ pound (1 stick) butter or margarine

3 eggs, at room temperature

Filling:

½ cup sugar

1½ teaspoons cinnamon

⅛ teaspoon nutmeg

1 tablespoon flour

1 cup fresh or frozen blueberries

In a mixing bowl thoroughly mix 1½ cups flour, sugar, salt, and yeast. Combine the milk, water, and butter in a saucepan. Heat slowly until very warm, about 120°F. Butter need not melt completely. Gradually add to dry ingredients and beat 2 minutes at medium speed in an electric mixer, using the flat beater, scraping down the sides of the bowl occasionally. Add the eggs and 1 cup of flour. Beat mixture at high speed 2 minutes. This will be the only kneading, so beat for the full amount of time. If preparation is made by hand, use a rubber spatula or your hand as explained on page 32. Stir in enough additional flour to make a stiff batter. Cover with a towel and let rise until doubled, about 1¼ hours.

To make the filling combine the sugar, cinnamon, nutmeg, and flour in a small bowl.

Stir down the batter and beat 30 seconds. Brush a Bundt pan thoroughly with melted butter or margarine. Spread half the dough in the pan. Sprinkle the sugar mixture over the dough and sprinkle the blueberries over the sugar. Spread remaining dough over the blueberries, cover, and let rise until doubled, about 1 hour.

Preheat the oven to 325°F. Bake the bread 45–50 minutes. Let cool in pan 5 minutes and turn out on a wire rack or a serving tray. Sally Lunn may be served hot, at room temperature, or saved for the following day.

Pennsylvania

I 've enjoyed exploring the many regions of this beautiful state, its rich farm lands, the mountains, historic inns, even the highly industrialized cities have all fascinated me. Entering from New Jersey, we were soon in mushroom country and then arrived in a unique section of America, the Pennsylvania Dutch country centered around Lancaster. The Pennsylvania Dutch, who are of Germanic origin, have given much to American cuisine with their "plain and fancy cooking."

Arriving in the late evening at the edge of Lancaster, we checked into a Holiday Inn. The following morning, I opened the door, intending to get something from our car, but snow whipping wildly through the air took my breath away. We waded to breakfast and discovered the motel had a Chinese restaurant with red bridge and gurgling brook. I had no intention of being caught in a blizzard with a Chinese cook of uncertain talent. Hastily I rummaged through my Pennsylvania file and came up with the answer—The Cameron Estates Inn. We called (9 A.M.) and to my great relief we were told to come now and were assured that a fire would be burning in our room. Hastily we threw everything into the car, hoping to make the fifteen-mile drive before snow stopped traffic. (Snow stops traffic in Oklahoma; we have no way to get rid of the stuff.) We had the great good fortune to be caught for the duration of a most unusual spring blizzard in this lovely historic inn amidst acres of Pennsylvania farm land. A king-size canopied bed, lovely armchairs, a big fireplace; all this charm was managed by a pretty young innkeeper whose husband is a superb chef.

Cameron Estates Inn could have captured me for weeks, but the snow stopped and we ventured out for a dinner at Betty and Abe Groff's, which was as delicious as I had anticipated. The return drive was hazardous, for strong winds had whipped snow across the one-lane country road. Half a mile from the inn, a car was stalled, almost covered with snow. My husband gunned our motor and made four attempts through a corn field before he got around the car. With snow spraying in every direction, I wondered if I should remove my shoes or keep them on for landing at the end of that last quarter mile. We plowed our way through and arrived intact. Snow flies into Oklahoma one day and out the next. This was an EXPERIENCE!

Old Horseshoe Road

T he roads became negotiable and Erica Shirk, a dedicated Mennonite, took us under her wing for a day of wandering through Pennsylvania Dutch country. We drove to a neat, modest home on Old Horseshoe Road in Leola where Anna and Christ Beiler, Old Order Amish, have added on a one-room bakery. Their daughters, Annie and Lydia, are the bakers, and, when they discovered I had written a book on bread, they asked questions about the freshness of their yeast. Soon I was behind the counter and rapidly tested the yeast to find it excellent. The two girls wore long black dresses with white aprons and caps. Their prayer caps were different from Erica's in that two long slender ribbons were attached to them to be worn either loose or gently tied. Soon we were all relaxed, discussing problems of breadmaking and becoming good friends.

Pennsylvania Dutch Sticky Buns

Makes 26 buns

A marvelous combination of Mennonite dough from Erica Shirk with a "sticky" topping from Lydia and Annie Beiler.

Dough:

1 cup warm water
2 packages active dry
   yeast
1 cup warm milk
½ cup melted butter or
   vegetable shortening

½ cup sugar
1½ teaspoons salt
2 eggs, beaten
7 cups flour,
   approximately

Topping:

1 cup packed brown sugar
2 tablespoons cornstarch
2 cups water
1 tablespoon butter
1 teaspoon vanilla

¼ teaspoon salt
1 cup chopped pecans
1 cup raisins, scalded,
   drained, and dried
   (optional)

Filling:

1½ cups packed brown
    sugar

4 teaspoons cinnamon

melted butter

Combine the water and yeast in a large mixing bowl, stirring until dissolved. Add the milk, butter, sugar, salt, and eggs and blend well. Beat in 3 cups of flour to make a smooth batter. Gradually add sufficient flour to form a soft, workable dough. Turn the dough out on a lightly floured surface and knead until smooth and elastic, about 8 minutes. Round into a ball and place in a warm buttered bowl, turning to coat the top. Cover loosely with plastic wrap and a towel and let rise until doubled, about 1 hour.

While the dough is rising, prepare the topping and the filling.

To make the topping, mix together the sugar and cornstarch in a saucepan. Add the water, butter, vanilla, and salt. Bring to a boil, stirring constantly. Let the mixture cool until it becomes the consistency of thin gravy (Annie's instructions!). Add more water or cornstarch if necessary. Divide the syrup between two 13 × 9-inch baking pans at least 1 inch deep. Sprinkle with pecans and raisins, if desired, and set aside.

To make the filling, blend the sugar and cinnamon in a small mixing bowl.

Punch down the dough, divide in half, and knead each piece lightly. Cover and let rest 10 minutes. Roll both halves into 13 × 9-inch rectangles. Brush with melted butter to within ½ inch of edges and sprinkle with the filling. Roll up fairly tightly (makes more swirls) from the long side, jelly-roll style. Cut into 1-inch slices and place cut side up in the pans on top of the syrup. Cover and let rise 30 minutes, or until the rolls are light and touch each other.

Preheat the oven to 350°F. Bake the rolls about 30 minutes. Remove from oven and turn out on racks set over aluminum foil to catch the drippings, or invert the pans directly onto a serving tray. Serve hot or at room temperature.

T he Mennonites and the Amish have common roots. In 1525, they began a separation from Roman Catholicism. They were nicknamed "Anabaptists" for their belief in being rebaptized as a confession of faith. They returned to the simplicity of the early church. Both devoutly believe in separation of church and state, and many were burned at the stake for that devotion. The Amish separated from the Mennonites because of their belief in a stricter code of everyday life.

It is charming to see a young Amish couple in a "courting buggy," which must be open, with, as a rule, the young girl wearing straight pins down the front of her dress. Driving through the fertile farm country, we saw a farmer driving ten handsome horses. The swift, magnificent buggy horses are purchased in Tennessee and Kentucky. To think that in those states the horses were rejects! Both the Mennonites and Amish, and also the Hutterites in the north, accept no welfare and no social security. When help is needed, such as to rebuild a barn, the whole community takes a day off. The men construct a handsome building and the women provide food for everyone.

Fastnachts

Makes about 40 doughnuts

If fastnachts are not eaten on Shrove Tuesday, the crops will suffer the following year. For the Pennsylvania Dutch, this square doughnut is made only for this special day just before Lent. There are many beliefs: that it should be square, that it should be a triangle, there must be a split in the middle. They love to dunk their fastnachts into hot coffee sometimes laden with molasses. The Lancaster Central Library has given me fascinating material on the folklore of Shrove Tuesday, not only for Pennsylvania but also New Orleans and Mobile. This excellent recipe is best if allowed to proof overnight.

2 cups milk, scalded
1 package active dry yeast
2 tablespoons warm water
¾ cup sugar
7 cups flour,
    approximately
¼ cup melted butter
½ teaspoon salt

2 eggs, beaten
½ teaspoon nutmeg
Oil or vegetable
    shortening for deep
    frying
Confectioner's or
    granulated sugar

Let the milk cool to lukewarm. In a mixing bowl combine the yeast and water, stirring until dissolved. Add the milk, 1 teaspoon of the sugar, and 3 cups of flour. Beat until batter is smooth. Cover loosely with plastic wrap and a towel and let stand overnight at room temperature.

The following morning, stir down the sponge. Add the remaining sugar, butter, salt, eggs, and nutmeg, blending well. Add sufficient flour to make a soft dough. Cover and let rise until doubled, about 1 hour.

On a floured surface roll out the dough ½ inch thick. Cut into squares, triangles, or use a doughnut cutter. Slash a slit in the squares or triangles. Cover and let rise 30 minutes. Heat 3 inches of oil or vegetable shortening to 370°F. Fry the *fastnachts* a few at a time—my deep fryer can hold 3—for 3–4 minutes on each side, or until golden. Drain on paper towels and roll in granulated sugar or sieve confectioner's sugar over them.

Pennsylvania Whole Wheat Bread

Makes 3 loaves

Urbane Peachy, a Mennonite and friend of my son Peter, made it possible for me to go to the home of Gertrude Habeggar, formerly a baker by trade but now retired. Each week this tiny woman kneads enough dough by hand to make six loaves of bread. I can barely handle a recipe for four! Hers is an excellent basic bread for sandwiches, to toast, and to enjoy warm from the oven with butter and homemade jelly as Gertrude served it to me.

2 packages active dry yeast
½ cup warm water
2½ cups water
2 tablespoons sugar
½ pound (2 sticks) butter

¼ cup honey
2 teaspoons salt
½ cup bran cereal
2 cups whole wheat flour
5½ cups white flour, approximately

Combine the yeast and warm water in a bowl, stirring until dissolved, and set aside. In a saucepan combine 2½ cups water, sugar, butter, honey, salt, and bran and heat to 115°F. Transfer to a large mixing bowl and stir to blend well. Add the yeast mixture. Beat in the whole wheat flour until smooth. Gradually add sufficient white flour to make a soft, workable dough that pulls away from sides of the bowl. Turn out on a floured surface and knead 8–10 minutes, until smooth and elastic. Round into a ball and place in a warm buttered bowl, turning to coat the top. Cover loosely with plastic wrap and a towel and let rise until doubled, about 1 hour and 10 minutes.

Punch down the dough and turn out on a lightly floured surface. Divide into 3 equal portions. Knead each, cover, and let rest 10 minutes. Butter three 8-inch loaf pans. Form the dough into loaves and place in pans. Cover and let rise until just curved over tops of pans, about 1 hour.

Preheat the oven to 425°F. Pat tops of loaves with cool water and bake 10 minutes. Reduce temperature to 350°F and bake 30 minutes more, or until golden brown. Let loaves cool on wire racks.

Philadelphia

L eaving the Pennsylvania Dutch area was difficult, for we had escaped the clutches of a motel Chinese cook, enjoyed being snow-bound, made new friends, met the gentle Mennonites and Amish, and obtained lovely recipes. But in all my eastern journeys, I had missed Philadelphia, and so we turned the car in the general direction of the City of Independence. Soon we were in steeply rolling country and joined the Pennsylvania Turnpike (in sad state of repair and the attendant shortchanged me at the toll booth). We checked in at a hotel on the north edge of the city and soon we were walking the inner city with a do-it-yourself-guide. I must admit to a thrill and an actual lump in my throat when I touched the "crack" in the Liberty Bell. Originally built in London and brought to the Colonies, it was rung for religious freedom. A crack appeared and was widened to improve the tone, but this made another hairline crack. The crack really opened after twenty-four hours straight of ringing for political freedom. Apparently there was a fault in the bell from the beginning, so perhaps the British had known what they were doing.

After a turtle soup luncheon at Bookbinder's Café by the bay, we went to an old, elegant section of the city to find a brownstone house that has been transformed into a private museum. A special showing of very old cookbooks, primarily from England, was displayed on the second floor. I relished seeing, even through glass, these lovely, elaborately printed books. The house is a joy to walk through. It was originally owned by two brothers who collected priceless artifacts all over the world.

Philadelphia is famous for its contributions to our history and for some simpler things. One of the best to be handed down through generations is its own sticky bun.

Philadelphia Cinnamon Sticky Buns

Makes about 30 buns

Dough:
1 package active dry yeast
1/4 cup warm water
1 cup warm milk
5 cups flour,
   approximately

1/2 cup sugar
1/4 cup melted butter
1/2 teaspoon salt
2 egg yolks

Filling:
Melted butter
7 tablespoons brown
   sugar

2 teaspoons cinnamon
1/2 cup raisins, scalded,
   drained, and dried

Topping:
1 pound brown sugar

3/4 cup Karo syrup

Combine the yeast and water in a small bowl, stirring until dissolved, and set aside. Pour milk into a large mixing bowl, add the yeast mixture and 2 cups of flour, and beat until smooth. Cover and let proof until light and bubbly, about 30 minutes.

Stir down the sponge and add the sugar, butter, salt, and egg yolks. Blend well and gradually add sufficient flour to make a very soft dough. Turn out on a lightly floured surface and knead 10 minutes. Round into a ball and place in a warm buttered bowl, turning to coat the top.

Cover loosely with plastic wrap and a towel and let rise until doubled, about 1½ hours.

Turn dough out on a floured surface and divide in half. Roll both pieces into 15 × 10-inch rectangles about ¼ inch thick. Brush with melted butter to within ½ inch of edges. To make the filling, combine the brown sugar, cinnamon, and raisins. Sprinkle half the filling over each rectangle. Roll up from the long side, jelly-roll style, and cut into slices 1¼–1½ inches thick. Brush a 14 × 10 × 2-inch baking pan with melted butter. Sprinkle thickly with 1 pound brown sugar and pour the syrup over the sugar. The pan must be covered completely with sugar. Place the rolls cut side up close together on the topping. Brush with melted butter and let rise 30 minutes.

Preheat the oven to 325°F. Bake the rolls 45 minutes. Turn them out on a tray brushed lightly with melted butter. Serve warm.

Bethlehem and Nazareth

A t the insistence of a Tulsa friend, we rose early on Easter morning and drove to Bethlehem to attend the special service at the First Moravian Church. By 9:30 we were settled in a pew and listened to the choir and a magnificent small orchestra practice in the balcony, and then enjoyed watching the congregation assemble. I had already fallen in love with the sanctuary, so simple in design and painted an off-white. The loft behind the pulpit had been filled with thick green ferns and palms, with a single dramatic spray of white lilies placed in the center. Many hymns and anthems were sung by the congregation and choir, accompanied by the orchestra. We listened with emotion as a perfect horn soared above the singing. Never have I seen or heard a lovelier Easter service.

Through a little research, I found Gwyneth Peischl of Nazareth, devoted to her church and to the Moravian Historical Society and a fine cook. Here is a portion of one of her letters to me: "From the founding of the Unitas Fratrum in March 1457 in Bohemia, through the leadership of John Amos Comenius and Count Ludwig von Zinzendorf, to the arrival of the first Moravian settlers in Nazareth in 1740 until today, the Moravian Church has been filled with the spirit of brotherly love and continued the outreach of our missions around the world. We are called Moravians because most of those in the early group who took refuge with Count Zinzendorf to escape religious persecution were from Moravia (a part of Czechoslovakia)."

It became a custom in the early Moravian church to have a simple meal before Holy Communion. This was revived in 1727 as the love feast, a service of worship, a sharing of a small "meal" in brotherly love in the Lord's house. It is now served by women in white and men in black, the women serving the raised sugar bun, the men serving coffee. The tradition is kept for Christmas Eve, Epiphany, Lent, Easter, and special commemorative festivals.

Love Feast Buns

Makes about 24 buns

¼ pound (1 stick) butter, at room temperature

1 cup sugar

1 cup warm mashed or riced potatoes (unseasoned and dry)

½ cup warm milk

2 eggs, beaten

¼ teaspoon nutmeg

½ teaspoon mace

2 packages active dry yeast

½ cup warm water

2 tablespoons grated orange rind

2 teaspoons grated lemon rind

2 tablespoons orange juice

1 teaspoon lemon juice

6 cups flour, approximately

Cream the butter and sugar together in a large mixing bowl. Add potatoes and mix well. Blend in the milk, eggs, nutmeg, and mace. In a separate bowl combine the yeast and water, stirring until dissolved. Add to the potato mixture. Stir in the grated rinds and juices. Beat in 3 cups of flour until batter is smooth. Gradually add sufficient flour to make a soft, workable dough. Turn out on a lightly floured surface and knead 5 minutes, or until smooth. Round into a ball and place in a warm buttered bowl, turning to coat the top. Cover loosely with plastic wrap and a towel and let rise until doubled, about 1 hour.

Punch down the dough, knead lightly, cover, and let rest 15 minutes. Butter 2 large baking sheets. The dough may be sticky; flour hands well and break or cut off 3-ounce pieces of dough, about ½ cup. Form into balls. Place on baking sheets ½–1 inch apart. Slash the tops to release air, cover, and let rise until doubled, about 45 minutes.

Preheat the oven to 350°F. Bake the buns 20–25 minutes. Remove and let cool on wire racks. The buns may be made smaller, if desired, but this is the classic size.

Moravian Sugar Cake

Makes 4 coffeecakes

Gwyneth tells me that this recipe dates back to the early 1700's, from a Marian Mease to Mary Sensenbach Mease to Marcie Freitag Sensenbach. A few adjustments have been made at Gwyneth's suggestion to turn this into one of the finest sugar cakes I've tasted. The topping belongs to Gwyneth, the cake to the 1700's.

Dough:

2 cups sugar
1 cup warm mashed or
   riced potatoes
½ cup melted butter
½ cup melted lard or
   vegetable shortening
2 eggs, beaten
1 teaspoon salt

1 cup warm milk
2 packages active dry
   yeast
1 cup warm potato water,
   page 184
6 cups flour,
   approximately

Topping:

1 pound brown sugar
1 tablespoon flour
2 tablespoons melted
   butter

Cold butter, cut into small
   nuggets
Cinnamon

Combine the sugar and potatoes in a large mixing bowl, stirring thoroughly. Add the butter, lard, eggs, salt, and milk. Combine the yeast and potato water in a separate bowl, stirring until dissolved. Add to the potato mixture. Beat in sufficient flour to "stiffen" the mixture—this is not a kneaded dough; it is a stiff batter. Cover loosely with plastic wrap and a towel and let rise until doubled, about 1 hour.

Butter four 8- or 9-inch round cake tins. Divide the dough among the tins, spreading it evenly. Cover with a light cloth and let rise until doubled, about 1 hour.

Preheat the oven to 350°F. To make the topping, combine the

sugar, flour, and butter. Sprinkle topping over the cakes. At about 1-inch intervals punch a deep hole into the dough with a chopstick or a knife and push a lima-bean-sized nugget of cold butter into each hole. Sprinkle the cakes lightly with cinnamon. Bake 20–30 minutes. Serve warm or at room temperature. The cakes freeze well.

Connecticut

A multitude of interstate highways circled us around the city of New York and into Connecticut. Leaving the fast highways, within minutes we were on winding country roads driving by huge outcroppings of rock, stone fences, beautiful trees, and houses and trees decorated with Easter eggs and ribbons for Easter. Our destination was Washington Depot, the home of Audrey and Jim Patterson.

My first encounter with Jim was in Lebanon, where he was an international banker in Beirut. The second time we met, Jim and Audrey were in Chester, Vermont. They had renounced the big city and purchased an inn. Jim became an innkeeper and Audrey, who possesses tremendous energy, an outstanding chef. Their third move was to Washington Depot to buy The Pantry, where Audrey increased her fame in the world of New England cuisine. Audrey made me taste many delicious tidbits and I fell in love with her light, airy brioche. Audrey and Jim, as a result of their success with The Pantry, have been featured in *Gourmet* magazine in an article about their area of Connecticut.

Audrey's Brioche

Makes 2 brioches

2 packages active dry
  yeast
⅔ cup warm water
⅓ cup sugar
5 cups flour,
  approximately
7½ tablespoons butter, at
  room temperature

6 large eggs, lightly
  beaten
1½ teaspoons grated
  lemon rind
1¼ teaspoons salt
1 egg plus 1 tablespoon
  milk for glaze

In the large mixing bowl of a heavy-duty mixer combine the yeast, water, and 1 tablespoon of the sugar, stirring until dissolved. Add the remaining sugar, 4½ cups, flour, butter, eggs, lemon rind, and salt. Using the flat beater, blend mixture at low speed until well combined. Stop the machine when necessary and scrape down the sides. When mixture is well combined, increase speed to moderate and beat the dough, adding more flour, 1 tablespoon at a time, until batter becomes glossy and pulls away from sides of the bowl. Increase the speed to high and knead the dough 3 minutes, or until smooth and silky. Scrape down the sides with a spatula, cover lightly with plastic wrap and a towel, and let proof 2 hours, or until triple in bulk. Punch down the dough, cover securely, and refrigerate overnight.

The following day, punch down the dough, divide in half, and cut off one third from each portion. Brush two 6-cup brioche tins with melted butter. Form the larger portions of dough into balls and place in pans. Make a deep indentation in the center of each ball. Mold smaller portions into pear shapes and press into the indentations with the tapered ends set into the dough. Let the brioches rise, uncovered, until tripled, about 1½ hours.

Preheat the oven to 450°F. Place the baking rack in the center of the oven. Brush the brioches gently with the glaze. Hold scissors vertically and snip around the bases of the topknots just where they fit into the larger mounds of dough. Bake the brioches on center rack of the oven 20 minutes. Reduce heat to 375°F and bake 12–15 minutes more. Remove from oven and let brioches cool in the tins on wire racks 15 minutes. Turn the breads out to cool. Serve sliced with butter and homemade jam.

I n northern Connecticut, we entered Caprilands, a fairyland of herbs created by a most unusual woman, Adelma Grenier Simmons. For thirty-five years she has grown herbs of all the seasons for mild medicines, for seasoning foods, for dyes, teas, wreaths, decorations, and the magic of her Caprilands festivals. A luncheon with Adelma Simmons is an experience. The short lecture on herbs before luncheon is both entertaining and informative. The luncheon is served in a very old house decorated everywhere with herbs of all descriptions. We were seated family style, enjoying visitors from many different states. Occasionally, during the serving of many courses, her gentle voice came over a loudspeaker, explaining the lore of the herb in the particular dish we were eating. Another building was stacked to the attic with colorful herbs, ending in a riot of rich purple lavender. In yet another small building, all the herb books she has written are for sale. I received a charming note from this great lady, explaining her many activities and wishing me the best of luck. And now for a bread with one of my favorite herbs.

Rosemary Bread

Makes 2 loaves

7–8 cups flour
2 packages active dry
  yeast
3 tablespoons sugar
2½ teaspoons salt
1 teaspoon dried
  rosemary, crushed in a
  mortar and pestle

1 teaspoon dried thyme
1 cup plus 1 tablespoon
  milk
1 cup water
4 tablespoons butter
2 eggs, lightly beaten
⅓ cup sesame seeds

In a large bowl of an electric mixer combine 2 cups of flour, yeast, sugar, salt, rosemary, and thyme. In a saucepan combine 1 cup milk, water, and butter and heat until warm, about 115°F. Add to the flour mixture and beat at medium speed 2 minutes, using the flat beater of a heavy-duty mixer. After the eggs are beaten remove 2 tablespoons and set aside. Add remaining eggs to the batter. Stir in 2 cups of flour and beat 2 minutes at medium speed.

Change to a dough hook or use a rubber spatula and gradually add sufficient flour to make a soft dough. Turn out on a lightly floured surface and knead until smooth and elastic, about 5 minutes. Round into a ball and place in a warm buttered bowl, turning to coat the top. Cover loosely with plastic wrap and a towel and let rise until doubled, about 1 hour.

Punch down the dough, divide in half, and knead each piece lightly. Cover and let rest 10 minutes. Butter 2 baking sheets. Divide each piece of dough into 3 equal portions. Roll each portion into a 12-inch rope. Place 3 ropes on a baking sheet and pinch edges together at one end. Braid and plump—do not stretch. The second portion may be braided as described or formed into a loaf and placed in a buttered 8-inch loaf pan. Cover and let rise 40 minutes.

Preheat the oven to 375°F. Combine the 2 tablespoons of egg with 1 tablespoon of milk and beat well. Brush braids with the glaze and sprinkle with sesame seeds. Bake 40 minutes. Let cool on racks. A beautiful aromatic bread!

Not many houses are visible when you follow the country roads of Connecticut, I felt as though Nathan Hale surely would stalk out of these Colonial woods at any moment. Then we drove into Hartford, the capital, and that dream burst! I immediately lost our route and we ended up in a dismal ghetto, feeling most conspicuous. We finally managed to extricate ourselves and found the Italian section, where we were aiming for lunch at a superb restaurant, Carbonne's. And there I found an outstanding bread. Eric Weiss, our waiter, immediately saw my dismay when I learned that the special Carbonne bread was not served at lunch. Soon a plate of hot bread, dripping with butter, was offered. We consumed every bit of it and begged for the recipe. When I returned home, the recipe was waiting for me. Now, there are a thoughtful waiter and superb restaurant!

Carbonne's Potato Sourdough Starter

Makes about 2 quarts starter

POTATO WATER

1 pound potatoes, peeled and cubed	1½ quarts water

Place the potatoes and water in a saucepan and cook until tender, about 30 minutes. Put potatoes and water through a sieve or a ricer into a clean bowl. Let cool to 110°F.

STARTER

1½ quarts warm potato water	2 teaspoons salt
4 cups bread flour	1 package active dry yeast
	2 tablespoons sugar

Mix potato water with remaining ingredients in a glass or ceramic bowl (not metal). Cover with a clean, damp towel and set aside in a cozy spot 2 days. The mixture will ferment during that time and then stop. Stir occasionally. Place in a 2-quart glass or ceramic jar and top with a loose lid. Refrigerate. When three quarters of the mixture has been used, make up a batch exactly as described and add to the remaining starter.

Carbonne's Sourdough Bread

Makes 4 regular or 5 smaller loaves

3½ cups warm water
1 package active dry yeast
1 tablespoon corn syrup
1 cup instant nonfat dry
    milk
¼ cup melted unsalted
    butter

2½ teaspoons salt
1½ cups sourdough
    starter, preceding
    recipe
11 cups flour,
    approximately
Melted butter (optional)

Combine the water, yeast, and corn syrup in a large mixing bowl, stirring until dissolved. Blend in the dry milk, butter, and salt. Add the starter and 4 cups of flour and beat until smooth, either by hand or in a heavy-duty mixer. Gradually add sufficient flour to make a soft dough that pulls away from sides of the bowl. Turn the dough out on a floured surface and knead 10–15 minutes. If you tire, cover the dough and rest 5 minutes. Round into a ball and place dough in a warm buttered crockery or plastic bowl, turning to coat the top. Do not use a metal bowl. Cover loosely with plastic wrap and a towel and let rise until doubled, about 1½ hours.

Punch down the dough, turn out on a floured surface, and knead 1–2 minutes. Divide into 4 or 5 portions. If you own baguette bread molds, they will be excellent to use. Or the dough may be shaped into regular loaves and placed in 5 buttered 8½-inch loaf pans. Cover and let rise until dough reaches tops of pans, about 45 minutes.

Preheat the oven to 375°F. Slash the breads and bake about 40 minutes. If you desire a more golden crust, brush tops of loaves with melted butter before baking. A beautifully textured bread.

Note: This recipe can be cut in half easily. If you do so, however, retain the entire package of yeast.

W e drove to New Haven and wandered once again over the grounds of Yale University, where two of our sons took degrees. Then to Mystic, the picturesque re-created whaling village, for a Sunday brunch that ended with a bowl of hot Indian pudding topped with ice cream. No New England journey is complete without a taste of that spicy Colonial dessert!

Rhode Island

E ven though Rhode Island is the tiniest state in the Union (Alaska is 475 times as large!), her history has been exciting. Massachusetts refugees came here to establish their religious independence and piracy plagued her shore and shipping. Providence and Newport are two completely contrasting cities only a few miles apart. The capital city is old but also highly industrialized, while the bay city of Newport is filled with rows of Colonial homes, each with a date posted on the front. Magnificent, later estates along the Newport shoreline remind us of great wealth past and are being redesigned into condominiums. We stayed in a charming inn close to the center of Newport and enjoyed one of the finest meals of our journey at The Black Pearl. Rhode Island is a lovely mini-state of yachts, forests, architecture, long Indian names—and of factories where flashy commercial jewelry is made.

In Bristol we met Helen Tessler, the strong, impressive president of The Society for the Propagation of the Jonnycake Tradition. And it is spelled JONNY. With Helen's guidance, I was to learn why there is such an organization. The three of us drove across the bay to Wakefield to meet Diane Smith.

Diane's brother, Dr. Robert C. Wakefield, an agronomist at the University of Rhode Island, joined us to explain the botanical intricacies of flint corn. He belongs to the third generation of scientists who have carried on the work of refining the local strain of flint corn inherited from the Narragansett Indians. An ear of flint corn becomes a pale golden color, almost translucent when it is ripe. The rock-hard kernels are set in eight straight rows on the cob, which is rounded at the tip. Flint corn is grown each year at the university, and seeds for planting are available free to anyone interested in growing real flint corn.

I could have listened to more, but Diane was ready to cook jonnycakes. A good-natured argument began between Diane and Helen over the proper thickness of a jonnycake. It seems that South County and Newport do not agree. Since this argument has been going on longer than Oklahoma has been a state, I did not feel at all qualified to join in the conversation. But I certainly was willing to try the fabled jonnycakes. Diane grows her own golden flint corn and ground some in her mill especially for our jonnycakes.

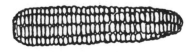

Diane Smith's Jonnycakes

Makes about 12 jonnycakes

Diane's jonnycakes are on the thin side (Diane lives in South County) with crisp edges. I loved every bite, smothered with butter and maple syrup.

1 cup flint cornmeal (see Sources of Supply, page 483)
1 tablespoon sugar
½ teaspoon salt

1 cup boiling water
2–3 tablespoons milk
1 tablespoon corn oil
2–3 tablespoons butter

Combine cornmeal, sugar, and salt in a mixing bowl. Stir in the water, taking care that the water wets all the meal. Add enough milk to make a batter that drops readily off the spoon. Place the oil and butter on a hot griddle. (Diane used an electric skillet, which seemed the perfect instrument.) When the oil and butter are piping hot, drop in 1 large tablespoon per cake. An electric skillet will hold this recipe. Cook at a moderate temperature about 6 minutes on each side, or until crisp and brown. Serve hot.

The oldest corn scientists have discovered was found under Mexico City and was estimated to be sixty-thousand years old. It has been accepted that corn originated in the jungles of Guatemala and the Yucatán. Slowly the use of corn moved to North America. Roger Williams, the patron saint of Rhode Island, found parched corn a "readie very wholesome food." He described how the men who traveled in early Colonial times carried small baskets on their backs, filled with little corn cakes. The Pilgrims were taught by the Indians to plant corn using fish for fertilizer. Diane maintains that tradition. She does use a modern hoe rather than the old Indian clam-shell hoe but she places one herring and five kernels of corn to a hill—one for the blackbird, one for the crow, one for the cutworm, and two to grow. The soil and atmosphere of Rhode Island are the only conditions that can actually produce the real flint corn. Plant the seeds in another state, and the corn soon becomes like any other corn.

Rhode Island jonnycake is unique. Originally "journey cake," which was abbreviated to "jo'rny cake" and pronounced "jarney cake," its final spelling changed to fit its New England sound—JONNYCAKE. Not even an act of

Congress can force an "H" into jonnycake. All this lovely information was compiled by the late W. L. Watson and given to me by the Jonnycake Society.

Jonnycake-in-the-Oven

Makes 1 corn bread

1 cup Rhode Island
   cornmeal (see Sources
   of Supply, page 483)
1 cup flour
2 teaspoons baking
   powder

½ teaspoon salt
⅓ cup sugar
2 eggs
1 cup milk
3 tablespoons melted
   butter

Preheat the oven to 425°F. Generously butter an 8-inch square baking pan.

In a mixing bowl combine the cornmeal, flour, baking powder, salt, and sugar, blending well. In a separate bowl beat the eggs and add the milk and butter. Pour the milk mixture all at once into the cornmeal mixture, stirring briskly to make a smooth batter. Pour into the baking pan and bake about 25 minutes.

Blueberry Jonnycake-in-the-Oven

Makes 1 corn bread

An old cook in Rhode Island emphatically stated that anything she "spized" was jonnycake without any blueberries. That's easily remedied. I have fallen in love with Rhode Island cornmeal and have made Jonnycake-in-the-Oven several times. Finally I added 1 cup of blueberries, lightly floured, to the batter and baked at 425°F for 25–30 minutes. We love it for breakfast.

New England Brown Bread

Makes 1 loaf

*Diane Smith shared this recipe from the files of
her mother-in-law, Elizabeth Barber Smith, born
in Hope Valley, Town of Richmond, Rhode
Island, in 1902.*

1 cup flour	¾ cup molasses
1 cup yellow cornmeal	2 cups buttermilk
1 cup whole wheat flour	½ cup raisins, scalded,
2 teaspoons baking soda	drained, and dried
1 teaspoon salt	(optional)

Combine the dry ingredients in a mixing bowl. Add the molasses
and buttermilk, stirring until smooth, and stir in raisins, if desired.
Brush a 1 pound coffee can with melted vegetable shortening, or use
one of the ceramic pots now available. Cover with foil and an elastic
band to hold it in place. Place on a rack set in a pan over 1 inch of
water, cover, and steam 2 hours. Check water occasionally so that it does
not evaporate. Uncover and let cool in the can on a wire rack.

Martha's Vineyard

W e left Helen Tessler and Diane Smith reluctantly to speed across the
state and a corner of Massachusetts in time to catch a 6:30 ferry at
Falmouth for "the Vineyard." As the Thirteen Colonies grew to become a
country, the whaling industry was at its height on Cape Cod, Nantucket, and
Martha's Vineyard. Wherever there were whaling ports, including the islands
of Hawaii, the Portuguese settled, for they were expert navigators and wandered all over the world. I knew that somewhere on this island there would be
a good Portuguese bread.

A reservation in Edgartown at The Charlotte Inn placed us in a suite on
the second floor of the carriage house, a charming vantage point. The day
after we settled in, our guides, my eldest daughter-in-law's parents, drove us
over the entire island, including to a faraway hill with a view of Jackie O's
compound on a lovely small inlet leading to the open sea. I loved the Edgartown streets lined with captain's houses, each posted with a name. Through a

local newspaper I located Edgartown's librarian, Jean M. Andrews, and hit the jackpot. Not only is Jean a native of Martha's Vineyard, she is also a fine cook. She was delighted to share her recipe file. The Bolo which follows is pronounced "Bull."

Bolo

Makes about 12–14 pancakes

Jean explained these are Portuguese cornmeal pancakes to be eaten with fish or chowder

1 cup cornmeal (see **Note**)	½ cup sugar
1½ cups boiling water	¼ cup plus 2–3
1½ cups flour	tablespoons milk
4 teaspoons baking	1 egg, beaten
powder	2 tablespoons melted
1½ teaspoons salt	butter

Gradually whisk the cornmeal into the water, stirring constantly to prevent lumps. Boil gently 5 minutes, stirring constantly. Transfer to a mixing bowl and let cool a few minutes. Sift the dry ingredients into the cornmeal mixture, beat in ¼ cup milk and the egg, and stir in the butter. The consistency should be that of a thick pancake batter. If too thick, add more milk to correct the consistency.

Heat a griddle or skillet, brush with butter, and drop in ⅓ cup batter to make 3-inch pancakes. (However, you can make the cakes any size desired.) Bake on one side over moderate heat until the pancake is light golden brown and flip to the other side. Serve hot.

Note: I found that if I used a stone-ground cornmeal, 1 cup of milk was needed, but with a regular commercial cornmeal only a small addition of milk was necessary.

Malasadas

Makes about 40 doughnuts

*A Portuguese doughnut great for dunking in
coffee or tea.*

1 cup milk, scalded
½ cup sugar
1 teaspoon salt
¼ pound (1 stick) butter
1 package active dry yeast

¼ cup warm water
2 eggs, beaten
5–6 cups flour
Oil for deep frying
Confectioner's sugar

In a large mixing bowl combine the milk, sugar, salt, and butter. Stir to dissolve the sugar. Melt the butter and let cool to lukewarm. Combine the yeast and water in a separate bowl, stirring until dissolved. Add to the milk mixture. Blend in the eggs and 2 cups of flour. Gradually add sufficient flour to make a very soft dough. Turn out on a lightly floured surface and knead about 5 minutes. Round into a ball and place in a warm buttered bowl, turning to coat the top. Cover loosely with plastic wrap and a towel. Let rise until doubled, about 2 hours.

Heat 3 inches of oil in deep fat fryer to 370°F. Break off—do not cut—chunks of dough and stretch slightly. These pieces can be made any size you like. I broke off chunks about the size of a Ping-Pong ball (¼ cup) that made about 2 or 3 bites. Remember, when that dough hits the hot oil, it will immediately expand. Stretch the pieces slightly and drop into the hot oil. Let brown on one side, turn, and brown on the other side. Drain on paper towels. Sieve confectioner's sugar over the doughnuts.

Martha's Vineyard
Portuguese Sweet Bread

Makes 3 loaves or 36 small rolls

1¾ cups milk, scalded
6 tablespoons butter
1 tablespoon vegetable
    shortening
2 cups sugar
1 teaspoon salt

3 large eggs
2 packages active dry
    yeast
¼ cup warm water
7–8 cups flour

Pour the milk into a large mixing bowl and add the butter, shortening, sugar, and salt. Stir to blend and cool to lukewarm. Beat the eggs and add to the milk mixture. Combine the yeast and water in a separate bowl, stirring until dissolved. Add to the milk mixture. Beat in 3 cups of flour to make a smooth batter. Gradually add sufficient flour to form a soft dough. Round into a ball and place dough in a warm buttered bowl, turning to coat the top. Cover loosely with plastic wrap and a towel. Let rise overnight in a cozy spot.

Turn the dough out on a floured surface and knead until smooth and elastic, about 8 minutes. Cover and let rest 15 minutes. Butter 3 baking sheets. Divide dough into 3 portions and form into smooth, round loaves. Place on sheets, cover, and let rise about 45 minutes.

Preheat the oven to 350°F. Bake loaves 35–40 minutes. Remove breads to cool on wire racks.

The dough is also excellent made into rolls, which should be served hot. Cut off pieces the size of a small egg and roll rapidly on a flat surface to form smooth buns. Place on buttered baking sheets and let rise until doubled, about 45 minutes. Bake in a preheated 350°F oven 20 minutes, or until golden.

I suggest that one-third of the dough be made into about a dozen rolls and the remainder into 2 loaves.

Cranberry Bread

Makes 1 large or 3 miniature loaves

Jean Andrews pointed out that I must have a cranberry bread from the Vineyard. Gratefully I accepted her recipe and found it to be one of the best I've tasted.

2 cups sifted flour
1 cup sugar
1½ teaspoons baking powder
½ teaspoon baking soda
1 teaspoon salt
¼ cup vegetable shortening or butter

¾ cup fresh orange juice
Grated rind of 1 large orange
1 egg, lightly beaten
½ cup coarsely chopped nuts (pecans or walnuts)
1 cup chopped raw or frozen cranberries

Preheat the oven to 350°F. Spray a 9-inch loaf pan with nonstick vegetable spray and brush with melted butter.

Into a mixing bowl sift the flour, sugar, baking powder, soda, and salt. Cut in the shortening with a pastry cutter. Or put the dry mixture and the butter into a food processor, pulse several times until mixture resembles cornmeal, and transfer to a mixing bowl. Combine the orange juice, grated rind, and egg and pour into the dry ingredients, stirring with a rubber spatula just long enough to dampen the mixture. Fold in the nuts and cranberries with about 4 thorough turns of a rubber spatula. Spoon batter into the pan and bake 1 hour, or until bread tests done. Place pan on a wire rack and let cool 10 minutes. Turn bread out on rack. Let it cool thoroughly before slicing.

Suggestion: Bake the bread in smaller pans, using three 7-inch loaf pans, or in small charlotte molds, 4 inches in diameter and 2½ inches deep. Fill a Christmas basket with an assortment of small breads. Baking time for smaller loaves is about 40 minutes.

Boston

I n all my journeys to Massachusetts, I had missed Plymouth. Despite having to negotiate a "cross at your own risk" bridge under reconstruction, a detour, and a huge traffic jam, to see 1620 carved on the side of Plymouth Rock and the tiny *Mayflower* was worth the effort. I knew the ship was small, but it was difficult to envision people sleeping, eating, loving, praying, and two babies born in such overwhelmingly narrow quarters! The Pilgrims' adventure obviously took the courage of the young and completely dedicated.

Then, into Boston, one of my favorite cities. On each visit I become enmeshed in its crooked streets and hopelessly lost, but someone always rescues me. My knights in shining armor have usually been huge Irish policemen. One officer gave me his rain cap to protect my hair from a cold drizzle at a Harvard/Yale football game. Once a motorcycle officer escorted me and two small sons through the city to find the beginning of the historic walking tour; I suppose he figured it was best for Boston traffic to get rid of me. On another visit, on October 11 with my sister I walked the "yellow brick line" that is set in the sidewalks of old Boston to guide visitors to historic landmarks. The Columbus Day parade appeared and we crisscrossed the marching bands ten times and plowed through crowds of huge, happy, noisy Italian families. Never shall I see such a wild, hilarious Columbus Day again.

Our hosts on this new journey were Shushan and Herb Teager, professors at the Massachusetts Institute of Technology. Shushan, sister of my daughter-in-law Annie, arranged for me to visit Lebanese, Armenian, and French bakeries, and what a treat all of them were.

A retired colonel, Jerry Engram, was persuaded by a friend to manage for him a Boston bread factory that was not doing well. Jerry knew little about bread, but he knew how to organize. As Jerry walked me through the plant, sixteen thousand croissants were just one item made daily by Vie de France for metropolitan Boston. Jerry pointed out a Frenchman who he said was the soul of his plant and worked long, tedious hours. He was a short, stocky, strong, black-headed baker, covered with flour. I grinned and he responded with that beautiful Gallic shrug. He was working with an enormous rolling pin wound with layered croissant dough over a foot thick, which would be fed into a cutting and molding machine. Tiers of croissants were in a huge proofing room, moist and warm, just the right temperature. Enormous vats bubbled with tomorrow's dough. The correct mixture of flour had been solved, and now Vie de France buys that mixture by the carload and butter to match. Jerry generously gave me handsome French breads and chocolate-filled croissants. Later, I would teach myself how to enveigle a food processor to make croissants (see page 76).

French Bread

Makes 4 loaves

4 cups warm water
2 packages active dry
  yeast
2 teaspoons salt

4 cups bread flour
6 cups unbleached white
  flour, approximately

Combine the water and yeast in a large mixing bowl, stirring until dissolved. Add the salt and 3 cups of the bread flour and beat until a smooth batter is formed. Stir in the remaining bread flour and gradually add sufficient unbleached flour to make a soft workable dough that pulls away from sides of the bowl. Turn out on a floured surface and knead until smooth and satiny, about 10 minutes. Lightly flour the kneading surface and your hands as needed. Round dough into a ball and place in a warm buttered bowl, turning to coat the top. Cover loosely with plastic wrap and a towel and let rise until tripled, about 1½–2 hours. Knead down in the bowl and let rise again, about 45–60 minutes.

Punch down the dough and divide into 4 portions. Knead each, cover, and let rest 10 minutes. Form into any of the loaves described on pages 39–41. Cover with a light towel and let rise 30–45 minutes.

Preheat oven to 425°F. Just before baking, spray water into the oven and close the door to trap the steam. Or, if you prefer, place a pan of hot water on lower rack. Slash loaves and brush with cool water. Bake 30 minutes, spraying every 5 minutes for the first 15 minutes. When loaves are golden, remove and let cool on wire racks.

Choereg (ARMENIAN SWEET ROLL)

Makes about 60 braided or 80 small buns

Visits to several Armenian bakeries, all within one small area of Boston, enticed me into including choereg *here, a round or braided roll made in two different flavors.*

2 packages active dry yeast	1 cup melted butter
½ cup warm water	Grated rind of 1 lemon
1 cup warm milk	1 teaspoon salt
½ cup sugar	4 eggs, beaten
1 teaspoon ground *mahleb* (see **Note** on page 285 and Sources of Supply)	7–8 cups flour
	1 egg beaten with 1 tablespoon water for glaze
	Sesame seeds

In a small bowl combine the yeast and water, stirring until dissolved, and set aside. In a large mixing bowl combine milk, sugar, *mahleb,* butter, grated rind, salt, and eggs. Blend well and add the yeast mixture. Beat in 3 cups of flour to make a smooth batter. Gradually add enough flour to make a soft, workable dough. Turn out on a lightly floured surface and knead 10 minutes, or until smooth and satiny. Round into a ball and place in a warm buttered bowl, turning to coat the top. Cover loosely with plastic wrap and a towel and let rise until doubled, about 1–1½ hours.

Butter 2 or 3 baking sheets. Punch down the dough and knead lightly. Cut off pieces of dough about the size of a walnut. Roll into pencil-slim ropes 8–10 inches long. Braid 3 ropes, cut the braid into thirds, and pinch the ends. Place on baking sheets ½ inch apart. Repeat directions with remaining dough. Cover and let rise until light, about 1 hour.

Preheat the oven to 375°F. Brush the braids with the glaze and sprinkle heavily with sesame seeds. Bake 15–20 minutes. Serve warm or let cool on wire racks.

Variation: Substitute ½ cup honey for the sugar. Before adding the flour, stir in 1 cup of finely chopped walnuts and 1½ cups raisins, scalded, drained, and dried. Proceed as directed until the molding. Cut off pieces the size of a walnut, cup in hand, and rotate quickly on counter top until smooth. Place the balls on buttered baking sheets, brush with the glaze, and sprinkle tops with sesame seeds. Let rise for 45 minutes. Bake in preheated 375°F oven 15 minutes. Remove to wire racks to cool or serve warm.

An arrangement made through my hostess Shushan allowed me to attend an evening meeting of The Culinary Historians of Boston, a pure-Harvard experience. This organization is composed of approximately thirty-five people intensely interested in the history of international cuisine and that of the United States. On this particular evening, elegant, very old French cookbooks, with drawings of elaborate table settings unfolded from the back of each, were arranged on a table for our pleasure. Plans were being perfected for an eighteenth-century dinner to be cooked and served from a table arrangement in the style of the time. Handsome folders were given to each visitor describing the cookbook collections that have been presented to the Arthur and Elizabeth Schlesinger Library. One that was of most interest to me is the personal library of Samuel and Narcissa Chamberlain, parents of my editor.

Before leaving Massachusetts, we drove the Old Post Road to the Wayside Inn at Sudbury, one of my favorite New England towns. After an excellent luncheon at the inn, we walked to the grist mill to meet Richard Gnatowski, who is writing a master's thesis on grist mills. Richard took us through the handsome mill, explaining every detail. He sliced a kernel of corn for me to see the germ and taste it—very sweet. Rye was the chief flour used in Colonial days, but corn was also popular. A little soft wheat was grown in the Connecticut River Valley, but hard wheat was unknown. Mr. Gnatowski is a charming young American, devoted to the study of our early way of life.

Maine

Although Maine is not one of the Original Thirteen, the territory was part of Massachusetts and sent some of the first soldiers into combat in 1776. One regiment from Maine was at Bunker Hill. From the beginning there were many who wished to separate from Massachusetts, but statehood was not achieved until 1820, when Maine became the twenty-third state.

As we drove, I jotted impressions in my journal. At Portland on the wharf, lobster stew with meat from a one-pound lobster for $7.50. Later a big lobster, so succulent the juice dripped down my chin. Lobster boats, inlets, peninsulas, innumerable islands (the name Maine was used to distinguish it as the mainland), outcroppings of huge rocks. As we drove north on the coastal route, antique stores popped up at every turn. Pussy willows were peeping out, spring flowers were beginning to bloom, and Maine has roads as lumpy as those in Alaska. We stopped three nights in Boothbay Harbor, as guests of Mary Louise and Howard Cowan. They introduced us to artists of the area and lobster rolls. We had a suite facing the colorful inlet. I unpacked my typewriter and could have stayed all summer.

Our hostess drove us to their new home under construction on stunning acreage facing the open sea. Nearby is a brick rabbit warren. When the door was opened, I thought surely this must be *Watership Down*. I had no idea rabbits could be so different, beautiful, and fascinating—long droopy ears, short ears, pink eyes, huge black eyes rimmed with black on a white bunny, sapphire eyes, a chinchilla with two babies, another with four babies each only one inch long snuggled into a nest.

Our final dinner with the Cowans was a luscious lobster roll and blueberry buckle topped with *crème fraîche*. Howard, who owns the *Boothbay Register*, sent us to another peninsula to meet one of his columnists, Allene White, who writes about food. Allene, born and raised in New Hampshire, majored in journalism at Boston University—a total New Englander. She returned to writing after her children grew up and began raising golden retrievers.

Blueberry Buckle

Makes 1 loaf

Now, to prepare one of the very best "buckles,"
given to me by Allene.

Batter:

½ cup vegetable
  shortening
½ cup sugar
1 egg, beaten
2 cups flour, sifted

2½ teaspoons baking
  powder
¼ teaspoon salt
½ cup milk
2 cups blueberries,
  preferably from Maine

Topping:

½ cup sugar
½ cup sifted flour

½ teaspoon cinnamon
4 tablespoons butter

Preheat oven to 350°F. Generously brush with butter an 11½ × 7½ × 1½-inch baking pan.

Cream shortening and ½ cup of sugar until fluffy. Beat in the egg. Sift together the flour, baking powder, and salt and add to creamed mixture alternately with the milk. Fold in the blueberries. Pour into pan.

Mix together all topping ingredients, either with a pastry blender or fingertips. Sprinkle over top of batter. Bake 45–50 minutes. Let cool slightly, cut into squares, and serve warm. The cake freezes well—bake several for Christmas made with fresh berries.

A llene and her husband live in a two-story house heated by two hand-some Swedish stoves. These amazing stoves heat the entire house, using either coal or wood, so the Whites are most self-sufficient. I could imag-ine how cozy her attractive kitchen would be in winter, especially when blue-berry muffins are baking.

Blueberry Muffins

Makes 12 regular or 24 miniature muffins

1½ cups flour
⅓ cup sugar
¼ teaspoon salt
¼ teaspoon baking soda
1 tablespoon baking
   powder

1 teaspoon grated lemon
   rind
½ cup milk
2 eggs
⅓ cup melted butter
1 cup fresh or frozen
   bluberries

Preheat the oven to 400°F. Butter twelve 2-inch muffin tins.

Sift dry ingredients into a mixing bowl. Stir in the grated rind. Combine the milk, eggs, and butter, blending well. Add milk mixture all at once to dry ingredients, stirring only until they are wet. Sprinkle a little flour over the blueberries, shake them in a bowl, and fold carefully into the batter. Spoon batter into muffin tins, filling them three quarters full. Bake 20–25 minutes. These make good miniature muffins—they will cook in half the time.

F arther north along the coast at Machais we indulged in a phenom-enal piece of fresh strawberry pie and one last gorgeous bowl of lobster stew. Then we headed inland through the Maine wilderness in the cen-ter of the state and into the White Mountains of New Hampshire.

New Hampshire and Vermont

N orth Conway seems to be just one long street, with enticing stores spaced far apart. We stopped for a most pleasant lunch at The Scottish Lion Inn, warmly decorated with plaid floors and plaid walls. Hot, crisp Scottish oatcakes, deliciously lavished with butter, were served immediately. I learned that the simple recipe had been handed down from Judy Hurley's grandmother, and the inn was delighted to share it.

Scottish Lion Inn Oatcakes

Makes 12 oatcakes

1 cup sifted flour
1 tablespoon sugar
1 teaspoon baking powder
½ teaspoon salt

2 cups quick rolled oats
¼ pound (1 stick) butter,
  at room temperature
½ cup milk

Preheat the oven to 375°F. Butter a large baking sheet.

Sift flour, sugar, baking powder, and salt into a mixing bowl. Blend in the oats. Cut in the butter thoroughly with a pastry blender. Gradually add the milk, stirring constantly until a dough is formed. On a lightly floured surface roll out the dough ⅛ inch thick. Cut into 12 squares and place on baking sheet ¼ inch apart. Bake 12–15 minutes, or until lightly browned. Let cool on wire racks, unless they disappear while being transferred there!

N ew Hampshire was a busy and active independent colony. Its people fought the Indians, established Dartmouth in 1769, and captured Fort William and Mary to steal gunpowder that was later used at Bunker Hill. New Hampshire became the ninth state to adopt the Constitution of the United States.

We enjoyed driving through the beautiful White Mountains and passed by Bretton Woods, where forty-four nations met after World War II to create a new international monetary agreement. Then we headed south and finally stopped at Jaffrey to spend a weekend at the Woodbound Inn, where I met Dot Flagg.

New Hampshire Cinnamon Rolls

Makes about 48 rolls

*Dorothy Flagg, a tall, handsome, angular
woman, looks every inch a New Englander. At
our first meal, a basket of warm cinnamon rolls
was served and I succumbed to all of them. Dot
makes hundreds of rolls every day, for each bus
group that stops to dine walks off with packages
of her cinnamon buns. Soon I was watching Dot
in her baking area in the large, bright kitchen
full of busy, friendly cooks. I was in my element
and loved chatting and punching the dough with
her.*

2½ cups warm water
2 packages active dry
  yeast
1½ cups instant nonfat
  dry milk
¼ cup melted butter
¼ cup sugar

2 teaspoons salt
7–8 cups flour
Melted butter
Cinnamon Sugar, page 46
Confectioner's Icing, page
  45

Combine ½ cup water and yeast in a small bowl, stirring until dissolved, and set aside. In a large mixing bowl blend 2 cups water with
dry milk, butter, sugar, and salt. Add the yeast mixture and 3 cups of
flour, beating until a smooth batter is formed. Gradually add sufficient
flour to make a soft, workable dough. Turn out on a lightly floured
surface and knead 5–8 minutes, or until smooth and elastic. Round into
a ball and place in a warm buttered bowl, turning to coat the top. Cover
loosely with plastic wrap and a towel and let rise until light and puffy,
about 1 hour.

Punch down the dough, turn out, and knead lightly. Cover and let
rest 10 minutes. Butter five 9-inch cake tins or 3 large baking sheets.
Divide dough into 3 portions. While working on 1 piece, keep the other
2 pieces covered. Roll into a 16 × 12-inch rectangle. Dot made up 25
pounds of flour at one time and simply slapped a piece of dough on her
table and rolled it out—no measuring. Roll the dough as large as you

wish—the larger the sheet, the more swirls. Brush the rectangle with melted butter to within ½ inch of edges. Sprinkle with Cinnamon Sugar. Roll up from the long side, jelly-roll style, and seal the seam. Slice into 1-inch rolls and place in pans ½ inch apart. Brush tops with melted butter. Repeat directions with remaining 2 portions of dough. Cover and let rise until the rolls are light and touch each other, about 35–40 minutes. Preheat the oven to 350°F. Bake rolls about 25 minutes. Remove from oven and brush with melted butter. Turn out on wire racks and frost with a light Confectioner's Icing.

Note: Dot's secret is to allow the dough to rise fully each time and to brush the rolls several times with melted butter to keep them moist.

Dartmouth

W e took beautiful drives around Mount Moandoah and long walks through the woods accompanied by the Woodbound Inn's water spaniel, who chased rabbits and dashed into the still, cold lake water. We enjoyed talking in the bar with a group of New Englanders about big ranches in Texas and Oklahoma, ate more good New England food, and we were soon rested and ready to start the drive north to Hanover and Dartmouth University.

Lunch at the venerable Hanover Inn was elegant and pleasant, by a window overlooking the grounds of the university. To my delight, behind the Hanover Inn we found The Upper Crust, a most innovative bakery and café.

The Preppie Alligator

Makes 2 alligators

Paul Davidson started his young career washing dishes and just "picked up the baker's trade." He prepares beautiful breads and pastries and has a delightful sense of humor. Residing in the glass showcase was a bread alligator made especially for his preppie customers. Paul had an alligator in the oven and showed me how to crinkle the skin;

it's great fun. When my youngest grandchild recognized the alligator I made, I felt I could share it with you!

2½ cups warm water
2 packages active dry
   yeast
2 tablespoons sugar
2 teaspoons salt
2 tablespoons melted
   butter

2 cups bread flour
5 cups unbleached white
   flour
Raisins for eyes
1 egg beaten with 1
   tablespoon water for
   glaze

In a large mixing bowl combine the water and yeast, stirring until dissolved. Add the sugar, salt, butter, and bread flour and beat to make a smooth batter. Gradually add sufficient unbleached flour to make a workable dough. Turn out on a floured surface and knead 5 minutes. Round into a ball and place in a warm buttered bowl, turning to coat the top. Cover loosely with plastic wrap and a towel and let rise until doubled, about 1 hour.

Punch down the dough and divide in half. Knead thoroughly, cover, and let rest 15 minutes. Spray 2 baking sheets with nonstick vegetable spray. From each piece of dough cut off a portion about the size of a tennis ball. Cover and set aside. Roll 1 large portion into a 20-inch rope. Using the illustrations as a guide, taper one end into a slender tail.

Shape the other end into a head, which should be wider at the forehead, with a long, blunt snout. Pinch the forehead in two places to make raised eyebrows and set in raisin eyes. Place on baking sheet and curve into the proper Izod shape. Pat the dough so that it is thicker in the center—a fat tummy for a well-fed alligator. Cut one of the smaller pieces of dough into 4 pieces, shape into feet, and place them just under the body so that the dough will stick. With scissors clip toes in each.

Repeat directions with remaining portion of dough. Cover and let rest 15 minutes.

Preheat the oven to 350°F. Bake the alligators 15 minutes. Remove from oven. Paul pinched ridges in the alligator's back with his fingers, but I could not handle the hot dough as easily as he. I use a pair of kitchen tongs and clip 2 ridges down the outside of the back and then down the center (if there is room). Two ridges are quite effective. Crimp the eyebrows. Brush heavily with the glaze. Return to oven and bake until golden brown, about 15–20 minutes more. Let alligators cool on baking sheets until they can be handled by children. If you wish the alligators to dry out more, reduce heat to 300°F after they have browned and bake 20 minutes more.

The first alligator I made I gave to my two-year-old granddaughter, who trotted around nibbling on it for two days.

Note: The use of unbleached white flour is strictly for nutrition.

A section of the Connecticut River to the east and, to the west, part of Lake Champlain and the common border with the state of New York outline the long, narrow state of Vermont. The verdant elegance of the very old Green Mountains occupies the center of the state. Settled mainly by the English from Massachusetts and Connecticut, the territory became an owner's battleground between New Hampshire and New York. Ethan Allen stepped in and organized the Green Mountain Boys to resist payment of taxes to either colony. Vermont was able to declare for independence on its own and captured Ticonderoga from the British, establishing the fame of Vermonters for their prowess in guerrilla fighting.

We followed the Connecticut River south from Dartmouth, and I chose Highway 9 to enter Vermont; it looked like a pleasant road. All at once, we were in a forest with a winding, lumpy road and decrepit houses, and I felt very uncertain where this would end. I thought things like this only happened in Oklahoma, but, the fact is, some of rural Vermont is very poor. After seemingly many miles, we found the Inn at Sawmill Farms, which turned out to be outstanding, both for good food and our room. Exploring the area, I found what I had hoped for—Coombs Beaver Brook Sugarhouse. The final preparation of maple syrup—it is made in four grades—was in production. I purchased the top grade for pancakes, small cans for gifts (this stuff is expensive!), and a huge can, grade C, for cooking (see Sources of Supply). These excellent recipes for scones and a health bread were given to me by Sally Coombs.

Maple Scones

Makes about 14 scones

2 cups flour
2 teaspoons baking
  powder
1 tablespoon maple sugar
½ teaspoon salt

4 tablespoons butter
2 eggs, well beaten
½ cup heavy cream

Preheat oven to 425°F. Butter a baking sheet.

In a large mixing bowl combine the flour, baking powder, maple sugar, and salt. Work in the butter with a pastry blender or fingertips until crumbly. Add the eggs and cream, stirring until well blended. Place the dough on a lightly floured surface and knead 1 minute. Pat out ½ inch thick and either cut into triangles or shape portions into balls and flatten slightly. Place on baking sheet and bake about 15 minutes, or until golden brown.

Blueberry Scones: Sally's scones were so successful that I could not resist trying them with fresh blueberries. When the butter has been cut into the dry ingredients, add 1 cup fresh or frozen blueberries. Proceed as directed.

Sally's Healthy Bread

Makes 2 loaves

*Sally uses this name, short and to the point, for
her multi-grain bread flavored with maple syrup,
and that is the New England way. Why waste
time on elaborate names—let's bake bread!*

¾ cup water
1 cup milk
2 tablespoons vegetable
 shortening
1 teaspoon salt
2 tablespoons maple syrup
1 package active dry yeast
¼ cup warm water

6 tablespoons soy flour
6 tablespoons instant
 nonfat dry milk
2 tablespoons toasted
 wheat germ
4 cups unbleached white
 flour
1 cup whole wheat flour

Bring the ¾ cup of water to a boil, combine with the milk, shortening, salt, and syrup in a large mixing bowl, stir, and let cool. In a separate bowl combine the yeast and warm water, stirring until dissolved. Add the yeast mixture, soy flour, dry milk, wheat germ, and 3 cups of white flour to the milk mixture and beat to make a smooth batter. Add the whole wheat flour and sufficient white flour to make a soft, workable dough. Turn out on a floured surface and knead 2 minutes. Cover and let rest 10 minutes. Knead until smooth and elastic, about 5 minutes. Place in a warm buttered bowl, turning to coat the top. Cover loosely with plastic wrap and a towel and let rise until doubled, about 1 hour.

Punch down the dough and divide in half. Knead each portion, cover, and let rest 10 minutes. Butter two 8-inch loaf pans. Shape the dough into loaves and place in pans. Cover and let rise to tops of pans, about 45–60 minutes. Preheat the oven to 375°F. Bake loaves 45 minutes. If they become quite brown, cover with aluminum foil during the last 15 minutes of baking. Let loaves cool on wire racks.

The State of New York

A drive through the Green Mountains took us to Lake Champlain, where we boarded a small ferry and crossed smoothly through the mist to Plattsburgh, New York. At a supermarket where we stopped for fresh fruit, I discovered that all the signs were in English and French for the French-Canadians who come across the border for American produce. The Adirondack Mountains cover a huge area of northern New York. They are ancient and low, covered with pines, maples, birch, and flowering trees. The roads are winding, waterfalls cascade down the mountainsides, there are innumerable small lakes, and signs are constantly posted to watch out for deer. The headwaters of the Hudson and the St. Lawrence, two great rivers in our history, both begin in New York State. It is a stunningly beautiful state.

Emerging from the Adirondacks, one has a choice of big cities that march across the center of New York: Albany, Utica, Rome, Syracuse, Rochester, Buffalo. My Utica Connection, Jo Spencer, lives just outside that city, in an historic area, in a very old house with a date posted on the front.

Honey-Currant Processor Bread

Makes 2 loaves

Jo Spencer is one of those wonderful women who can cope with any situation. She has five children, a handsome husband, and can do any kind of job from sewing to food processor demonstrations. Her success in using this marvelous machine has led to many good recipes. Here is an elegant bread that can be quickly prepared for a dinner party.

4½ cups flour
1 teaspoon salt
4 tablespoons butter, at
    room temperature and
    cut into pieces
1 package active dry yeast

¼ cup warm water
1 cup warm milk
¼ cup honey
1 egg
2 cups currants, scalded,
    drained, and dried

Combine the flour, salt, and butter in bowl of food processor. Pulse several times to blend ingredients. Combine the yeast and water in a bowl, stirring until dissolved. Add milk, honey, and egg. With the motor running pour the milk mixture through the feed tube. The dough will mass into a ball; knead 1 minute. If mixture is too soft, add a small amount of flour through the tube. Remove and lightly knead by hand about 2 minutes. Round into a ball and place in a warm buttered bowl, turning to coat the top. Cover loosely with plastic wrap and a towel and let rise until doubled, about 1 hour.

Remove dough to a lightly floured surface and pat into a circle. Pile the currants in the center, fold dough over the fruit, and begin to knead. Knead 1 minute, cover, and let rest 10 minutes. Knead until currants are distributed throughout dough. This is a bit messy—but worth the effort! Butter two 8½-inch loaf pans. Divide the dough in half, shape into loaves, and place in pans. Cover and let rise to tops of pans, about 45 minutes.

Preheat the oven to 350°F. Brush tops of loaves with melted butter and bake 30–35 minutes. Let loaves cool on wire racks.

Kaiser Rolls

Makes 12–16 rolls

The kaiser roll originated in the East. Jo Spencer remembers that when she was a child kaiser rolls were served in every hotel in Syracuse, as well as in the elegant dining cars of fifty years ago. Jo agreed to test this roll, which turned out just as she remembers it.

2 packages active dry
   yeast
2½ cups warm water
2 tablespoons sugar
2 teaspoons salt
1 small egg, beaten

5½ cups unbleached
   white flour,
   approximately
1 egg white beaten with 1
   tablespoon water for
   glaze (optional)
Poppy seeds (optional)

In a mixing bowl combine the yeast and ½ cup of warm water, stirring until dissolved. Add the sugar, salt, and egg. Blend in the remaining water and gradually add sufficient flour to form a soft dough. Turn out on a floured surface and knead 5–8 minutes, using more flour, if necessary, to cut the stickiness. Round into a ball and place in a buttered bowl, turning to coat the top. Cover loosely with plastic wrap and a towel and let rise until doubled, about 45 minutes. Punch down the dough and let rise again, about 45 minutes.

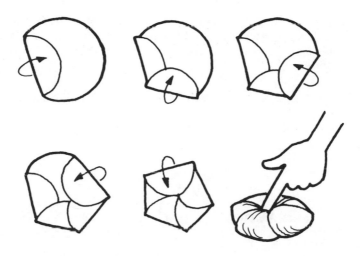

Punch down the dough, knead lightly, and divide into 12–16 pieces, however large you wish the rolls to be. If the dough is divided into 16 portions, the rolls will be about the size of small hamburger buns—good for family serving. On a lightly floured surface roll each piece into a ball. Cover and let rest 15–20 minutes. Brush a large baking sheet with melted butter. Roll each ball into a circle ¼ inch thick. Using the illustrations as a guide, fold the edges of circle into the center, making a total of 5 folds. When the final edge has been folded in, punch your forefinger down firmly into the center. Arrange rolls ¾ inch apart on the baking sheet. Cover and let rise until doubled, about 30 minutes.

Preheat the oven to 425°F. Brush rolls with cold water and bake 20–25 minutes. Serve hot.

Note: If a crisper crust is desired, spray the rolls with water 3 times during the baking period. To create a shiny finish, brush the rolls with the glaze just before baking and sprinkle with poppy seeds.

We followed the Hudson River south, making one detour to see an exceptionally well maintained Shaker village. That evening, after an energetic swim in the indoor swimming pool of our motel near Hyde Park, we dined in the Escoffier Room at the Culinary Institute of America. It was a hilarious, delightful evening. We watched the student waiters hovering anxiously over their notes and could see into the kitchen, where the student chefs worked under the eagle eye of a supervisor who never moved from his post. We enjoyed seven beautiful courses of carefully prepared continental cuisine. It was worth every penny, and in fact we considered the final bill quite reasonable. An elaborate Chinese dragon made of salt dough dominated the foyer, but he was much too intricately wired for me to attempt.

The following day, we unexpectedly found Delhi, New York, where a well-designed state agricultural college is located at the top of a steep hill. There I met a professor who introduced me to Ruth Kasmierski. Ruth and her friend Barbara Onasch have shared their "absolutely favorite homemade bread."

Honey Whole Wheat Bread

Makes 3 loaves

3 cups warm water
½ cup honey or molasses
2 packages active dry
  yeast
4 cups whole wheat flour

½ cup instant nonfat dry
  milk
1 tablespoon salt
2 tablespoons light oil
4–4½ cups unbleached
  white flour

In a large mixing bowl combine the water, honey, and yeast, stirring until dissolved, set aside, and let bubble well, about 20 minutes. Add 3 cups of the whole wheat flour, dry milk, salt, and oil and stir to make a smooth batter. Add the remaining whole wheat flour and sufficient white flour to make a soft, workable dough. Turn out on a floured surface and knead until smooth and elastic, about 8 minutes. Round into a ball and place in a warm bowl brushed with melted butter, turning to coat the top. Cover loosely with plastic wrap and a towel and let rise until doubled, about 1–1½ hours.

Punch down the dough, turn out on a floured surface, and knead 1 minute. Cover and let rest 10 minutes. Butter 3 9-inch loaf pans. Divide the dough into 3 portions, mold into loaves, and place in the pans. Cover and let rise until just curved over tops of pans, about 1 hour.

Preheat the oven to 350°F. Bake the loaves 35–40 minutes. Remove and let cool on wire racks.

C lose to the Finger Lake District, the hills became steeper and were clad completely with apple orchards in full bloom. Acres and acres of white, airy trees created a misty fairyland around Skeantles. We made an enchanting discovery: the New Hope Grist Mill on a clear rushing stream, with a huge water wheel that actually works. Dale Weed, the young miller, proudly told me that his mill had been in existence and in constant use for more than two hundred years. A small covered bridge crosses the stream just where it becomes a waterfall. What a restful, picturesque spot. Dale mills excellent flours (see Sources of Supply) and agreed to share his recipes.

New Hope Oatmeal Bread

Makes 2 loaves

This is a crusty bread, great for toasting.

1 package active dry yeast
½ cup warm water
1 cup rolled oats
1½ cups boiling water
½ cup honey or molasses
⅓ cup vegetable
   shortening

2½ teaspoons salt
6¼ cups New Hope bread
   flour, approximately
   (see **Note**)
2 eggs, lightly beaten

In a small bowl combine the yeast and warm water, stirring until dissolved, and set aside. In a large mixing bowl combine the oats, boiling water, honey, shortening, and salt and let cool to lukewarm. Stir in 2 cups of flour and the yeast mixture. Add the eggs and beat to make a smooth mixture. Gradually add sufficient flour to make a workable dough. Turn out on a floured surface and knead until smooth and elastic, about 10 minutes. Round into a ball and place in a bowl brushed with melted butter or shortening, turning to coat the top. Cover with plastic wrap and a towel and refrigerate at least 2 hours, but preferably overnight.

Butter two 8-inch loaf pans. Turn the dough out, knead lightly, and divide in half. Form into loaves and place in pans. Cover and let rise about 3 hours. The dough will need this much time to come to room temperature and rise to tops of pans.

Preheat the oven to 375°F. Bake loaves about 40 minutes. If the bread browns too quickly, cover with aluminum foil during the last 15 minutes of baking. Let cool on wire racks.

Note: The New Hope Mill is one of the few grist mills that grinds a bread flour. An unbleached white flour may be substituted.

New Hope Herb Bread

Makes 1 loaf

1 package active dry yeast	1 egg, beaten
¼ cup warm water	1 teaspoon caraway seeds
¾ cup milk, scalded	1 teaspoon sage
2 tablespoons honey	2 teaspoons celery seeds
2 tablespoons vegetable	1 teaspoon nutmeg
shortening	3–3½ cups bread or
1 teaspoon salt	unbleached white flour

Combine the yeast and water in a small bowl, stirring until dissolved, and set aside. In a large mixing bowl combine the milk, honey, shortening, and salt. Let cool to lukewarm. Add the yeast mixture. Blend in the egg, caraway seeds, sage, celery seeds, and nutmeg. Beat in 2 cups of flour to make a smooth batter. Gradually add sufficient flour to make a soft dough. Turn out on a lightly floured surface and knead until smooth and elastic, about 8 minutes. Round into a ball and place in a warm buttered bowl, turning to coat top. Cover loosely with plastic wrap and a towel and let rise until doubled, about 1 hour.

Punch down the dough, knead lightly, cover, and let rest 10 minutes. Butter an 8- or 9-inch cake tin. Shape dough into a round loaf and place in tin. Cover and let rise until doubled, about 45 minutes.

Preheat the oven to 400°F. Bake the bread 35 minutes. Let cool on a wire rack.

The Sovereign State of Virginia

O ur final night in New York State was in the handsome city of Corning. Each time I return, more has been added to the magnificent

Corning glass museum, and always there is such pleasure in watching some of our finest American craftsmen and artists making the exquisite Steuben crystal. We crossed into the center of Pennsylvania and drove through the preserves of forests and mountain ridges. Pennsylvania is the Keystone State, battleground of the French and Indian War, the Revolution, and the Civil War. The area we drove through was at one time a vast frontier, and much of it is still covered with forest. Crossing through a tiny portion of western Maryland and West Virginia, we entered Virginia at its northernmost point on the map and stopped at Middletown to spend the night at the Wayside Inn.

The opening year of the Wayside Inn was 1797. It offered bed and board to travelers on the Black Bear Trail. Twenty years later, the inn also became a stagecoach stop, where fresh relays of horses were maintained. The inn survived Civil War battles and many owners and in the twentieth century became "America's first Motor Inn." The bed and board were all I had hoped for, but I also found here one of the finest-textured white breads ever. Through the manager, Charles Alverson, The Wayside Inn has graciously shared this very old recipe, which has been used for five generations—since 1797.

Old-Fashioned Yeast Bread

Makes 2 loaves

2 packages active dry yeast	2 tablespoons butter
½ cup warm water	2 teaspoons salt
1 cup milk	5–5½ cups flour
¼ cup sugar	1 egg, well beaten

In a small bowl combine the yeast and water, stirring until dissolved, and set aside. Heat the milk, sugar, butter, and salt until just warm, about 110°F, and butter is almost melted. Pour mixture into a large mixing bowl. Stir in 2 cups of flour, beating well. Add the egg and blend in the yeast mixture until smooth. Gradually add sufficient flour to make a soft, workable dough. Turn dough out on a floured surface and knead until smooth and elastic, about 8 minutes. Round into a ball and place in a warm buttered bowl, turning to coat the top. Cover loosely with plastic wrap and a towel and let rise until doubled, about 1¼ hours.

Punch down the dough, turn out on a floured surface, and divide in half. Knead each piece thoroughly, cover, and let rest 10 minutes. Butter two 8-inch loaf pans. Form dough into loaves, place in pans, cover, and let rise until nearly doubled, about 45–60 minutes.

Preheat the oven to 375°F. Bake loaves about 35 minutes. Cover with foil during the last 10 minutes of baking. Remove loaves from pans and let cool on wire racks.

T he magnificence of the Shenandoah National Park and the Skyline Drive never ceased to thrill me with their extraordinary beauty. In the Blue Ridge foothills, we stopped to tour the homes of Thomas Jefferson and James Monroe. I had missed Monticello on previous journeys, and happily there were only ten of us on this tour. Considering all Mr. Jefferson's architectural ability, I wondered about his reasons for building two such very narrow staircases—hardly room on them for his wife's petticoats. President Jefferson, a true southern host, offered his guests many splendid meals. One of the cakes that is so much a part of Virginia tradition, Sally Lunn bread, surely was in his cook's repertoire.

The day Mr. Jefferson was married, he and his bride rode one hundred miles to Monticello, where the great house was barely off the ground. They arrived to find all the servants asleep. Our future President had to stable his own horses. Mr. and Mrs. Jefferson lived in a tiny outbuilding for two years before his beautiful home was liveable. Mrs. Jefferson must have been a very patient woman.

Sesame Seed Sally Lunn Bread

Makes 2 loaves

With the assistance of my Kansas City Connection toasted sesame seeds, a delightful addition, have been added to the usually rather bland Sally Lunn. Serve it warm for breakfast with raspberry preserves, or as a base for a dessert of fresh strawberries and thick cream.

2 packages active dry
   yeast
½ cup warm water
¼ cup sugar
3 large eggs, beaten

1½ cups warm milk
1 cup melted butter
2 teaspoons salt
6½ cups flour
Toasted sesame seeds

Combine yeast and water in a large mixing bowl, add 1 tablespoon of sugar, and stir until dissolved. Add the remaining sugar, eggs, milk, and butter. Stir in the salt and gradually add 4 cups of flour, beating well until the batter falls in sheets from a spoon. This may be accomplished with a heavy-duty mixer, using the flat beater. Stir in remaining flour and scrape down the bowl. Brush top of dough with melted butter, cover with a towel, and let rise until doubled, about 1 hour.

Punch down the dough, cover, and let rest 10 minutes. Brush two 8-inch ring molds with melted butter. Sprinkle heavily with sesame seeds. Place half the dough in each ring, cover, and let rise until ¼ inch from the top of pans, about 45 minutes.

Preheat the oven to 350°F. Bake loaves about 1 hour. Turn cakes out on wire racks to cool.

North Carolina and a Portion of South Carolina

We left Monticello and Charlottesville and drove south to Lynchburg and Danville, through the rich farming area of Virginia. When the Colonists discovered how well tobacco grew here, the area boomed, but they almost depleted the soil. A larger variety of crops was finally introduced, including peanuts, which pigs adore, and that crop became the source of the famous Virginia hams. The land continued gently rolling into North Carolina where we stopped at Winston-Salem.

"Wachovia" was the name of an area purchased by the Moravians from Pennsylvania in 1753. In 1766 they built the nearby town of Salem. Winston was established in 1849, and the two towns were merged in 1912. In 1950, the Moravians undertook to re-create "Old Salem," which has become an outstanding restoration. We went through all the buildings, including the working bakery and the Single Brothers House, which served as a home for unwed male members of the Moravian Society. The Moravians have that love for good, wholesome food which is so much a part of the authentic American tradition.

Moravian Christmas Bread

Makes 4 loaves

3 cups milk
1 package active dry yeast
8–9 cups flour
1 cup melted butter
¾ cup sugar
1 teaspoon salt
1 cup currants, scalded,
    drained, and dried
½ cup chopped candied
    pineapple

½ cup chopped candied
    lemon rind
½ cup chopped candied
    orange rind
1 egg beaten with 1
    tablespoon water for
    glaze
Sliced almonds

Scald 2 cups of milk and let cool to lukewarm. Pour into a mixing bowl, sprinkle with yeast, and stir to dissolve. Beat in 3 cups of flour to make a smooth batter. Cover with plastic wrap and a towel and let proof overnight at room temperature.

The next morning, scald the remaining cup of milk. Let cool to lukewarm and add to the sponge with the butter, sugar, and salt. Gradually add sufficient flour to make a soft, workable dough. Turn out on a floured surface and flatten into a circle. Combine fruits and rinds and sprinkle with a little flour. Pile on top the dough and pull dough over the fruit to knead. Knead thoroughly until fruits are well distributed, adding more flour if necessary. Place dough in a warm buttered bowl, turning to coat the top. Cover loosely with plastic wrap and a towel and let rise until doubled, about 1 hour.

Punch down the dough and divide into 4 equal portions. Knead each piece, cover, and let rest 10 minutes. Butter four 8-inch loaf pans. Shape dough into loaves and place in pans. Let rise until dough reaches tops of pans, about 45–60 minutes.

Preheat the oven to 350°F. Brush tops of loaves with the glaze and sprinkle with almonds. Bake 30–35 minutes. Turn out on wire racks to cool. Properly wrapped (page 44) the breads will store beautifully in the freezer.

N orth Carolinians are fortunate in their state's rugged mountains, vast agricultural areas, the long, fascinating seashore with fine resorts, and the famous swamp lands that provide breeding grounds for fish and excellent hunting. Something in North Carolina created unusual and fierce independence in its people, for they bitterly objected to the royal government long before 1776, and North Carolina became the first state to declare its independence. But, now, we are going to slip south into the neighboring state of South Carolina and have some old-fashioned grits.

Hunters from many other states come to the forests of South Carolina, for the deer season here lasts several months (versus Oklahoma's four days). Along the coast, wild turkey and quail, wild rabbit, opossum, fox, and raccoon abound in the forest areas. Later we shall circle around to see the coastal region, but now our route is a lovely drive through portions of Sumter National Forest and into Georgia, for there are friends in Atlanta I want you to meet. Before we leave, here is a recipe for one of my favorite foods, prepared in a most elegant fashion for a Southern dinner.

Baked South Carolina Grits

Serves 8

3 cups water	4 eggs, well beaten
1 teaspoon salt	½ cup melted butter
1 cup instant grits	½ cup grated Cheddar
1 cup milk	(optional)

Bring the water to a boil in a saucepan and add the salt. Sprinkle in the grits, stirring constantly; the mixture will thicken rapidly. Keep stirring until thickened and smooth. Remove from burner and let cool 15 minutes, stirring occasionally.

Preheat the oven to 350°F. Generously butter a 2-quart soufflé mold or casserole.

Add the milk, eggs, and butter to the grits, stirring until mixture is smooth. Pour into soufflé dish and bake 1 hour. Test for doneness with a cake tester. If desired, sprinkle the cheese over the top during the last 10 minutes of baking. Serve hot.

Note: For leftover baked grits: Reheat the next morning, covered, and serve with a poached egg.

Georgia

W hen we sailed on the *Mississippi Queen* (which you'll read about later), we were invited to dine at the captain's table on the last evening. My dining companion, across the table, was a handsome young man from Atlanta. Somehow, bread became a topic of conversation (I'm good at maneuvering!). I asked this charming young man what would be the most popular bread of the sophisticated, aggressive city of Atlanta. "Why, ma'am, CAWNBREAD, of course!" So that's it.

Southern Buttermilk Corn Bread

Makes 1 corn bread

1 cup unbleached white flour	¼ teaspoon baking soda
1 cup cornmeal	2 tablespoons sugar
2 teaspoons baking powder	2 eggs
¾ teaspoon salt	1 cup buttermilk
	¼ cup melted butter

Preheat the oven to 450°F. Generously butter an 8- or 9-inch square pan.

Combine all dry ingredients in a mixing bowl, stirring to blend. In a separate bowl beat the eggs and add the buttermilk and butter. Make a well in the center of dry ingredients and pour in the milk mixture all at once. With a rubber spatula stir quickly to moisten the dry ingredients. Pour into the pan and bake until golden brown, about 25 minutes. Serve hot.

Note: I have no intention of becoming embroiled in the argument about the virtues of yellow cornmeal versus white cornmeal. For corn bread I usually prefer the yellow—prettier color. Sometimes, if I have whole dried corn kernels, then I grind my own on my Magic Mill and make up the corn bread immediately. The corn flavor is greatly enhanced.

S outherners enjoy breads other than just the quick ones. Join me to meet my Atlanta Connection, Lois Powell. Lois, like many Americans, has moved around a bit. She was born in the South, had to live for ten freezing years in Chicago, and has been happy in Atlanta for many years. The focal point of her life is her gardens. Lois owns a ravine with a creek, fish pond, and beautiful walkways. She raises everything from day lilies, black-eyed Susans, azaleas, and roses to wild flowers—and even blueberries! What season is best to visit Georgia? April, reports Lois, for the air is cool and azaleas are in full bloom. Lois has given me a whole grain bread recipe, and through her we shall meet another breadmaking Atlantan.

Colonial Georgian Bread

Makes 2 loaves

½ cup cornmeal
⅓ cup packed brown
  sugar
2½ teaspoons salt
2 cups boiling water
¼ cup light oil
2 packages active dry
  yeast
½ cup warm water
¾ cup whole wheat flour

½ cup rye flour
¼ cup instant nonfat dry
  milk
¼ cup soy flour
2 tablespoons toasted
  wheat germ
4½ cups unbleached
  white flour,
  approximately

In a large mixing bowl combine the cornmeal, sugar, salt, boiling water, and oil, stirring rapidly to keep mixture smooth. Let cool to lukewarm, about 30 minutes. Combine the yeast and warm water in a small bowl, stirring until dissolved. Add to the cornmeal mixture with the whole wheat and rye flours. Stir in the dry milk, soy flour, and wheat germ and beat until mixture is smooth. Gradually add sufficient white flour to make a soft, workable dough. Turn out on a floured surface and knead until smooth and elastic, about 8 minutes. Round into a ball and place in a buttered bowl, turning to coat the top. Cover loosely with plastic wrap and a towel and let rise until doubled, about 1 hour.

Punch down the dough and turn out on a lightly floured surface.

Divide in half, knead each piece, cover, and let rest 10 minutes. Butter two 9-inch loaf pans. Shape dough into loaves and place in pans. Cover and let rise until just curved over tops of pans, about 45 minutes.

Preheat the oven to 375°F. Bake loaves 45 minutes. If the bread browns too rapidly, cover loosely with aluminum foil during the last 15 minutes of baking. Let loaves cool on wire racks.

A visit to Atlanta can be a "happening." It is known as a progressive city and has handsome shopping centers and fascinating tiny restaurants that delight visitors. But Atlanta grew to be like this through her people. Sally Nichols stands out as a perfect example of an American success story, as well as of an independent young woman. A college dropout, Sally borrowed $1,000 from her mother, Jane, and opened the Good Ol' Days Restaurant, where she featured breads and "sandwiches" baked in simple clay pots. Her first attractive café with outdoor tables is on Peachtree Road, almost as notable an address as Pennsylvania Avenue. Now, Sally, with her mother, working long, hard hours has opened three more restaurants. Sally has been written about in *People* and *Glamour* magazines and has been approached by McDonald's chairman of the board to sell her restaurants. Sally refused. Good for her!

Fast Flowerpot Bread

Makes 12 small breads

Part of Jane's secret is the use of natural ingredients. At the end of her recipe there are directions for seasoning flowerpots.

2 packages active dry
   yeast
1 cup warm water
1 teaspoon salt
⅓ cup honey
⅓ cup instant nonfat dry
   milk
½ cup vegetable oil

4 cups flour
3 eggs, at room
   temperature
½ cup raisins, scalded,
   drained, and dried
   (optional)
Slivered almonds
Candied cherries

Combine yeast and water in a mixing bowl, stirring until dissolved. Add the salt, honey, and dry milk, blending well. Stir in the oil and mix well. Add 2 cups of the flour, beating until a paste forms. Add the eggs and beat thoroughly. Beat in ⅓ cup flour and beat 1 minute. If you have a heavy-duty mixer, use the flat beater. Add remaining flour and beat for 3 minutes, or until dough is quite elastic. If desired, beat in raisins at this time. Line the bottoms of 12 seasoned 3-inch clay pots with rounds of aluminum foil and generously butter pots and foil. Fill each half full of batter, cover, and let rise 20 minutes. Gently press slivered almonds and candied cherries on top of the dough. Place the pots on a baking sheet and put into a cold oven. Turn oven to 350°F. As Jane suggests, baking time can vary from 30–45 minutes. Test for doneness.

How to Season Clay Pots: Wash new pots thoroughly in hot soapy water. Rinse and let drain. Wipe dry. Brush each all over with salad oil and place in a preheated 275°F oven 2 hours. Remove and let cool. The pots should be washed by hand after each baking—do not put in a dishwasher.

Doc's Dough!

Makes 3 loaves

Arthur E. Lesesne, M.D., was inspired to start baking by a New York dentist he met who made all his own bread. After being "molded" by medical school, internship, and residency, a great deal of one's creativity is "kneaded out," he says. Breadmaking has helped restore Arthur's creativity and establish a new rapport with his family and patients. Minnie Lee Horton of Atlanta gave Arthur a recipe that originally came from the Pennsylvania Dutch country and made twenty-five loaves. The name for this version? Arthur thought that if he retired from medicine and opened his own bakery, he'd call it Doc's Dough!

3 cups warm water	1 cup melted vegetable
2 packages active dry	shortening
yeast	1 cup toasted wheat germ
¼ cup sugar	8 cups unbleached white
1 tablespoon salt	flour, approximately

Combine the water, yeast, and sugar in a large mixing bowl, stirring until dissolved. Add the salt, shortening, and wheat germ and beat in 3 cups of flour until batter is smooth. Gradually add sufficient flour to make a soft, workable dough that pulls away from sides of the bowl. Turn out on a floured surface and knead 8–10 minutes. Place in a warm bowl brushed with melted shortening, turning to coat the top. Cover loosely with plastic wrap and a towel and let rise until doubled, about 1 hour.

Punch down the dough, turn out on a floured surface, and knead 5 minutes. Cover and let rest 15 minutes. Brush three 8-inch loaf pans with melted shortening. Divide dough into 3 equal portions. Shape in loaves and place in loaf pans. Cover and let rise until doubled, about 30 minutes.

Preheat oven to 425°F. Bake loaves 30 minutes. Let cool on wire racks.

Cheese Bread: After wheat germ is added, beat in 2 cups grated sharp Cheddar and ⅓ cup sesame seeds.

The Coastal Areas of South and North Carolina

W e drove across Georgia to the state's main seaport, Savannah, established in 1733 and captured twice during the War for Independence. During the Civil War, it was evacuated before General Sherman reached the sea, thus saving many lovely old homes, most of which today have been restored. Again, this is a city to enjoy at your own pace with a do-it-yourself tour. South of Savannah lies a series of beautiful islands and the famous Okefenokee Swamp where the fictitious Pogo used to live. We began a drive north along the coast of South Carolina. I did some reading and became fascinated with the exploits of General Francis Marion, known as the "Swamp Fox," during the Revolution. It seemed to me our military today could still learn a few things about guerrilla warfare from this Southern gentleman, for he kept the British in an uproar. They never knew how or when he would create uncomfortable situations.

Huge, prolific pecan trees grow all across the Southern states, including both the Carolinas. Here is a most delicious coffeecake, encrusted with chopped pecans. The cake freezes well.

Carolina Pecan Coffeecake

Makes 1 coffeecake

Topping:

3 tablespoons light corn syrup
3 tablespoons butter
½ cup packed brown sugar

1 teaspoon cinnamon
1 cup coarsely chopped pecans

Batter:

2 cups sifted unbleached white flour
3 teaspoons baking powder
¼ pound (1 stick) butter, at room temperature

1 cup granulated sugar
2 eggs
1 cup milk
1 teaspoon vanilla

Preheat the oven to 350°F. Butter a Bundt pan.

To make the topping, combine corn syrup and butter in a small saucepan. Mix the brown sugar and cinnamon and add to the saucepan. Stir well, bringing just to a simmer to dissolve ingredients. Pour mixture into Bundt pan. Sprinkle pecans on top and set aside.

Sift together the flour and baking powder. In bowl of an electric mixer cream the butter and granulated sugar until light and fluffy. Beat in the eggs one at a time, stirring well after each addition. Add the dry ingredients alternately with milk, beating well after each addition. Beat 1–2 minutes, or until light and fluffy. Add the vanilla and spoon batter over the topping. Bake 40 minutes. Remove and let cool in pan 5 minutes. Turn out on a serving tray and serve warm or at room temperature.

C ontinuing along the coastal plains, we crossed to the outlying islands to see Cape Hatteras and Kitty Hawk. The Wright brothers picked quite a spot. It's windy! During this journey, we gorged on excellent seafood, always served with hush puppies, corn pone, or cornsticks.

Carolina Cornsticks

Makes 14 cornsticks

The secret for crisp cornsticks is a piping hot cornstick pan—that's the way my mother always made them. I can still hear that sizzle as she poured the batter into those little grooves.

1 cup yellow cornmeal	½ teaspoon salt
1 cup flour	1 egg, beaten
¼ cup sugar	1 cup milk
1 tablespoon baking powder	¼ cup melted vegetable shortening

Preheat the oven to 425°F. Brush 14 cornstick molds with melted shortening and heat in the oven while you make the batter.

Sift cornmeal, flour, sugar, baking powder, and salt into a mixing bowl. Combine the egg, milk, and shortening. Make a well in the center of dry ingredients and pour the milk mixture in all at once. Stir quickly just to wet all ingredients. Remove cornstick pans from the oven and pour the batter into the molds. Bake 15–20 minutes, or until golden and crisp. Serve immediately.

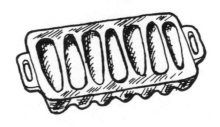

T hrough Georgia, the Carolinas, and now back in Virginia, we relived both the War for Independence and the black days of the Civil War. Constantly, I begged my husband to stop at just one more plaque or monument. Now our return to Virginia was through Norfolk and Newport News. Then we took Interstate 44 to spend a night at Colonial Williamsburg. Several journeys had taken us before to this magnificent re-created village. I believe the most memorable time was riding a tandem bicycle with one of my sons, while another peddled ahead of us. We covered every building and ate in each restaurant and loved it all. For three centuries, the coffeehouses and inns of Williamsburg and the state of Virginia have served excellent food, so here's one more recipe from Virginia before we drive back to Washington, D.C.

Virginia Buttermilk Rolls

Makes about 48 rolls

I'm certain every Virginia housewife has her own special hot roll she enjoys serving. Buttermilk is a favorite ingredient in the South, and you can see why in these light, tender rolls with a lovely crust.

1 package active dry yeast
¼ cup warm water
2 cups warm buttermilk
¼ teaspoon baking soda
¼ teaspoon baking
   powder

1 teaspoon salt
1 tablespoon sugar
3 tablespoons light oil
5 cups flour,
   approximately

Combine the yeast and water in a large mixing bowl, stirring until dissolved. Add the buttermilk, baking soda and powder, salt, sugar, and oil. Add 3 cups of flour and beat until batter is smooth. Gradually add sufficient flour to make a soft dough. Turn out on a lightly floured surface and knead until smooth and elastic, about 10 minutes, adding as little flour as possible during the kneading process. Round into a ball and place in a warm bowl brushed with melted butter, turning to coat the top. Cover loosely with plastic wrap and a towel and let rise until doubled, about 1 hour.

Punch down the dough, knead lightly, cover, and let rest 10 minutes. Butter 2 baking sheets. Roll dough out ½ inch thick. Cut with 2½-inch biscuit cutter to make Parker House rolls (page 42). Or use a 1½–2-inch cutter for plain rolls. Place on baking sheet about ½ inch apart. Cover and let rise until light and puffy, about 1 hour.

Preheat oven to 400°F. Bake rolls 15 minutes. If a softer crust is desired, the rolls may be brushed with melted butter before baking. Serve hot.

An entire month, or more, could be spent in the state of Virginia alone, enjoying the variety of the scenery, dining in fine country inns, learning about all the magnificent building and planting Thomas Jefferson did for his state and for his country, and admiring the man who held our tiny nation together at the beginning, George Washington.

During this long journey through the Original Thirteen, I read prodigiously, from stories of the "Swamp Fox" to detailed accounts of the battles of Lexington, Concord, and Bunker Hill. Driving through these states, it is impressive to see historical names everywhere—those of heroic men on bronze plaques and of historic towns and villages now routinely emblazoned on interstate highway exit signs. I was raised in a very young state, so it was a special thrill for me to drive through the densely populated areas of Boston, New York, and Philadephia and attempt to imagine them still rural and agricultural, as they were when Paul Revere rushed madly down a country lane to sound the great alarm. As a citizen, I am most grateful to the state governments and the individuals who have re-created and restored so many of the old areas—and to those who have preserved the old recipes that are also part of our early history.

THE SUNBELT
AND HAWAII

MILEAGE—10,230 MILES

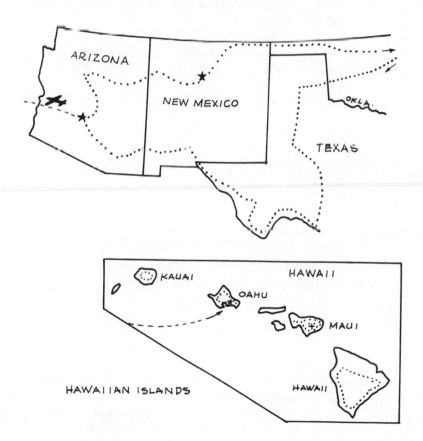

Western Texas

T hrough the wheat fields of western Oklahoma we drove to the Texas Panhandle, where I chose to turn south off Interstate 44 to Hereford, Texas, known as the "City Without a Toothache" because of the discovery of natural fluoride in the water supply of Deaf (pronounced deef) Smith County. This stirred up an old-fashioned "gold rush" of people wanting to move there or to buy the water. Hereford may not be all things to all teeth, but it is one of the neatest, best designed small cities in Texas. At the edge of town is Arrowhead Mills, owned by Frank Ford, a six-foot-two Texan who gave us a tour of the plant. He packages and distributes superb flours of every kind, plus granola, cereals, cooking and salad oils—everything health food and natural food devotees could wish for. The plant is spotless and the personnel friendly and eager to show off each department.

After a conference with Boyd Foster, an executive vice-president, and Mr. Ford, I left happily with a stack of recipes and bags of flour, crunching happily on fresh, crisp granola.

Extra-Rich Vitamin B Bread

Makes 3 loaves

½ cup Arrowhead Mills, or other, wheat berries
3 cups stone-ground whole wheat flour
2 packages active dry yeast
1½ teaspoons salt

1 cup milk
¼ pound (1 stick) butter
½ cup honey
2 large eggs
3–3½ cups unbleached white flour

Place the wheat berries in a 1-quart jar and fill three quarters full with water. Let soak, covered, 24 hours and drain off water—according to Arrowhead the water is fine to drink (probably will help your teeth!)—refill with fresh water and let soak 24 hours more. When ready to prepare bread, drain and set berries aside; there will be 1 full cup.

In a large mixing bowl combine 2 cups whole wheat flour, yeast, and salt and mix well. In a small saucepan heat milk and butter until warm, about 115°–120°F. Be certain butter is melted. Let cool to 100°F. Add the milk mixture to flour mixture and beat well. Blend in the honey and eggs and beat at low speed with an electric mixer or by hand until well mixed. Beat 3 minutes at medium speed or by hand until the mixture is smooth. Gradually stir in the wheat berries, remaining whole wheat flour, and enough white flour to make a workable dough. Turn out on a floured surface (use white flour) and knead until dough is smooth and elastic, about 5–8 minutes. Round into a ball and place in a warm buttered bowl, turning to coat top. Cover loosely with plastic wrap and a towel and let rise until doubled, about 1½ hours.

Punch down the dough and divide into 3 portions. Knead lightly, cover, and let rest 10 minutes. Butter three 8½-inch loaf pans. Form dough into loaves and place in pans. Cover and let rise until doubled, about 1 hour.

Preheat the oven to 375°F. Bake the loaves 35–40 minutes. Turn out on racks to cool.

Note: The addition of ½–1 cup of chopped nuts will increase richness and flavor. Also a topping may be added: just before baking, brush tops of loaves with 1 egg yolk mixed with 1 tablespoon of water and sprinkle with oats, sesame seeds, finely chopped nuts, wheat germ, or bran cereal.

A rrowhead Mills has worked out several fascinating recipes containing such flours as millet and soy, spiced with delicious flavorings to help people confront the problem of celiac sprue. Celiac sprue (gluten allergy) is a permanent intolerance for gluten. It is inherited, although there has been no determination of the mode of genetic transmission. Usually the condition occurs during the first two years of life, but may be delayed for years in some people. Once a positive diagnosis has been made, the family and ultimately the child must realize there can be no toleration of wheat, barley, rye, and oats. Psychologically, it is best to accustom children to the restrictions before the age of understanding. They will simply have to cope with eating entirely different breads than you and I. Let's take a look at several short, easy recipes.

Pineapple Bread

Makes 1 loaf

1 cup unsweetened
  dessicated coconut
1 cup canned crushed
  pineapple and juice
4 large eggs

½ cup honey
2½ cups millet flour
1 teaspoon sea salt
1 tablespoon baking
  powder

In a large mixing bowl combine the coconut and pineapple. Add the eggs and honey and beat until light either with an electric mixer or a wire whisk. Combine millet flour, salt, and baking powder, blend thoroughly with the pineapple mixture, and let the batter stand 15 minutes.

Preheat the oven to 325°F. Butter well a 9-inch loaf pan. Stir batter and pour into the pan. Bake 1 hour, or until the bread tests done.

Banana Rice Bread

Makes 1 loaf

2½ cups rice flour
½ teaspoon sea salt
1 tablespoon baking
  powder
¼ pound (1 stick) butter,
  at room temperature

⅔ cup honey
2 eggs
1½ cups mashed bananas
½ cup chopped nuts

Preheat the oven to 350°F. Generously butter a 9-inch loaf pan.

Combine rice flour, salt, and baking powder and set aside. In an electric mixer cream the butter and honey. Add the eggs and beat well. Blend in the bananas and the dry ingredients. Stir vigorously and add the nuts. Pour mixture into the pan and bake 1 hour, or until the bread tests done.

Nongluten Bread

Makes 1 loaf

A basic recipe for nongluten bread with many ingredients was given to me in Milwaukee, but it had little flavor. Unfortunately most breads of this kind are dry and crumbly, but, after a few trials, I am pleased with the results of this recipe. Rice flour and rice polish are available at health food stores.

¼ cup mashed or riced potato
4 tablespoons butter, at room temperature
¼ cup sugar
6 medium eggs, separated
1½ cups brown or white rice flour
½ cup rice polish
2 tablespoons soy flour

1 teaspoon baking powder
1 teaspoon baking soda
1 teaspoon cream of tartar
½ teaspoon salt
⅛ teaspoon ground pepper (optional)
¾ cup milk, soy milk, or frozen nondairy creamer

Preheat the oven to 350°F. Spray a 9-inch loaf pan with nonstick vegetable spray and brush with butter. (The batter has a tendency to stick.)

In mixing bowl of electric mixer cream potato with the butter and sugar until light and fluffy. Add the egg yolks one at a time, beating after each addition.

In a separate bowl sift together the rice flour, rice polish, soy flour, baking powder, baking soda, cream of tartar, salt, and pepper, if desired. Add to the potato mixture alternately with the milk, stirring after each addition.

Beat the egg whites until softly stiff. Fold into the batter. Pour into the pan and bake 1 hour. Turn loaf out on wire rack to cool.

Innovations: Whirl 1 cup of sunflower seeds in a food processor until coarsely chopped. Add to the batter just before the egg whites are folded in. Do not attempt to use whole seeds in batter breads as they will all end up in the middle of the loaf.

A second loaf and my favorite: Add 2 teaspoons of cinnamon when sifting the dry ingredients. Add 1 cup of coarsely chopped pecans and ½ cup currants, scalded, drained, and dried, before folding in the egg whites.

Triticale Bread

Makes 2 loaves

Triticale (rhymes with daily), a grain created by man, is a cross between wheat and rye. Triticale has been in existence over a hundred years, but little was done to further its development until recently. Now, researchers feel the grain could be the hope of undeveloped countries because of its unusual, sturdy qualities. Unfortunately, it has a minimum of gluten and should be combined with other flours. The flavor is similar to that of a light rye. I have tried a bread using just triticale flour only; the result was a small dense loaf, but with good flavor.

2 packages active dry
  yeast
½ cup warm water
2 cups warm buttermilk
¼ cup molasses
½ cup melted butter

2 teaspoons salt
1 tablespoon caraway
  seeds (optional)
3 cups triticale flour
3 cups unbleached white
  flour, approximately

Combine yeast and water in a small bowl, stirring until dissolved. In a large mixing bowl combine the buttermilk, molasses, butter, salt, and seeds, if desired, blending well. Add the yeast mixture and beat in the triticale flour to make a smooth batter. Gradually add sufficient white flour to make a soft dough. Turn out on a lightly floured surface (use white flour) and knead lightly. Triticale flour is fragile since there is little gluten, and it should be kneaded only lightly, just enough to smooth the dough. Leave the dough on the floured surface and let it rise 15 minutes.

Butter two 8½-inch loaf pans. Divide dough in half and form into loaves. Place in the pans, cover, and let rise to top of pans, about 1 hour.

Preheat the oven to 350°F. Bake loaves 40 minutes. Remove and let cool on wire racks.

The Ranch Country of Texas

Our next goal was Del Rio on the Mexican-American border, a bit over five hundred miles from Hereford, passing through Lubbock, a cotton capital, and San Angelo (fortunate to have a lake here in the middle of West Texas), and through rolling hills and stunning Texas ranch country, where there is always evidence of someone's sense of humor. We stopped at a huge ranch gate that sported two mailboxes; a big fat one sat on a fencepost, while the second, that only a bird could reach, was perched high in the air on a pole and marked "AIRMAIL." Finally, we drove into Del Rio to spend a night with our friends, Fred and Frankie Lee Harlow. They had just taken possession of a big, gorgeous Lincoln in which we drove sixty miles through sheep ranch country to drink a Coke—and sixty miles back. The road was like a roller coaster, and during this whole drive we passed only one truck and two or three Mexicans, but lots of sheep.

Tex-Mex Bread

Makes 3 regular or 16 miniature loaves

Texans are weaned on hot peppers. I knew one Texas woman who carried a miniature bottle of Tabasco sauce in her purse—everything she ate was spattered with Tabasco. I have devised a Tex-Mex bread that should appeal to all Texans and Frankie Lee has given me a corn bread variation.

2 packages active dry
  yeast
1½ cups warm water
½ cup warm milk
1 tablespoon sugar
2 teaspoons salt
¼ cup melted butter
2 eggs, lightly beaten
6–7 cups flour
½ cup sour cream
¼ cup chopped black
  olives

¼ cup finely chopped
  onion
1 cup grated Cheddar
1 clove garlic, finely
  chopped
2 tablespoons canned hot
  salsa, or 2–4
  tablespoons finely
  chopped jalapeño
  peppers

In a small bowl combine the yeast and ½ cup warm water, stirring until dissolved, and set aside. In a large mixing bowl combine 1 cup warm water, milk, sugar, salt, butter, and eggs, blending well. Add the yeast mixture and beat in 2 cups of flour until batter is smooth. Stir in the sour cream, olives, onion, cheese, garlic, and *salsa.* Gradually add sufficient flour to form a soft dough. Turn out on a floured surface and knead until smooth and elastic, about 8 minutes. Round into a ball and place in a warm buttered bowl, turning to coat top. Cover loosely with plastic wrap and a towel and let rise about 45 minutes.

Butter three 8½-inch pans. Punch down the dough and turn out on floured surface. Knead lightly, divide into 3 portions, form into loaves, and place in pans. Cover and let rise to tops of pans, about 40 minutes.

Preheat the oven to 375°F. Bake the loaves 30 minutes. Turn out on wire racks to cool.

Note: You can also mold the bread in sixteen 4-inch miniature pans. Let rise 45–60 minutes and bake about 25 minutes. Let cool and slice for appetizers—the slices can be topped with more peppers!

Jalapeño Corn Bread

Makes 1 corn bread

One could just call this Texan Bread, for every native Texan I've met loves this "hot" corn bread, especially served with black-eyed peas and fresh scallions.

1 cup cornmeal
½ teaspoon baking soda
¾ teaspoon salt
1 cup buttermilk
2 eggs, beaten
½ cup melted butter or
  bacon drippings

1 medium onion, finely
  chopped
17-ounce can yellow
  cream style corn (about
  3½ cups)
1 cup grated Cheddar
1 jalapeño pepper,
  chopped

Preheat the oven to 350°F. Brush a 9-inch square baking pan heavily with vegetable shortening and place in the oven until piping hot.

In a large mixing bowl combine the first seven ingredients, beating quickly and thoroughly. Fold in the corn. Pour half the batter in the hot baking pan. Sprinkle the cheese over the batter and top with the jalapeño pepper. Top with remaining batter and bake 45 minutes. Let cool slightly before serving.

Note: Frankie Lee suggests using green chilis instead of jalapeño peppers if a milder flavor is preferred. But not for this Texas lady, born and raised on a ranch so close to the border that she has always been able to cross over and purchase enormous jars of hot peppers.

I t must boggle the mind of the Mexican government to think that it once owned the state of Texas. The dollars here are no larger than in the other forty-nine states, but there certainly seems to be more of them. The Texans declared their independence and almost lost it at the Alamo, but became the Lone Star Nation after their victory at the battle of San Jacinto. I had a great-grandpa whose name is engraved on the huge monument that dominates the battlefield. Texas joined the Union in 1848 and seceded during the Civil War, re-entering in 1878.

Our departure from Del Rio took us west to Great Bend National Park, a mountain and wilderness area wrapped in a huge bend of the Rio Grande, then back to Interstate 10, which crosses the vastness of Texas east and west. Fort Stocton, surrounded by wind-swept fields, was a stop on the old Butterfield stage line. Now it is a remote motel stop, where Texas-size steaks are served with potatoes to match. After the final three hundred miles through desert and mountains, we entered El Paso, next to Juarez across the Rio Grande. Cupped in a great bowl of surrounding mountains, the entire area is covered with a violet haze that emanates from Juarez, where there is no smoke control.

Ysleta and Mesilla

The oldest settlement in Texas, established in 1662, Ysleta is the last stronghold of the surviving members of the Pueblo tribe of Texas. Their crafts are preserved in a re-created village. I watched a Pueblo Indian woman, dressed in a red satin blouse and full black skirt and swathed in heavy turquoise jewelry, knead twenty-five pounds of dough in an enormous bowl. She wore red nail polish, half of which had disappeared. Later we shall meet another Pueblo baker in Isleta, New Mexico, with a recipe to share.

Thirty miles north of El Paso is the tiny village of Mesilla, now a suburb of Las Cruces. Mesilla, built in the Mexican fashion around a colorful town square, once served as the capital of Arizona and New Mexico territory, creating great activity in the area. Katy Camuñez, owner of La Posta de Mesilla, told me the ancient adobe building that houses the restaurant was a stagecoach stop on the Butterfield trail, and many western heroes and outlaws such as Kit Carson, Judge Roy Bean, and Billy the Kid walked the floors of La Posta, sometimes to flirt with a Mexican señorita, sometimes to deal at both ends of a six-shooter. This was the scene for Billy the Kid's famous trial, and a portion of the restaurant was his prison. There are lots of exciting tales in the west!

For twenty-five years on journeys west, our family has always stopped at La Posta for a fine Mexican dinner. On a recent trip, I finally met Katy. A waitress pointed her out to me, an exuberant woman just at that moment marching through the dining rooms, headed I couldn't tell where. So we trotted after her, single file, while I tried to get across to Katy what I was doing and handed her a copy of *Mary's Bread Basket*. That seemed to amaze her, but it didn't break her stride; we continued our parade through the last dining room, into the gift shop, and right through the kitchens to a back door. Katy extracted keys from her pocket, opened the door, and invited us into her home. I was stunned, for nothing showed from the outside that this interior existed. A huge living room, thickly carpeted, lavish with soft chairs and divans, led into a garden room complete with swimming pool and, next to it, a raised dining room. From there we walked into her bedroom, furnished with a tremendous round bed covered with a white fur spread. "Katy, this looks like a Hollywood set!" She laughed, we chatted, and she gave me a small paperback cookbook of the foods of La Posta, saying with a wave of her hand, "Mary, use anything you like."

Food-Processor Sopaipillas

Makes about 9 sopaipillas

2 cups flour
2 teaspoons baking
 powder
1 teaspoon salt
1 teaspoon sugar
2 tablespoons lard or
 vegetable shortening

1 egg
⅓ cup lukewarm water,
 approximately
Oil for deep frying
Honey
Confectioner's sugar
Cinnamon

Place the flour, baking powder, salt, and sugar in bowl of food processor fitted with steel blade. Whirl 3 times to blend ingredients. Add the lard and pulse 3 or 4 times, blending well. With the motor running drop the egg down the tube and add just enough water to form the ingredients into a mass. Do not overprocess. The dough should be slightly damp. Remove from bowl and with floured hands knead several times. Cover with a towel and let rest 30 minutes.

In a deep fryer heat 2 inches of oil to 370°F. On a lightly floured surface roll out the dough about ⅛ inch thick. Cut into 3-inch squares or 4 × 3-inch rectangles (I like to cut them on the bias). Drop 2 or 3 sopaipillas at a time into the fat and cook about 2 minutes on each side, until they are puffed and browned. Drain on paper towels. Serve hot, drizzled with honey or sprinkled with confectioner's sugar and cinnamon.

T here is in Texas, New Mexico, Arizona, and southern California, a great mix of Mexican, ancient Spanish, and Indian cultures that still influence the way of life, including food. *Sopaipillas* actually originated in New Mexico, rather than across the border. For festivals, which they love, Mexican-Americans in these states make a special coffeecake, similar to one made in New Orleans for Mardi Gras.

Mexican King's Bread Ring (ROSCA DE REYES)

Makes 2 loaves

2 packages active dry yeast
½ cup warm water
1 cup warm milk
1 cup sugar
1 cup melted butter or vegetable shortening
1 teaspoon salt
Grated rind of 1 lemon
6 eggs, beaten

2 tablespoons orange flower water
8–9 cups flour
¾ cup raisins, scalded, drained, and dried
½ cup chopped pecans
1–2 dried beans, covered in foil
Confectioner's Icing made with lemon juice, page 45

Combine yeast and water in small bowl, stirring until dissolved, and set aside. In a large mixing bowl combine the milk, sugar, and butter, stirring until dissolved. Add the salt, grated rind, eggs, orange flower water, and yeast mixture and blend thoroughly. Beat in 3 cups of flour to make a smooth batter. Add the raisins, pecans, and sufficient flour to make a soft dough. Turn out on a floured surface and knead 8 minutes, or until smooth and elastic. Round into a ball and place in a warm buttered bowl, turning to coat top. Cover loosely with plastic wrap and a towel and let rise until doubled, about 1–1½ hours.

The bread may be formed in two different shapes: free-form round loaves or molded rings. Punch down the dough and divide in half. Knead the bean or beans (which will bring good luck to the person or persons who receive that slice) into one or both halves. Round into loaves and place on a buttered baking sheet. Cover and let rise until doubled, about 1 hour.

Preheat the oven to 375°F. Bake the loaves 15 minutes. Reduce heat to 350°F and bake 30 minutes. Let loaves cool on wire racks and frost with Confectioner's Icing while warm.

To prepare rings, divide dough in half and roll each piece into a rope 24–26 inches long. Place in 2 buttered 5½-cup ring or Savarin molds, pinching ends together. Cover and let rise until doubled, about 1 hour.

Preheat the oven to 350°F. Bake rings about 40 minutes. Remove and let cool on wire racks. Frost as directed above.

Tucson, Arizona

P ronounced TOO-sawn, this fine city promises 3,800 hours of sunshine a year and is the home of the state university. Nearby are the singular Saguaro National Forest, an outstanding desert museum, Old Tucson, showing how the Old West lived (which is in constant use as a location for western movies), and superb desert resorts. Hacienda de Sol Ranch began as a small private school for girls, passed through several hands, and is now well established as an incomparable inn with fine cuisine.

Lettuce Bread

Makes 1 loaf

A quick bread, light and unusually attractive, to serve with morning coffee. A lovely gift from the Hacienda de Sol Ranch.

½ cup safflower or corn
  oil
1 cup sugar
2 eggs
1 teaspoon lemon juice
1½ cups flour
1 teaspoon baking powder
½ teaspoon baking soda

½ teaspoon salt
⅛ teaspoon ginger
1 cup packed finely
  chopped lettuce,
  preferably garden or
  leaf lettuce
Melted butter

Preheat the oven to 350°F. Brush a 9-inch loaf pan with butter and dust it lightly with flour.

In a large mixing bowl beat together the oil and sugar until well mixed. Add the eggs and lemon juice, blending well. Combine the dry ingredients and stir into the oil mixture. Add lettuce and mix well. The batter will be thick and smooth. Spread in the loaf pan and bake 55 minutes, or until bread tests done. Let cool in pan on a wire rack 10 minutes, remove from pan, and let cool on rack. The bread will slice better the next day.

F rom June Gibbs, extension specialist at the University of Arizona, I received information on the Mexican-Indian contribution to Arizona foods, which are not only delicious, but also interesting nutritionally. The difference between Mexican and Indian foods frequently is in name only, such as Mexican popovers and Indian fry breads. The ingredients are basically the same, though the techniques may vary. The addition of ash to Indian dishes increased the iron content of the Indians' diet.

Navajo Taco

Makes 1 taco

The base for a Navajo Taco is Navajo Fry Bread. That recipe will be found later in this chapter (page 381) and comes from the Navajo nation's capital at Window Rock. The directions are very simple and the recipe makes a full meal!

Place 1 warm fry bread on a large warm plate. Add ⅓ cup hot chili stew, top with ⅓ cup cooked pinto beans, 2 tablespoons chopped onion, ¼ cup chopped tomatoes, ⅓ cup shredded crisp lettuce (iceberg is the best for this dish), and ½ green chili torn into strips. Sprinkle ¼ cup grated cheese over all. Truly a meal in itself.

Phoenix and Scottsdale

A rizona is a land of canyons, mountains, and deserts, an Indian nation, and rapidly growing cities, a state we've enjoyed roaming for years. The northwest canyon country can be overwhelming in its brilliance. Driving over the Mogollon crest into green forests thick with snow in the winter is like being on top of the world, while cool, colorful Oak Creek Canyon is an artist's paradise.

In both Phoenix and Scottsdale are many restaurants that have maintained their fine cuisine for years. One, established over forty years ago, is the El Chorro Lodge. By the outdoor fireplace is an ideal spot for a predinner cocktail, where one can watch the play of the fire as the clear, deep blue evening sky begins to sparkle with stars. El Chorro is one of the few restaurants that still serves a traditional rack of lamb on a board, surrounded by spring vegetables. Always, there is a basket of breads and among them a moist, luscious dark cinnamon bun. I've noticed customers leaving, taking a doggie bag of buns with them. Evie and Joe Miller, the owners of El Chorro, have shared this fabulous recipe.

El Chorro Sticky Buns

Makes 42 buns

When measuring the brown sugar for both the topping and filling, do not pack tightly or there will be sugar bubbling on the floor of your oven!

Dough:

2 packages active dry
   yeast
1½ cups warm milk
⅓ cup melted butter
1 teaspoon salt

¼ cup sugar
2 eggs, beaten
1 teaspoon vanilla
6 cups flour,
   approximately

Topping:

⅜ pound (1½ sticks)
   butter, at room
   temperature
2 cups loosely packed
   brown sugar

3 tablespoons light corn
   syrup
2 tablespoons hot water

Filling:

⅜ pound (1½ sticks)
   butter
2½ cups loosely packed
   brown sugar

⅓ cup cinnamon
¼–½ cup hot water

In a large mixing bowl combine the yeast and milk, stirring until dissolved. Add the butter, salt, sugar, eggs, and vanilla, blending well. Gradually add sufficient flour to make a soft, workable dough that pulls away from sides of the bowl. Turn out and knead on a lightly floured surface 8–10 minutes, or until smooth and satiny. Round into a ball and place in a buttered bowl, turning to coat the top. Cover loosely with plastic wrap and a towel and refrigerate overnight.

The next day, prepare the topping. Cream the butter and sugar until fluffy. Add the corn syrup and slowly blend in the water. Spread in two 14 × 10 × 2-inch baking pans.

To make the filling, cream the butter, sugar, and cinnamon unttil fluffy. Slowly add sufficient water to make a spreadable mixture. Let the filling cool and refrigerate 30 minutes.

Preheat the oven to 375°F. Remove dough from refrigerator and divide in half. Roll one portion into a 21 × 12-inch rectangle. Spread half the filling over the dough to within ½ inch of the edges. Roll up from the long side, jelly-roll style. Cut into 1-inch slices and place cut side down on the topping, leaving ½ inch between the rolls. Repeat with remaining dough. Cover the rolls with a wet cloth in order to keep them the same height as the pan: Wet a muslin teacloth, wring it out, and lay it over the rolls. Place the pan in the oven. After 5 minutes rewet the cloth, place over the rolls again, and bake 5–10 minutes. Rewet the cloth a third time, replace it over the rolls, and bake the rolls 25–30 minutes more. Remove the cloth during the last 10–15 minutes. Turn the rolls out on a tray with a raised rim to catch drippings. If you like luscious rolls thick with topping and filling—these are for you!

Our Fiftieth State—Hawaii!

We parked our car in a garage at the Phoenix airport and left by plane to soar over the blue Pacific for our third visit to Hawaii. During the thrilling approach to Honolulu, the sentinel of Diamond Head appears, casting its shadow over Waikiki Beach, and, beyond, the old pink Royal Hawaiian maintains its dignity among the string of towering and unimaginative (but functional) new hotels. The sight of Pearl Harbor always brings a few tears; from the air one can clearly see portions of the rusting *Utah* beneath the long white memorial reaching across the water.

My adventures seeking out the breads of Hawaii began with Mary Cooke, a native Anglo-Hawaiian and food editor of the *Honolulu Advertiser*, who is most knowledgeable about all the foods of her state. Since she is a native and married to a man descended from an early missionary family, I valued her advice. From her I learned that Portuguese bread, popular over all the islands, evolved evidently into another bread, *malasadas*, which are frequently sold on the street. Someone made a batch of Portuguese dough that did not rise properly and, so as not to waste it, pulled off hunks and threw them into hot fat. Hawaiians love their *malasadas* hot and sprinkled with powdered sugar. On Martha's Vineyard I found a similar recipe (page 317).

Maui

Flying from island to island is pure delight. As we approached Maui, the sea dashed against the cliffs. Lush rows of sugar cane climb up the hills and converge with fields of pineapple. Later we stopped at a pineapple field to buy fresh, ripe slices to dip in salt—a true taste thrill. A curving, narrow road leads up the towering Haleakai, through the clouds, to a national park. At ten thousand feet the view is unbelievable from this giant slumbering volcano painted in its swirls of colors. We picnicked on a tiny beach pounded by exciting waves that crashed perilously close to a tiny missionary church. In the graveyard, each small monument was adorned with color photographs of the departed. We stumbled on a pillbox covered with trees and wiggled inside to try to imagine World War II from such a spot. All this and more is Maui.

Maui Onion Bread

Makes 1 loaf

Leslie Jackson, a teacher of cooking in the continuing education program at the University of Hawaii, has shared bread recipes of her state with me. This onion bread is delicately flavored and has an unusually fine texture.

¼ cup warm water
1 package active dry yeast
1 cup warm cottage
   cheese
2 tablespoons sugar
1 tablespoon butter, at
   room temperature
1 teaspoon salt

¼ teaspoon baking soda
1 egg
2¼ cups flour,
   approximately
2 tablespoons finely
   chopped Maui (or
   sweet) onion

Combine the water and yeast in a small bowl, stirring until dissolved. In a mixing bowl combine the cottage cheese, sugar, butter, salt, baking soda, egg, and yeast mixture and blend thoroughly. Stir in the flour and most of the onion, saving a small bit to place on top the bread. Turn dough out on a floured surface and knead 5 minutes, lightly flouring hands and work surface if needed. Round into a ball and place in a warm buttered bowl, turning to coat top. Cover loosely with plastic wrap and a towel and let rise until doubled, about 1 hour.

Spray a 1-quart soufflé dish with nonstick vegetable spray and brush with melted butter. Knead the dough and form into a round loaf. Place in the soufflé dish, press the remaining onion on top, cover, and let rise about 45 minutes.

Preheat the oven to 350°F. Bake 40–50 minutes. Let bread cool on a wire rack.

The bread also may be baked in a 9-inch loaf pan, but my preference is the round loaf.

The Island of Kauai

T he volcanoes of Kauai were quieted millions of years ago, allowing the sea, wind, and rain to carve wondrous sights. The summit of the island receives 460 inches of rain each year and literally lives in the clouds much of the time. We stood at the brink of Waimea Canyon, open to the sea, waiting for the mist to clear to see what we were told is one of the loveliest views in the world. We waited forty-five minutes, but the canyon remained a gray, swirling void.

My friend Gail Worstman, whom I introduced briefly in The Oregon Trail chapter, decided that city life had become too complicated and that she was depriving her family of a valuable different life style. The Worstmans moved to Kauai, purchased a natural foods store (which was almost wiped out in a hurricane), and now love every minute of their new life in Hawaii. Natural, flavorful foods are Gail's life. She has given me two superb recipes.

Tropical Kauai Papaya– Banana Bread

Makes 1 loaf

*A bread that combines the mellowness of papaya
with the sweetness of banana for a perfect tropical
marriage of flavors—a moist, luscious loaf.*

¼ pound (1 stick) butter,
   at room temperature
½ cup honey
1 egg
1½ cups whole wheat
   flour
½ cup unbleached white
   flour
2 teaspoons baking soda

¾ teaspoon sea salt
¾ cup mashed papaya
½ cup mashed banana
¼ cup buttermilk
⅛ teaspoon cinnamon
¼ teaspoon vanilla
¼ teaspoon grated orange
   peel

Preheat the oven to 350°F. Generously butter a 9-inch loaf pan.

Cream the butter and honey until fluffy. Beat in the egg. Combine the 2 flours, baking soda, and salt and add to butter mixture, stirring well. Combine papaya, banana, and buttermilk and blend into flour mixture until smooth. Stir in remaining ingredients and pour into loaf pan. Bake 50 minutes, or until the bread tests done. Remove from pan and let cool on a wire rack.

Old-Fashioned Portuguese Sweet Bread

Makes 2 loaves

From Martha's Vineyard to Kauai, Portuguese immigrants, laborers, and sailors have brought their culture with them. Originally, according to Gail, this was an Easter bread, but now it is made for everyday consumption. It is prepared with whole wheat flour, which may have been the way sweet bread was originally made.

¼ cup mashed or riced
  potatoes
½ cup boiling water
½ cup honey
¼ cup instant dry skim
  milk
¼ pound (1 stick) butter
2 packages active dry
  yeast
¼ cup warm water

4½–5 cups whole wheat
  flour
3 eggs, beaten
1 teaspoon sea salt
½ teaspoon vanilla
Grated rind of 1 lemon
1 cup chopped candied
  orange peel
1 egg, beaten, for glaze
Freshly grated nutmeg

Combine the potatoes, boiling water, honey, dry milk, and butter in a mixing bowl, stirring well. Let cool to 110°F.

In a small bowl combine the yeast and warm water, stirring until dissolved, and add to potato mixture. Beat in 2 cups of flour to make a smooth batter. Blend in the eggs, salt, vanilla, grated rind, and candied peel. Gradually add sufficient flour to form a workable dough. Turn out on a floured surface and knead until smooth and elastic, about 8 minutes. Round into a ball and place in a warm buttered bowl, turning to coat the top. Cover loosely with plastic wrap and a towel and let rise until doubled, about 1½ hours.

Punch down the dough, knead lightly, cover, and let rest 10 minutes. Butter 2 baking sheets. Divide dough in half and shape into round loaves. Place on baking sheets, cover, and let rise until doubled, about 1 hour.

Preheat the oven to 350°F. Brush the loaves with the glaze, sprinkle tops with nutmeg, and bake 30 minutes. Let cool on wire racks. Excellent served with butter and marmalade.

The Big Island

A loha to Gail and Kauai and off to the Big Island of Hawaii. To me, Hawaii is the most intriguing of all the islands. There are dramatic black beaches made of volcanic rock ground and eroded to silken sand by the sea. Fiery eruptions in Hawaii Volcanoes National Park can be safe to see. Once we arrived shortly after an eruption, to be awed by lava flows high above our heads; it was still steaming, green trees stuck out of it at odd angles, and had completely obliterated one of the park's paved roads. This big island cradles one of the world's largest cattle ranches, which sports a tiny manmade beach. The southern tip of the island is the southernmost point of the United States, reached by a lonely road that ends on huge rocks pounded by heavy ocean waves. We stayed in a charming new hotel built on lava rock high above the Pacific, where we enjoyed excellent lamb, luscious papaya, sweet bananas, and macadamia nut pie.

Hawaiian Coffeecake

Makes 1 coffeecake

8-ounce can crushed
  pineapple, not drained
½ cup packed brown
  sugar
⅜ pound (1½ sticks)
  butter, at room
  temperature
1 teaspoon cinnamon
1 teaspocn light corn
  syrup
½ cup canned flaked
  coconut

2½ cups sliced bananas
  (about 4 medium
  bananas)
¼ cup warm water
1 package active dry yeast
½ cup granulated sugar
½ teaspoon salt
3 eggs, beaten
¼ cup milk
2 cups flour

In a saucepan combine pineapple, brown sugar, 4 tablespoons of the butter, cinnamon, and corn syrup and bring mixture to a boil over moderate heat, stirring until ingredients are dissolved. Spoon into a 9-inch square or round cake tin. Sprinkle with the coconut and top with banana slices.

Combine water and yeast in a small bowl, stirring until dissolved. Cream remaining butter with granulated sugar until fluffy. Add the salt, eggs, milk, and yeast mixture and beat until well blended. Stir in the flour, beating until smooth. Spoon batter over topping and let rise 1 hour.

Preheat the oven to 375°F. Bake the cake 40 minutes, or until done. Let stand in pan on wire rack 15 minutes and invert on a cake plate.

Oahu

M ark Twain spent four months exploring these beautiful islands. His description cannot be surpassed, "the loveliest fleet of islands . . . anchored on any ocean." Back in Honolulu, we suddenly discovered a special charm of Oahu quite unconnected to tourist Waikiki—that we could never get lost. The main U.S. highway (obviously not an interstate) goes all around the island; turn left or right, you still can't go astray. What sights there are to see— huge breakers crashing on the leeward side (or was that windward?), the fun of the surf boarders riding the crests of waves, the beauty of a Mormon church surrounded by brilliant flowers, the tiny missionary museums filled with fascinating artifacts, and the extraordinary, intricately made feather capes in the Bishop Museum. Orchid leis and the hot Portuguese *malasadas* Mary Cooke told me about are sold on street corners. And a fruit that no other state grows in such abundance (except California, probably) is the perfumed mango that can be used to make a fresh-flavored bread.

Deluxe Mango Bread

Makes 2 loaves

The mango trees are so prolific at certain seasons that people place the fruit by the side of the road for anyone to take, according to my friend Leslie Jackson. I checked with my produce grocer and learned that mangoes are the most common tropical fruit in the world; to an Oriental, our common apple is a rarity. He buys mangoes from Hawaii and Haiti and sometimes from South America. Be sure to dice the mangoes—do not put them in either a food processor or a blender.

2 cups diced mangoes and juice
1 tablespoon lemon juice
2 cups flour
2 teaspoons cinnamon
2 teaspoons baking soda
1 cup sugar
½ teaspoon salt

3 eggs, lightly beaten
1 teaspoon vanilla
¾ cup light oil
½ cup chopped walnuts
½ cup canned flaked coconut
½ cup raisins, scalded, drained, and dried

Preheat the oven to 325°F. Spray two 8-inch loaf pans generously with nonstick vegetable spray.

Place the mangoes in a mixing bowl and marinate in the lemon juice about 10 minutes. Sift together the flour, cinnamon, baking soda, sugar, and salt. Add to the mangoes the eggs, vanilla, and oil, blending well. Stir in the dry ingredients until well mixed. Add the walnuts, coconut, and raisins, stirring to blend. Pour the batter into the loaf pans and bake 55 minutes, or until bread tests done. Remove from oven and place pans on wire racks to cool 10 minutes. Remove breads and let cool. They may be frozen successfully.

W hile I was testing recipes for this chapter, I discovered that the Mauna Loa Macadamia Nut Corporation markets jars of "Bits of Macadamia Nut"—just what I needed. A correspondence ensued, and the company was kind enough to offer me several recipes. There are three, two delicious quick breads, the third an outstanding Christmas cake. Refer to Sources of Supply regarding macadamia nuts.

Bits O' Mac Banana Bread

Makes 1 loaf

¼ pound (1 stick) butter,
  at room temperature
1 cup sugar
2 eggs
1 teaspoon vanilla
1⅔ cups sifted flour
1 teaspoon baking soda

½ teaspoon salt
1 cup mashed ripe
  bananas
½ cup sour cream
½ cup macadamia nut
  pieces

Preheat the oven to 350°F. Generously butter and flour a 9-inch loaf pan.

In bowl of an electric mixer cream the butter, sugar, eggs, and vanilla until fluffy. Sift the flour, soda, and salt together and add to butter mixture, beating for 30 seconds and scraping down sides of bowl with a rubber spatula as necessary. Fold in the bananas, sour cream, and nuts. Pour batter into the loaf pan and bake 1 hour, or until bread tests done. If the bread browns too fast, cover with aluminum foil during the last 10 minutes. Turn out carefully on a wire rack to cool.

Cinnamon-Crumb Coffeecake

Makes 1 coffeecake

A charming cake that brings the Pennsylvania Dutch influence to Hawaii!

2½ cups flour
1 cup packed brown sugar
¾ cup granulated sugar
¾ cup melted butter
2 teaspoons cinnamon
1 teaspoon baking powder

1 teaspoon baking soda
1 cup buttermilk
1 egg, beaten
½ cup chopped
   macadamia nuts

Preheat oven to 350°F. Butter a 9-inch square baking pan.

In a large mixing bowl stir together the flour, brown and granulated sugars, butter, and 1 teaspoon of the cinnamon to make a crumbly mixture. Measure ¾ cup of the crumb mixture and set aside. To the remaining mixture add the baking powder and soda, buttermilk, and egg and combine thoroughly (the batter will not be smooth). Pour into the baking pan. Mix nuts and remaining cinnamon with reserved crumb mixture and sprinkle over top of batter. Bake 35–45 minutes, or until cake tests done. Cut into squares and serve warm.

Macadamia Nut Fruitcake

Makes 2 large or 5–8 smaller loaves

Four 3½-ounce cans whole macadamia nuts
1 cup coarsely chopped candied pineapple
1½ cups golden raisins, scalded, drained, and dried
½ pound candied cherries, cut in half
4 cups sifted flour

¾ pound (3 sticks) butter, at room temperature
2 cups sugar
6 eggs, separated
¾ cup fresh orange juice
Grated rind of 1 orange
1 teaspoon cream of tartar
Candied cherries, pineapple, and whole nuts for decoration

Preheat oven to 275°F. Generously butter two 9-inch loaf pans. Line bottoms of pans with parchment or wax paper. Brush butter over the paper.

In a large mixing bowl combine macadamia nuts, pineapple, raisins, and cherries with ½ cup flour. Mix or shake gently to coat all the fruit with flour. Cream butter until fluffy. Gradually add the sugar and continue beating until creamy. Beat the egg yolks in a separate bowl and add to the butter mixture, mixing thoroughly and scraping down sides of bowl with a rubber spatula. Add the orange juice alternately with remaining flour, blending well after each addition. Fold in grated rind and nut and fruit mixture. Beat the egg whites until glossy, add the cream of tartar, and beat 1–2 minutes. Fold egg whites into the batter. Spoon batter into the pans and arrange nuts, pineapple, and cherries on top. Bake until cake tests done, about 1½–2 hours. Let stand in pan on a rack 1 hour. Turn cakes out and remove the paper carefully from bottoms. When thoroughly cooled, wrap in foil and, if they are to be kept longer than 3 days before serving, refrigerate or freeze the cakes.

If you prefer to make smaller cakes, this amount of batter will make four 7-inch loaves plus one 5½-inch loaf, *or* eight 5½-inch loaves. Prepare pans as directed above.

O ne more lovely dinner at Michel's in Honolulu, a restaurant we consider one of the top ten of the fifty states, an evening walk in the soft air of Oahu, and it was time to pack for the flight back to Los Angeles, Phoenix, and the Sunbelt.

Albuquerque, New Mexico, and Window Rock, Arizona

W|e blew the Arizona dust off our car and drove northeast over the Mogollon crest, passing the tiny hamlets of Strawberry, Punkin Center, and Happy Jack, to Albuquerque, New Mexico. Shirley and Earl Stewart, close friends who have lived near the Navajo Indians for more than thirty years, arranged two adventures—with recipes.

Following the Rio Grande south of Albuquerque, we came into the Pueblo village of Isleta, where I found a friendly, darling Pueblo woman, Sophie Lente. Sophie bakes Pueblo bread in free-standing, cone-shaped outdoor ovens, fifty loaves at one time. Mesquite wood is piled on the floor of the oven, then slowly reduced to ashes. By that time the oven's temperature is close to 500°F. Using a wet gunny sack on a stick, Sophie raked out the ashes. The bread, which had been rising in aluminum cake tins (used many times), was then placed on the floor of the huge oven. A board covered with a wet gunny sack was placed over the opening. Thirty minutes later, golden crusted loaves were removed. Two daughters and a granddaughter, Patricia Abeita, with whom I fell in love, helped carry the loaves inside to cool. We sat at Sophie's simple table in her one-room adobe house, broke open a hot loaf of bread and had a feast!

Patricia has sparkling black eyes and was wearing lovely Indian jewelry her mother had made. She soon pulled me back into her grandmother's backyard, for in addition to the two ovens it contained a veritable zoo—goats, sheep, chickens, cats—and Patricia had her own baby goat that I had to pet.

Sophie's Pueblo Bread

Makes 3 loaves

2½ cups warm water
1 tablespoon active dry
   yeast
⅓ cup lard or vegetable
   shortening

2 teaspoons salt
6 cups flour,
   approximately

Combine the water and yeast in a mixing bowl, stirring until dissolved. Melt the lard or shortening and blend into the yeast mixture with the salt. Beat in 3 cups of flour to make a smooth batter. Gradually add sufficient flour to form a very soft dough. Knead lightly in the bowl or on a floured surface just long enough to gather the dough together. Place in a warm bowl brushed with melted lard or shortening, turning to coat top. Cover loosely with plastic wrap and a towel and let rise overnight at room temperature.

The next morning, knead down the dough and divide into 3 equal portions. Shape into round loaves or into this delightful molding, which Sophie says the tourists like: Roll one portion of dough into a circle ½ inch thick. Using the illustrations as a guide, fold over like a big Parker

House roll so that the top does not quite meet the bottom. Cut deeply into the rounded edges twice. When baked, this puffs like a butterfly. Sophie maintains that the shaping has no Indian meaning—it's just pretty. Place loaves on buttered baking sheets and let rise 30 minutes.

Preheat the oven to 425°F. Bake the loaves about 25 minutes. Let cool on wire racks.

Note: The use of lard creates the crust typical of Pueblo Bread, but vegetable shortening does very well. Again, notice the similarity between this and Puerto Rican and Cuban breads.

T he following day, Earl drove us to Window Rock, Arizona, just over the border from western New Mexico. This small village is the capital of the Navajo Nation and is composed primarily of government buildings and a single motel. A huge rock formation with a hole in the center dominates the landscape and provided the name of the village. The Navajos are a nation within a nation, with their own tribal laws and an elected president and board that govern Navajo affairs, their finances, and the protection of their rights. We stayed in the motel and there I met Jayne Hawthorne. Jayne, an Anglo, married a handsome Navajo and the two have raised four huge sons. The family manages the motel. Jayne piloted me into the motel kitchen and gave me a lesson in Navajo Fry Bread, which we promptly ate piping hot with a good steak.

Navajo Fry Bread (DAH DI NIEL HYASH)

Makes 5 breads

4 cups flour
½ cup instant dry milk
2 teaspoons salt
1 tablespoon baking
  powder

1½ cups warm water
Lard or vegetable
  shortening

Combine the flour, dry milk, salt, and baking powder in a mixing bowl, blending thoroughly. Gradually add sufficient water, stirring constantly, to make a soft dough. Knead in the bowl just long enough to gather all the dough together. Cover and let rest 1 hour.

Divide dough into 5 pieces, each the size of a tennis ball. Fill a large skillet ½ inch deep with lard for best results, but vegetable shortening may be substituted. Jayne suggests that a liquid shortening is best. Do not use oil. Heat shortening until smoking hot, about 350°F. Jayne pats each ball into a thin sheet by throwing the dough between her hands. This is tricky and it takes practice, but you can fudge a little and use a rolling pin. Drop the sheet of dough into the hot fat and fry quickly on both sides until golden and puffy. Serve immediately.

When you conquer the fry bread, make the Navajo Taco on page 366.

Santa Fe and Taos

O ne could easily succumb to the enchantment of both Santa Fe and Taos. Santa Fe, the capital of New Mexico, is presumably the oldest colonial seat of government in the United States. The Spanish ruled from Santa Fe, the Indians reconquered their city, then the Mexicans interfered, and finally came the Americans. Archaeological discoveries now show that the ancient Indian lived here four hundred years before the arrival of the Spanish. Today, the architecture of the whole city has a golden glow of the pueblo and the desert.

Through Rosalie Talbott, a lifelong friend and Taos buff, I contacted Virginia Dooley, director of the Navajo Gallery and right-hand woman for the Navajo artist R. C. Gorman. Virginia, a superb cook, often hosts parties for Mr. Gorman's visiting VIPs. Generously, she has shared recipes for several fascinating breads.

Taos Pueblo Pumpkin Bread

Makes 2 loaves or 40–45 rolls

Canned or fresh pumpkin may be used, but the canned gives a stronger, more intense flavor.

1 package active dry yeast
1½ cups warm water
½ cup honey
1 teaspoon salt
⅔ cup melted butter
2 eggs, beaten

1 cup warm pumpkin
  purée
4 cups bread flour
4 cups unbleached white
  flour

In a large mixing bowl combine the yeast and water, stirring until dissolved. Add the honey, salt, butter, eggs, and pumpkin and blend very well. Beat in 3 cups of the bread flour to make a smooth batter. Gradually add the remaining bread flour and sufficient unbleached white flour to form a soft dough that pulls away from sides of the bowl. Turn out on a lightly floured surface and knead 5–8 minutes, or until smooth and elastic. Round into a ball and place in a warm buttered bowl, turning to coat the top. Cover loosely with plastic wrap and a towel and let rise until doubled, about 1 hour.

Butter a large baking sheet or two 9-inch cake tins. Punch down the dough, turn out on a floured surface, and knead lightly. Divide in half and form into round loaves. Place on the baking sheet or in cake tins. Cover and let rise until doubled, about 30–40 minutes.

Preheat the oven to 375°F. Bake loaves about 1 hour. Let cool on racks.

Rolls: Pull off pieces about the size of a small egg. Roll by cupping hand over ball of dough on a counter top to make a smooth round ball. Remember that whatever size you make the ball of dough, it will be twice as large when baked. Place the rolls in buttered cake tins. Cover and let rise until doubled, about 30–40 minutes. Bake in a preheated 375°F oven about 30 minutes.

Multi-Grained Hippie Bread

Makes 2 loaves

A quote from Virginia Dooley, who knows Taos well. "There are three different but co-existing cultures in Taos—Indian, Spanish, and Anglo. Each has made its own contributions to our culinary tradition. In the late 1960's, there was the Great Hippie Invasion of Taos by a generation of colorfully garbed 'Anglos' who eventually had jobs, mortgages, and station wagons just like everyone else. They made a culinary contribution with their interest in natural and unprocessed foods."

2 packages active dry
    yeast
1 cup warm water
3½ cups warm water
2 tablespoons honey
2 tablspoons light
    molasses
1 teaspoon salt
¼ cup light oil
2 cups unbleached white
    flour
3 cups stone-ground
    whole wheat flour

1 cup unprocessed bran
    (miller's bran)
Approximately 2 cups of
    the following in a
    mixture: soy flour,
    cornmeal, oatmeal,
    cracked wheat, brown
    rice flour, raw wheat
    germ
Melted butter (optional)

In a large mixing bowl combine the yeast and water, stirring until dissolved. Blend in the honey, molasses, salt, and oil. Add the white and whole wheat flours, beating until smooth, and beat in the bran. Make your own choice of grains for the mixture of the 6 flours and wheat germ. When the recipe was tested in my kitchen, this was the most successful mixture: ½ cup soy flour, 1 cup oatmeal (whirled in a food processor), 2 tablespoons cracked wheat, ¼ cup cornmeal, and ¼ cup wheat germ. Add the desired mixture of whole grains and enough white flour (it will take very little) to form a soft workable dough. Turn out on a lightly floured surface (use white flour) and knead with abandon (isn't that the hippie way?) 8–10 minutes, or until smooth and elastic. Round into a ball and place in a warm bowl lightly brushed with oil, turning to coat top. Cover loosely with plastic wrap and a towel and let rise until doubled, about 1 hour.

Butter a large baking sheet or two 8½-inch loaf pans. Punch down the dough, cut in half, and form into loaves—either round free-form or regular 8-inch loaves. Place in pans or on baking sheet, cover, and let rise until doubled, about 45 minutes.

Preheat oven to 375°F. Bake loaves 45 minutes, or until bread sounds hollow when rapped on the bottom. Brush with melted butter, if a soft crust is desired, and let cool on wire racks.

Biscochuelos

Makes 3 loaves

R. C. Gorman's housekeeper, Rose Roybel, sent me a recipe for a marvelous cookie using Scotch, which could not be used in a bread book. After rereading the recipe, I converted the ingredients into a sweet bread that all my volunteer assistants loved.

2 packages active dry
   yeast
1 cup warm water
1 cup warm milk
1 cup plus 1 tablespoon
   sugar
6–7 cups flour
½ cup melted lard or
   vegetable shortening

2 eggs, beaten
1 teaspoon salt
¼ cup Scotch
1 teaspoon anise seeds
Melted butter or vegetable
   shortening (optional)

Combine the yeast and water in a bowl, stirring until dissolved. Add the milk, 1 tablespoon sugar, and 3 cups of flour, beating until batter is smooth. Cover and let proof 30 minutes.

Stir down the sponge and add the lard, 1 cup sugar, eggs, salt, Scotch, and anise seeds. Gradually add sufficient flour to make a soft, workable dough that pulls away from sides of the bowl. Turn out on a lightly floured surface and knead 8 minutes, or until smooth and satiny. Round into a ball and place in a warm bowl brushed with vegetable shortening, turning to coat the top. Cover loosely with plastic wrap and a towel and let rise until doubled, about 1 hour. Punch down, knead lightly, and let rise about 30 minutes.

Brush three 8-inch loaf pans with melted shortening. Punch down the dough and divide into 3 equal portions. Form into loaves and place in pans. Brush tops of loaves with melted butter, if a soft crust is desired. Cover and let rise until just curved over tops of pans, about 30 minutes.

Preheat the oven to 400°F. Bake loaves 10 minutes, reduce heat to 350°F, and bake 20 minutes more. Remove and let cool on wire racks.

Variations: Divide one loaf into 3 portions, roll into ropes, and braid. Place on baking sheet brushed with melted shortening, cover, and let rise until doubled, about 30 minutes. Bake in a preheated 350°F oven 30 minutes.

Divide one portion of dough into 16 pieces. Stick some chocolate chips or a piece of chocolate in the center of each, roll into small balls, and place on prepared baking sheet. Cover and let rise until doubled. Bake in a preheated 350°F oven about 20 minutes.

A gain we drove back through the sweeping ranch lands of eastern New Mexico and the panhandle of Oklahoma, thrilled by the great variety of our country, from the tropical beauty of Hawaii to the deserts and ranches of the Southwest. Meeting Indians of different tribes and observing the complex mix of ethnic groups had enriched my understanding of our culture and of the exciting variety in the art of preparing bread.

MICHIGAN, WISCONSIN, AND THE MIGHTY MISSISSIPPI

MILEAGE—4,253 MILES

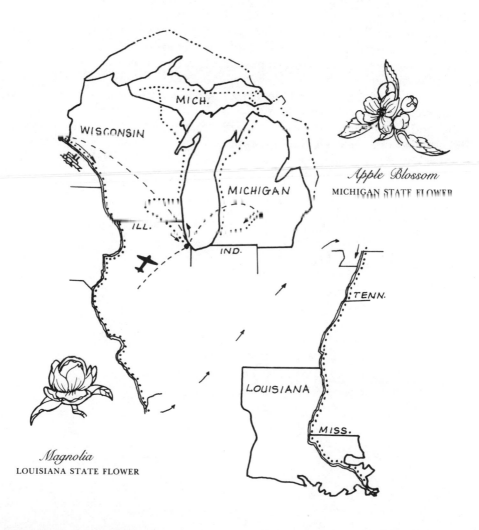

Apple Blossom
MICHIGAN STATE FLOWER

Magnolia
LOUISIANA STATE FLOWER

Michigan and Wisconsin

F our hours after leaving the Tulsa airport, our jet landed in Chicago, and we boarded a small commuter plane for Lansing, Michigan, where we began a journey filled with great beauty during which I would discover some of my finest breads. In our comfortable rental car, we drove through the center of Lansing, curved around the old capitol with its unusual dome on a high, slender tower. A stop at the tourist bureau provided packets of material and information, for there is an organized effort all over the state to boost tourism.

I suppose I could have been reading the map upside down. Anyway, I lost us attempting to find the Michigan State campus ("losing" a mere thirty thousand students) and we became trapped on some wild interstate that obviously would thrust us into the heart of industrial Detroit, never to be heard from again. Finally an exit appeared, we fled down the ramp, circled back onto the same jammed highway, and escaped the way we had come. Through great perseverence, we did find the campus, checked into a pleasant motel, and prepared for dinner.

The Pretzel Belle (despite its name) presented us with an excellent salad, fresh, fresh northern pike, and a superb black bread. Naturally I asked questions, and I ended up with a loaf of bread, but no recipe. I ate the whole loaf and decided that surely it could be repeated in my kitchen. Our waitress scurried back with the information that it was Russian black bread baked in Detroit.

Russian Black Bread

Makes 3 loaves

I inquired and searched for black bread when we were in Moscow and Kiev, but there was nothing but white bread and a pale rye. Perhaps all the fine Russian bakers have immigrated to Detroit.

3½ cups dark rye flour
3½ cups bread flour
1 teaspoon sugar
2 teaspoons salt
2 cups whole bran cereal
2 tablespoons crushed
    caraway seeds
½ teaspoon crushed
    fennel seeds
2 teaspoons instant coffee
2 teaspoons onion powder
2 packages active dry
    yeast

2½ cups water
¼ cup vinegar
¼ cup dark molasses
1 square unsweetened
    chocolate
¼ cup safflower oil
4 tablespoons margarine
1 egg white beaten with 1
    tablespoon water for
    glaze
Sesame seeds (optional)

Combine the rye and bread flours. In a large mixing bowl combine 2½ cups of flour mixture with the sugar, salt, bran, caraway and fennel seeds, coffee, onion powder, and yeast. In a saucepan combine the water, vinegar, molasses, chocolate, oil, and margarine and cook over low heat until warm, about 120°F. Margarine and chocolate need not melt completely. (Chocolate and coffee are added strictly for color. Both can be omitted, but then you won't have a black bread.)

Gradually add the liquid mixture to dry ingredients and beat thoroughly. Gradually stir in sufficient flour mixture to form a soft, workable dough. Turn out on a floured surface (use bread flour) and knead 10 minutes, or until smooth and elastic. Round into a ball and place dough in a warm bowl brushed with melted margarine, turning to coat top. Cover loosely with plastic wrap and a towel and let rise until doubled, about 1 hour.

Punch down the dough and divide into 3 portions. Knead each, cover, and let rest 10 minutes. Spray a baking sheet with nonstick vegetable spray. Form dough into baguette loaves (page 39) 16–17 inches long. Place on the baking sheet, cover, and let rise 1 hour.

Preheat the oven to 350°F. Brush loaves with the glaze, sprinkle with sesame seeds, if desired, and bake 45 minutes. Let loaves cool on wire racks.

Note: The sesame seeds are certainly optional, but the Detroit baker splashed them on heavily, which I love. Use any seeds of your choice.

I have long wondered how corn flakes are ironed into those flat little pieces. After an excellent breakfast at the Kellogg Center in Lansing, which is actually a lovely hotel for student management training, we drove west to Battle Creek. The eleven o'clock tour was ready to begin. We donned nets—even my husband's rather elaborate sideburns and mustache had to be covered. I thought it was hilarious. We looked like a group from outer space.

The tour was noisy, fascinating, and everything was so clean one could have dined on the floor. Finally we were led into a huge room where enormous pressure cookers can process 2,100 pounds of corn grits and 93 gallons of flavoring together at one time. The sticky, gummy mixture is dumped on a conveyor belt below, fed into an enormous dryer, and finally thrust into a hopper that funnels it onto rollers that flatten everything into corn flakes. More machines pop them into boxes that are automatically folded and sealed, ready for delivery. The entire process is monitored electronically; one woman watching a small screen can spot any error made by people or machines.

Accidentally, in 1894, a laboratory experiment with cooked wheat was interrupted, the wheat dried, and when it was run through rollers, the result was a sheet of wheat that broke into flakes. The highly successful Kellogg company was organized in 1906. In 1930, the W. K. Kellogg Foundation was formed, one of the ten largest philanthropic foundations in the United States, which makes grants in the fields of health, education, and agriculture.

Kellogg's Corn Flakes Muffins

Makes 12 muffins

*Kellogg Company in Battle Creek, Michigan, has
given me permission to use the following recipe.
I have made the muffins, they are delicious, and
the added variation is zippy!*

1⅓ cups flour
1 tablespoon baking
   powder
½ teaspoon salt
¼ cup sugar

2 cups Kellogg's Corn
   Flakes
1¼ cups milk
1 egg
⅓ cup light oil

Preheat the oven to 400°F. Butter twelve 2½-inch muffin cups.

Combine the flour, baking powder, salt, and sugar and set aside. Measure corn flakes and milk into a large mixing bowl, blending well. Let stand about 2 minutes, until cereal is softened. Add the egg and oil and beat well.

Add the flour mixture to the corn flakes mixture, stirring only until combined. (As with any muffin mixture, the mixing should be done quickly.) Divide batter among the muffin cups. Bake about 25 minutes, or until lightly browned. Serve hot.

Cheesy Hot Pepper Muffins: Add ½ cup shredded Monterey jack with chopped jalapeño peppers to egg mixture before adding flour mixture.

After extricating ourselves from the city of Battle Creek (I always manage to lose us in a city, but give me fifty miles of wide open spaces and I know exactly where I am), we drove to Lake Michigan, picking up fresh Michigan peaches at a fruit stand on the way. They were rosy and juicy and tasted the way a peach should. We chose a rambling route north. Hints of color, an occasional red maple already bursting into scarlet, gave me that very early fall feeling of just being glad to be alive.

We stopped at roadside markets looking for more lush Michigan peaches and found one small market with a bakery, clean rest rooms, and beautiful fresh produce. A couple passed me carrying a whole quart of fresh red raspberries. Never one to hesitate, I asked them where I should look for the raspberries. We started to talk, they asked if I were on vacation, and, after I explained my reason for traveling, the wife volunteered to let me have her recipe for a coffeecake with lots of cream, butter, and eggs. She promised to mail it and, bless her heart, I did receive this rich, lovely coffeecake recipe from Ruth and Al Korinek of Custer, Michigan.

Rich Coffeecake Dough

Makes enough dough for 2 coffeecakes

*As well as I could determine, this recipe came
from Al's mother and is very old. It can be
topped with fresh fruit or a cottage cheese filling.*

1 package active dry yeast	2 eggs
1 cup warm milk	2 egg yolks
7 cups flour	⅛ teaspoon nutmeg
½ teaspoon salt	1 tablespoon grated
1½ cups fresh or frozen	orange rind
orange juice	1 teaspoon grated lemon
1½ cups sugar	rind
½ pound (2 sticks) butter,	1 cup light cream
at room temperature	

In a large mixing bowl combine the yeast and milk, stirring until dissolved. Beat in 2 cups of flour and the salt to make a smooth batter. Cover and let rise until doubled and bubbly, about 1 hour.

Combine orange juice and sugar, stirring to blend, and let stand until sugar is dissolved. Cream the butter in an electric mixer until fluffy. (Use a flat beater if you have a heavy-duty mixer.) Add the whole eggs and egg yolks and blend well. Stir in the orange juice mixture, nutmeg, and orange and lemon rinds and add to sponge. Add the remaining 5 cups of flour alternately with the cream until they are incorporated. Ruth wrote a note not to overbeat. This will be a thick dough, similar to batter bread dough, not one to knead. Transfer to a warm buttered bowl, cover loosely with plastic wrap and a towel, and let rise 2 hours.

Stir down the dough with a rubber spatula just enough to take out the bubbles. The dough is ready to make into any of the following coffeecakes.

Cottage Cheese Coffeecake

Makes 1 coffeecake

2 cups well-drained
cottage cheese
½ cup sugar
2 egg yolks
½ cup raisins, scalded,
drained, and dried

½ recipe Rich Coffee
Cake Dough, preceding
recipe
Freshly grated nutmeg

Combine the cheese, sugar, egg yolks, and raisins until well blended. Spread the dough in a buttered 13 × 9 × 2-inch baking pan or Pyrex dish. Drop the cottage cheese filling by spoonfuls over the batter. Sprinkle lightly with nutmeg. Let rise 40 minutes.

Preheat the oven to 350°F. Bake cake 40–45 minutes. The coffeecake is delightful served hot or warm.

Fruit Coffeecake

Makes 1 coffeecake

Streusel Topping:
⅓ cup packed brown
sugar
½ cup flour

4 tablespoons butter, at
room temperature

½ recipe Rich Coffee
Cake Dough, page 392

Fruit Options:
2–3 peeled, cored, and
thinly sliced cooking
apples; *or* 3–4 cups
pitted raw cherries,
sliced Italian plums, or
peeled and sliced
peaches

To prepare the streusel topping, combine the brown sugar and flour in a small mixing bowl. Cut in the butter with a pastry blender or your fingertips. Set aside.

Butter a 13 × 9 × 2-inch baking pan. Spread the dough in the pan and top with neat rows of fruit, slightly overlapping. Sprinkle streusel over the fruit. Let the cake rise 40 minutes.

Preheat the oven to 350°F. Bake the cake 40–45 minutes. Remove baking pan to a wire rack and let cool or serve immediately.

Bundt Coffeecake

Makes 1 coffeecake

½–¾ cups slivered
  blanched almonds
½ recipe Rich Coffee
  Cake Dough, page 392

1 cup golden raisins,
  scalded, drained, and
  dried

Brush a Bundt pan thoroughly with melted butter. Sprinkle almonds over the bottom—at least ½ cup or more to make a pretty, crunchy top. Stir the golden raisins into the dough until well distributed. Spread the batter in the pan over the almonds. Cover and let rise 1 hour.

Preheat the oven to 350°F. Bake the cake about 50 minutes, or until it tests done. If the top becomes too brown, cover with a piece of aluminum foil during the last 15 minutes of baking. Turn out on a wire rack to cool. The coffeecake freezes well.

W e left the Korineks with their lovely red raspberries (a whole quart!) and drove to Bear Sand Dunes National Lake Shore and then on to Traverse City, the cherry capital of the world. When it was first settled, lumber and shipping were the main industries, but cherry trees had been planted in the 1800's, and in this century fruit has become the dominating industry of the area. Branches of apple and pear trees drooped to the ground, they were so heavily laden. On Saturday evening the resort section of the city was jammed. In the dining room of our hotel, which looks out over a magnificent bay, balloons were popping as children and adults celebrated birthdays and anniversaries.

During the drive north on Highway 131, the trees slowly became more vivid with color among many hues of green. After lunch in Petosky we finally crossed the Mackinac Bridge, a magnificent masterpiece. We parked our car at St. Ignace, purchased ferry tickets, and boarded for a misty twenty-minute ride to Mackinac Island.

A bellman from our hotel met us at the boat, loaded his bicycle with our luggage (a most amazing show of dexterity), and we went on foot along Main Street. It smells of horses and fudge; every other store sells elaborate kinds of fudge, and only horses are allowed to pull conveyances. We hailed a likely looking horse and driver and toured the island. Our driver and tour director was Irish, the father of seven children. His family arrived here in 1852. We learned that the Grand Hotel, one of the country's most elegant resort hotels, was built by two railroad companies. Those who stay on the island during the winter are icebound, but the women drive snowmobiles to one spot closest to mainland, zip over the ice for groceries, and are back within an hour. There are three hundred horses, four blacksmiths, two veterinarians, and fifty-seven varieties of lilacs on the island. Highway 181, which circles the island, is the only United States highway with no cars. The people here are a mixture of French, Irish, Indian, and English. But our driver, Jack, a Roman Catholic, married a Finnish Lutheran, even though both their families objected. So, now that you know the fascinating facts about this island without cars, let's take a look at a marvelous Finnish bread. One more interesting fact—the horses come from Indiana and Iowa.

Finnish Pulla

Makes 1 large or 2 smaller loaves

1 package active dry yeast
¼ cup warm water
1⅓ cups warm milk
1 egg, beaten
⅓ cup melted butter
½ cup sugar
½ teaspoon salt

6 cups flour,
 approximately
1 teaspoon cardamom
1 egg mixed with 1
 tablespoon water for
 glaze
¼ cup slivered or sliced
 almonds

Combine the yeast and water in a small bowl, stirring until dissolved. Measure milk into a large mixing bowl. Add the egg, butter, sugar, and salt. Add the yeast mixture and stir well. Beat in 2 cups of flour and add the cardamom. Add 2 more cups of flour and beat well. Add sufficient flour to make a soft, workable dough that pulls away from sides of the bowl. Turn out on a floured surface and knead until smooth and elastic, about 8 minutes. Round into a ball and place dough in a warm buttered bowl, turning to coat the top. Cover loosely with plastic wrap and a towel and let rise until doubled, about 1 hour.

Punch down the dough and divide into 3 equal portions. Knead each and let rest 10 minutes. Brush a 15½ × 14-inch baking sheet with melted butter or spray with nonstick vegetable spray. Roll each piece of dough into a 16–17-inch rope. Pinch three ends together and braid the ropes (see page 36 for braiding instructions). The finished loaf should be very long—a huge, beautiful braid. Place the bread diagonally on baking sheet, cover, and let rise until doubled, about 1 hour.

Preheat the oven to 350°F. Brush the loaf with the glaze and sprinkle with almonds. Bake about 30 minutes, or until golden brown. Let cool on a wire rack.

Note: If desired the dough may be cut into 6 portions and made into 2 smaller braids. Baking time will be about the same. This is a magnificent bread for a dinner party and toasts unusually well.

O n January 26, 1837, Michigan gained admittance to the Union as a state. Settlers poured into the agricultural southern section. It is one of our most beautiful states, with shore lines on four of the Great Lakes, divided into two portions at the straits of Mackinac. Michigan is rich now in planted forests, but depleted of the iron that once drew thousands of immigrant workers to the northern peninsula. We left the main highway to drive through the Hiawatha Forest and to see both the upper and lower Tahquamenon Falls. The former is a spectacular fifty-foot drop from a great rocky crest two hundred feet wide. The water is colored a rich golden brown by iron deposits. I could have stayed a week just to see the glorious fall foliage, but after two lovely days we entered the neighboring state of Wisconsin, equally stunning, but with completely different exciting adventures in store for us.

Milwaukee

M ahanawaukee-Seepe, "the gathering place," was a strategic area, for here the Kinnikinnik, Menomonee, and Milwaukee rivers converge and empty into Lake Michigan. Fur trading began the growth of this tiny Indian village that is now a vigorous city of 640,000. Before World War I, seventy percent of the city's population was German. Still the home of the famous Milwaukee brewers who make some of the finest beer brewed in America, it has become a refuge for tremendous numbers of immigrants seeking freedom and peace. One fifth of the population of Milwaukee is foreign born. At the International Institute of Milwaukee, where immigrants are helped to adjust to their new country, I was informed that Germans are still the largest group, followed by Poles, Italians, Austrians, and Russians. Sixty-five ethnic groups and other Americans are represented in the spectacular annual festival. The city is an international mosaic.

The sun shone brightly as I walked the one block from the old, elegantly redone Pfister Hotel to Universal Foods. Two well-informed Milwaukeeans, Laura Erwin and Robert Mantsch, for two hours patiently answered my questions about breads and Red Star yeast. Much of my information concerning yeast in the first chapter of this book stems from our conversation. I returned to my hotel happily laden with material, my brain buzzing with ideas and the information that Port Washington is the place for smoked fish.

Red Star Yeast was born on December 4, 1882, as part of a small distilling company that gradually grew into the conglomerate of Universal Foods. All my testing has been done with Red Star Yeast for two reasons. It contains no additives and the product is very widely available. Permission has been given by Universal Foods for me to use three recipes that I particularly wanted to share with you.

Old Milwaukee Rye Bread

Makes 2 loaves

Although the preparation of this bread requires three days, there is nothing difficult about the process. Since this is a sourdough procedure, just a little tender care, stirring the sponge occasionally, is required before you construct the final bread—one of my favorites.

Sponge:

1 package active dry yeast
1½ cups warm water
2 cups rye flour

1 tablespoon caraway
  seeds

3–4 cups white flour
1 cup rye flour
1 package active dry yeast
1 tablespoon salt
1 tablespoon caraway
  seeds

1 cup water
¼ cup molasses
3 tablespoons vegetable
  shortening
Cornmeal

Prepare the sponge (similar to a sourdough starter) 2–3 days before baking the bread. Combine the yeast and water in a mixing bowl (nonmetal), stirring until dissolved. With a rubber spatula stir in the rye flour and caraway seeds. Cover loosely with plastic wrap and a towel. Set aside in a cozy spot 2–3 days; the longer the sponge works, the more bite to the bread. Stir twice a day—the aroma will be delicious.

On the third day, combine 1 cup of white flour, the rye flour, yeast, salt, and caraway seeds in a large mixing bowl and blend well. In a saucepan heat the water, molasses, and shortening until warm, about 120°–130°F. The shortening need not melt completely. Add to the flour mixture, stirring well. Stir down the sponge, add to the flour mixture, and beat well to blend. Using the dough hook of a heavy-duty mixer, beat 3 minutes at medium speed. Gradually add sufficient white flour to make a workable dough that pulls away from sides of the bowl. Turn out on a lightly floured surface and knead about 5 minutes, or until smooth and resilient. Round into a ball and place the dough in a warm bowl brushed with melted shortening, turning to coat the top. Cover loosely with plastic wrap and a towel and let rise until doubled, about 1 hour and 15 minutes.

Brush a baking sheet with melted shortening and sprinkle with cornmeal. Punch down the dough and divide in half. On a lightly floured surface shape each portion into a round loaf. Place loaves on a baking sheet, cover, and let rise 15 minutes. Slash each loaf ¼ inch deep with a razor. Cover and let rise 15 minutes more.

Preheat the oven to 375°F. Bake the loaves 40–45 minutes. Let cool on a wire rack.

Red Star Christmas Coffeecake

Makes 1 coffeecake

When I baked six of these cakes for holiday gifts,
the aroma permeated my home; the cakes smelled
like Christmas and tasted like Christmas!
Originally the cake was named Queen Ann
Holiday Brunch Cake, but I have changed the
title; it did seem the cake deserved a special star!

3–4 cups flour
2 packages active dry
  yeast
¾ cup sugar
1 teaspoon salt
¼ teaspoon ginger
1 tablespoon grated
  orange rind
½ cup milk
½ cup water
½ pound (2 sticks) butter
  or margarine

4 eggs, lightly beaten
3-ounce package cream
  cheese, at room
  temperature
½ cup currants
½ cup chopped mixed
  candied fruit
¼ cup chopped candied
  cherries
½ cup coconut flakes
½ cup sliced almonds

Orange Glaze:

1 cup confectioner's sugar
1 teaspoon grated orange
  rind

¼ teaspoon vanilla
5–6 teaspoons orange
  juice

In a large mixing bowl combine 1½ cups flour, yeast, sugar, salt, ginger, and grated rind and mix well. In a saucepan heat the milk, water, and butter until warm, about 120°–130°F. The butter need not melt completely. Add the mixture to the flour mixture. Blend in the eggs and cream cheese. If you have a heavy-duty mixer, use the flat beater and blend at low speed until all ingredients are well moistened. Turn machine to medium speed and beat 3 minutes. If beating by hand, use a rubber spatula. If you tire, cover the bowl and rest a few minutes.

Gradually stir in the currants, fruit, cherries, coconut, and sufficient flour to make a stiff batter. Brush a Bundt pan with melted butter, dust with flour, and arrange almonds on bottom. Spoon the batter into the pan. Cover and let rise in a warm spot until doubled, about 1 hour. The cake should rise only to within 1 inch of the top of the pan. Otherwise luscious batter will slurp all over on the oven floor!

Preheat the oven to 375°F. Bake the cake 35–40 minutes, or until it is golden brown and tests done. Remove from oven and let cool in the pan on a wire rack 15 minutes. Remove from pan. If planning to serve immediately, cover with the glaze, made by combining the sugar, orange rind, vanilla, and sufficient orange juice to form a smooth icing. Pour over the cake. Freeze the coffeecake without the glaze.

Raisin-Orange Holiday Trees

Makes 3 Christmas trees (33 rolls)

Luscious rolls that could be served for a morning coffee, but are also perfect for a Christmas tree breakfast. The formation of the tree is delightfully easy.

Dough:

2 packages active dry yeast

5–5½ cups flour

½ cup sugar

2 tablespoons grated orange rind

1 teaspoon salt

1 cup milk

½ cup water

4 tablespoons butter or margarine

2 eggs

1½ cups raisins, scalded, drained, and dried

Filling:

½ cup packed brown sugar

½ cup chopped toasted almonds

1 teaspoon cinnamon

3 tablespoons melted butter

Orange Glaze, preceding   Candied cherries
   recipe

In a mixing bowl combine the yeast, 2½ cups flour, sugar, orange rind, and salt and mix well. Heat the milk, water, and butter until warm, about 120°–130°F. The butter need not melt completely. Add the mixture to the flour mixture and add the eggs. If using a heavy-duty mixer, blend at low speed with the flat beater until the dry ingredients are moistened. Beat at medium speed 3 minutes. If mixing by hand, use a rubber spatula and rest when tired—the dough will be fine. Gradually stir in the raisins and sufficient flour to make a soft dough that pulls away from sides of the bowl. Turn out on a lightly floured surface and knead 5–8 minutes. Round into a ball and place the dough in a warm buttered bowl, turning to coat the top. Cover loosely with plastic wrap and a towel and let rise until doubled, about 1 hour.

To make the filling, mix together the brown sugar, almonds, and cinnamon. Set aside.

Punch down the dough, knead lightly, and divide into 3 portions. Cover and let rest 10 minutes. Butter three 15½ × 14-inch baking sheets. On a lightly floured surface roll 1 portion into an 11-inch square. Brush with melted butter and sprinkle with one third of the filling. Roll up tightly and seal seam and ends. Cut the roll into 11 slices. To form a tree, place the slices cut side up and edges touching on a baking sheet as follows, using the illustrations as a guide: Place 1 roll at

the bottom for the trunk; for the second row use 4 rolls; for the third row use 3 rolls; for the fourth row use 2 rolls; and top with the last roll. Repeat directions with remaining dough. Cover and let rise until almost doubled, about 30–40 minutes.

Preheat the oven to 350°F. Bake trees 10–25 minutes. Let trees cool on baking sheets set over wire racks. When cooled they can be removed without a roll tumbling off. Brush with Orange Glaze and decorate with cherries.

Slovenian Potica

Makes 2 coffeecakes

From the Milwaukee Public Library I received this fascinating recipe. I had to check in the encyclopedia to find out exactly where the Slovenes had been located. Between the two world wars, Slovenia was part of Yugoslavia, Istria, Friuli, and a tiny slice of Hungary. Then I discovered that my Utica Connection is of Slovenian background. Together we carefully tested the recipe.

Sponge:
2 packages active dry
   yeast
¼ cup warm milk

1 teaspoon sugar
3 tablespoons flour

1 cup warm milk
3 tablespoons sugar
1 teaspoon salt

4 egg yolks, beaten
5 cups flour,
   approximately
½ pound (2 sticks) butter

Filling:
¾ cup heavy cream
3 cups ground walnuts
1 tablespoon butter
¼ cup sugar
1 tablespoon honey

1 egg, beaten
Grated rind of 1 lemon
½ teaspoon cinnamon
¼ cup raisins

1 egg beaten with 1
   tablespoon water for
   glaze

To make the sponge, in a small mixing bowl combine the yeast and milk, stirring until dissolved. Beat in the sugar and flour and let proof 20 minutes.

In a large mixing bowl combine the milk, sugar, and salt. Blend in the egg yolks and the sponge.

Into a separate bowl sift 4 cups of flour and cut in the butter with pastry blender or use a food processor. Gradually add the flour mixture to the liquid mixture, beating with rubber spatula or the dough hook of a heavy-duty mixer. Keep mixing, adding spoonfuls of flour until dough pulls away from sides of the bowl. Turn the dough out on a lightly floured surface and knead about 5 minutes, or until smooth and elastic. Round into a ball and place in a warm buttered bowl, turning to coat the top. Cover loosely with plastic wrap and a towel and let rise until doubled, about 2 hours.

To make the filling, heat cream to scalding, remove from the heat, and add the walnuts. Add the butter and let cool. Blend in the sugar, honey, egg, lemon rind, cinnamon, and raisins, mixing well.

Generously butter two 9-inch cake tins, or 1 cake tin and a Bundt pan. Punch down the dough and divide in half. Roll 1 portion into a 24 × 12-inch rectangle. Spread half the filling over the dough, leaving ½ inch of free edge all around the rectangle. Roll from the long side, jelly-roll style. Pinch the seam to seal and form into a snail. Place the snail seam side down in a cake tin. Repeat directions with the remaining portion of dough. If using a Bundt pan, overlap the ends and pinch them to seal. Cover and let rise 1 hour.

Preheat the oven to 350°F. Brush the loaves with the glaze and bake about 45–60 minutes. If the *potica* becomes too brown, cover with foil during the last 15 minutes of baking. Let cool in pan set over a wire rack 15–20 minutes. Remove to a serving tray or let cool further to freeze.

New Glarus, Wisconsin

A fter gorging on smoked fish, fresh fish, *Wiener Schnitzel,* liver dumpling soup, and potato dumplings, we waddled out of Milwaukee and drove west to Madison, the capital. We admired the handsome capitol building, which is unfortunately scrunched between other buildings, and the huge University of Wisconsin campus, where we promptly got lost. After carefully examining the map (right side up!), we finally managed to find a highway south into Frank Lloyd Wright country—beautiful low hills, where the trees were just coming into color and we saw more of his fine buildings which have weathered the years so well. Then we headed into dairy farm country—southern Wisconsin is all cows. We saw endless acres of feed crops ready for harvesting and, on the rich grazing land, thousands and thousands of the big, handsome Holsteins that produce Wisconsin milk, cream, and butter.

When we drove into New Glarus, we could have been in some tiny village in Switzerland, where my husband's family came from. Flower boxes filled with gaily colored blossoms were at every window, and I spotted a bakery—or rather, The Bakery. I bought a pumpernickel raisin loaf and an apple-cinnamon bread. Then we checked into a lovely Swiss motel. Our room was huge and had a Persian rug in the pretty sitting area. I could tell that it was going to be difficult to extricate me from this place. At dinner we had some of the best veal sausage I've ever tasted, made with local veal and rich fresh cream. We also splurged and had beef fondue.

The following morning, on the breakfast buffet were sweet rolls and a coffeecake. I took one bite of the coffeecake and asked about the baker. The hostess phoned immediately to arrange for me to meet Howard Weber at The Bakery.

Howard is one of the most delightful young men I've met in all my travels and simply tops as a baker. Not only does he make gorgeous breads and coffeecakes, but he also creates elegant desserts and some of the best chocolates I've ever popped in my mouth. Howard has a delightful American sense of humor. There was one bread that puzzled me. "Oh, that's an udder bread," he said. "This is dairy land, you know." Then he promptly showed me how to form the "udder bread." I could hardly wait to make that for some of my ranching friends (see page 412)! But let's start at the beginning with Howard's recipes that he makes each day for The Bakery (owned and operated by him, as it turned out) and that he patiently taught me.

Howard Weber's Apple Bread

Makes 3 loaves

*I called Howard for this recipe after eating
practically a whole loaf he had given me because
it was so moist and just plain good. His method is
very practical for him. When he is through for
the day, he throws all his leftover pieces of dough
in a pile and makes apple bread with them. You
and I don't normally have pieces of dough left
over, so I worked out a different method.*

2 packages active dry
  yeast
¼ cup warm water
2½ cups warm buttermilk
½ cup melted butter
2 teaspoons salt
¼ cup sugar
2 eggs, beaten

6 cups flour,
  approximately
2 cups peeled, cored, and
  thinly sliced apples
  (enough for 1 loaf only)
¼–½ cup Cinnamon
  Sugar, page 46 (enough
  for 1 loaf only)
Melted butter

In a small bowl combine the yeast and water, stirring until dissolved, and set aside. In a large mixing bowl combine the buttermilk, butter, salt, sugar, and eggs, blending well. Add the yeast mixture. Beat in 2 cups of flour. Gradually add sufficient flour to make a soft, workable dough that pulls away from sides of the bowl. Turn out on a floured surface and knead 8 minutes, or until smooth and satiny. Round into a ball and place in a warm buttered bowl, turning to coat the top. Cover loosely with plastic wrap and a towel and let rise until doubled, about 1 hour.

Punch down the dough and divide into 3 equal portions. Knead each piece thoroughly, cover, and let rest 10 minutes. Butter one 9-inch and two 8½-inch loaf pans. Roll or pat out 1 portion of dough into a 12 × 8-inch rectangle—don't worry about being precise. Place the apples over the dough and sprinkle with as much Cinnamon Sugar as you like. With a dough scraper immediately and carefully cut into the apples in 3 straight lines across the dough. Chop the apples and cinnamon sugar

lightly into the dough. Do not chop completely through the dough or you will have an awful mess. Continue chopping until liquid begins to form and the dough wells up through the chopped apples. Roll up the mess—I mean dough—from the short side, using that trusty dough scraper to help, into something that looks like a loaf and plop it right into the 9-inch loaf pan. Tuck down the corners and brush with melted butter. If you want 2 more loaves of apple bread—prepare more apples. Repeat directions with remaining portions of dough (they freeze well). Cover and let rise 30 minutes.

Preheat the oven to 350°F. Bake the apple loaf 35–40 minutes, the plain loaves 30 minutes. Brush again with melted butter and place loaf pans on a wire rack to cool 10 minutes. Turn bread out on wire racks to cool. The simplest things with leftovers can turn out to be so delicious.

Note: The bread can be prepared with Basic Sweet Dough (page 432).

Mandel Ring,
an Almond Coffeecake

Makes 4 coffeecakes

One of the finest coffeecakes I've encountered is this one created by Howard Weber. Working back from the large amount of ingredients that he uses to make just two cakes was a challenge I enjoyed. In testing, I found that the cake can be made with two different doughs—one a classic Danish dough, which Howard uses, and the other a simpler rich basic dough. Both doughs are refrigerated overnight. Read the directions carefully and gather all ingredients together before beginning.

DANISH COFFEECAKE DOUGH

1¼ pounds (5 sticks) unsalted butter, at room temperature
½ cup sugar
3 tablespoons instant nonfat dry milk
1 teaspoon salt
1 teaspoon cardamom

4 large eggs
4 egg yolks
⅓ cup light corn syrup
2 packages active dry yeast
½ cup warm water
1½ cups cake flour
5 cups bread flour

Cream 1 stick butter, sugar, dry milk, salt, and cardamom until light and fluffy. If you are working with a heavy-duty mixer, use the flat beater. In a small bowl combine the whole eggs, egg yolks, and corn syrup, beat well, and add to the butter mixture. Combine the yeast and water in a small bowl, stirring until dissolved. Change from the flat beater to a dough hook. Add the yeast mixture and cake flour, beating until smooth. Gradually add sufficient bread flour to make a soft, workable dough that pulls away from sides of the bowl. Turn out on a floured surface and knead by hand 10 minutes, or with the dough hook about 8 minutes. Divide the dough in half. Keeping each portion sepa-

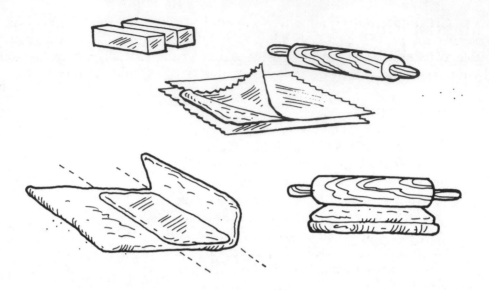

rate, shape into small rectangles, cover with plastic wrap, and refrigerate 30 minutes.

The remaining 1 pound of butter should be soft enough to mold. Place ½ pound of the butter between 2 sheets of wax paper and roll into a 12 × 8-inch rectangle. Refrigerate. Repeat with remaining portion of butter.

Remove 1 portion of dough and roll the small rectangle into a 16 × 9-inch rectangle. Remove 1 sheet of butter, peel off the wax paper, and place butter in center of rectangle, using the illustrations as a guide. Fold into thirds. Turn so that open side is toward you and roll into a 16 × 8½-inch rectangle. Fold into thirds again. Turn so open side is toward you and roll into a rectangle. Repeat the folding and rolling one more time. Wrap the dough carefully in plastic wrap and refrigerate overnight. Repeat directions with remaining dough and butter.

ALMOND FILLING

¼ pound (1 stick)
   unsalted butter, at room
   temperature
¼ pound almond paste

½ cup sugar
1 egg white, if necessary
Sliced almonds (optional)

Cream the butter, almond paste, and sugar in the small bowl of an electric mixer and beat until light and fluffy. It should be of a spreadable consistency, like creamy peanut butter. If stiff, add a little egg white. Do not add the egg white unless necessary to thin the mixture.

RUM SYRUP

1 cup light corn syrup
1 cup sugar
½ cup water

2 ounces dark or light
rum (optional)

Combine the syrup, sugar, and water in a saucepan and bring to a boil, stirring occasionally to brush down the sugar from sides of saucepan. As the syrup begins to bubble, place a lid on the saucepan for 1 minute so that the condensed steam will clean off sides of pan. Remove from burner and add rum, if desired.

Final Preparation: Remove 1 portion of Danish dough from refrigerator, place on a floured surface, and roll into an 18 × 12-inch rectangle. Spread half the almond filling down center of dough and sprinkle with sliced almonds, if desired. Fold one long side over filling and fold over the other side to make 3 layers. Seal the open side. Cover with plastic wrap and place in freezer 30 minutes. Repeat with remaining dough and filling.

Butter 2 Savarin pans and two 11-cup ring molds. Remove 1 filled portion of dough and roll (do not hesitate to sprinkle table with flour) into a 20 × 8-inch rectangle. With a dough scraper or sharp knife divide the rectangle into 6 lengthwise slices. Roll the ropes a little to give a

better shape. Braid 3 of the ropes and place in a Savarin pan. Braid the second 3 ropes and place in a ring mold. Repeat with remaining portion of dough.

Cover the pans and let rise until light, about 1–1¼ hours.

Preheat the oven to 350°F. Bake cakes 30 minutes. Remove from oven and, if serving at once, brush the warm rum syrup over top of cakes thoroughly. Turn the cakes out on a wire rack (with foil underneath) and brush the bottom of cakes with syrup. Howard dips his cakes into the syrup—but then he makes lots of cakes with a huge pan of syrup. Let cakes cool until syrup is set. Amazingly, the syrup is not sticky and it prevents this luscious cake from drying out. The cakes keep very well for several days without refrigeration. Freeze the cakes without the syrup.

Note: There will be syrup left over. Place in container, cover, and label; it will keep indefinitely.

Cardamom Coffeecake

Makes 2 coffeecakes

*This is easier to prepare than the Danish dough—
no folding of butter and rolling. The dough
should be prepared the night before, refrigerated,
and then filled and molded, following the
directions in the recipe for Mandel Coffeecake.
There is more dough here than in Mandel
Coffeecake, so all the filling will be needed, but
once again there will be syrup left over.*

2 packages active dry
  yeast
½ cup warm water
¼ cup sugar
1 teaspoon salt
1 teaspoon cardamom
1 cup warm milk

1 cup melted unsalted
  butter
2 egg yolks, beaten
5 cups flour,
  approximately
Almond Filling, page 408
Rum Syrup, preceding
  recipe

Combine the yeast and water in a small mixing bowl, stirring until dissolved. In a large mixing bowl blend the sugar, salt, and cardamom. Add the milk and butter, stirring until dissolved. Blend in the egg yolks and yeast mixture. Beat in 3 cups of flour until mixture is smooth. Gradually add sufficient flour to make a workable dough that pulls away from sides of the bowl. Turn out on a lightly floured surface and knead 5 minutes. Round into a ball and place in a buttered bowl (do not warm the bowl), turning the dough to coat it with butter. Be certain to use a large bowl as the dough will expand during the night. Cover securely with plastic wrap and a towel. Refrigerate overnight.

Remove the dough, knead, and divide in half. Follow the same directions for filling, molding, and baking the coffeecakes as instructed in the Final Preparation for the Mandel Ring. This dough is easy to handle. Use flour when rolling on either a board or pastry cloth. Brush with warm syrup just after the cakes have been removed from the oven.

Suggestion: In testing, I found this dough makes an especially lovely cake if baked in a Bundt pan. To be certain that the filled dough will be long enough to braid and fit into a Bundt pan, roll the rectangle about 5 inches longer.

A special friend at Fort Atkinson gave me further understanding of this portion of Wisconsin. From their home on top of a knoll in the midst of six lovely acres, one can see tree-covered ridges far across the countryside, evidence of the last glacial movement that receded and left behind not only the ridges but rich black soil ten inches deep between them, the soil that supports today's dairy farming. My host guided me to a neighboring farm, where I watched fifty enormous cows placidly walk into their modern milking stalls. First the quantities of tubes installed on the ceiling are automatically flushed and cleaned. Then one young man cleaned udders, the other hooked up the milking machine, and milk poured through the tubes overhead into a cooling vat. Two people can milk all those cows in an hour!

Wisconsin Udder Bread

Makes 1 loaf

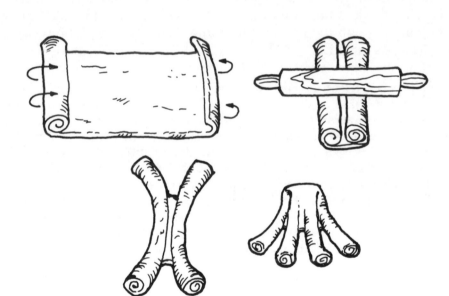

This very simple procedure that Howard Weber taught me is loads of fun!

¼ recipe French Bread dough after second rising (page 321)

1 egg yolk beaten with 1 tablespoon milk (optional)

Spray a baking sheet with nonstick vegetable spray. With a rolling pin roll the dough into a 20 × 8-inch rectangle. With your hands roll one of the narrow ends toward the middle, using the drawing as a

guide. As you roll, stretch the dough slightly toward the edges. (This makes the udder ultimately.) Stop in the center of the rectangle. Now, roll from the other end toward the center. There are now 2 long rolls of dough touching in the center. With a rolling pin roll back and forth just in the center to flatten that portion. Lift one end of the dough and flip it over so that it lies in the center of the other 2 rolls. There are now 4 rolls side by side. Spread them, shape a bit, and you have 4 spigots. Place on the prepared baking sheet, cover, and let rise 30 minutes.

Preheat the oven to 425°F. Brush the udder with the glaze, if desired, to make it shiny and golden. Bake about 20–25 minutes. Let cool on a wire rack. A wonderful gift for a rancher or a farmer!

The Mighty Mississippi

A short drive back to Chicago, and we flew to St. Paul where we boarded the *Mississippi Queen*. Our booking for this journey down the Mississippi River had been made one year previously, for there are just so many cabins, and the boat makes the complete trip of the river only once a year.

Directions to our cabin were given by "J. J." Johnson, the maître d', and we explored everything from the paddle wheels and the calliope to the "brain box," or pilot house. At 9 P.M., the majestic boat slowly began to move past the city of St. Paul and down the tree-lined river. Her enormous searchlights played over the riverbanks and the water, the calliope played at full steam, and every passenger on board, I am sure, was thrilled actually to be traveling down the historic Mississippi. Surely, through the mist, I saw a birch-bark canoe with an Indian moving swiftly beyond us. . . . Sleep came almost instantly, for I've never been on a smoother-riding boat.

When we docked at Wabash, the crew had great difficulty in adjusting the long gangplank. Finally the contact was correctly made, and everyone on shore clapped—a typical American scene. A sign read, "Tour the Mississippi Queen for 1 Dollar." And that's what the people were waiting for. Tours were offered all the way to St. Louis, so tourists were constantly stumbling over tourists.

From St. Paul to St. Louis the river has in the past been treacherous, swift during floods, blocked by rocks and rapids, and never dependable. In 1830, the federal government realized the importance of river transportation and made attempts to remove huge boulders and make a navigable channel for boats. Gradually through the years, but particularly between 1930 and 1940, a series of locks and dams was constructed by the Army Corps of Engineers. They are rather like a series of steps leading down to St. Louis. The locks and dams have made a beautiful playground of this portion of the river. We saw every possible kind of pleasure boat—you couldn't miss them, for the *Queen* was constantly surrounded by a flotilla of sightseers. At each lock, the boat went past a series of grandstand seats, and they were always filled. We talked to people and gave them candies and pens from the boat. The arrival of the *Mississippi Queen* always puts everyone in a holiday mood!

Early morning mist curled off the water each day as we walked the deck for a morning mile. The *Mississippi Queen* is 385 feet long, white, completely made of steel, fireproof, and has a paddle wheel that really works and the finest steam calliope on the river. The captain blew the huge whistle, which can be heard for miles up and down the river, and everyone who lived close to the riverbank came out to watch her. Captain Gabriel Chengery, a big handsome man, six foot two, has been on the river for fifteen years. His charming purser, Tom Murphy, and J.J. seemed to be everywhere at once on that boat!

The hotel manager, Mr. Marcou, took me for a tour of the kitchen. There are two head chefs and thirty-two people work in the galley. The day begins at six and ends at midnight, and three meals a day are made for 415 passengers and crew. Mr. Marcou took me down, by elevator, into the dungeons of the boat where the crew bunks, to the officers' quarters, and into the two huge walk-in freezers packed with food to last until St. Louis—everything from steak to strawberries. In one week on the *Queen*, 1,100 dozen eggs, 500 pounds of bacon, and 2,500 pounds of shrimp are prepared. Unfortunately, all the bread was purchased from bakeries and nothing was outstanding.

But, soon we would dock at Hannibal, Missouri, where on an earlier journey I had watched President Carter arrive on the sister ship, the *Delta Queen*. After almost a week on the river, we walked down the gangplank into this delightful town made forever famous by Mark Twain, and met a good friend, Susan Clayton Stark. She had a recipe ready for me. Susan's heritage goes back for three generations in Hannibal. She is not only an excellent executive, but also a fine writer and cook.

Half Time Hamburger Buns

*Makes 16 hamburger buns or 32 dinner rolls
or about 60 appetizer rolls*

*A wonderfully easy bun to prepare, one that can
be made into a regular size hamburger bun or
miniatures.*

4 tablespoons butter	½ cup warm water
1 cup milk	1 cup whole wheat flour
1 teaspoon salt	2½ cups white flour,
2 tablespoons honey	approximately
2 packages active dry	
yeast	

In a saucepan melt the butter over low heat. Add the milk, salt, and honey and heat mixture to 100°–110°F. Remove from burner. Combine the yeast and water in a mixing bowl, stirring until dissolved. Add the milk mixture. Stir in the whole wheat flour and 1 cup of white flour and beat until batter is smooth. Gradually add sufficient white flour to make a soft, workable dough. Turn out on a lightly floured surface and knead until smooth and elastic, about 5 minutes. Round into a ball and place the dough in a warm buttered bowl, turning to coat the top. Cover loosely with plastic wrap and a towel. Place the bowl in a pan of warm water, about 98°F, and let proof 15 minutes.

Butter 2 large baking sheets. Punch down the dough and divide into 16 portions. Cup each in your hand and rotate quickly to make a smooth bun. Place on baking sheets 1 inch apart and flatten each bun slightly. Cover and let rise 15 minutes.

Preheat the oven to 375°F. Bake the buns 15–20 minutes, or until golden brown.

Dinner Rolls: These are easy, light, and quick. Divide dough in half and cut each piece into 16 portions. Roll into smooth buns and place ½ inch apart on large buttered baking sheets. Cover and let rise 15 minutes. Bake about 12–15 minutes.

Appetizer Rolls: Divide the dough into quarters and cut each into about fifteen 1-inch ("silver dollar" size) rolls. Place ½ inch apart on large buttered baking sheets, cover, and let rise 15 minutes. Bake about 12 minutes.

A s we approached St. Louis, we were nearing the end of the "stairway of water." We had floated down the series of lakes created by the locks and dams and "supervised" the mechanics of passing through the locks many times, sometimes seeing huge tug boats go through, pushing twelve to sixteen barges filled with grain on their way to the port of New Orleans. When two of our sons canoed the Mississippi years ago, they, too, had gone through each lock. Now I could easily visualize their tiny canoe, *The Nike*, bobbing along in the locks with those huge barges. Colonel Francis Wilson, formerly of the Corp of Engineers, had given the boys a set of maps, two packets each two inches thick, with every town, well, lock, farm, and curve of the river on them, so that they always knew exactly where they were except once when they got lost on Lake Winnibigoshish. We had those maps with us now and from notes the boys had jotted down we could even tell where they had camped.

The *Queen* docked at St. Louis, close to the soaring, silvery arch. Trucks of every description were waiting on the cobbled riprap with supplies for the

Queen for the following week. My artist and niece, Pat Biggs, with husband Bill, joined us for an early dinner at Al's, a superb restaurant close to the river that St. Louisans have enjoyed for years. To my delight I was given a marvelous loaf of pumpernickel bread—no recipe, but after a bit of testing, I like the following recipe for a similar bread.

St. Louis Pumpernickel Bread

Makes 2 large or 3 smaller loaves

There is no such thing as pumpernickel flour, except a mixture any miller might throw together and give such a name to. There is no pumpernickel seed, therefore no pumpernickel grain. Supposedly, long ago, there was a German gentleman by the name of Pumper Nickel, who invented a mixture of flours that was given his name. In any event, pumpernickel is now a famous whole grain bread based on rye flour.

3 packages active dry
   yeast
½ cup warm water
2 cups warm buttermilk
½ cup molasses or honey
¼ cup light oil
2 teaspoons salt
2 teaspoons caraway seeds
3 cups rye flour

½ cup cornmeal
½ cup bran cereal
2½ cups bread flour,
   approximately
1 egg white beaten with 1
   tablespoon water for
   glaze
Caraway or fennel seeds

In a small bowl combine the yeast and water, stirring until dissolved. In a large mixing bowl combine the buttermilk, molasses, oil, and salt, blending well. Add the yeast mixture. Separately combine caraway seeds, rye flour, cornmeal, and bran, add to the buttermilk mixture, and beat to make a smooth batter. Gradually add sufficient bread flour to make a soft, workable dough. Any dough with rye flour will be sticky. While kneading, sprinkle kneading surface and hands with flour as needed. Turn the dough out on a floured surface (use bread flour) and knead until smooth and resilient, about 8–10 minutes. Place in a bowl brushed with melted vegetable shortening or butter and turn dough to coat top. Cover loosely with plastic wrap and a towel and let rise until doubled, about 1¼ hours.

Punch down the dough, knead lightly, cover, and let rest 10 minutes. Divide dough in half and mold into round loaves, or divide into 3 portions and form into baguettes (page 39). Place on baking sheets sprayed with nonstick vegetable spray, cover, and let rise about 45 minutes.

Slash the loaves, brush thoroughly with the glaze, and sprinkle with seeds. The bread from Al's was sprinkled heavily with coarse salt and was marvelous if you are not on a no-salt diet. Use the coarse Kosher salt available in all big supermarkets.

Preheat the oven to 375°F. Bake the loaves 35–40 minutes. The round loaves may take 5 minutes longer.

I n 1767, bread was in such short supply around the tiny French settlement of St. Louis that it became known as *paincourt* (short loaf). An outpost for the early fur traders, it was controlled by the French, then the Spanish, then the French again. The tiny encampment grew to become "The Gateway to the West." During the famine in Ireland in the 1840s, the Irish flocked in, and Germans soon came in even greater numbers. In 1850, one third of the population was German. The great influx of immigrants helped St. Louis gradually to become an industrial, railroad, and Mississippi port center.

The *Queen* slowly pulled away from St. Louis at 9 P.M., its witching hour, with calliope playing and whistle blowing. Cruising the next morning, we saw that our river was completely different—wide and muddy, constantly curving, no more locks and dams, but great levees on both sides. The scenery became monotonous, but there were twice as many barges to watch, pushed by tug boats of all sizes. Fishermen held up their catch of the day for us to see—big, whiskered catfish!

The *Queen* turned slowly at the entrance of the Ohio River where its green waters meet the muddy Mississippi. We docked at Cairo, Illinois, to take on water. Darkness came early and the pilot constantly played those huge searchlights on the shore, looking for markers (they are on our maps) or whatever it is a pilot looks for. We made another stop at Caruthersville, Missouri, for the garbage to be taken out and water taken in. Our next big stop would be Memphis, Tennessee.

Built on the high Chickasaw Bluffs, Memphis was an "industrial center" in 1541, when DeSoto erected a shipyard here for the construction of barges and pirogues to cross the Mississippi—at that time seven miles wide. Railroads, logging, the rich delta farmlands, as well as its situation as a river port, have been the making of this lovely Southern city. Chris Arpe Gang, food editor for the Memphis *Commercial Appeal,* came aboard to join us for lunch. J.J. was most attentive and now became interested in my project. Through Chris, I contacted Doris Belcher of Memphis. Doris has sent me several very good, real Southern recipes.

Cracklin' Bread

Makes 1 corn bread

1¾ cups pork fat or salt
    pork
2 cups cornmeal,
    preferably white
½ teaspoon baking soda

½ teaspoon salt
1 egg
1½ cups buttermilk
Vegetable shortening

To make the cracklin's, sauté the pork fat until golden brown and very crisp. Remove from pan with a slotted spoon and drain on paper towels until cool. Place the cracklin's in the bowl of a food processor and process with the steel blade until ground. If the cracklin's are made from salt pork, omit the ½ teaspoon of salt from the ingredients.

Preheat the oven to 400°F. Combine the cracklin's, cornmeal, baking soda, and salt in a mixing bowl. In a separate bowl beat the egg and add buttermilk. Add to the cornmeal mixture and stir until smooth. Add sufficient vegetable shortening to cover the bottom of a 9-inch cast-iron skillet and heat until piping hot. The mixture should sizzle when poured into skillet—this keeps the bread from sticking. Bake 25–30 minutes. Serve hot. Baking in a heavy skillet gives a marvelous thick crust.

Southern Spoon Rolls

Makes 24 rolls

A light, spongy roll, excellent for receiving that homemade blackberry jelly you've been hoarding.

1 package active dry yeast
2 cups warm water
  (110°F)
4 cups self-rising flour

⅜ pound (1½ sticks)
  butter, at room
  temperature
¼ cup sugar
1 egg

In a large mixing bowl combine the yeast and water, stirring until dissolved. Beat in the flour to make a smooth batter and set aside. In the bowl of an electric mixer cream the butter and sugar until light and fluffy. Add the egg and beat well. Stir in the yeast mixture and beat until smooth. If using a heavy-duty mixer, beat 2 minutes with the flat beater. Place in a bowl, cover with plastic wrap and a towel, and refrigerate overnight.

Preheat the oven to 375°F. Brush twenty-four 2-inch muffin tins with melted butter.

When ready to bake, remove dough from refrigerator. Drop by spoonfuls into the muffin tins, filling them about three quarters full. Let rise 30 minutes. Bake 15–20 minutes. Serve immediately.

Note: These are not high-puffing rolls, but they do have a lovely soft texture. Self-rising flour is used extensively in Southern states. If a plain all-purpose flour is used, add 1 teaspoon baking powder and ½ teaspoon salt.

T he river becomes even wider as it flows south. Soon we passed the great confluence where the Arkansas River joins the Mississippi. Our sons indicated on their map the locations of sand bars that were their camping grounds. Fortunately for them, when they reached this part of the river, it was in flood and for several days they splashed along at a rate of eighty miles each day, versus their speed at the beginning, after leaving Lake Itasca in Minnesota, when they were lucky to make 10 miles in a day.

Vicksburg, Mississippi, was our next stop. The river cut away from Vicksburg, which is built on high bluffs, but the old river bed was used to build the Yazoo Canal. Friends of many years met us for breakfast, and we reminisced about the time when they fetched our sons off the river and onto a barge they owned, took them home, washed their clothes (through three cycles), and fed them fresh vegetables. I had joined them at that point, and when I saw those two boys cast off again in their clean clothes on that huge swollen river, my heart skipped a few beats. From the high bluff, they were just two tiny dots in their tiny canoe.

A Civil War battle raged around Vicksburg for months and the citizens were finally starved out and made to surrender on July 4, which has not exactly endeared that day to them. The battlegrounds around the city have been made into a continuous park that is meticulously laid out and beautifully cared for. And there is some mighty good eating in Vicksburg. The most famous restaurant, built by Mary McKay and continued by Warren Asher, is The Old Southern Tearoom. Both Warren and the Tearoom have given me permission to use the two recipes that follow.

Aunt Elvira's Little Hot Biscuits

Makes about 30 biscuits

The recipe is for a large quantity, but may easily be cut in half (use the entire amount of lemon juice). In the Tearoom, the biscuits were made constantly, so that they were always available hot and fresh.

3 cups flour
2 teaspoons baking
   powder
1 teaspoon salt

11 tablespoons vegetable
   shortening or lard
1½ cups milk
½ teaspoon lemon juice

Preheat the oven to 425°F. Butter 2 fluted ceramic plates, 9 or 10 inches in diameter, or use two 9-inch cake tins.

Combine the flour, baking powder, and salt in a mixing bowl. Cut in the shortening with a pastry blender. With rubber spatula or wooden spoon mix in the milk and lemon juice quickly until dry ingredients are wet. Turn out on a floured surface and roll out ½ inch thick. Fold in half, using extra flour if necessary, and roll again. Cut with a 1-inch biscuit cutter and place on baking sheet. Bake about 12–15 minutes. Serve hot in the baking dishes.

Aunt Fanny's Spoon Bread

Makes 1 spoon bread

A spoon bread recipe that produces a different texture, because it uses both grits and cornmeal.

1 cup cooked grits	5 tablespoons butter,
1 cup cornmeal	melted
1 cup boiling water	1 teaspoon baking powder
1 cup milk	1 teaspoon sugar
2 eggs, separated	1 teaspoon salt

Preheat the oven to 350°F. Butter a 2-quart soufflé dish or casserole.

Combine the grits and cornmeal in a mixing bowl using a whisk and beat until smooth. Slowly add the water, whisking constantly. Stir in the milk. Beat egg yolks, add butter, and whisk into the cornmeal mixture. Add the baking powder, sugar, and salt, stirring to distribute evenly. Beat egg whites until softly stiff and fold into the cornmeal mixture. Pour into the soufflé dish. Place dish in a shallow pan filled with hot water and bake 1 hour. Serve immediately with lots of sweet butter and strawberry preserves.

T he *Queen* cruised quietly now between Mississippi and Louisiana. Our last evening aboard was festive. We and our traveling companions, Agnes and Nat Janco, dined at the captain's table. We dressed elegantly to suit the occasion. As we entered the dining room, the bus boys were standing at attention in a row and waiters stood behind our chairs. J.J. was in command and all was perfection. To my delight, I sat at Captain Chengery's right, and I must say he is a charmer. We could not have had a more delightful last evening to climax two such superb, relaxing, informative, nostalgic weeks.

The following morning we passed Baton Rouge, the capital of Louisiana. A pause here to mention that I met Grace Balcom, a native of this lovely Southern city, on another boat trip, in Alaska, cruising Glacier Bay National Park. When Grace returned to Baton Rouge, she mailed me an excellent recipe for Strawberry Bread.

Strawberry Bread

Makes 2 loaves

For this moist, densely textured bread, I have tried both fresh and frozen strawberries and the frozen are best, but should be unsugared.

3 cups flour	4 eggs
1 teaspoon baking soda	1¼ cups light oil
1 teaspoon salt	2 cups thawed sliced
1 teaspoon cinnamon	strawberries
2 cups sugar	1¼ cups chopped pecans

Preheat the oven to 350°F. Generously butter two 9-inch loaf pans.

In a large mixing bowl sift together the flour, baking soda, salt, cinnamon, and sugar. In a separate bowl beat the eggs and add the oil, strawberries, and pecans. Make a well in the center of the dry ingredients and add the liquid mixture, stirring thoroughly. Pour into loaf pans and bake 1 hour, or until cakes test done. Let cool 10–15 minutes in the pans set over wire racks. Remove bread and let cool on wire racks. Do not attempt to slice until thoroughly cooled—it's best to wait until the following day. The bread freezes well.

F or more than one thousand miles the *Mississippi Queen* had cruised so smoothly that only occasionally did a tiny ripple remind me we were moving over water. We passed by the states of Wisconsin, Minnesota, Iowa, Illinois, Missouri, Kentucky, Tennessee, Mississippi, and Louisiana, on the great center line of the continental United States. To sail this mighty river had been a dream of ours, even before our sons accomplished their well-organized

Huck Finn adventure. Now we left the *Queen* at New Orleans, a city we have visited often through the years.

We stayed a short time, in an old inn in the French Quarter built around a central garden, shopped in the numerous antiques stores, gawked at a sign (Girlies wanted—$250.00, see Big Daddy), listened to the clip-clop of horse-drawn carriages, lunched at K-Paul's on superb Cajun cuisine, passed by the ever-present waiting line outside Antoine's, and had breakfast at Brennan's.

Owen Brennan was a flamboyant Irishman who couldn't cook, but with his wife, an extremely gifted cook, together with an imaginative chef, Paul Blangé, he opened Brennan's and served Creole food with a French flair. It was not long before they realized that there were no restaurants that served breakfast, and that began the most elaborate menu for breakfast in the United States. I had toured the kitchens on another trip, watched twenty-four eggs being poached at one time, and wondered what the egg consumption was here. The present manager, David Wilson, provided me with some fascinating statistics—here are a few: each year—1,000,000 eggs, 4,700 quarts of whipping cream, 1,000,000 rusks (for all the egg dishes), and 8,400 quarts of banana liqueur plus 35,000 pounds of bananas for a specialty, Bananas Foster.

My favorite spot, Morning Call, serves hot square doughnuts, strong hot Creole coffee with hot milk, and has long been the place to go after a night in the Quarter. Our most delightful time there was once at six in the morning. We had driven to New Orleans to meet our sons and their canoe at the foot of Canal Street. They spent the night at our hotel, and at dawn the following morning we drove to Morning Call, where they each had six cups of hot milk and six plates of hot doughnuts sprinkled with confectioner's sugar. Then back they went to continue 150 miles south of New Orleans, canoeing one of the five fingers made by the river. We followed in a crew boat until they tasted salt-water, and finally plucked both boys and the canoe from the water.

New Orleans French Square Doughnuts (BEIGNETS)

Makes about 36 doughnuts

1 cup boiling water
¼ cup vegetable
   shortening
½ cup sugar
½ teaspoon salt
1 cup evaporated milk
1 package active dry yeast

½ cup warm water
2 eggs, well beaten
7–8 cups flour
Shortening or oil for
   frying
Confectioner's sugar

In a large mixing bowl pour the boiling water over shortening, sugar, and salt. Add the milk and let cool to lukewarm. Combine the yeast and warm water, stirring until dissolved, and add to the milk mixture. Blend in the eggs. Beat in 3 cups of flour to make a smooth batter. Gradually add sufficient flour to make a soft, workable dough. Turn dough out on a lightly floured surface and knead lightly. Round into a ball and place in a buttered bowl, turning to coat top. Cover loosely with plastic wrap and a towel. Refrigerate about 8 hours or overnight.

Roll the dough out about ⅛ inch thick. Cut into 2- or 2½-inch squares. In a deep fryer heat at least 3 inches of shortening or oil to 370°F. Add the doughnuts, a few at a time, and cook 3–4 minutes on each side, or until golden brown. Drain on paper towels. Sprinkle with confectioner's sugar and serve hot.

THE
GULF COAST STATES

MILEAGE—6,621 MILES

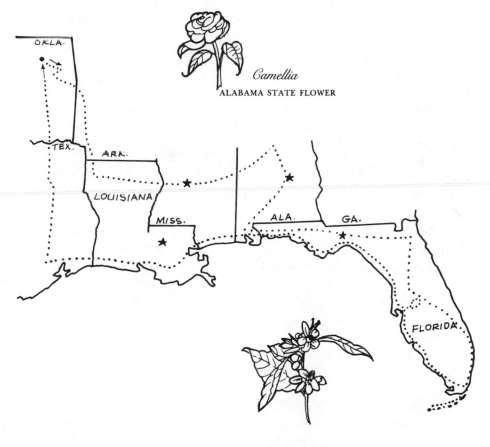

Camellia
ALABAMA STATE FLOWER

Orange Blossom
FLORIDA STATE FLOWER

Northern Louisiana

A n eastern Oklahoma state highway leads to Tahlequah, the capital of the Cherokee Nation, and joins a highway that winds south through the low, rugged Ouachita Mountains, where men escaping from the law can still find places to hide. A few more miles and we were driving through the low, rolling, piney woodlands of northern Louisiana. The famous gray moss began to appear, hanging from the pine branches.

A personal friend suggested that I write to Bobbie McFatter of Louisiana State University in Baton Rouge. Bobbie provided a number of recipes indigenous to her state. As often happens in Southern states, most of the recipes are for quick breads, fast and easy to make but full of Southern flavor.

Louisiana Corn Pone

Makes 24 muffins

3 cups cornmeal	1 cup milk
1½ cups boiling water	1 egg
2 tablespoons lard or	2 teaspoons baking
vegetable shortening	powder
1 teaspoon salt	

Place the cornmeal in a mixing bowl and add the boiling water, stirring constantly. Add the lard and salt, mixing well. Blend in the milk and egg and set aside to cool for 1 hour, covered with a towel.

Preheat the oven to 375°F. Generously brush twenty-four 2-inch muffin tins with melted shortening. Beat the cornmeal mixture thoroughly and add the baking powder. Pour into muffin tins, filling each cup about two-thirds full. Bake 40 minutes. Serve hot.

I nterestingly, two states in entirely different areas lead the nation in production of sweet potatoes—New Jersey and Louisiana. (California, no doubt, also raises the golden tuber, since anything grows in those fertile valleys.) Bobbie gave me an outstanding recipe for a yeast doughnut made either with canned yams or freshly cooked sweet potatoes. I found the doughnuts best when glazed and allowed to cool.

Raised Yam Doughnuts with Orange Glaze

Makes 18–24 doughnuts

1 package active dry yeast
¼ cup warm water
¾ cup milk, scalded
¼ cup vegetable
  shortening
1 cup sugar
1 cup mashed yams (or
  sweet potatoes)

1 teaspoon salt
1 egg
4½–5 cups flour
Oil or vegetable
  shortening for deep
  frying

Orange Glaze:

1 teaspoon grated orange
  rind
3 tablespoons orange juice

2 cups sifted
  confectioner's sugar

In a small bowl combine the yeast and water, stirring until dissolved, and set aside. In a large mixing bowl combine the milk, shortening, sugar, yams, and salt, stir well, and let cool to lukewarm. Blend in the yeast mixture and egg. Beat in 2 cups of flour to make a smooth batter. Gradually add sufficient flour to make a soft, workable dough. Turn out on a floured surface and knead until smooth and satiny, about 8 minutes. Round into a ball and place dough in a buttered bowl, turning to coat the top. Cover loosely with plastic wrap and a towel and let rise until doubled, about 1¼ hours. Punch down the dough, knead lightly in the bowl, cover again, and let rise 55 minutes.

Turn dough out on a lightly floured surface and roll out ⅓ inch thick. Cut with a floured doughnut cutter. Re-knead the scraps, roll out, and cut. Cover the doughnuts and let rise until doubled, about 30 minutes.

In a deep fryer or heavy saucepan heat 3 inches of fat to 375°F. Fry only 2 or 3 doughnuts at a time; do not crowd them. Brown 3–4 minutes on one side and turn to cook on the other side. Drain on paper towels. Combine the Orange Glaze ingredients in a shallow bowl. Dip the warm doughnuts in the glaze and place on wire racks to cool.

Mississippi and Alabama

A raised highway took us through Louisiana swamps and over the wide, muddy Mississippi south of Vicksburg, and then plunged immediately through high loess bluffs shrouded with wind vines. The beautiful trees, dripping gray moss, and the solid, lush greenness of the vines gives one the feeling of being in the land of Jack the Giant Killer. Closer to Jackson, the capital of Mississippi, farms slowly take over the land. As my friend at "Ole Miss" explained, zucchini has become a popular cash crop. To my delight, I discovered a zucchini muffin instead of the usual sweet bread.

Zucchini Muffins

Makes 12 muffins

2 cups flour
2 teaspoons baking
   powder
¼ teaspoon baking soda
¼ cup sugar
½ teaspoon salt

1 cup buttermilk
1 egg
¼ cup light oil
1½ cups grated zucchini
½ cup sunflower seeds

Preheat the oven to 375°F. Generously butter twelve 2½-inch muffin tins.

Sift the dry ingredients together into a mixing bowl. In another bowl combine the buttermilk, egg, and oil, beating thoroughly. Make a well in the center of dry ingredients and add the buttermilk mixture all at once, stirring quickly with a rubber spatula. Fold in the zucchini and sunflower seeds. Distribute the batter among the muffin tins and bake 25 minutes. Serve hot.

A labama has an early pioneer history, myriad beautiful rivers, Appalachian foothills, a big busy seaport, fresh oysters, honey, and hot biscuits. February to April are exquisite months over all the state, but particularly so in the famous Bellingrath Gardens southwest of Mobile. Originally a massive jungle, sixty-five acres have been turned into a glorious horticultural fairyland. Two rivers, the Tombigbee and the Alabama, converge just above

Mobile to form the Mobile River, which empties into the Gulf of Mexico. Montgomery, today the epitome of a lovely, gentle Southern town and the capital of the state, is where the secessionists organized the Confederacy. Here I easily found those wonderful hot biscuits served fresh from the oven accompanied by good sweet butter and honey.

Southern Buttermilk Biscuits

Makes 10–12 plain or 12–14 cheese biscuits

I loved watching my mother throw biscuit dough together; she could whip up a batch and have them hot on the table in fifteen minutes.

2¼ cups flour
½ teaspoon salt
1 tablespoon baking
  powder
½ teaspoon baking soda

5 tablespoons vegetable
  shortening or butter
1 cup buttermilk
Melted butter (optional)

Preheat the oven to 450°F. Butter a large baking sheet.

Sift 2 cups of the flour with the dry ingredients into a shallow mixing bowl. Cut in the shortening with a pastry blender until mixture resembles cornmeal. Make a well in the center, pour in the buttermilk all at once, and stir quickly with a rubber spatula until a dough is formed. If it seems very sticky, add the remaining flour. Turn dough out on a floured surface and knead lightly for a dozen strokes. Pat out ½ inch thick. Cut with floured 2-inch biscuit cutter or glass and place on baking sheet. If desired, brush biscuits with melted butter. Bake about 12 minutes. Serve immediately.

Innovations on a Biscuit: Add ¾ cup grated Cheddar to the dry ingredients. Combine as described, but pat the biscuit dough out thinner—¼ inch thick. Split the biscuits immediately after baking and spread with a deviled Smithfield ham for a quick hot appetizer.

A t one time the main highway through the center of Mobile was a long beautiful street lined with enormous live oaks whose branches met overhead to make a living green arch. Many of the trees were destroyed in an especially violent hurricane. The French and Spanish influences bring excitement to the city during Mardi Gras, and the superb cooking features Gulf fish and oysters. For the French, Mobile was the second most important city in the Louisiana Territory, after New Orleans, because of the deep harbor at the mouth of the Mobile River. When Alabama became a state, the harbor was further developed by the federal government, and shipbuilding advanced as fast as the flourishing fish industry. Today, to best enjoy the Gulf waters along this portion of the coast, including that of Mississippi, take a boat about ten miles out to the offshore islands. Our sons loved this adventure, for the sands are white and there are all kinds of funny crabs to catch.

What with shore dinners that include fried oysters, shrimp, and snapper throats, hush puppies of some kind are inevitable. But, occasionally, there will be a restaurant that makes hot muffins—a welcome change.

Bran Wheat Germ Muffins

*Makes about 1 gallon batter, or enough
for 48 regular or 96 miniature muffins*

*A most popular muffin batter in the South, which
keeps for weeks refrigerated. I have taken the
liberty of adding a further nutritional twist, the
bran and wheat germ. When house guests descend
on you, it's marvelous to have four jars filled with
ready-to-cook muffins in a variety of flavors.
Children love them baked in miniature muffin
tins.*

2 cups unprocessed bran
   (miller's bran)
2 cups boiling water
1 cup melted butter
1 cup granulated sugar
1½ cups packed brown
   sugar

4 eggs, beaten
1 quart buttermilk
5 cups unbleached white
   flour
4 cups bran cereal
½ cup toasted wheat germ
5 teaspoons baking soda
2 teaspoons salt

Measure unprocessed bran into a mixing bowl. Cover with boiling water, stir well, and set aside to cool. In a large mixing bowl combine the butter, sugars, eggs, and buttermilk, beating well. Add the bran mixture. In a separate bowl blend the flour, bran cereal, wheat germ, soda, and salt. Stir into the liquid mixture until well mixed. Muffins may be baked immediately or the batter may be chilled. Store batter in four 1-quart glass or plastic containers, leaving space at the top for the mixture to thicken and expand. Each quart will make twelve 2-inch muffins or twenty-four 1-inch muffins. Label, cap, and refrigerate. The batter will keep for as long as 6 weeks.

To bake the muffins, preheat the oven to 400°F. Brush 2-inch or miniature muffin tins with melted butter. The batter may be used directly from the refrigerator. Optional additions are chopped nuts, dates, and candied orange peel, or raisins that have been scalded, drained, and dried. Fill the muffin cups three quarters full. Bake 2-inch muffins about 20 minutes, miniature muffins 10 minutes. An easy addition for morning coffee.

The Peninsula of Florida

L eaving Mobile, the highway flows in a long curve into the state of Florida. The northern panhandle with its tall pines retains much of the gentle, relaxed atmosphere of the South. I've enjoyed many journeys to Florida, and each has offered a different and distinct kind of pleasure. Perhaps the most outstanding was a three-week trip with my sister, Kay Loring, who was a restaurant columnist for the *Chicago Tribune*. What an adventure it was to dine in two fine restaurants each day, from Palm Beach, south and around the peninsula, across the everglades, and north to Tampa. And I only gained five pounds!

Ponce de Leon discovered Florida in 1513, searching for the fountain of youth. People from many states and South America still come to Florida looking for the same magic wand in the soft sunshine and warm breezes. On this new journey, we chose highways through the center of the state to enjoy the gentle, rolling hills covered with orange, grapefruit, lemon, and lime trees. It appeared the crop would be prodigious, for every green, waxy tree was burdened with fruit. But on our return a few weeks later, after a devastating winter storm, the whole picture would be changed. Interestingly, I found few citrus breads or rolls in Florida. With a little imagination, that could easily be remedied, especially with limes. No other state produces limes in the quantity nor of the quality that Florida does.

Lime-Almond Rolls

*Makes 36–40 large or
about 70 miniature rolls*

*Not enough of the flavor of fresh lime is used in
the baking world. Since it is a favorite of mine, I
experimented and produced a luscious, sticky,
melt-in-your-mouth roll that also freezes well.
The Basic Sweet Dough is highly adaptable and
may be used for the Growly Bear (page 159),
Howard Weber's Apple Bread (page 405),
Cinnamon Rolls (page 105), and other fillings
that strike your fancy.*

Basic Sweet Dough:

2 packages active dry yeast	½ cup melted butter
½ cup warm water	5 cups flour, approximately
1 cup warm milk	2 eggs, beaten
½ cup sugar	Grated rind of 1 lime
1 teaspoon salt	

Lime-Almond Topping:

1 cup sugar	Grated rind of 1 large lime
5 tablespoons butter	¾–1⅛ cups sliced or slivered almonds
¼ cup light corn syrup	
3 tablespoons fresh lime juice	
Melted butter	1 cup Cinnamon Sugar, page 46

Combine the yeast and water, stirring until dissolved, and set aside.
In a large mixing bowl combine milk, sugar, salt, and butter. Add the
yeast mixture and 2 cups of flour and beat thoroughly. Stir in the eggs
and grated rind. Gradually add sufficient flour to make a soft, workable

dough. Turn out on a lightly floured surface and knead until smooth and satiny, about 8 minutes. Round into a ball and place dough in a warm buttered bowl, turning to coat the top. Cover loosely with plastic wrap and a towel and let rise until doubled, about 1 hour.

While the dough is rising, make the topping. Combine sugar, butter, syrup, lime juice, and rind in a saucepan and bring to a boil, stirring constantly. Let boil 1 minute and remove from burner. To prepare individual rolls, butter thirty-six to forty 2-inch muffin tins and spoon 1 tablespoon of topping into each cup. Add 1½ teaspoons almonds per cup. If preferred, the topping may be spread in three 9-inch cake tins and each pan sprinkled with one third of the almonds. Set aside.

To make large rolls, punch down the dough, knead lightly, cover, and let rest 10 minutes. Divide dough in half. Roll each piece into an 18 × 9-inch rectangle. Brush with melted butter to within ½ inch of edges and sprinkle with ½ cup of Cinnamon Sugar. Roll up from the long side jelly-roll style. Seal the seam and turn so that the roll is placed seam side down. Smooth out the roll slightly with your hands and cut into 1- to 1½-inch slices.

Place rolls cut side up in prepared muffin tins. Cover and let rise 45–60 minutes, or until dough is light and rolls in cake tins touch.

Preheat the oven to 350°F. Bake rolls 30 minutes. Place a sheet of aluminum foil under a rack and turn the rolls out to cool.

Miniature Rolls: Divide the dough into 6 equal portions and roll each into a 15 × 9-inch rectangle. Follow directions for larger rolls, cutting them into slices ½–¾ inch thick. Place in tiny muffin cups containing topping. The small rolls may be frozen and thawed quickly for an emergency coffee.

Puerto Rico

H appily, my husband had a business meeting scheduled in Puerto Rico. We parked our car in Orlando and flew to San Juan. At first, the city seemed too American. Our hotel looked like any hotel in Tulsa. After a little research, I found what I wanted in the old section of the city. Here were Old World charm and delightful restaurants that prepared native foods. Primarily, this is a mild Spanish cuisine, centered around fresh seafood, rice, and lots of pimiento. Always, a simple white bread was served, similar to a French baguette.

But a tour within the Caribe Hilton International was offered, which meant admission to the kitchens. I watched two chefs prepare exquisite dessert pastries filled with colorful fresh island fruit arranged in beautiful perfection. Finally, I asked if there was a Puerto Rican bread and, if so, would the recipe be available.

The men in the kitchen all grinned and pushed forward Antonio Perez. Now, Antonio could speak no English and I no Spanish; but we were surrounded by eager interpreters. I scribbled on the back of a menu a recipe for fifteen pounds of flour, one gallon of water, one pound of lard, and a "handful" of yeast. Back in my own kitchen, I finally dwindled down these interesting measurements to a workable recipe. There is a short proofing period and you have instant bread! As I've mentioned before, see how similar this bread is to Indian Pueblo bread (page 379), Hutterite bread (page 146), and the Cuban bread later in this chapter.

Puerto Rican Bread

Makes 2 loaves

3 cups warm water	¼ cup melted lard or
2 packages active dry	vegetable shortening
yeast	7½ cups flour,
2 tablespoons sugar	approximately
2 teaspoons salt	

In a large mixing bowl combine the water and yeast, stirring until dissolved. Blend in the sugar, salt, and lard. Beat in 3 cups of flour to make a smooth batter. Gradually add sufficient flour to make a workable dough. Blend well, turn out on a floured surface, and knead just enough to pull the dough together. Form into 2 baguette loaves (page 39) and place on a baking sheet brushed with melted shortening. Cover and let rise 20 minutes.

Preheat the oven to 400°F. Bake loaves 25–30 minutes, or until golden brown and crunchy. Certainly a simply made and amazingly good, peasant bread. Use unbleached white flour for better nutrition.

W e walked through the incredibly enormous Spanish El Morro Castle, dating back to 1539, which is ringed with forts placed at high, strategic points overlooking the ocean. A relaxing drive through a portion of the

Caribbean National Forest, dripping with ferns, rare flowers, and exquisite waterfalls tumbling down the mountainsides, ended our short, productive trip—more pleasure than business to me.

We retrieved our car at Orlando and drove to the Atlantic coast and elegant Palm Beach. This is the kind of town where a Rolls Royce can roll slowly down Worth Avenue with a Marmaduke type of dog patiently loping alongside, leashed to the dapper driver. On our first evening, we dined in the home of a gentleman whose living room was fittingly designed for a baronial palace and contained a fireplace I could walk into. He had a marvelous cook by the name of Lucky who served miniature sticky buns for breakfast and luscious hot muffins.

Orange-Blueberry Muffins

Makes 12 muffins

*These are an adaption of what Lucky could do.
The lavish use of Florida oranges provides a
piquant and luscious flavor.*

1 cup sugar
¼ pound (1 stick) butter,
   at room temperature
2 eggs
2 cups flour
1 teaspoon baking soda

½ teaspoon salt
1 cup buttermilk
Grated rind of 1 large
   orange
1 cup fresh or frozen
   blueberries

Glaze:
Juice of 1 orange

2 tablespoons sugar

Preheat the oven to 400°F. Generously butter twelve 2-inch muffin tins.

Cream the sugar and butter in bowl of an electric mixer until fluffy. Add the eggs one at a time, beating well after each addition. Sift flour, baking soda, and salt together. Add alternately to butter mixture with buttermilk, beating well after each addition. Blend in the grated rind, dust a little flour over the blueberries, and fold them into the batter. Spoon into the muffin tins, filling them three quarters full. Bake 25 minutes, or until golden brown.

To make the glaze, combine the orange juice and sugar in a small saucepan and bring to a boil, stirring constantly. Remove from heat and immediately brush the glaze over tops of muffins. Serve hot.

W e joined a stream of cars on the Florida Turnpike to avoid jam-packed Fort Lauderdale and the gilt and glitter of Miami, and for the third time took one of the most beautiful ocean drives in our land, to Key West. There we enjoyed two unique specialties of the area, stone crab and Key lime pie. Years ago, turtle steaks were abundant, too, but no longer; man has almost wiped out the enormous sea turtle. A windy area once made famous because Harry Truman had a second White House here, Key West is now occupied by artists, writers, and fishermen.

Leaving the main highway, we drove into the compound of the Everglades National Park. Long, raised, board paths lead into the mysteries of the quiet swamp areas, sanctuaries for birds and occasional alligators. I should not call this a swamp; it is an extraordinarily wide and very shallow river. Approximately six hundred Seminole Indians still live in its jungles, the descendants of those that refused to leave for Oklahoma Territory in 1832. For a small price, a Seminole Indian will take you for a never-to-be-forgotten ride on an airboat that skims over the shallow water filled with sawgrass, to see the hundreds and hundreds of birds. Osceolo was the Seminole chief who held the band together and refused to recognize the United States. Not until this century, when the federal government finally paid this remaining group a sum of money, would the Florida Seminoles sign a treaty recognizing the United States as a legitimate government.

From the Everglades we headed north to Naples, then to Fort Myers and across the toll bridge to spend a few days on one of our favorite islands, Sanibel. On the tiny spit of land between Sanibel and Captiva flourishes a most unusual and innovative restaurant called the Bubble Room. It sports an electric train running around overhead and waitresses dressed in Girl Scout uniforms and wearing saddle shoes. The Bubble Room serves tremendous quantities of amazingly excellent food, accompanied by Bubble Rolls. These inspired the following handsome coffeecake that is easily transformed into a holiday cake or individual breads.

Orange Bubble Coffeecake

Makes 1 coffeecake

My Old Order Amish friends would call this a Plucket cake. Bubble or Plucket, it is redolent with the flavor of Florida oranges.

Dough:

2 packages active dry yeast
¼ cup warm water
1½ cups warm milk
3 eggs, lightly beaten
½ cup sugar

¼ cup melted butter
Grated rind of 1 lemon
½ teaspoon salt
6½ cups flour, approximately

Topping:

½ cup melted butter
1 cup sugar
Grated rind 3 large oranges

Golden raisins (optional)
Slivered almonds (optional)

Combine yeast and water in a small bowl, stirring until dissolved, and set aside. In a large mixing bowl blend the milk, eggs, sugar, butter, grated rind, and salt. Add the yeast mixture and 3 cups of flour and beat well to make a smooth batter. Add sufficient flour to form a soft dough that pulls away from sides of the bowl. Turn out on a lightly floured surface and knead until smooth and satiny, about 10 minutes. Round into a ball and place dough in a warm buttered bowl, turning to coat the top. Cover loosely with plastic wrap and a towel and let rise until doubled, about 1½ hours.

Punch down the dough, turn out on a lightly floured surface, and knead lightly. Cover and let rest 10 minutes.

To make the topping, combine the melted butter, sugar, and grated orange rind.

Brush a 10-inch tube pan with melted butter. With a dough scraper cut off pieces of dough about the size of a walnut. Roll into rough balls and dip each into the topping mixture. Place in the pan topping side up. When a layer is finished, sprinkle with raisins and almonds, if desired. Cover and let rise about 30 minutes, or until dough has risen to within ½ inch of the top of the pan. Of the dough rises too high, some of the balls will fall off onto oven floor.

Preheat the oven to 350°F. Bake the bread 45 minutes. Remove from oven and let cool 15 minutes in the pan set over a wire rack. Turn out on a serving plate, if serving warm. Otherwise let the cake cool and freeze it.

Christmas Bubble Cake

Makes 1 coffeecake or 6–8 individual coffeecakes

¼ cup sugar
2 tablespoons butter
2 tablespoons light corn syrup
2 tablespoons fresh orange juice or frozen concentrate

Whole blanched almonds
Candied cherries
1 recipe Orange Bubble Coffeecake dough and topping, preceding recipe

Brush a 10-inch tube pan with melted butter. Combine the sugar, butter, syrup, and orange juice in a saucepan and bring to a boil, stirring constantly. Remove from burner and pour into the pan. Sprinkle heavily with almonds and cherries. Proceed as directed for the Orange Bubble Coffeecake. When the cake is turned out, the top will be glazed with the Christmas confection.

Note: Individual breads for gifts may be prepared in small charlotte molds or large custard cups—any small, deep ovenproof container. These may be tucked in the freezer when finished and given with container as presents. The baking time for a small charlotte mold will be about 25 minutes.

T housands of shells are washed onto the shores of Sanibel with every tide. We joined the beachcombers for two days, and after much walking and bending felt limbered enough to return to the crowded Florida highways filled with the cars of grandparents from almost every state in the Union. After the sparkling city of Sarasota, where the Ringling Brothers Circus stages test performances each Sunday during the winters, we made our next stop in the tri-city area of St. Petersburg, Clearwater, and Tampa.

Tampa

T ampa has an excellent deep-water port in a secluded bay, which created an exciting history. It was from here that DeSoto began his long journey to the Mississippi river. Pirates used the hidden bay to hide and sell their plunder. The Gasparillo Festival reenacts the daring of the pirate, Jose Gaspar, who roamed the seas and cached his booty in this area; each February, law-abiding Tampa citizens, dressed in piratical style, sail into the bay to capture the city. During the Civil War, the Union navy actually did capture the city. Later, after Florida rejoined the Union, Tampa was the port of embarkation to Cuba during the Spanish-American War.

Within Tampa is Ybor City, the Latin section. For a long time the area flourished as a center for cigar factories, and then it slumped, as so many inner cities have. But through all the ups and downs, the old Columbia Restaurant has stayed open. Flamenco dancers whirl during the late dinner hour, and the food centers around fish stews made of stone crabs, oysters, and red snapper, accompanied by a crisp Cuban bread. The Columbia has always been one of our favorite spots to dine in Florida.

Cuban Bread

Makes 2 loaves

2 packages active dry
   yeast
2⅔ cups warm water
1 tablespoon salt
1 tablespoon sugar

3 cups bread flour
3 cups all-purpose or
   unbleached white flour
Cornmeal
Melted butter

In a large mixing bowl combine the yeast and water, stirring until dissolved. Blend in the salt and sugar. Add the bread flour, beating until batter is smooth. Gradually add sufficient all-purpose flour to form a soft, workable dough that pulls away from sides of the bowl. Turn the dough out on a floured surface and knead 10–15 minutes. Round into a ball and place the dough in a warm buttered bowl, turning to coat the top. Cover loosely with plastic wrap and a towel and let rise until doubled, about 1 hour.

Punch down the dough, turn out on a floured surface, and divide in half. Knead each, cover, and let rest 10 minutes. Form into baguette loaves (page 39) and place on a heavy baking sheet sprinkled with cornmeal. Slash both loaves with a razor, as for French bread, and let rest 5 minutes. Brush with melted butter. Place in a cold oven. Turn the temperature to 400°F and bake 40–45 minutes, or until bread is golden brown and has a good crust.

B efore leaving Tampa, we drove to a spot unique in the state of Florida. Close to Lake Wales, not far from Disneyworld and in the center of the citrus country, is Chalet Suzanne, built over fifty years ago. From a distance it has the shimmering appearance of one of Mr. Disney's fantasy castles. Chalet Suzanne is advertised as an "inn," but an evening of dining there is truly a "happening." The combination of Southern-Continental cuisine, served in seven courses, delighted one of our grandsons. He assured us at age nine, that this was the finest meal he had ever had!

Outside, the picture was different. The winter storm had struck the state, and we were appalled at the condition of acres and acres of frostbitten orchards we had seen not long before. All those lovely green leaves had turned ugly and brown, smudge pots were everywhere, and crews of emergency workers were picking the fruit as quickly as possible to save the year's crop.

My husband returned to Tulsa for business engagements, and I traveled alone along the western coast. At a favorite spot in Tarpon Springs, I stopped to savor a Greek salad redolent with fresh herbs and greens piled in perfect confusion around a hearty potato salad. I walked across the street to watch a big sponge boat cast off, laden with tourists eager to see a Greek-American don his cumbersome diving suit and plunge into Lake Tarpon to obtain some of the few natural sponges in the United States.

Tsoureke (GREEK EASTER BREAD)

Makes 1 or 2 braided loaves

Sponge:

2 packages active dry
   yeast
1 cup warm water

2 teaspoons sugar
2 cups flour

1 cup warm milk
1 cup sugar
1 teaspoon salt
¾ cup melted butter
3 eggs, lightly beaten
Grated rind 1 orange
Grated rind 1 lemon

¼ cup orange juice
½ cup golden raisins,
   scalded, drained, and
   dried
8 cups flour,
   approximately

Topping:

1 egg white beaten with 1
   tablespoon water for
   glaze

Sliced almonds (for braids
   only)

To make the sponge, in a small mixing bowl, combine yeast, water, and sugar, stirring until dissolved. Add the 2 cups of flour and beat until smooth. Cover and allow to proof for 30 minutes.

In a large mixing bowl, blend the milk, sugar, salt, butter, eggs, grated rinds, orange juice, and raisins. Beat in 2 cups of flour to make a smooth batter. Stir down the sponge and add to the milk mixture. Gradually add sufficient flour to make a soft, workable dough that pulls away from sides of the bowl. Turn out on a lightly floured surface and knead for 8–10 minutes, or until smooth and satiny. Round into a ball and place dough in a warm, buttered bowl, turning to coat the top. Cover loosely with plastic wrap and a towel and let double in bulk, about 1½ hours.

Punch down the dough, turn out and knead lightly for about 1 minute. Cover and let rest for 10 minutes. This delicious dough can be molded into braids, plain loaves, or an Easter ring. First, for a stunning braid to use for entertaining or Easter dinner, mold into a 6-braid loaf, page 37. The amount of dough is exactly right. Place the braid, which will be quite large, diagonally on a buttered baking sheet, 15½ × 14 inches, cover, and let rise until almost double in bulk, about 1 hour.

Preheat the oven to 350°F. Brush the loaf with egg white glaze, sprinkle heavily with almonds, and bake for about 1 hour. If the braid becomes too brown, cover with aluminum foil during the last 15 minutes of baking. The dough may also be divided in half and molded into two 3-strand braided loaves. Reduce baking time by about 15 minutes.

Easter Ring: During a visit to Boston, in an Armenian bakery I watched the preparation of a tremendous Greek Easter bread. The dough had been wound into a large coil, filling a large baking sheet, and in the center was a single red egg, which symbolizes a blessing and good luck. For this braid, dye 3 hard-cooked eggs red. Place 2 eggs opposite each other in a circle of braided dough and place the third egg equidistant from the other two. Gently push the eggs into the dough, cover and let rise about 45 minutes.

I drove north to Tallahassee, which was declared the territorial capital in 1824 under the governorship of Andrew Jackson and where a log cabin capitol was soon built among the beautiful pine trees that grace the rolling hills of this portion of Florida. I joined relatives for a splendid Greek dinner. (Greek immigrants flocked to Florida, and they are superb in the preparation of fish.) Then a quick drive took me to the white sands of the panhandle, the summer resort area of the state. To me there is nothing lovelier in the state than the white beaches of northern Florida. I watched the waves pound the white shores, and soon my husband rejoined me to drive west into New Orleans.

South Louisiana

A great international port, the fabled city of New Orleans is rich with Spanish, French, and American history, stories of pirates, steamboats, and exciting battles, and of course is the home of Dixieland jazz. I am convinced the whole world must know "When the Saints Come Marchin' In." In Yerevan, Armenia, thousands of miles away, where few people even speak English, we once asked a hotel swing band if they could play New Orleans' famous tune. After a few minutes, the musicians started, and all the Americans in the room formed a "congo" line—it was unbelievable! We had dinner at Galatoire's, a favorite, and then spent two hours listening to great jazz at Preservation Hall.

Before we start wandering the bayous, I want to include here a delicious hot roll that Southerners love.

Featherbeds

Makes 24 muffins

¼ cup warm water	1 tablespoon sugar
1 package active dry yeast	½ teaspoon salt
3 tablespoons safflower oil	1 egg, beaten
1 tablespoon melted	3½ cups flour,
butter	approximately
¾ cup warm milk	Melted butter

Combine the water and yeast in a small bowl, stirring until dissolved, and set aside. In a large mixing bowl mix the oil, butter, and milk. Stir in the sugar, salt, and egg. Blend in the yeast mixture. Gradually add sufficient flour to make a soft, workable dough. Turn out on a very lightly floured surface and knead 8 minutes, adding as little flour as possible. Round into a ball and place the dough in a warm buttered bowl, turning to coat the top. Cover loosely with plastic wrap and a towel and let rise until doubled, about 1 hour. Punch down the dough, knead lightly in the bowl, cover again, and let rise about 45 minutes.

Turn the dough out on a lightly floured surface and knead lightly. Cover and let rest 10 minutes. Brush twenty-four 2-inch muffin tins with melted butter. Break off small pieces of dough about the size of an egg, roll lightly, and place in muffin tins. Cover and let rise until light and puffy, about 30–45 minutes.

Preheat the oven to 400°F. Brush rolls with melted butter and bake 15 minutes. Serve immediately.

The Evangeline Country

S oon after leaving metropolitan New Orleans, heading west toward New Iberia, the highway narrows and the landscape changes immediately to rural countryside coursed with bayous, the term used for creeks in the Gulf Coast areas. At one point, we joined a lovely Southern lady who drove us through cane fields to Oaklawn, one of the most beautiful antebellum homes. The house has been completely restored and stands on a sweep of green lawn surrounded by incredibly high live oaks. At our hostess's suggestion, we found a restaurant in "Cajun country," perched beside Bayou Teche, and there enjoyed crawfish prepared eight different ways. There are good breads in Cajun country. Again, I must thank Bobbie McFatter for her assistance.

Cajun Hush Puppies

Makes about 20 hush puppies

Many stories have been told about the origin of hush puppies and they all have to do with men sitting around a campfire ready to cook the evening's catch of fish. Where there are hunters or fishermen, there are pups, and they whine mightily when the smell of that food permeates the air. The men would roll up bits of wet cornmeal, fry them quickly, toss them to the pups, with the command to "Hush, puppies."

2 cups cornmeal
1 tablespoon flour
1 tablespoon sugar
½ teaspoon baking soda
1 teaspoon salt

½ cup finely chopped
  onion
½ cup buttermilk
¼ cup melted bacon fat
1 egg, beaten
Oil for deep frying

Combine the cornmeal, flour, sugar, soda, salt, and onion, blending well. Add the buttermilk, fat, and egg. Beat well. If too dry, add a bit more buttermilk.

In a deep fryer or heavy saucepan heat 3–4 inches of oil to 325°F. The hush puppies can be dropped from a spoon, formed by hand into cylindrical balls, or forced from a pastry bag. Drop a few hush puppies into the hot fat and cook 3–4 minutes on each side, or until golden brown. Drain on paper towels. Hush puppies are best served immediately, but they can be reheated and still taste very good.

Note: If desired, add 2 or 3 drops of Tabasco sauce. I've tried this, and I'm certain that is what my Catfish Man added in southern Texas. This is an excellent recipe—light and tasty.

Hot Water Corn Bread

Makes about 12 small corn breads

When my mother made hot water corn bread, it was always with white cornmeal. There was no reason given, but that was the way it was supposed to be done, and I loved it. Moist and piping hot on the inside, with a crusty crust on the outside.

2 or 3 tablespoons
  vegetable shortening
1 cup white cornmeal

½ cup flour
1 teaspoon salt
Boiling water

Preheat the oven to 375°F. Put the shortening into a heavy cake or pie tin and place in the oven while preparing the cornbread.

Combine the cornmeal, flour, and salt in a mixing bowl. Slowly add sufficient boiling water to make a soft mixture, which, when dropped, will hold its shape. Remove the cake tin from the oven and drop big tablespoons of dough into the hot shortening. Return to the oven and bake until the tops begin to brown, about 20–25 minutes. Serve immediately with butter.

Note: This bread is similar to hoe cake, except that the hoe cake mixture is allowed to cool and then formed by hand into cakes and fried. Hot water corn bread is more sophisticated in that it is baked and is not as greasy.

A t St. Martinsville we stopped to see again the tremendous and beautifully shaped Evangeline Live Oak that commemorates the fabled lovers immortalized by Longfellow. Nearby a re-created Acadian village beside a bayou shows how the early settlers of Louisiana lived and is extremely well done. A few miles to the south, we crossed a tiny bridge and suddenly we were on Avery Island. Here a man found that he could plant a special pepper and perfect plants would grow in this soil. The straight rows of beautifully tilled plants continue for acres and acres. A small building houses the manufacturing of Tabasco Pepper Sauce, but exactly what goes into the huge vats inside is a secret. Avery Island smells spicy and is the only source for the hot Tabasco pepper.

Another Portion of Texas

F rom Avery Island we drove north to gain access to Interstate 10 West for Texas. Soon after the border, there is a series of Texas towns, Orange, Beaumont, Port Arthur, Baytown, before the highway enters sprawling Houston. During the year 1901, the Spindletop oil field near Beaumont was discovered. Up until that year, Baku on the Caspian Sea in Russia had the largest oil field in the world. All America had was a few oil discoveries in Pennsylvania, Ohio, and Indiana. A wild gusher at Spindletop completely changed the oil picture for the United States and the world, and it is here that many of the huge oil companies originated. I saw the field years ago, before the derricks were removed, and even though I was used to oil equipment, Spindletop seemed incredible to me, with its derricks crowded almost on top of each other. What an amazing difference there is in the way Americans have handled old oil fields, versus the Russians at Baku. In 1979, we saw the Baku area—the land looked burned and the Caspian Sea horribly dirty and ugly.

Later when I read the book *Spindletop,* an idea popped into my head for a fun way of forming rolls that would rise up to simulate an oil field.

Spindletop Rolls

Makes 12–18 rolls

1 recipe Basic Sweet
    Dough, page 432
Melted butter
1 cup sugar
2 teaspoons nutmeg

1 cup currants marinated
    in ½ cup brandy for 30
    minutes and drained
Confectioner's Icing made
    with lemon and brandy,
    page 45

Prepare the dough as instructed, omitting the grated lime rind. If a more intense flavor is desired, use the grated rind of 1 lemon or orange—or even both! After the dough has risen, divide in half, knead each piece, cover, and let rest 10 minutes. Butter twelve to eighteen 2-inch muffin tins or two or three 9-inch cake tins. The muffin tins are more fun—try them and see. Roll each portion of dough into an 18 × 12-inch rectangle. Brush with melted butter to within ½ inch of edges. Combine sugar and nutmeg. Sprinkle each rectangle with ½ cup each of nutmeg sugar and currants. Roll from the long side, jelly-roll style. Seal the seam and cut the rolls into 2- or 3-inch lengths. Place in muffin tins or arrange in cake tins, cover, and let rise 1 hour. The center swirls of the rolls will puff high—ready for a gusher!

Preheat the oven to 375°F. Bake rolls 25 minutes. Top with Confectioner's Icing and give them to your favorite oil man!

IN MY OWN BACKYARD

MILEAGE—712 MILES

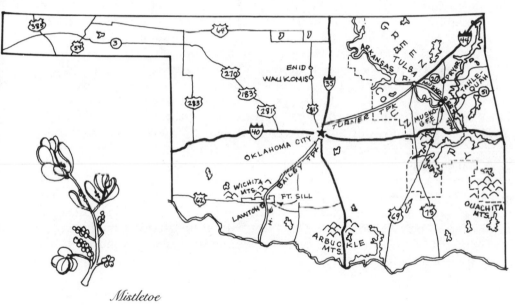

Mistletoe
OKLAHOMA STATE FLOWER

Oklahoma!

[O]n a recent New England journey, I was asked by a gentleman of traditional Boston background, "Now, just where is Oklahoma?" Pull out a map of the United States and there, located almost in the center of the lower "forty-eight," is the state of Oklahoma. You may think of it as dusty (because of the ruinous 1930's) and landlocked, but neither is true. The eastern half of the state is called "Green Country," for now there are at least a baker's dozen manmade lakes that have changed the landscape, Tulsa has a port, open for barge traffic to the Gulf of Mexico. Oklahoma has an assortment of distinctions. We are in the Sunbelt, Bible Belt, Dry Belt,* Tornado Alley, Oil Belt, Gas Belt, Prairie Belt, and Wheat Belt.

Oklahoma farmers grow a high-protein winter wheat rich in gluten, excellent for breadmaking. We are second in production of hard red winter wheat, occasionally outranked by North Dakota, but our neighbor, Kansas, always ranks first. Many of the wheat-growing states ship wheat to the city of Enid, an Oklahoma agricultural center, where it is tested periodically.

Connie Hunter, born on a western Oklahoma wheat farm, married a wheat farmer who lived just six miles from her home. Connie's husband, Losco, works several wheat farms for the family, growing hard red winter wheat and alfalfa hay for feed, and also runs some cattle. Connie purchased a small mill (see Sources of Supply) equipped with miniature grindstones and began processing her own wheat to bake bread. Through Connie and Losco, I have learned how the gluten content can vary by a small percentage each year. When there is too much rain as the wheat ripens, cheat, a wheatlike grass, grows and is harvested with the wheat, which lessens the quality of the harvested grain. A perfect year will have early spring rains to help the development of the wheat kernels and no rain just before the harvest. Connie became so fascinated with milling that she began demonstrations for children to develop their interest in the use of whole grains.

---

*Dry Belt does not mean Dust Bowl; we conquered those problems and have become a booming agricultural state. But we have been far behind other states in our liquor laws until September of 1984, when we finally entered the twentieth century and voted to legalize liquor by the drink instead of liquor by the "wink."

Oklahoma Hard Winter Wheat Bread

Makes 2 loaves

Connie ground some freshly harvested wheat and mailed it to me with her recipe and the necessary cracked wheat. I received the package the following day and immediately baked the bread. The loaves were superb, of a good texture, earthy, and flavorful. One loaf set aside for two days I found made excellent sandwich bread.

⅓ cup cracked wheat
1 cup water
1 cup warm milk
½ cup melted butter
½ cup honey
2 teaspoons salt
½ cup warm water

2 packages active dry yeast
2 eggs, beaten
4 cups stone-ground whole wheat flour
2 cups unbleached white flour, approximately.

Combine the cracked wheat and water in a saucepan. Slowly bring to a boil, stirring constantly until thickened. Let simmer 10 minutes, or until liquid has evaporated. Remove from burner and let cool to lukewarm.

In a large mixing bowl combine the milk, butter, honey, and salt, blending well. Combine the warm water and yeast, stirring until dissolved. Add to the milk mixture with the eggs. Beat in the cracked wheat mixture and 3 cups of the whole wheat flour. Add the remaining cup of whole wheat flour. Gradually add sufficient white flour to make a workable dough that pulls away from sides of the bowl. Turn out on a floured surface (use white flour) and knead until smooth and elastic, about 10 minutes. Round into a ball and place in a warm buttered bowl, turning to coat the top. Cover loosely with plastic wrap and a towel and let rise until doubled, about 1 hour.

Punch down the dough and divide in half. Knead each piece thoroughly, cover, and let rest 15 minutes. Butter two 9-inch loaf pans. Mold the dough into loaves and place in pans. Cover and let rise to tops of pans, about 45–60 minutes.

Preheat the oven to 350°F. Bake the loaves 40 minutes. Turn out on wire racks to cool.

Sheaf of Wheat

Makes 2 sheaves

Forming a sheaf of wheat with Connie's bread dough is a natural next step. My students in western Oklahoma and Texas have been enthusiastically molding facsimile sheaves with their own wheat. A favorite student in Cleburne, Texas, owns several wheat farms. She formed a group of wheat sheaves which were placed on her church altar for an Easter service.

Prepare Oklahoma Wheat Bread as directed. After the bowl rising, divide in half and cover the portion not being used.

Divide 1 piece of the dough into 18 equal pieces. Roll 2 of the pieces into 13-inch ropes; twist ropes together and set aside. Roll 8 of the pieces into 18-inch ropes and roll the remaining 8 pieces into 15-inch ropes. Spray a baking sheet with nonstick vegetable spray.

The longer ropes make up the base of the sheaf of wheat, with 2 shorter ropes to fill in. The remaining ropes are placed on top of the base where they are needed to fill in to make the sheaf solid and attractive. Using the drawings as a guide, place 1 of the 18-inch ropes length-

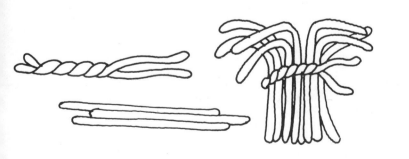

wise on center of baking sheet and bend top third of rope to the left at a 45-degree angle. Place a second 18-inch rope on sheet, touching first rope, but bend top third off to right. Repeat procedure, using 2 of the 15-inch ropes. Fill out the bottom layer of the sheaf with the 6 remaining long ropes, spreading them out on the baking sheet. Over this layer place the 6 remaining 15-inch ropes, making shorter bends in the uppermost ropes.

Arrange twist across center of sheaf and tuck ends underneath. Repeat directions with remaining portion of dough. Cover and let rise 30 minutes.

Preheat the oven to 350°F. With scissors make diagonal snips along bent "stalks" of wheat. Beat 1 egg with 1 tablespoon water and brush both sheaves thoroughly. Bake about 25 minutes, or until golden brown. Let sheaves cool on baking sheets set over wire racks. Remove when cool. If you wish to dry the sheaves so that they will keep longer, lower oven temperature to 250°F and bake 30 minutes more.

Lawton and Fort Sill

When Oklahoma Territory was finally thrown open to the Boomers and Sooners, the last frontier disappeared. Most of those front runners in the last "run" of 1889 were a mixture of Scotch, Irish, German, and English ancestry, plus a few Bohemians and Lebanese. As a result of this mixture, there are few distinct ethnic groups in Oklahoma, but one of the largest is the population of approximately 169,000 Indians. I grew up with the singsong, "Chickasaw, Choctaw, Cherokee, Creek, and Seminole," the five "civilized tribes." We did not enter the Union as a state until 1907.

In the southwestern portion of our state, close to the low hills called the Wichita Mountains, are our third largest city, Lawton, and the artillery school of the United States Armed Forces, Fort Sill. Soldiers from all over the free world are sent to Fort Sill for training. Often their wives accompany them and some of the American servicemen have brought home foreign born wives. A constant flow of international guests has created a stimulating society, both on the base and in the town.

Erika Watkins, a GI bride, brought her expertise for homemade breads to America from Germany, where she worked in a bakery. Erika says that German people eat not so differently from Americans, but that on Easter, in her native area, they love rabbit dishes or roasted baby goat rubbed with garlic and flavored with bacon. The following bread from Erika would be a perfect addition to such dinners.

Swielbrot (ONION BREAD)

Makes 2 loaves

1 tablespoon finely
  chopped onion
3½ cups white flour
3½ cups rye flour
2 cups warm water
2 packages active dry
  yeast
1 teaspoon salt

3½ tablespoons melted
  lard or vegetable
  shortening
2 tablespoons light
  molasses
1 teaspoon fennel seeds
½ teaspoon caraway seeds

To prepare the onion, preheat the oven to 375°F. Spread the onion in a small baking dish and roast a few minutes, or until slightly browned.

Combine the white and rye flours. In a large mixing bowl combine the water and yeast, stirring until dissolved. Add 2 cups of the flour mixture, beating until mixture is smooth. Cover and set aside until sponge is bubbly, about 30 minutes.

Stir down the sponge and add the salt, lard, onion, molasses, and fennel and caraway seeds. Gradually add sufficient flour mixture to form a soft dough that pulls away from sides of the bowl. Turn the dough out on a floured surface (use white flour) and knead 10 minutes. Rye flour always makes a dough quite sticky; sprinkle white flour on the kneading surface and your hands as needed. Cover with a towel and let rest 15 minutes. Brush a large baking sheet with melted shortening or spray with nonstick vegetable spray. Divide dough in half and round into balls. Place on baking sheets, cover, and let rise until doubled, about 1 hour.

Preheat the oven to 375°F. Bake the loaves about 45 minutes. Let cool on wire racks.

Tahlequah and Northeastern State University

T wo hundred miles across the state from Lawton—in an area where the trees are beautiful, clear tumbling streams invite canoeists, and the many small lakes are loved by fishermen and water-skiers—is the pretty town of Tahlequah. Many elderly Cherokees who live in the region speak only their native language—an *American* language, don't forget! On the campus of the small but active university is an unusually fine cafeteria maintained at the Student Union. A unique "Bishop's Bread" is baked for sale each week. The bread of the same name (page 217) made in Southern states is quite different. Here is the charming story of Northeastern State's Bishop's Bread.

Annually a Boare's Heade Feaste, sponsored by the art, drama, and music departments, features good-natured improvisations by student actors in the style of the entertainments of sixteenth- and seventeenth-century England. Lavish period costumes, beautiful choral and instrumental performances, and rowdy good fun highlight the evening. On the elegant dinner menu, Bishop's Bread has become an obvious favorite among the guests. Bishop's Bread was called "Pull-A-Part Bread" years ago. It was made to bring good luck and a blessed year ahead, and, as the university catering service pointed out, it is an ideal holiday bread.

Bishop's Bread

Makes 4 or 5 loaves

4 cups warm water
3 packages active dry
  yeast
2½ teaspoons salt
¾ cup sugar
1 cup instant nonfat dry
  milk
½ cup melted butter or
  vegetable shortening

9–10 cups flour
1 cup melted butter
1½ cups Cinnamon
  Sugar, page 46
Confectioner's Icing, page
  45
Chopped nuts
Candied cherry halves

In a large mixing bowl combine the water and yeast, stirring until dissolved. Add the salt, sugar, dry milk, and butter, blending well. Beat in 3 cups of flour until batter is smooth. Gradually add sufficient flour to form a soft, workable dough. Turn out on a floured surface and knead 5 minutes. Cover and let rest 15 minutes.

Butter four 8½-inch loaf pans. Roll out dough 1 inch thick and cut out rounds with a 2-inch biscuit cutter. Dip each round in melted butter

and then in Cinnamon Sugar and place on edge in prepared pans, 12 rounds to a pan, 6 on either side. The recipe may make as many as 5 loaves, depending on how you have rolled and cut the dough. If necessary, butter another 8-inch pan. Cover loaves and let rise in a warm spot until dough reaches almost to tops of pans, about 45 minutes.

Preheat the oven to 300°F. Bake the loaves 45 minutes. Let them cool in the pan set over a wire rack 10 minutes, turn out on a decorative platter, and frost with Confectioner's Icing. Sprinkle with chopped nuts and cherries. The breads freeze well without the icing.

Pryor

N orth of Tahlequah, the land changes to open prairie. Pryor, in the center of productive farm lands (many owned by Mennonites and Amish), is subject to high winds and tornadoes. It was almost totally destroyed several years ago, when an exceptionally devastating storm roared down the main street. Within two years, Pryor was rebuilt and looked like a new town. Here resides a native Oklahoman whom I consider one of the finest cooks in the state, Elizabeth Morgan. She sent me the recipe for her favorite sweet rolls. They are light and puffy, and I have enjoyed them with Elizabeth, while sipping coffee in her kitchen.

Orange Sweet Rolls

Makes about 64 rolls

Dough:

1 cup milk, scalded
¼ pound (1 stick) butter
½ cup sugar
1 teaspoon salt
1 package active dry yeast

¼ cup warm water
3 eggs, beaten
6 cups flour,
    approximately

Filling:

¼ pound butter (1 stick),
    at room temperature

2 cups sugar
4 heaping tablespoons
    grated orange rind

In a large mixing bowl combine the milk, butter, sugar, and salt. Stir until ingredients are dissolved and let cool to lukewarm. Combine the yeast and water in a bowl, stirring to dissolve. Add to milk mixture and blend in the eggs. Beat in 3 cups of flour to make a smooth batter. Gradually add sufficient flour to form a soft dough. Knead lightly in the bowl. Round into a ball and place in a warm buttered bowl, turning to coat the top. Cover loosely with plastic wrap and a towel and let rise until doubled, about 1–1½ hours.

Combine the filling ingredients, mix thoroughly, and set aside.

Brush three 8-inch square or round baking tins with melted butter. Punch down the dough and divide into 4 equal portions. Keeping the rest of the dough covered, roll 1 portion into a 16 × 4-inch rectangle. Spread with one quarter of the filling to within ½ inch of edges. Roll up from the long side, jelly-roll style. Seal the seam. Cut into 1-inch slices and place in baking pan cut side up. Repeat directions with remaining 3 portions. Cover and let rise until doubled, about 45 minutes.

Preheat the oven to 350°F. Bake rolls 20 minutes, or until light golden brown. Turn out immediately on a serving tray or, if freezing, on aluminum foil.

Tulsa

O f course you knew that, after all my journeys in search of breads in America, eventually I must settle down in my own backyard. At this writing, I have lived in my city for more than fifty years. Tulsa began with a few mud streets at the turn of the century and is now a truly beautiful city built on bluffs in a curve of the Arkansas River. Our history has been rugged. Oklahoma was just a prairie that had to be built into a state and make good on its discovery of oil, its capacity for abundant agriculture, and opportunities in aviation. I love my state and would live nowhere else. The wide open spaces are a part of my heritage. Travel is easy to both coasts and to Mexico and Canada, via air or automobile. We are part of the Sunbelt, fortunate today and in our promise for the future.

I've found fascinating special breads in Oklahoma and breads for every day family use. Each bread in this chapter, and all the recipes in this book, has been tested either in my kitchen or by one of my volunteer assistants. They have never let me down, despite all that dishwashing.

The first bread comes from Judy Klos. She was born in Hungary and had a happy childhood, but tragic difficulties began to separate the family when her father was taken prisoner by the Germans. Judy came to the United States and married an American. Her story is like so many caused by World War II, but with a happy ending. Judy still yearns for her beloved Hungary. She told me eagerly about this Hungarian poppy seed roll, an excellent coffeecake similar to others made in many of the Balkan countries.

Makos Kalacs (HUNGARIAN POPPY SEED ROLLS)

Makes 6 coffeecakes

Dough:

2 packages active dry
    yeast
¾ cup warm milk
½ pound (2 sticks) cold
    butter

4½–5 cups flour
2 eggs, lightly beaten
¼ cup sugar
¼ teaspoon salt

Filling:
3 cups poppy seeds, or
    ground pecans or
    walnuts
¾ cup sugar
¼ cup flour
½ cup warm milk

½ cup raisins marinated
    in 2 tablespoons rum
    and drained
½ teaspoon vanilla
Grated rind of 1 lemon
1 tablespoon lemon juice
    or rum

1 egg, separated

Combine the yeast and milk in a small bowl, stirring until dissolved, and set aside. In a large mixing bowl cut the butter into 3 cups of the flour using a pastry blender, or whirl the ingredients in a food processor and turn into a mixing bowl. Add the yeast mixture to the flour mixture with the eggs, sugar, and salt and stir thoroughly. Gradually add sufficient flour to form a soft, workable dough. Turn out on a floured surface and knead until smooth and elastic, about 5–8 minutes. Round into a ball and place in a warm buttered bowl, turning to coat the top. Cover loosely with plastic wrap and a towel and let rise until doubled, about 2 hours.

Punch down the dough, divide into 6 equal portions, knead each piece, cover, and let rest.

To make the filling, if you do not have a poppy seed grinder, grind the seeds, ⅓ cup at a time, in a blender at high speed. Mix the sugar and flour and combine with the milk, raisins, vanilla, grated rind, and juice. Add the ground poppy seeds and mix thoroughly.

Roll 1 portion of dough into a 12 × 8-inch rectangle. Spread one sixth of the filling over the dough to within ¼ inch of the edges. Roll up from the long side, jelly-roll style. Seal the seam and place on an unbuttered baking sheet seam side down. Seal the ends and tuck under. Repeat directions with remaining portions of dough. Beat the egg yolk and brush on the rolls. Let rise 1 hour. Beat the egg white until frothy and brush on rolls. Refrigerate 30 minutes.

Preheat the oven to 350°F. Prick sides of rolls with a fork to permit steam to escape and bake 25–30 minutes, or until light golden brown. Let rolls cool on wire racks. The rolls freeze very well.

Magic Mill Hamburger Buns

Makes 24–36 rolls

During the testing of recipes for America's Bread Book, *one of my associates whipped up these hamburger buns when my eldest grandsons came for a visit. They were such a complete success that I contacted the Magic Mill Company in Salt Lake City for permission to use this delicious, fast way of producing hamburger buns. They graciously assented. What is a Magic Mill? A superb little machine that will grind wheat and other grains in a matter of seconds (see Sources of Supply).*

3½ cups warm water
1 cup light oil
½ cup honey
6 packages active dry
  yeast (See **Note**)
2 teaspoons salt

3 eggs, lightly beaten
10½ cups whole wheat
  flour, approximately
  (preferably freshly
  ground; see **Note**)

In a large mixing bowl combine the water, oil, honey, and yeast. Stir thoroughly and let rest 15 minutes. Stir in the salt and eggs. Beat in 4 cups of the flour to make a smooth batter. Gradually add sufficient flour to make a workable dough. Turn out on a lightly floured surface (use white flour) and knead 5 minutes.

Spray 2 or 3 large baking sheets with nonstick vegetable spray. Preheat the oven to 425°F.

On a floured surface roll out the dough ½ inch thick. Cut into any size you prefer for hamburger buns; 3- and 4-inch buns are standard. Place ½ inch apart on the baking sheets. Cover and let rise 10 minutes. Bake 10 minutes. Let cool on racks. This recipe can easily be cut in half, or freeze leftover buns.

Note: A yeasty taste does not result from using too much yeast but from the yeast being too warm. Less yeast may be used in this recipe but there will be a longer rising time in the pan. If you are not using freshly ground flour, warm the flour in the oven following the directions on page 200.

Kathy's Pumpernickel Hamburger Buns

Makes 24 large or 36 smaller buns

Kathy Major, a native Oklahoman, from the Oklahoma City area, worked for six months with me testing myriad breads. Kathy is a meticulous, happy, natural chef. I asked her to work on a pumpernickel bun somewhat similar to the Magic Mill Hamburger Bun. In no time, she proudly came into my kitchen with her creation—just what I wanted.

3½ cups warm water
6 packages active dry
   yeast
½ cup molasses
1 cup light oil
3 squares unsweetened
   chocolate, melted and
   cooled
2 teaspoons salt

3 eggs, lightly beaten
2 tablespoons caraway
   seeds
3 cups rye flour
3 cups whole wheat flour
3½–4½ cups unbleached
   white flour
Sesame seeds

In a large mixing bowl combine the warm water and yeast, stirring until dissolved. Add the molasses and oil and let rest 15 minutes.

Combine the chocolate (used strictly for color), salt, eggs, and caraway seeds, blending well. Add to the yeast mixture. Stir in the rye flour to form a smooth batter. Add the whole wheat flour and beat thoroughly. Gradually add sufficient white flour to form a workable dough. Turn out on a floured surface (use white flour) and knead until smooth and elastic, about 10–15 minutes.

Preheat the oven to 425°F. Spray 2 or 3 baking sheets with nonstick vegetable spray. Roll out dough about ½ inch thick. Cut into large circles 3–4 inches in diameter. Place on baking sheet and let rise 10 minutes. Brush tops with water, sprinkle with sesame seeds, and bake 10 minutes.

Irene's Pear Bread

Makes 2 loaves

*My friend Howard Weber, in New Glarus,
Wisconsin, told me about this bread. Many years
ago there was a terrible drought in Switzerland.
About the only thing that survived agriculturally
was the pear trees, and so pears came to be used
for many things, including a luscious bread. This
one was designed by Irene Holland, a beautiful
woman born in French Switzerland, who married
an American; by now she could almost be a native
Tulsan, except for her lovely, lilting accent.
Irene, an exquisite cook, prepares breads, or any
special recipe, so professionally that they could be
published anywhere. She has the "touch" for
making bread by hand.*

Filling:

1 pound dried pears
½ pound dried pitted
   prunes
1 cup finely chopped
   walnuts

1 cup raisins, scalded,
   drained, and dried
1½ teaspoons ground
   anise
¼ cup Kirsch
½ cup sugar

Dough:

1 package active dry yeast
½ cup warm water
1 cup warm milk
¼ teaspoon salt

½ cup melted butter
¼ cup sugar
4–5 cups flour

1 egg plus 1 tablespoon
   water for glaze

Cook the pears and prunes separately in water to cover until tender. Drain and let cool slightly. Place both fruits in bowl of a food processor and whirl several times. Remove to a mixing bowl and add the walnuts, raisins, anise, Kirsch, and sugar. Mix well and set aside.

In a large mixing bowl combine the yeast and water, stirring until dissolved. Blend in the milk, salt, butter, and sugar. Beat in 2 cups of flour to make a smooth mixture. Gradually add sufficient flour to form a soft dough. Turn out on a floured surface and knead 5–8 minutes, or until smooth and elastic. Round into a ball and place in a warm buttered bowl turning to coat the top. Cover loosely with plastic wrap and a towel and let rise until doubled, about 1½ hours.

Punch down the dough, knead lightly, cover, and let rest 10 minutes. Divide dough in half and cover 1 portion while you work with the other.

Butter a baking sheet. Roll 1 portion of dough into a 15 × 12-inch rectangle. Spread with half the filling to within ½ inch of edges. Roll up from the long side, jelly-roll style. Seal the seam and ends. Place the roll seam side down on baking sheet.

Butter an 8-inch loaf pan. Pat the second portion of dough into a large circle. Place remaining filling on top. Bring dough up over the filling and begin kneading the fruit into the dough. This will be quite a sticky process, but eventually you will be able to form a loaf. Pick up the dough, sticky as it is, and place in loaf pan. Cover both loaves and let rise about 1½ hours.

Preheat the oven to 350°F. Brush loaves with the glaze and bake about 45 minutes. Turn out on wire racks to cool.

Laura's Breakfast Puffs

Makes 12 muffins

*My youngest daughter-in-law handed me a recipe
card and insisted that I try her buttery puffs. I
did and loved every single delicious calorie!*

5 tablespoons butter, at
  room temperature
½ cup sugar
1 egg
1½ cups unbleached
  white flour, sifted
2 teaspoons baking
  powder

½ teaspoon salt
¼ teaspoon nutmeg
½ cup milk
¾ cup melted butter
1 cup Cinnamon Sugar,
  page 46

Preheat the oven to 350°F. Butter twelve 2-inch muffin tins. Cream the butter and sugar in bowl of an electric mixer until light and fluffy. Add the egg, beating well. Sift together the flour, baking powder, salt, and nutmeg. Add dry ingredients to butter mixture alternately with milk, beating well after each addition. Fill muffin tins two thirds full and bake 20–25 minutes, or until golden brown. Remove from oven and immediately dip each puff in melted butter and roll in the Cinnamon Sugar. Serve immediately.

F or eleven years, while our three sons were struggling through the teenage phase of life, we spent summer weekends on a huge house-boat called the *Queen Mary*. Accommodations were almost limitless and we often had five to seven water-skiing boats roped to the sides as we floated around the lake, teenagers also dripping on all sides. Twenty guests could sleep inside, on the deck, and on the roof. Our tricolor collie patiently watched all the confusion from the middle of the front deck. The kitchen had room for only one person, but it was delightfully convenient. To my left was the stove, in front of me, the sink with window above, to the right, a bar and the only working surface, and behind me, the refrigerator operated by butane—most of the time. The meals that came from that tiny kitchen were fun to prepare and, with assistance of our friends, each was a feast. The favorite was Sunday morning brunch. Early risers slipped into the water for an invigorating swim. The first to get up, started the coffee. Melons were cut on deck and handed around to eat hanging over the side. My husband prepared Orange Flips for those who cared to start the day in a spin, while I heated our favorite rolls—and the teenagers couldn't get over the idea that the recipe came from the Tulsa public school system!

Tulsa School Day Cinnamon Rolls

Makes about 200 miniature or 72 large rolls

These were our favorites on the Queen Mary. *Through the Tulsa Public Schools I was given permission to use their recipe. I have adapted and tested it for both miniature and regular size rolls. The recipe may be cut in half.*

4 packages active dry
    yeast
2 cups warm water
½ cup sugar
¾ cup melted butter
½ cup instant nonfat dry
    milk

2 teaspoons salt
3 eggs, beaten
9 cups flour,
    approximately
Melted butter
Cinnamon Sugar, page 46

Frosting:
2 cups confectioner's
    sugar

1 teaspoon vanilla
Warm coffee

In a large mixing bowl combine the yeast and water, stirring until dissolved. Add the sugar, butter, milk, salt, and eggs, blending thoroughly. Beat in 3 cups of flour to make a smooth batter. Gradually add sufficient flour to form a soft, workable dough. Turn out on a floured surface and knead until smooth and elastic, about 8 minutes. Round into a ball and place in a warm buttered bowl, turning to coat the top. Cover loosely with plastic wrap and a towel and let rise until doubled, about 1 hour.

Miniature Rolls: Butter 16 miniature muffin tins (twelve muffins per tin) or five 9-inch cake tins. Punch down the dough, knead lightly, and divide into 8 portions. Roll each portion into a 20 × 5-inch rectangle. Brush with melted butter to within ¼ inch of edges. Sprinkle each rectangle with about ¼ cup Cinnamon Sugar. Roll up from the long side and seal the seam. Cut into ¾-inch slices and place in prepared tins. Let rise 15 minutes.

Preheat the oven to 350°F. Bake rolls about 20 minutes, or until just lightly colored.

Large Rolls: Butter 6 muffin tins (twelve 2-inch muffins per tin) or six 9-inch cake tins. Divide the dough into 4 equal portions. Roll each piece into an 18 × 10-inch rectangle. Brush with melted butter and sprinkle heavily with Cinnamon Sugar. Roll up from the long side (the tighter you make the roll, the more swirls you will get), jelly-roll style, and seal the seam. Cut into 1-inch slices and place in prepared tins. Cover and let rise until light, about 30 minutes. Bake in a preheated 350°F oven 25 minutes.

To frost, combine the confectioner's sugar and vanilla. Whisk in sufficient warm coffee to make a thin icing. When the rolls have baked, turn them out on a serving tray and frost with the warm icing.

Dora's Microwave Muffin Loaves

Makes 2 loaves

A discussion arose during a bread session with my associates about the pros and cons of using a microwave oven to bake breads. Dora Malone was willing to try. She came up with such a variety of recipes, I was stunned. This bread has a texture very close to that of an English muffin— full of holes to accept all that butter!

2 packages active dry yeast	¼ teaspoon baking soda
5 cups flour	2½ cups water
1 tablespoon sugar	10 tablespoons instant dry milk
1½ teaspoons salt	Cornmeal

Combine the yeast, 3 cups of the flour, sugar, salt, and soda in a large mixing bowl. Heat the water to 120°F and add the dry milk. Add the liquid mixture to the flour mixture, beating very well. Stir in the remaining flour to make a stiff batter. Spray two 8½-inch glass loaf pans with nonstick vegetable spray and sprinkle with cornmeal. Divide the dough between the pans, spreading batter into the corners. Sprinkle tops with cornmeal. Cover with a towel and let rise 45 minutes.

Microwave each loaf on high power for 7 minutes. Remove from oven and let rest 5 minutes before removing from pans. The loaf will be quite pale in color—don't let that bother you, for there is another step. Cut into fairly thick slices and toast. Now, enjoy with cream cheese and strawberry jam.

Variations on the Microwave Muffin Theme:
Substitute 2 cups of yogurt for 2 cups of the water.
Substitute 2 cups of warm milk for 2 cups of the water.
Add 2 cups shredded sharp Cheddar—very attractive!
Add 1½ cups raisins, scalded, drained, and dried—delicious toasted and served with hot applesauce for breakfast.
Substitute 1 cup of orange juice for 1 cup of water. Add grated rind of 2 oranges.

Lucy's Flour Tortillas

Makes about 72 tortillas

Lucy Lombardo volunteered to bring her expertise and griddle into my kitchen to teach my testing group how to prepare flour tortillas. Lucy's parents immigrated from Mexico to Oklahoma, before she was born, so Lucy, now a great-grandmother, is a native Oklahoman and Tulsan. I shall give you the recipe as Lucy prepared it; the result is many dozen tortillas, but they can be frozen and, if wrapped properly, keep well in the refrigerator. If you want to cut the recipe in half, use the entire tablespoon of shortening.

5 pounds flour
5½ tablespoons baking
   powder
1 tablespoon salt

1 tablespoon vegetable
   shortening
5½–6 cups warm water

In a very large mixing bowl combine the flour, baking powder, and salt. Now, Lucy started to dump everything in, But Dora Malone, one of my assistants, grabbed a bowl, pencil, and paper, and we finally got under way. The dry ingredients were mixed well by hand. The shortening was dropped in the center. Carefully, Lucy broke a tiny piece of shortening between two fingers and rubbed flour in it. Slowly she worked the shortening with her fingertips until it vanished, mixed into the flour. Lucy made a well in the center and began to pour in the water, mixing flour down in that well with her hands. A dough began to take shape, and she picked up 1 piece and placed it on a floured surface. Then a second large piece of dough was on the table. Finally all the flour was mixed into dough, which was kneaded together and returned to the bowl. Lucy covered the bowl and then sat down to relax and have a cigarette.

After the dough had rested, we began to make it into *tostales,* small pieces of dough, about 2 tablespoons, that are rounded into the shape of a small fat egg, dipped lightly in flour, and stacked in a bowl. When the bowl was filled with *tostales,* we covered them and everybody rested 30 minutes.

Have ready an ungreased heavy griddle (preferably cast iron) and a rolling pin. Lucy's rolling pin was a very heavy cylinder, once part of a printing press, that she had picked up at a garage sale—perfect for rolling *tostales* into tortillas. I used my favorite rolling pin. Dip the *tostale* lightly in flour again and place on a flat surface. Roll forward and then backward once, then turn the *tostale* over, and press and roll forward and backward. Turn and repeat this pressure rolling. The *tostale* must be rolled paper-thin. Place on a moderately hot griddle (you will have to learn to test your own heat), cook the tortilla quickly on one side, then flip to the other. The tortilla should just barely take color and show a few bubbles on the surface. Stack immediately one on top of another. As they bake, make 3 or 4 stacks and, when finished, cover with a wet cloth. Leave the tortillas covered until completely cooled. They may be wrapped for freezing or refrigeration for use at any time.

That was a fun day with Lucy Lombardo!

Lefse

Make 4 breads

Millie Lillegard, raised in Minnesota but now transplanted to my "backyard," lives in Oral Roberts Retirement Village. Accompanied by Dora Malone, one of my volunteers, we spent a morning with Millie to watch and help her make this Norwegian pancake bread. Although it is thin and cooked like a tortilla, the similarity ends there.

5 cups packed hot riced potatoes	3 tablespoons melted butter
1 teaspoon salt	2 tablespoons sugar
	2½ cups flour

Combine the potatoes, salt, butter, and sugar. Mix well and let cool to lukewarm. Add the flour, stirring thoroughly. Divide into 4 portions for easy handling. Cover and chill the dough.

Place 1 portion on a floured surface and roll. Turn over, pat with more flour, and roll until the dough is ⅛ inch thick and about 12 inches in diameter. If you have access to a grooved Norwegian *lefse* rolling pin, the process will be simpler. Keep the rolling pin floured. Bake on an ungreased hot grill or in an electric skillet heated to 500°F. The breads may be eaten plain, or you may sprinkle sugar over one quarter of a pancake, then roll and set aside while preparing the remaining breads.

Swedish Limpa Bread

Makes 3 loaves

Bernice Hallquist, of Swedish ancestry and born in Milwaukee but now an Oklahoman, has been making this bread for more than forty years. It adapts well for "flowerpot" sandwiches. See page 347 for seasoning ceramic flowerpots.

2 cups water
½ cup packed brown
  sugar
1½ teaspoons caraway
  seeds
1 teaspoon anise seeds
1 tablespoon lard or
  vegetable shortening

2 packages active dry
  yeast
3½ cups white flour,
  approximately
1 teaspoon salt
2 cups rye flour

Combine the water, sugar, caraway and anise seeds, and lard in a small saucepan. Heat just to the boiling point, remove from burner, stir, and let cool to lukewarm, about 100°F. Transfer to a mixing bowl and sprinkle in the yeast, stirring until dissolved. Beat in 2 cups of white flour to make a smooth batter. Add the salt and rye flour and sufficient white flour to form a workable dough. Turn out on a floured surface and knead 8–10 minutes, or until smooth and elastic. Round dough into a ball and place in a warm bowl brushed with melted shortening, turning to coat the top. Cover loosely with plastic wrap and a towel and let rise until doubled, about 1 hour.

Punch down the dough, knead lightly, cover, and let rest 10 minutes. Brush three 8½-inch loaf pans with melted shortening. Divide dough into 3 portions and mold into loaves. Place in pans, cover, and let rise until doubled, about 45 minutes.

Preheat the oven to 400°F. Bake loaves 20 minutes. Reduce heat to 350°F and bake 35 minutes. Turn loaves out on wire racks to cool.

Rye Flowerpot Loaves: Use one third of the dough for 2 well-buttered 4-inch seasoned flowerpots. (The complete recipe will make 6 flowerpots.) Roll each portion into a 12 × 4-inch rectangle. Brush with a good French mustard. Spread 2 ounces of grated Swiss cheese over the dough. If desired, add thinly sliced ham and even some well-drained sauerkraut—not too much or the sandwich will be soggy. Experiment a bit to see what you like. Roll up from the short end and place in flowerpots. Repeat with remaining two thirds of the dough, if desired. Cover and let rise about 30–40 minutes.

Preheat the oven to 350°F. Bake the loaves 40 minutes. Remove from pots and let cool on wire racks.

Jo's Processor Wheat Berry Bread

Makes 1 loaf

Jo Spencer, my third associate and now my Utica, New York, "Connection," lived in Tulsa for several years before going back to Yankee country. For her large family, Jo experimented with quick yeast breads. Together we worked out this food processor whole grain bread.

1 cup wheat berries
1 cup whole wheat flour
1 package active dry yeast
2 tablespoons honey
¼ cup melted butter

¼ cup instant nonfat dry milk
1 teaspoon salt
1½ cups unbleached white flour

Place the wheat berries in a 1-quart jar and add sufficient water to fill jar three quarters full. Set aside 12 hours.

Drain the berries, reserving 1 cup of the water. Add the berries to bowl of food processor with the whole wheat flour. Process using steel blade 4 or 5 times. Heat the reserved water to 100°F. Add the yeast, honey, and butter and stir to dissolve. To the flour mixture add the dry milk, salt, and white flour. Whirl just to blend. Slowly pour in the yeast mixture, pulsing the machine until the dough forms a mass. Pulse 30 seconds more. If the dough seems too wet, add a very small amount of white flour and process to absorb. Remove dough from bowl and knead by hand about 1 minute. Round into a ball and place in a warm buttered bowl, turning to coat the top. Cover loosely with plastic wrap and a towel and let rise until doubled, about 1 hour.

Butter an 8½-inch loaf pan. Punch down dough, form into a loaf, and place in pan. Cover and let rise to the top, about 45 minutes.

Preheat the oven to 375°F. Bake the loaf 30 minutes. Turn out on a wire rack to cool.

Jenk's Popovers

Makes 24 popovers

Jenkin Lloyd Jones, publisher, editor, raconteur, and syndicated columnist, has a hidden talent. He loves to make popovers. To quote Jenk, "Popovers are overheated Yorkshire pudding baked most successfully in cups 2 inches deep, slightly conical, and about 2¾ inches across the top. Variations in the contents of a recipe make little difference, but cooking method does. Baked at 450°F for 20 minutes, plus 15 minutes at 350°F, would guarantee a panful of blackened cinders in my oven. Placing them in a cold oven and baking at 425°F for 40 minutes would still overdo them, and I yank them out in 25 minutes. The trick is to bake them without scorching." I tried several methods and here is the result.

| 3 large eggs | 1¼ cups flour |
| 1¼ cups milk | ½ teaspoon salt |

Throw everything into a food processor and pulse several times to make a smooth batter, or put the ingredients into a mixing bowl and beat with a whisk until smooth. Muffin tins, shallow custard cups, or heavy cast-iron popover pans can be used. To start with a cold oven, it is better to use muffin tins rather than popover pans. If baking at a high temperature, use the popover pans. Brush the pans or cups (enough to make 24 popovers) with melted shortening. Fill the cups two thirds full. Place muffin tins in a cold oven and turn oven heat to 425°F. The popovers will be golden brown in about 25 minutes. If using the cast-iron popover pans, which are now available in most cookware stores, preheat the oven to 450°F. Bake popovers 20 minutes, reduce heat to 350°F, and bake 15 minutes more. Popovers should be eaten hot out of the oven—they do not hold well.

Note: Crystal Glenn of Aspen, Colorado, suggests that for popovers baked at high altitudes the popover pan should be heated and the milk warmed to 100°F.

For Men Only

Makes 10 loaves

No doubt ERA supporters will flip over this title, but I know of only two Amazons who could handle the quantity. My youngest son, Michael, has carefully created this highly nutritional family bread which he prepares once a month. Mike maintains that only REAL men can handle this amount of dough! To tell the truth, he bought one of those huge bread makers that looks like an ice-cream freezer; I can't lift it. My youngest grandchildren love the bread and will eat their peanut butter on it. I shall give Mike's original recipe and, following it, one divided down for the feminine sex.

8 packages active dry yeast	½ cup honey
2 cups warm water	4 cups stone-ground whole wheat flour
2 quarts warm buttermilk	4 cups gluten flour
1 pound (4 sticks) butter, melted	26 cups unbleached white flour, approximately
2½ tablespoons salt	

Combine the yeast and water in a mixing bowl, stirring until dissolved. If you just happen to have one of those big mixers, then start dumping everything in. Otherwise, buy the largest mixing bowl you can find or use a baby's bathtub—that should be nice and sterile! Combine the buttermilk, butter, salt, honey, and whole wheat and gluten flours. Add the yeast mixture and stir vigorously. Start adding the white flour until a workable dough is formed. If attempting this by hand (the Pueblo women handle this amount with ease, fingernail polish and all) knead for a while, rest, and start kneading again. Or divide the dough into several batches (keeping them covered) and knead each one separately putting them all together at the end. The dough will not be harmed by resting; it will probably rather enjoy the whole process. If using a mixer, throw a towel over the top and let rise until doubled, about 1 hour. Punch down or run the machine for a short time, recover, and let rise again about 30 minutes.

If you want to bake some of the breads right away and freeze the rest, divide the dough into 10 portions, knead each briefly, cover, and let rest 10 minutes. Butter ten 8½-inch loaf pans. Form the dough into loaves, wrap those you wish to freeze in plastic wrap, and place in the freezer (see **Note**). Cover the remaining loaves and let rise until curved over the tops of the pans, about 45–60 minutes.

Preheat the oven to 375°F. Bake the loaves 30 minutes. Turn out on wire racks to cool.

If you are baking all the loaves on the same day, mold half the dough into loaves and place the other half in the refrigerator to await the baking of the first batch. Remove the second portion of dough from the refrigerator and proceed as directed (the dough will take about 30 minutes longer to rise since it is cold).

Note: The frozen unbaked loaves will keep about 1 month. Remove from the freezer about 6 hours before baking to allow time for dough to defrost and then rise.

For Women Only

Makes 3 loaves

2 packages active dry
  yeast
½ cup warm water
2 cups warm buttermilk
½ cup melted butter
2 teaspoons salt

2 tablespoons honey
1 cup stone-ground whole
  wheat flour
½ cup gluten flour
6–7 cups unbleached
  white flour

Combine the yeast and water in a small bowl, stirring until dissolved. In a large mixing bowl, combine the buttermilk, butter, salt, and honey, blending well. Add the yeast mixture. Stir in the whole wheat and gluten flours. Gradually add enough white flour to form a soft dough that pulls away from sides of the bowl. Turn out on a lightly floured surface and knead until smooth and elastic, about 8 minutes. Round dough into a ball and place in a warm buttered bowl, turning to coat the top. Cover loosely with plastic wrap and a towel and let rise until doubled, about 1 hour. Punch down, knead lightly in the bowl, re-cover, and let rise until doubled again, about 30 minutes.

Punch down the dough and divide into 3 equal portions. Knead each, cover, and let rest 10 minutes. Butter three 8-inch loaf pans. Form the dough into loaves, place in pans, cover, and let rise until just curved over pans, about 45 minutes.

Preheat the oven to 375°F. Bake the loaves 30 minutes. Let cool on wire racks.

Creating Your Own Breads

Frequently I've been asked how to change a bread recipe. Can deletions or substitutions be made, such as omitting salt or sugar, or perhaps adding more whole wheat flour than is called for? The answer is a resounding yes. A favorite recipe can accept a special ingredient to produce a flavor or texture you desire. Study the balance of a well-written recipe and from that begin constructing your own version. Let me show you what can be done with the preceding bread, For Women Only. I shall change it, using two different patterns but still retaining the basic premise of the recipe. This is an adaptable family bread, good for toast, sandwiches, or just to accompany a meal.

Although For Women Only is nutritious, the bread is not over-powered by heavy flours. The flavor is best when it is made with stone-ground whole wheat and unbleached white flour, butter, and good buttermilk. Buttermilk is one of my favorite liquids in building a bread, for it seems to impart that old-fashioned flavor people love. The basic ingredients are 3 cups of liquid, 7–8 cups of flour, and 2 packages of yeast. This ratio of ingredients results in a smooth-textured bread that is a bit moist—it will not crumble.

For the first variation, Buttermilk Batter Bread, I cut down the amount of white flour and added extra honey and enough eggs to make a very thick batter. I upped the amount of whole wheat flour simply because I enjoy the flavor. The resulting batter bread has the texture of a coarse cake and is even more like a cake when dried fruits are added.

Here are a few points to remember when converting a regular bread to a batter bread. The baking pan or bowl should be brushed thoroughly with melted butter and sprayed with nonstick vegetable spray because batter bread has a tendency to stick. Batter bread needs a little extra help in rising; in this recipe the baking soda gives the bread a final push. Or, instead, I could have added ¼ cup of gluten flour, which helps a heavy bread rise and provides more protein. A slightly higher oven temperature is the final inducement for the bread to rise.

Batter bread always seems to taste better soon after baking. I al-ways reheat cold batter bread.

The second variation, Buttermilk Multi-Grain Bread—what we now think of as a "health" bread—has the same ratio of liquid to flour and yeast as For Women Only. However, because it contains so many different flours, the texture is coarser and drier. The bread has a slight tendency to crumble, but will be good for sandwiches if held for a day or two before slicing.

To arrive at the final recipe, I jotted down special nutritional ingre-dients I thought would make a good bread. Then, as I put it together, I changed a few items, adding wheat sprouts and cashew nuts. Rye flour used in any amount tends to make sticky dough, so the total addition had to be carefully noted. Soy flour was limited to ½ cup, for it is a dense flour and can make a bread heavy. Cornmeal is great to give flavor and a crunchy texture—but not too much in this kind of bread;

no single ingredient should overwhelm the others to obtain the correct balance. Don't forget—if you are on a no-salt diet, leave it out. There will be no affect on the texture. If there is a diabetic in your family, omit the sugar—I've made this bread with no salt and no sugar and it was amazingly good.

To create your own breads, gather all the ingredients that you particularly like in a bread and then begin, for it is great fun and highly stimulating. Just remember the wise remark of my friend in Oregon, Virginia Morgan: "Don't put too many goodies all in one bread, or you'll muddy up the taste!" It is best to prepare two or three breads with different ingredients, rather than to cram everything into one and end up with a heavy bread that lands in a lump in your tummy.

Buttermilk Batter Bread

Makes 2 loaves

½ cup warm water
2 packages active dry
   yeast
2 cups warm buttermilk
½ cup melted butter
½ cup honey
2 eggs, lightly beaten
2 cups stone-ground
   whole wheat flour

2 teaspoons salt
¼ teaspoon baking soda
2 cups unbleached white
   flour
1 cup chopped mixed
   dried fruit or raisins,
   scalded, drained, and
   dried

Combine the water and yeast in a small bowl, stirring until dissolved, and set aside. In a large mixing bowl combine the buttermilk, butter, honey, and eggs. In a separate bowl mix the whole wheat flour, salt, and soda. Add the yeast mixture to the buttermilk mixture and blend well. Beat in the whole wheat flour mixture. If using a heavy-duty mixer, beat with the flat beater 2 minutes. If stirring by hand, keep beating until your arm is tired! Add the white flour, 1 cup at a time. The consistency should be that of a thick pancake batter. When all the flour has been added, beat with a mixer 2 minutes more or by hand for as long as you can. This is the only kneading the batter bread receives, so beat hard. Add the dried fruit.

Spray two 2-quart casseroles with nonstick vegetable spray and brush with melted butter. Pour the batter into the casseroles, cover, and let rise until ½ inch from the top, about 50–60 minutes but watch it.

Preheat the oven to 375°F. Bake breads 40–45 minutes. If the tops become too brown, cover with aluminum foil during the last 15 minutes of baking. Turn loaves out on a wire rack to cool.

A quicker bread, with excellent nutrition, and an entirely different texture than its sister recipe.

Buttermilk Multi-Grain Bread

Makes 3 loaves

A well-balanced, health-oriented recipe that gives you a choice of flavors. One thick slice with a hearty bowl of soup will keep your tummy happy for hours.

1 cup stone-ground whole
    wheat flour
1 cup stone-ground rye
    flour
½ cup stone-ground
    cornmeal
½ cup soy flour
2 teaspoons salt
¼ teaspoon baking soda
½ cup warm water
2 packages active dry
    yeast

2 cups warm buttermilk
½ cup safflower oil
¼ cup light molasses
½ cup toasted sesame
    seeds, sunflower seeds,
    or wheat sprouts, *or* 1
    cup coarsely chopped
    cashew nuts
5 cups unbleached white
    flour, approximately

Combine the whole wheat and rye flours, cornmeal, soy flour, salt, and baking soda and mix well. In a small bowl combine the water and yeast, stirring until dissolved. In a large mixing bowl blend the buttermilk, oil, and molasses. Add the yeast mixture. Beat in the flour mixture to make a smooth batter. Add the seeds. Gradually add sufficient white flour to form a workable dough that pulls away from sides of the bowl. Turn out on a floured surface and knead until smooth and resilient, about 10 minutes. Round into a ball and place in a warm buttered bowl, turning to coat the top. Cover loosely with plastic wrap and a towel and let rise until doubled in bulk, about 1½ hours.

Punch down the dough, turn out on a floured surface, and divide into 3 portions. Knead each, cover, and let rest 10 minutes. Butter three 8½-inch loaf pans. Form the dough into loaves and place in pans. Cover and let rise until curved over edges of pans, about 1 hour.

Preheat the oven to 350°F. Bake the loaves 40 minutes, or until golden brown. Remove and let cool on wire racks.

D uring a series of student classes, I awakened at 2 A.M. one night and conceived a brilliant idea! My plan worked exceedingly well. There had been many questions about whole grains and how to put them together. When the class gathered, I had a complete array of ingredients arranged on the counter. This was during a big election year, so we held a "Convention," with me as chairman—I pushed that right through the rules committee. Each ingredient to go into the bread would be voted on. There was a bit of wrangling over the basic "platform," but together we made the bread and declared it a complete success (probably better than the result of the real election!). The bread belongs to my class and the students chose the name. I offer you the final bread in my book.

"Our Bread"

Makes 3 loaves

2½ cups warm water
2 packages active dry
 yeast
¾ cup instant nonfat dry
 milk
½ cup safflower oil
½ cup honey
2 teaspoons salt

¼ cup toasted wheat germ
½ cup toasted sesame
 seeds
¼ cup millet flour
3 cups stone-ground
 whole wheat flour
5 cups unbleached white
 flour, approximately

Combine ½ cup warm water and yeast in a small bowl, stirring until dissolved, and set side. Measure 2 cups of warm water into a large mixing bowl and blend in the dry milk, oil, honey, salt, and wheat germ. Add the yeast mixture. Stir in the sesame seeds and millet and whole wheat flours until smooth. Gradually add sufficient white flour to make a soft, workable dough that pulls away from sides of the bowl. Turn the dough out on a lightly floured surface and knead until smooth and elastic, about 10 minutes. Round into a ball and place the dough in warm buttered bowl turning to coat the top. Cover loosely with plastic wrap and a towel and let rise until doubled, about 1½ hours.

Punch down the dough, turn out on a floured surface, divide into 3 equal portions, and knead each piece. Cover and let rest 10 minutes. Butter three 8½-inch loaf pans. Shape dough into loaves and place in pans. Cover and let rise until rounded over edges of pans, about 45–60 minutes.

Preheat the oven to 350°F. Bake breads 35–40 minutes, or until dark golden brown. Remove loaves from pans and let cool on wire racks.

In each state of the Union, there is a special beauty and a slightly different way of life, evidence of how people adjust to their environment. Wherever we stayed, I purchased newspapers to read local editorials and the society pages. This quickly showed me the problems of the state, while gossip columns and wedding announcements contained the names of families that had been in a city for generations and gave a hint of the many Old World countries represented in the population.

The contrasts are stupendous. The incredible scenery of the West stretches the mind and relaxes everyday tensions. The eastern seaboard excited me as a history buff, seeing the towns where our independence began. One can drive hundreds of miles in New Mexico and Arizona, crossing only dry arroyos, while the northwest at the end of the Oregon Trail is green and lush. The enormous valleys of California could feed the world, Hawaii is an escape to tropical beauty, and Alaska, one of the most awesome states, is still pioneer country.

Throughout our country, I found an intense desire for personal independence, and a positive expression of that is making one's own bread at home. The breads differ in all the various areas, the result of environment and the diversity of ethnic backgrounds. But many breads are favorites of all Americans, the whole grain breads, French breads, and sourdoughs—and cinnamon rolls! The actual preparation of any homemade bread, and then removing the fragrant loaves from the oven, gives you a true sense of the pioneer spirit, for here is bread, a universally loved food, that you have made with your own independent ingenuity.

Sources of Supply

FLOURS AND GRAINS

Akins Special Foods (health-food
   store)
6570 East 51st
Tulsa, Oklahoma 74145

Arrowhead Mills, Inc.
Box 2059
Hereford, Texas 79045

Brumewell Flour Mill
South Amana, Iowa 52334

Burnt Cabins Grist Mill
Burnt Cabins, Pennsylvania 17215

B. F. Clyde's Grist Mill
R.F.D. 1A
Mystic, Connecticut 06355

Archer Daniels Flour Milling
Route 23B
Hudson, New York 12534

Edwards Mill
School of the Ozarks
Point Lookout, Missouri 65726

Elams Mills
2625 Gardner Road
Broadview, Illinois 60153

Great Grains Milling Company
P.O. Box 427
Scobey, Montana 59263

Floyd Harwood
Log Village Grist Mill
R.D. #2
Granville, New York 12832

El Molino Mills
P.O. Box 2250
City of Industry, California 91746

New Hope Mills
R.D. #2
Moravia, New York 13118

Shiloh Farms
Sulphur Springs, Arkansas 72768

Walnut Acres
Penns Creek, Pennsylvania 17862

War Eagle Mill
Route 1
Hindsville, Arkansas 72738

HERBS, SPICES, AND IMPORTED PRODUCTS

Al's Food Store (import store)
6900 Greenville Avenue
Dallas, Texas 75231

Caprilands (herbs)
Adelma Grenier Simmons
Coventry, Connecticut 06238

The Cedars Import Company, Inc.
5055 South Yale
Tulsa, Oklahoma 74135

Eastern Lamejun Bakers, Inc.
   (mideastern spices)
145 Belmont Street
Belmont, Massachusetts 02178

Thomas Market (spices)
2650 University Boulevard West
Wheaton, Maryland 20902

Mecca Coffee Company (import
   store)
3509 South Peoria
Tulsa, Oklahoma 74105

NUTS AND MAPLE SUGAR PRODUCTS

Coombs Beaver Brook Sugarhouse
Box 503
Junction Routes 9 and 100
Wilmington, Vermont 05363

Mauna Loa Macadamia Nut
   Corporation
Suite 200
1833 Kalakaua Avenue
Honolulu, Hawaii 96815

SPECIAL EQUIPMENT

Country Engineering (large electric
   dough mixer)
Box 202
Kiel, Wisconsin 53042

Magic Mill
3971 South 900 East
Salt Lake City, Utah 84101

Ozark Mill Company
Stone Ground Mills
Vian, Oklahoma 74962

Pantry Products (pastry cloths)
201 North Link Lane
Fort Collins, Colorado 80524

Index